Islamist Occidentalism
Sayyid Quṭb and the Western Other

Islamic Studies at Gerlach Press

Colin Turner
The Qur'an Revealed: A Critical Analysis of Said Nursi's Epistles of Light. With a Foreword by Dale F. Eickelman
ISBN 9783940924285, 2013

Aziz Al-Azmeh
The Arabs and Islam in Late Antiquity: A Critique of Approaches to Arabic Sources [Series: Theories and Paradigms of Islamic Studies]
ISBN 9783940924421, 2014

Sadik J. al-Azm
On Fundamentalisms
ISBN 9783940924223, 2014

Sadik J. al-Azm
Islam – Submission and Disobedience
ISBN 9783940924247, 2014

Sadik J. al-Azm
Is Islam Secularizable? Challenging Political and Religious Taboos
ISBN 9783940924261, 2014

Sadik J. al-Azm
Critique of Religious Thought. First English Translation of Naqd al-fikr ad-dini. With a New Introduction by the Author
ISBN 978394092444, 2014

The Caliphate and Islamic Statehood – Formation, Fragmentation and Modern Interpretations (3 Vols Set)
Ed. by Carool Kersten
ISBN 9783940924520, 2015

Nasrin Rouzati
Trial and Tribulation in the Qur'an. A Mystical Theodicy. With a Foreword by Colin Turner
ISBN 9783940924544, 2015

Wahhabism - Doctrine and Development (Critical Surveys in Islamic Denominations Series, 2 Vols)
Ed. by Esther Peskes
ISBN 9783940924506, 2016

Muhammad Shahrour
Islam and Humanity: Consequences of a Contemporary Reading. First Authorized English Translation of Al-Islam wa-l-insan by George Stergios. With a Foreword by Dale F. Eickelman
ISBN 9783959940184, 2017

Seyfeddin Kara
In Search of Ali ibn Abi Talib's Codex: History and Traditions of the Earliest Copy of the Qur'an. With a Foreword by James Piscatori
ISBN 9783959940542, 2018

Mahshid Turner
The Muslim Theology of Huzn: Sorrow Unravelled (With a Foreword by Alparslan Açıkgenç)
ISBN 9783959940405, 2018

Imène Ajala
European Muslims and their Foreign Policy Interests: Identities and Loyalties (Islam and International Relations Series, Vol. 1)
ISBN 9783959940603, 2018

The Fatwa as an Islamic Legal Instrument: Concept, Historical Role, Contemporary Relevance (3 Vols)
Ed. by Carool Kersten
ISBN 9783959940207, 2019

Mohsen Mirmehdi
Systematische Theologie des Korans. Systematic Theology of Qur'an. Text in German with English Summary
ISBN 9783959940443, 2019

Nadia Duvall
Islamist Occidentalism: Sayyid Qutb and the Western Other
ISBN 9783959940627, 2019

Sadik J. al-Azm
Occidentalism, Conspiracy and Taboo. Collected Essays 2014-2016
ISBN 9783959940467, 2019

Abdel-Hakim Ourghi
Reform of Islam. Forty Theses for an Islamic Ethics in the 21st Century
ISBN 9783959940566, 2019

Islamic Theological Discourses and the Legacy of Kalam. Gestation, Movements and Controversies (3 vols)
Ed. by Mustafa Shah
ISBN 9783959940481, 2019

www.gerlach-press.de

Nadia Duvall

Islamist Occidentalism

Sayyid Quṭb and the Western Other

GerlachPress

First published 2019
by Gerlach Press
Berlin, Germany
www.gerlach-press.de

Cover Design: Frauke Schön, Hamburg
Set by Anne Jeschke, Gerlach Press
Printed and bound in Germany

British Library Cataloguing in Publication Data.
A catalogue record for this book is available from the British Library.

Bibliographic data available from Deutsche Nationalbibliothek
http://d-nb.info/1169676944

ISBN: 978-3-95994-062-7 (hardcover)
ISBN: 978-3-95994-063-4 (eBook)

Contents

Acknowledgements

The completion of this study would have been impossible without the support and guidance of my PhD supervisor Professor Kate Zebiri. I owe her a great debt of gratitude for her insights and meticulous review of my work over the many years which took me to complete this monograph.

I wish also to express my heartfelt gratitude to Professor Walid Kazziha for his support, and to both Professor Robert Gleave and Professor Carool Kersten for enriching this study by suggesting new perspectives, and encouraging me to widen the pool of secondary sources I consulted.

Last, but not least, I wish to thank all of the marvellous librarians at SOAS, Senate House and the British Library. Special thanks go to Professor Gilbert Achcar for all the support he offered me towards publishing this work; to my friend, Penelope Vita-Finzi, for lending me and entrusting me with her late father's copy of the Oxford translation of the Bible; to my friend, David Hazan, for offering me his copy of a 2003 edition of *Siddur Farhi: Daily Prayers* (1914) which he obtained in Cairo. I had the privilege of obtaining Alan Farhi's approval to quote freely from the fourth edition of the aforementioned work which was published by the Farhi Foundation in New Jersey.

I dedicate this work to my maternal grandmother and my mother for instilling in me the belief in the value of knowledge.

Introduction

The era in the aftermath of the September 11 attacks on America saw the emergence of a plethora of literature and articles addressing Muslim anger against a grieving and deeply-wounded America. The refrain which gained prominence in the American media following the attacks of 2001 was: "Why do they hate us?"[1] "Us" being used here as an essentialist category which includes the "West" with "they" being the counterpart category designating an alien Muslim "other" who supposedly lives under the umbrella of a monolithic Islamic cultural entity. The answer was, at times, simplistic and reflected old biases which dismissed the Muslim terrorists as barbaric, insane and violent who are following an "extremist" version of Islam which is bent on destroying the West for no other reason than sheer "envy",[2] although all of the nineteen hijackers, mostly from Egypt and Saudi Arabia, came from privileged backgrounds and were highly-educated young men.[3] Bernard Lewis was particularly criticised by Edward Said for "attempting to supply a medieval religious ancestry for modern hijackings."[4]

President Bush was quick to declare that the attacks on America were an "attack on freedom itself" by a "faceless coward", promising that freedom will be defended,[5] and went on to divide the world into a camp standing for freedom and one supporting terrorists famously warning: "either you are with us or you are with the terrorists".[6] Bush called initially for the imposition of democratic ideals in the Islamic world.[7] However, this particular enterprise was overtaken by an all-out-war on Islamic "terror" using America's substantial military arsenal. This heavy-handed American approach had serious repercussions. Militant Muslims residing in Europe launched a series of terrorist attacks targeting innocent civilians in Madrid in May 2004 and London in July 2005. According to one study, these attacks came as a "direct response" to America's "War on Terror",[8] which continued unabated under Obama's administration (2009-2017) with one American homeland-security expert reportedly calling it "repackaged Bush".[9]

On the other side of the divide, there was an equal failure to issue an unequivocal condemnation of the violent attacks: a position which almost bordered on a tacit endorsement of the terror attacks on America and the world-view of the hijackers which was partly revealed in a chilling four-page document found in the baggage of the suspected Egyptian-born ringleader Muḥammad 'Aṭṭa. Of particular significance to this study are the numerous references to prophetic traditions, and Qur'anic injunctions, (extracted from *Sura* VIII, *al-Anfāl,* and *Sura* IX, *al-Tawba*) condoning martyrdom, and the necessity to slaughter flight passengers if they show any resistance and loot their possessions in accordance to prophetic traditions. The act of slaughter itself is considered an act of grace from God and those committing it are enjoined to offer it to their parents.[10] Here, as in Quṭb's discourse in his later writings, non-Muslims are objectified as mere spoils of war in accordance to qur'anic prescriptions and *sunna*.

Ziauddin Sardar, for instance, blamed the West for its failure to understand non-western societies and wrote of the bankruptcy of Western thought in dealing with the non-Western world. He criticised Buruma and Margalit's work *Occidentalism: The West in the Eyes of its Enemies* (2004) for putting forward the view that Occidentalism, being "the dehumanising picture of the West painted by its enemies", has its origin in the West itself, with "the poor sods", the "Orientals", having nothing to say for themselves. He also pointed out the danger of such a view which considers that radical *jihadis*, as well as anti-globalisation protestors, are merely "acting out a perverted Western fantasy".[11]

Sardar's concerns are certainly noteworthy in as far as there is indeed an urgent need to understand Islamist Occidentalism to attempt to bridge the increasing wide gap between the Islamic world and the West. I deem it necessary to address such a need which provides the *raison-d'être* behind my choice to undertake such a study. Such an undertaking, however, was to represent several initial challenges, not least of which was the need to meet the epistemological challenge posed by Said's critique of Orientalism in relation to studies which deal with the "we-other" problematic which is at the centre of this study.

1. The Western "Other" in Quṭb's Thought, and Humanism in Islamic Culture

When I set out to undertake this study, I was particularly concerned about the sheer brutality of the hijackers, and their use of the Qur'an and Prophetic sayings to justify their murderous acts.[12]Equally disconcerting is their inclination to objectify non-Muslims as mere objects of booty to be slaughtered in the name of God. Of particular significance is the evidence which was furnished by a recent study of jihadis' websites which reveals that Quṭb is the most quoted Islamist next to the thirteenth century Hanbalite theologian Ibn Taymiyya.[13]

As indicated in Lifton's study, radicalised Muslim youth in the West today are "more disposed than average to use splitting" in reference to the "other" as a manifestation of strong anger.[14] Alarmingly, Muslim leaders were also found to speak of their opponents at times in less than personal terms, with the adversary being seen merely "as part object, like pain or ugliness".[15]

Recently, it emerged that the now deposed President of Egypt Muḥammad Mursi, a member of the Muslim Brothers' organisation, referred to the "Jews" as swine and apes (in accordance to a literal reading of the two qur'anic verses 2:65 and 5:63),[16] in the same way that Quṭb did in his commentary on these two verses in *Ẓilāl*.[17] It is noteworthy that there is reference in the 1947 edition of *al-Manār*, which was taken over by al-Banna from Rashīd Riḍa's heirs,[18] to the Jews as having fallen in a "beastly" state (*al-bahīmiyya*); comparisons are also drawn in the journal between the "Jew" and an ape in "his vagarious impulses", and swine in "his concupiscence".[19]

Clearly, the above extreme dehumanising views of the "other", in this instance, "the Jew", by political Islamists who are affiliated with the Brothers, including Quṭb, hardly fall under the rubric of what Buruma and Margalit refer to as "religious Occidentalism".[20] In this line of argument, these two writers argue that Quṭb, as well as Mawdūdī and Taleqani, shared "a similar view of the world" in their depiction of the West as "the source of the new *jāhiliyya*, as the hotbed of idolatry."[21] Apart from the questionable use of the word "religious" in relation to Quṭb, who objectified Islam as an "idea", or a "concept", and Mawdūdī, who objectified it as a "system",[22] I agree with Ayubi that political Islamism is conceptually just as modern a phenomenon as Arab nationalism even though it draws intellectually from older sources such as the ideas of the *Khawārij* and Ibn Taymiyya.[23]

By situating Quṭb's thought on the "other" in the broader context of Islamic humanist "cumulative traditions" of the classic age of Islamic piety,[24] my main concern in contributing this monograph is to attempt to illuminate modern-day Islamist Occidentalism, and to put in question the assumption that Quṭb's brand of Islamism is representative of "religious Occidentalism". As I demonstrate in the course of this study, Quṭb's thought on the "other" in general, and "the Jew" specifically, marks a clear departure from a long-standing tradition, especially in Sufi Islam, which Nettler argues, showed much openness to Judaism.[25]

It is noteworthy that, unlike European humanism, which developed much closer relations with art and philosophy than with religion,[26]humanist elements were an integral part of Islamic culture fairly early on in the classical period of Islamic history. Arkoun makes the point that in the course of Miskawayh's life (945-1030), the concept of *adab* is said to have been studied by renowned authors, poets, historians, grammarians, geographers, and secretaries (*Kuttāb*) of great services (*dīwān*) of the caliphate.[27]

In applying the term "humanism" to Islamic cultural history, one is inevitably to lay the emphasis on the rational component of that culture in relation to Greek translations into Arabic in Abbasid Baghdad between the 8th and 10th centuries. Würsch argues that considering that this intellectual movement aimed to revive the philosophical and scientific heritage of Greek antiquity, it is quite apt to designate it as "humanist". She notes further that the Arabic translation movement showed much openness toward Syrian, Persian and Indian texts; thus, it broadened its outlook compared to the *litterae humaniores* in Europe.[28]

The argument is made, however, that the idea of humanism, as applied to Islam's cultural history, is highly problematic when it makes exclusive reference to philosophy; thus, becoming intimately connected with terms like "rationality" or "secularisation". Secularisation, of course, makes reference to a particular development which followed the Enlightenment. Similarly, exclusive reference to rationalist philosophy, as a value-concept of humanism, is at odds with Islamic mysticism. In Würsch's words,

> One would be doing more justice to Islamic mysticism if one applied the idea of humanism as a value-concept (with a religious connotation) to a more generalising idea of Mankind and its place in the scheme of creation. Such a notion of "humanism" would come close to that of humanity"... The origin of "humanism" as well as "humanity" is formed by *Humanitas*: a term that ultimately stands for "being human". If, therefore, we understand "humanism" in the sense of "*humanitas*" as the defining concept of being human i.e. an anthropology determining how humans can attain their full humanity and dignity (according to Schöller), then there are no obstacles to linking "humanism" and Islamic mysticism.[29]

Put differently, Anne Marie Schimmel puts forward the view that the humanist concept underlying Sufism encompasses key forms including:

> reflections upon the position of man within creation, his relationship with God, the intense preoccupation of the mystic with his own self; the education of the instinct-driven soul (*nafs*) seeking nothing but sensual gratification as a precondition of man's capacity to attain higher aims; instruction in ethics and a finely tuned system of rules concerning proper behaviour (*adab*).

Among the other aspects of Sufi "humanity", Schimmel finally lists "hospitality, serving fellow humans and the sacrificing of the self on behalf of others".[30]

In analysing the otherness formulations targeting the West in Quṭb's writings within the time-frame of this study (1939-1966), I aim to challenge and deconstruct the finished Quṭbian product that has been presented to us, at times, as an emblem of puritanical Islam.[31]In illuminating the influences which came to bear on the unfolding of Quṭb's thought against the West, culminating in a condemnation of humankind as living in a state of idolatrous *jāhiliyya*: a doctrine which was unknown to great humanists of Islam such as the Arab philosopher, Miskawayh, and the great Andalusian mystic, Ibn 'Arabī (d. 1240). Würsch argues that Ibn 'Arabī's concept of "the Perfect Man" can be regarded as a humanist one. The Perfect Man as "the highest stage of being human" constitutes "the ideal of a true humanitas". Furthermore, she writes, "the idea of mankind's special place in the scheme of creation is something not altogether alien to the European epoch of humanism".[32]

On another level of the discussion, I aim to elucidate the point that much of the extreme otherness formulations in Quṭb's late edition of his commentary on the Qur'ān, *Fī Ẓilāl al-Qur'ān* (*In the Shade of the Qur'ān*), targeting especially "the Jew", appear to be of a fairly late development in Quṭb's 1960s discourse as he joined forces with the then main ally of the United States, Saudi Arabia, to topple Nasser's secular regime. As will be discussed in the course of this study, it is my contention that it is Quṭb's younger brother, Muḥammad, who assumed the role of being "the primary custodian and official interpreter of his older brother's legacy",[33] who revised Quṭb's late writings to reflect his own more extreme views, especially in *Ẓilāl*.[34]

Throughout the work, the thrust of my argument revolves around the novelty in Quṭb's thought which marks him out as the main contributor to a modern-day trend of thought which I consider to be an almost complete rupture with Islamic thought in its classical and pre-modern age of piety. As I argue in the work, Quṭb's dehumanising views of the Western 'other', as he adopts the simplistic spiritual-East and materialist-West duality in his early 1940s writings, for instance, set him on a collision course with the leading humanist of the day, Ṭaha Ḥusayn (d. 1973), in the early part of the twentieth century. In situating Quṭb's thought on the Western "other" in the broader context of Islamic humanist traditions of the classical age of Islamic piety, I am making the argument that Quṭb's deprecating and essentialising views on "the Jew" in his later writings is a drift away from a long-standing tradition, especially in Sufi Islam, which showed much openness to the Jewish tradition.

As I pointed out in chapter 5, Quṭb's vehement dismissal of Ezra (otherwise known as the second Moses in Jewish tradition), as the pharaoh who opposed Joseph, breaks away from an enduring "cumulative tradition", especially in Sufi Islam, which, according to Nettler's study of Ibn 'Arabī's Discussion of 'Uzayr (Ezra), incorporated figures, such as Ezra, in the Islamic canon.[35] Unlike early mystics, such as Muqātil Ibn Sulaymān (d. 767), who, Nwyia argues in *Exégèse Coranique et Langage Mystique,* did not hesitate to quote the Bible to illuminate the Qur'ān,[36] Quṭb dismisses Judeo-Christian scriptures, which are considered 'authoritative' by 'Abduh, as 'corrupted' (*muḥarafa*) in his later writings. Crucially, Quṭb's depiction of the Jews as 'apes' in the revised section of *Ẓilāl,* in accordance with a literal reading of the Qur'ānic verse 2:65, is a clear departure from 'Abduh's interpretation of the same verse in accordance with the exegesis of Mujāhid (d. 772) who argued that the verse makes reference to only those Jews who desecrated the Sabbath.[37]

2. Identity Formation and the "Cumulative Traditions" of Islam

In analysing Quṭb's discourse on the Western "other", I adopted an interdisciplinary approach, relying mainly in my theoretical assumptions on the insights provided by Wilfred Cantwell Smith, lauded chiefly as "one of the past century's most influential contributors to interfaith dialogue and the comparative study of religions";[38] and those provided by Erik H. Erikson (1902-1994), who is mainly renowned for his contribution to human development theory on culture, identity and social order.[39]

Firstly, I would like to make the point that, although I consider that Quṭb's discourse falls under the rubric of Islamist Occidentalism, which in recent times descended to sheer vulgarity,[40]it is the case that the term "Occidentalism", denoting a system of representation of the Occident, appears to be quite a novelty in the Islamic world[41] and is not clearly defined in Western Academia.[42]According to Varisco, "the standard pre-post-colonial definitions of 'Occidentalism' in English all refer to the process of making something Western, just as the earlier meaning for 'Orientalism' originally connoted an Oriental custom".[43] In agreement with Varisco, I am particularly opposed to Edward Said's assumption that Occidentalism represents a kind of linguistic tit-for-tat binary in relation to Orientalism.

> Said, like a number of binary-blinded writers, errs in assuming that the opposite of the Orientalism he is describing would be an Occidentalism, a kind of linguistic tit- for-tat à la Orient versus Occident...As Orientalism is reduced to what Westerners hate or reject about the Eastern other, so an equally complicit Occidentalism can be seen merely as what Orientals hate about the West.[44]

In analysing the system of representation of the Westerner in Quṭb's discourse in the early Islamist stage of his life, I find that it falls in what Wilfred C. Smith identifies in *Islam in Modern History* (1957) as "a leaning towards apologetics to defend Islam [as an idea] in history in the Arab(ic-speaking) world.[45] Smith explains that in view of the "mordant feeling of contemporary decline", the purpose of historiography is "not investigation but aggrandizement, not intellectual accuracy but emotional satisfaction".[46] In his analysis of al-Azhar journal, Smith detects that, as early as the 1930s, the spirit of the defence of Islam is strikingly "Westernizing" with Islam being defended not only against "Western disparagement", but it is also defended by means of "Western approval".[47]

It is noteworthy that Smith singles out Quṭb's early Islamist work *Social Justice in Islam* (1949) as a good example of Brotherhood literature which shows "no grappling with the more intricate responsibilities of modernity". Furthermore, he adds, the *Ikhwān* programme rests on the conviction that "Islam in history already has extant and precise answers to all problems". Smith argues that such an attitude was found by other Muslims, such as Ṭaha Ḥusayn, to be both "morally arrogant and practically disastrous".[48]

In agreement with Smith, I find it important to avoid talking of "religions" as "reified" as though they are mere "things" or "entities".[49] Smith argues that a scientific study of religion must deal with "meaning", not "object".[50] In *The Meaning and End of Religion* (1964), Smith invites us instead to ponder on the key concept of "the cumulative tradition" as being "the mundane result of the faith of men in the past and the mundane cause of the faith of men in the present". Every religious person, Smith argues, "is the locus of an interaction between the transcendent which is presumably the same for every man, and the cumulative tradition which is different for every man."[51] Put differently, Smith argues that "each person is presented with a cumulative tradition, and grows up among other persons to whom that tradition is meaningful".[52] In this line of thought, Smith suggests that terms such as Christianity, Buddhism, and the like must be dropped as "untenable".[53] (In the instances when I make use of these terms in the course of this study, it is rather to reflect Quṭb's or other thinkers' usage.)

Theoretically speaking, I am particularly in favour of Smith's "cumulative tradition" thesis which somewhat converges with Erikson's theory which places an emphasis on the importance of establishing an "average expectable continuity" with the past in delineating outside-inside divisions. Under the heading "A Community of Egos", Erikson observes that the matter of establishing "unchartered areas", or an "outer world", is both a necessity and a peculiarity of human societies whereby humans create an outside-inside division by "placing on the 'outside' what fails to be on the 'inside' in a vague and yet omnipresent 'outerness' which, by necessity, assumes a number of ideological connotations". Furthermore, Erikson stresses the point that the outerness process is necessarily predicated on ideological foundations which are central for social order especially at a time of immense upheaval due to rapid technological changes in the modern age. As he puts it, "the matter of establishing and preserving inflexible forms as 'average expectable continuity' for child rearing and education everywhere has become a matter of human survival".[54]

Put differently, Erikson states that "the older generation needs the younger one as much as the younger one depends on the older for the strength of their respective egos". In all cases, elites and leaders are called upon "to meet their period's specific need for a re-synthesis of the prevalent world image" to provide certain basic and universal values which are "indispensable" for the ego development of the younger generations.[55]

On the whole, as Smith points out, there have been a great many Muslim liberals in the early part of the twentieth century, and a considerable liberal exposition of Islam; but, relatively little Islamic exposition of liberalism. As an example, Smith makes the case that, as individuals, liberal Muslims met with members of other faiths, on terms of personal "equality"; however, while liberals occupied key leadership positions, liberalism remained weak.[56] Giving the example of key Egyptian literati figures of the older generation who encountered Quṭb, such as Ṭaha Ḥusayn, Muḥammad H. Haykal, and 'Abbās al-'Aqqād, Smith argues that these three men conveyed in their literature "a creative synthesis" which related their liberalism to their "Muslim-ness".[57]

As we shall see in the course of this study, Quṭb remained largely unreceptive to that "creative synthesis", which was the brainchild of Egypt's intellectual luminaries of the day. Consequently, he remained on the "outside" of the "outside-inside" division which was chartered by the older generation of literati in the course of his literary career. Significantly, even in his youth, Quṭb failed, as well, to develop what Erikson describes as a "sense of comradeship" with other men and women of different pursuits and of distant times who have left a heritage conveying human love and dignity which are essential components of both "identity formation" and "integrity of the mind".[58]

According to Erikson, it is only in achieving this sense of comradeship" that one can map out, in any given society, the formation of a "vision quest" which is not necessarily derived from religion. To illustrate this point, Erikson gives the example of Europe's romantic period when European youth, writers and artists engaged with and retrieved "the ruins left by a dead past" in formulating a "vision quest" for the present in which they lived.[59]

Lastly, I would like to point out that in such instances of "severe identity confusion" (as in Quṭb's case), Erikson observes that the situation is further compounded when one experiences "extreme work paralysis [which] is the logical sequence of a deep sense of the inadequacy of one's general equipment". In such cases, when a given individual comes to develop "a deep sense of the inadequacy of one's general equipment", one's "ego ideal" would settle for nothing less than making the unrealistic demand of commanding "omnipotence" or "omniscience". Such a sense of inadequacy, he argues, "may express the fact that the immediate social environment does not have a niche for the individual's true gifts".[60]

Broadly speaking, Erikson explains, "extreme work paralysis [is] the logical sequence of a deep sense of the inadequacy of one's general equipment" which detracts from a person's need to confirm a "work identity" which, unfulfilled, leads inevitably to destructive tendencies.[61] As an example of an extreme case of identity confusion, Erikson makes reference to Hitler who, as a youth, had wanted desperately to be a city planner. It was when a prize committee ignored his plans for a new opera house in Linz, that he broke with society only to reappear subsequently as an "avenger", showing "excessive destructive needs" to the end of his days.[62]

As we shall see in this study, I find that, at different intervals of Quṭb's life, he often exhibits "excessive destructive tendencies" as he finds himself in a situation of 'extreme work paralysis'. Starting in the mid-1930s, when he first challenged the Francophile humanist Ṭaha Ḥusayn, and subsequently experienced a situation of 'extreme work paralysis', he targeted the French and the Christian West as an 'other', while he expressed a clear affinity with the Jewish tradition. In the 1940s, the rift with the literati in general, and the dispute with al-'Aqqād in particular, led to another experience of "extreme work paralysis" followed by a scathing attack on "the Greek" and philosophy. This development was followed by a marked attraction to the Christian West and a recognition of the refinement of the French in opposition to the brutishness of the American. As an Islamist ideologue, in the early 1960s, Quṭb was particularly threatened by both 'Abduh and Iqbal. Consequently, his polemics target both these thinkers.

Finally, in challenging Nasser's secular regime in *Ma'ālim fī al-Ṭarīq*, Quṭb ends up identifying "the Jew", as his main "other" "pseudo-species", as he insists on the concept of *Ḥākimiyya* (god's sovereignty) and the implementation of *Shari'a.* Here, we see the development in Quṭb's thought of a recognition of what Arkoun describes as "the famous alliance of *Yahve* with the Jewish people, later the new alliance with the Christian people and the Qur'anic pact".[63] In developing what Erikson refers to as "an age old awareness of man's division into pseudo-species",[64]Quṭb bypasses what Erikson explains is "a certain degree of 'identity-consciousness', and becomes aware of man's division into 'pseudo-species', as he did before in tribal life". The example of national-socialist Germany is given here as "the most flagrant manifestation of the murderous mass 'pseudologia' (a form of lying) which can befall a modern nation" in realising its own "pseudo-species".[65] It is important to stress the point here that a universal concept of humanity involves "a conscious move beyond the deep-rooted norms of ethnocentricity", which give pre-eminence to one's own ethnic or cultural in-group. "Humanism is based on an extension of these values ... to every member of the human race".[66]

Finally, Quṭb conjures up the idea of a Judeo-Christian conspiracy against Islam which he associates with Orientalism following developing an awareness of Smith's views in *Islam in Modern History* which dismiss, not only his own thought but also the *Ikhwān*, as well as the *Jama'at-i Islami* of Pakistan, as mere "fanatical outbursts".[67]

3. The Book

This book is based on my PhD thesis *The Evolution of the Otherness Process targeting the West in Sayyid Quṭb's Discourse (1939-1966).* It is offered as a contribution to illuminate contemporary thought in the Islamic World. In contributing this book, I aim to offer new insights into the thought of the leading Islamist ideologue, Sayyid Quṭb, by investigating his views on the Western other as he grappled with the retreat of European colonialist powers and the onset of American expansionism and influence in the Islamic world in the mid-twentieth century. I deem it particularly important to illuminate Quṭb's views on the West especially in light of the escalation in violent attacks by militant Islamists targeting the West starting 9/11, 2001, in the United States.

Throughout the work, the thrust of my argument revolves around the novelty in Quṭb's thought which marks him out as the main contributor to a modern-day trend of thought which dehumanises the Western 'other', setting him on a collision course with the leading humanists of the day, Ṭaha Ḥusayn and Aḥmad Shawqī (d.1932), in the early part of the twentieth century. Both Shawqī and Ḥusayn are recognised for a "truly humanist merger" of Western and Arabic cultural values in the classical poetry of the former and in the life and works of the latter.[68] In situating Quṭb's thought on the Western "other" in the broader context of Islamic humanist traditions of the classical age of Islamic piety, I am making the argument that Quṭb's deprecating and essentialising views on "the Jew" in his later writings is clearly in opposition to the views expressed by 'Abduh and Mujāhid as he descended into dehumanising polemics which targeted the Jews as another "pseudo-species" which competed with the Muslims as God's chosen "pseudo-species": a notion that Quṭb develops fairly early on in his Islamist writing based on the Qur'anic verse 2:143, which considers Muslims to be an "*Umma*" acting as "witnesses" over all others; and Q3:110 singling out Muslims as the "best *Umma*" in relation to all other humans.

Broadly speaking, I conjecture that Quṭb made his own interpretation of Islam, which he objectifies mostly as an "idea", or a "concept", a tenet of faith without however establishing any discernible continuity with its past "cumulative traditions". It is, therefore, my contention that Quṭb's works fall under the rubric of a genre of modernist literature which, W. C. Smith argues, saw some Muslim writers give more attention to Islam than to God.

> A true Muslim, however, is not a man who believes in Islam – especially Islam in history; but one who believes in God and is committed to the revelation through His Prophet.[69]

4. Synopsis, and Structure of the Book

Having familiarised myself with Quṭb's works within the time-frame of this study (1939-1966), I deemed it necessary to adopt a thematic approach in deconstructing the otherness formulations targeting the West in his discourse. In addition to two historical background chapters, I identified three main themes in Quṭb's thought on the Western other which I covered in corresponding core chapters (3, 4 & 5). These themes relate to Quṭb's views on the modern civilisation of the West which I tackle in chapter 3; in chapter 4, I deal with the "West-East" duality in Quṭb's discourse, and his early views on "Islam" in relation to the Christian and the Jewish traditions; finally, in chapter 5, I deal with Quṭb's later radical views with special emphasis on the development of the doctrine of *jāhiliyya* (presupposing the barbarity or ignorance of modern-day civilisation). My emphasis in this chapter is to bring to the fore the construction of 'the Jew' as his main 'other' in his later writings. As discussed in this chapter, I've put forward the view that, contrary to his younger Brother Muḥammad, who was particularly unnerved by 'the three Jews' – Durkheim, Marx and Freud – Quṭb was particularly rattled by Ezra and Henri Bergson.

In chapter 1, I focus on the shock encounter between the West and the world of Islam in Egypt starting the three-year occupation of Egypt by the French (1798-1801) when the egalitarian ideals and norms of the French Revolution clashed with those of traditional Islam in relation to gender and non-Muslim outsiders. As discussed in this chapter, these egalitarian ideals took root in the early part of the twentieth century in the westernised intellectual elites' circles in Egyptian society; unlike Quṭb, these intellectuals were mostly educated in Europe but they were also firmly grounded in traditional Islam. As a graduate of *Dār al-'Ulūm*, which was a failed attempt to modernise al-Azhar, Quṭb was accused by Ḥusayn, of being suspended between "the modern" and "the traditional".

In chapter 2, I give an overall survey of Quṭb's life stressing his feud with Egypt's literati and the confusion in his thought in relation to his reception of the modern thought-world of the West as synthesised by Egypt's senior literati. I also give an overview of Quṭb's works, stressing the point that some of his later works, specifically his 6-volume commentary on the Qur'ān, *Fī Ẓilāl al-Qur'ān*, bears clear signs of revision by his younger brother, Muḥammad, to accommodate the Saudi Wahhābī kingdom which sought to topple the Nasserite secular regime in the 1960s. It is my contention that Quṭb, through his younger brother's revision of his works, contributes to a modern trend in Islamic thought which, Arkoun argues, saw "obedience towards a God further away than ever, which ensures the transfer of obedience to the absolute master representing the installed government".[70]

In chapter 3, I offer a historical background section under the title 'Quṭb's Schooling Years in Musha, and the Clash between the Modern and the Traditional Worlds' in addition to three other sections. In the second section, 'The Literary Stage in Quṭb's Life and his Early Attitude towards the Civilisation of the West', I attempt to cover Quṭb's career, as a teacher and a littérateur, stressing the confusion in his thought starting the mid-1930s. In the third section, 'Quṭb's Turn to Islamism & his Early Discourse against the Thought-world and the Civilisation of the West', I am making the argument that Quṭb's turn to Islamism seems to be an extension of his feud with the literati as he drifted away from the orbit of his mentor, 'Abbās M. al-'Aqqād. In the last section, 'Quṭb's Sojourn in America (1948-1950) and Encountering the American "Other"', I sketch out some of the caricatured accounts which were given by him as he embarks on essentialising the American as his main 'other', while claiming for himself the refinement of the French.

In chapter 4, I tackle Quṭb's early views in relation to spirituality, in general, while giving special attention to the "spirit" of the East, and the "matter" of the West duality in his discourse in particular. This chapter includes three sections in addition to a historical background section under the title 'First Views of Religious Traditions and Folk-beliefs in Musha'. In section two, 'Quṭb's Views on "*Religions*" and the East-West Dichotomy in the Early Literary Stage of his Life', I discuss the spiritual "East" imaginary construct in Quṭb's mid-1940s discourse which he associates mostly with the traditions of India. In section three, 'Quṭb's Early Studies of the Qur'ān and Reflections on Islam in Comparison with "Other" *Religions*', I make the argument that Quṭb was rather preoccupied by the artistic imagery in the Qur'ān and recognised both the Jews and the Christians encountered by the early Muslims as 'learned men', only to reject them in his later writings as polytheists. In the fourth section, 'Rethinking the Christian and the Jewish Traditions in Quṭb's Discourse (1947-1948)', I discuss Quṭb's apparent attraction to the New Testament and to the Christian tradition.

In chapter 5, I look at Quṭb's first use of the doctrine of *jāhiliyya* to condemn the "Material Spirit" of modern-day civilisation in the historical background section. Although the condemnation of modern-day civilisation is an integral part of Quṭb's discourse, the novelty in his thought lies in the claim he makes that, while Muḥammad encountered barbarity in the early days of Islam, he purports that he is facing refinement (*irtiqā'*), revealing clear Darwinist influences which permeate his thought. Significantly, Quṭb goes on to express the view that Islam is a blending of Christianity and Marxism as he collides with the USA which objectified Islam as an ideology to combat communism. In section two, 'The Otherness Formulations Targeting the West in Quṭb's Early 1960s Discourse with Special Emphasis on the Doctrine of *Jāhiliyya*', I attempt to bring to the fore Quṭb's changing perceptions of the USA, to the negative, as he becomes aware of the CIA's open intervention in the Middle East in an effort to combat communism. It is, however, clearly the case that Quṭb's clear attraction to Christianity remains unabated as he ventures to invite the West to accept Islam as a means towards "salvation" (*khalāṣṣ*): a concept unknown in Islamic thought which rather places an emphasis on "intercession" (*shafā'a*). In this section, I also tackle Quṭb's pronounced animosity towards Muḥammad 'Abduh and Muḥammad Iqbal.

In the third section, 'The Construction of "the Jew" as the "Other" "Pseudo-Species" in Quṭb's Later 1960s Writings', I place an emphasis on how 'the Jew' is constructed as the main 'other' in his later writings. I also make the point that, although 'the Jew' is considered by Quṭb to be the main culprit in a conspiracy involving Orientalism and the Christian West, the most extreme formulations against 'the Jew', which only emerge in some sections of his commentary on the Qur'ān, Fi *Ẓilāl al-Qur'ān*, such as the commentary on Q5:82 in which there is reference to his younger brother's article "the Three Jews", is perhaps rather the work of the latter.

In keeping with Smith's guideline, I attempted, to the best of my ability, to read texts which were read by Quṭb to "listen to what people leave 'unsaid'".[71] I also adopted the methodology adopted by Shepard in his critical analysis of the various editions of *Social Justice in Islam* (1949-1964), which I consider to be the most central work in illuminating the evolution of Quṭb's thought on the West. Inevitably, my starting point was to endeavour to read the above text thematically while comparing the three different editions of the work (1949-1958-1964) in my possession, and consulting Shepard's study.

By applying this methodology to *al-'Adāla*, and different editions of other works, it became apparent to me that the 1960s marks a watershed in Quṭb's Islamist thought, as we shall see in chapter 5 later. Throughout the work, I attempted to respond to the key question of whether Quṭb attempted in his otherness formulations targeting the West to establish an "average expectable continuity" with any of Islam's "cumulative traditions", and "comradeship" with men and women of the Islamic past.

5. Notes on Translation and Transliteration

Unless otherwise indicated, all translations of Arabic texts are my own, except for *al-'Adāla*, which is translated by Shepard. For translations of the Qur'ān, I made use mainly of Professor Abdel Ḥaleem's translation. At times, I consulted Yusuf Ali's translation and al-Azhar-approved translation by Dr. Aḥmad Ḥamid and Professor Muḥammad Ḥamed (2004). Occasionally, I offered my own translation. For translation of the Bible, I made use of an Oxford University Press translation The Holy Bible, containing the Old and New Testament (1882?).

In transliterations, I followed the rules of *The International Journal of Middle East Studies* using ā, ū, ī for long vowels and a, u, i for short vowels; for doubled vowels in the middle of a word I used iyy (final form ī) and uww (final form ū). On certain occasions, I will supply the original Arabic texts for long sentences. I also included a glossary to provide some details or further explanations of terms used in the body of the main text. These terms are marked by an asterisk.

1

Historical Background I: The Discovery & Perceptions of the West in the Modern Age

> Described as the most brilliant cavalry of the age, the Mamluks entered battle expecting to face the enemy in a normal hand-to-hand combat at which they excelled, and for which they had been trained. Instead they were met by a deadly hail of gunpowder that decimated their ranks before they even got within hailing distance of the enemy. Mamluks who were captured alive raged at the Ottomans, asking them to give them a fighting chance, to fight like men in hand-to-hand combat instead of aiming these fire-sweeping instruments at them. The Ottomans, who were not fighting a war for fun, but for profit, contemptuously laughed at the Mamluks who believed there was a "code of honour" in fighting a war which had to be respected or the soldier "disgraced".[1]

The scene is one depicting the encounter between the Egyptian Mamluks and the Ottoman forces on the battlefield in the plain of Marj Dabiq North of Aleppo on 24 August 1516 which ended with the Mamluk forces suffering a resounding defeat: one which was down to the Ottomans' use of what they firstly considered to be "infidel" and "un-chivalrous" weapons. The scene also marks the passing of the old order and the advent of a new age where chivalry could only win one ridicule. As Lewis remarks, following an initial resistance to these "un-chivalrous" Western weapons, the Ottomans were quick to adopt them on a vast scale gaining an enormous edge over other Muslim forces such as that of Egypt's Mamluks.[2]

The adoption of Western weapons by the Ottomans was to mark one of the turning-points in the power relationship between Islam and Christendom as the Islamic world became increasingly dependent on the importation of Western firearms which became in Lewis' words "by far the most important contribution of the West to life, and death, in the Islamic world".[3] Following a series of crushing defeats, and the withdrawal of the Ottoman armies from Vienna before the victorious Habsburg forces at the end of the seventeenth century, a debate was now to be conducted for the first time in the course of Islamic history in terms of "us" and "them" posing the question: "why were the miserable infidels, previously always vanquished by the victorious armies of Islam, now winning the day, and why were the armies of Islam suffering defeat at their hands?"[4]

On the whole, the initial debate was to prove to be a downright failure with regard to objectivity as the Ottomans seemed to be unable to recognise the moral, social and cultural merits lying behind the military, technological and material strength of their rivals propounding only military remedies and opening as Lewis puts it: "a sluice in the barrier that had for long separated Islam from Christendom – a sluice with a limited and regulated flow" which allowed only for the importation of European weapons and technology.[5]

As Rahimieh finds, early Ottoman historians were "to abandon all pretence of objectivity in their accounts of encounters between East and West" seizing every opportunity to amplify the moral "flaws" of the Europeans.[6] According to Lewis, the Arabic word "*kafir*" (infidel), which was customarily used to designate all those who disbelieve in the truth of the Islamic message, came to be virtually synonymous with "Christian" in Persian, Arabic and Turkish usage.[7]

With the intellectual and the material balance of power clearly tilting in favour of a superior Europe, Moosa observes that the Muslims' awareness of the "self" and the "other" in the new changed world in which they were now dominated on every front by the European Christian "other" was seriously flawed by an inability to bypass what he refers to as an "ideology of Empire" which is essentially grounded in a triumphalist and deeply-ingrained body of thought reflecting an earlier age when Islam was a strong political entity and an empire.[8]

For the most part, Moosa finds, the benefits of technology and science were brought to Muslim societies with far-reaching consequences for culture with some societies adopting modernity in a pragmatic manner, which resulted in disruptions with the existing traditional heritage, while other societies attempted a degree of fusion with the past to maintain a certain degree of "continuity" with their heritage.[9]

Although, as Wilfred C. Smith argues, historical Islam flowered afresh, both geographically and spiritually, in Persian and Turkish forms in the sixteenth century which he considers to be a period marking "a new zenith" in Islamic history, this period has not been generally regarded by the Muslims as "fully intrinsic to Islam" as the classical period is.[10] For one thing, Smith remarks that as mysticism gained ground an "incipient sense of separateness between mundane history and spiritual life" set in

> Sufism differs from the classical Sunni *Weltanschauung* radically: and not least in its attitude to history, the temporal mundane. It stresses the individual rather than society, the eternal rather than the historical, God's love rather than His

> power, and the state of man's heart rather than behaviour. It is more concerned that one's soul be pure than that one's actions be correct.[11]

It is worth mentioning here that, although Quṭb included Turkey, as well as Iran, in the category of "the East" in refuting Ṭaha Ḥusayn's *Mustaqbal al-Thaqāfa fī Miṣr* (1938) in 1939,[12] he did not accept the Turks as fellow Muslims at the later Islamist stage of his life. Instead, Quṭb included the Turks, along Circassians and Dailamites, in a category of races whose hearts were "sealed" (*ghuluf*) and opposed to "the spirit of Islam" in all six editions of his first Islamist work *al-'Adāla* (1949-1964).[13]

In contrast to "the jubilant proclamation of the death of God" in the West, followed by "the death of the human subject",[14] Quṭb connected God and Islam with power especially as he veered, as Jomier finds, to anthroporphism (*tashbīh**) in *Ẓilāl*.[15] He envisaged that purity is *not* that of the soul, but can only be achieved by exacting harsh punishments, such as stoning, on sinners.[16] Unlike Kant's philosophical hermeneutics to rethink God and religion which led to the abolition of harsh laws on blasphemy and paved the way for new possibilities of emancipation of the human condition,[17] Quṭb's thought was firmly grounded in what Arkoun describes as a trend of thought in Islam that was both "dogmatic" and "obscurantist".[18]

In bringing to the fore Quṭb's above views on God and Islam, I hope to bring to the reader's attention the vast gap that came to separate political Islamism from the humanist movements in both Europe and Islam. In Pico della Mirandola's *De dignitate hominis* (1478), one of the key texts of Western humanism, Würsch points out that the Italian humanists were engaged in speculation about God. In accordance to this text, "the purification of the human soul leads to the true knowledge of God as the ultimate aim and perfection of humanity". In the same vein, humanist Islamic philosophers who were making reference to the heritage of ancient Greece in their works, never failed to include God in their thought – not even Abū Bakr al-Rāzī (d. 925) who is highly critical of some of the aspects of religion (e.g. prophecy).[19]

1. Egypt's Early Encounter with the Challenge of the Modern West

Described as the biggest maritime expedition that had crossed the Mediterranean since the Crusaders,[20] Napoleon's three hundred vessels expedition targeting Egypt in 1798 carried some 32,000 troops - including some of France's best soldiers - and a hundred of France's scholars, artists and technicians who brought with them the first printing press with Arabic type.[21] It was perhaps this printing press which was France's biggest contribution in shaking what Gibb describes as the "dull monotony" which, according to him, was particularly discernible in the Arabic-speaking provinces of the Ottoman empire starting in the sixteenth century. He notes that, following the period of the Ottoman conquests, "a general lethargy seems to settle on Islam and especially on the Arabic-speaking provinces".[22]

With the landing of Napoleon's troops on Egyptian shores in 1798, the full intellectual and technological might of Europe seems to have been suddenly thrust upon Egypt's population. France's well-equipped army was as much a military force just as it was a cultural one with the French proclaiming that the expedition was led by

> a new chivalry of intellectual and military nobility which envisaged to bring to life a global empire of Light in the same line of thought of 1789 under the commandment of Bonaparte.[23]

In his account of the French three-year occupation of Egypt (1798-1801), the great historian al-Jabartī (1756-1825) did not fail to recognise some of the merits of French rule such as their commitment to justice.[24] Al-Jabartī was however quick to recognise that the coming of the French to Egypt was the beginning of the reversal of the "natural" order and the corruption or destruction of all things, specifically making reference to the "pernicious" innovations introduced into the legal system, the corruption of women, the arming and training of Christian soldiers and the powers given to Coptic tax-collectors under French rule in Egypt.[25]

Al-Jabartī remained particularly averse to the idea of emancipating non-Muslim Egyptians which would be tantamount to a *de facto* termination of the *dhimma* pact[26] which traditionally regulated the relationship between the Muslim State and its non-Muslim subject communities. Under the terms of the *dhimma* pact, certain restrictions were imposed on non-Muslim subject communities who, in accordance with the holy law, were expected to recognise the primacy of Islam and the supremacy of the Muslims since the early days of Islamic history.[27] In Nettler's words, non-Muslim communities were kept in a position of "natural inequality".[28]

One expression of such relation of "natural inequality" between the ruling Muslims and their subject non-Muslims is symbolised in the payment of a poll tax by the latter to the ruling Muslim *élite* under the terms of the *dhimma* pact. According to Lewis, such a payment amounted to a "fiscal penalization" of the unbeliever[29] and was also seen as a symbolic expression of "subordination" of the non-Muslim subjects to their Muslim rulers. The subordination of the non-Muslims is in accordance to some Qur'anic commandments, such as Q9:29 & Q11:61. Islamic traditions as well often made use of the word *dhull* or *dhilla* (humiliation or abasement) to indicate the status God has assigned to those who reject Muḥammad[30] whose acceptance, in pre-modern Qur'anic exegesis, according to McAuliffe, became an integral part of faith, contrary to explicit Qur'anic statements.[31]

According to Lewis, al-Jabartī was not the only one to voice a negative reaction to the egalitarian ideas of the French Revolution. From 1798, when hostilities began between the French Republic and the Ottoman Empire, Ottoman documents make frequent allusions to the "absurd and preposterous" ideas of equality among mankind. In the course of the nineteenth century, however, the new egalitarian ideals of Europe gained momentum and the new concept of equal citizenship had gradually gained strength and was to be finally enshrined in the Ottoman Empire's great reform *(fermān)* of February 1856 which repealed the age-old restrictions imposed on the non-Muslims and all subjects of the Ottoman state were formally declared to be equal.[32]

By the mid-nineteenth century, thinkers in both Constantinople and Egypt were beginning to address the burning issue of the place of Islam in the modern world. According to Hourani, the consensus by a great number of thinkers was to set a high value on the social norms of Islam while adopting western institutions on the grounds of their conformity to the "true" spirit of Islam.[33] One such thinker is the Azharite Rifa'a al-Ṭahṭāwi (1801-73) who, like many of his generation, came into contact with Western civilisation through being a member of one of Muḥammad 'Ali's (r. 1805-48) first scholastic missions to Paris between 1826-31.[34]

Al-Ṭahṭāwi stressed the need to interpret *shari'a* in light of modern needs. He suggested that there was not much difference between the principles of Islamic law and those underlying natural law on which the legal codes of modern Europe were based and was to go on to incorporate the element of equality into legislation in Egypt based on the French legal system.[35] It is noteworthy that the Egyptian Islamist thinker, Ṭāriq al-Bishri, quotes Rashīd Riḍā (d. 1935) as asserting that the rigidity of *shari'a* laws in the nineteenth century was such that the people at the time, including the shaykhs of al-Azhar, chose to resort to courts which applied French laws which, they thought, were more conducive to justice than *shari'a* courts.[36]

Beyond the efforts of al- al-Ṭahṭāwi to modernise the legal system in Egypt, I find it crucial here to attract the attention of the reader to the ability of this great thinker to circumvent, in his translation endeavour from French into Arabic, what seemed to be a weakness of the Arabic language, and culture, in conveying equivalent terms and socio-democratic concepts of European bourgeois thought, such as *Liberté, Humanité, Fraternité* which, according to Tibi, were non-existent in the social life of Islam.[37] Notwithstanding the existence of notions of equality of sorts among the believers, Lewis points out that these excluded unbelievers, slaves and women.[38]

Al-Ṭahṭāwi was to go even further than that by probing, along with other writers of his time, including the Christian Ḥunayn al-Khūri and, somewhat later, 'Abd Allah al-Nadīm (1845-1896), what Cachia describes as "the foundation of a regionally-based loyalty" that would cut across ethnic and religious divisions.[39] According to another study, this thinker was to extend the notion of Islamic brotherhood to include other humans which translated into the formulation of the idea of "equality in being human" which he promoted alongside the idea of Egyptian "national brotherhood".[40]

From the perspective of this study, I must emphasise here that it is indeed a credit to al-Ṭahṭāwi that he attempted no less than a fusion between traditional Islamic thought and the modern thought of Europe; thus, the modern idea of "*ḥubb al-waṭan*" (*l'amour de la patrie)* being the basis of political virtues, which he most probably owes to Montesquieu (1689-1755), is equated with the idea of *'aṣabiyya* (solidarity) binding together people living in the same community in the doctrine of Ibn-Khaldūn (1332-1406).[41]

There is no hint here of the "intellectual compromise" which, according to Ayubi, marked the thought of the next generation of Muslim reformers- including Jamal al-Dīn al-Afghānī (1839-97) and Muḥammad 'Abduh (1849-1905) – who "borrowed eclectically" and claimed for Islam Western concepts – such as liberty, individualism, and social contract – without however accepting the ideological underpinnings of these Western ideas.[42] Nowhere do we see in al-Ṭahṭāwi's thought the defensive attitude that we see unfolding against the triumph of "Christian" Europe in the latter part of the nineteenth century, as we shall see below.

Instead, al-Ṭahṭāwī's discourse did imply that the moral virtues which provide the foundation of civilisation, such as he found them in both Europe and Ancient Egypt, might in fact supersede religion. Hourani finds that al-Ṭahṭāwī accepted as it were "the idea of change as a principle of social life and the idea of welfare and its link to progress in accordance to the thought-world of nineteenth-century Europe".[43] Al-Ṭahṭāwi was also to recognise that modern Europe, and specifically France, provided the norm of civilisation.[44] According to one study, al-Ṭahṭāwi went as far as claiming that although French laws were not derived from scripture they supported justice and human rights.[45] While maintaining that Islam is the "final religion" and that the Muslims are the "best community" (*khayr umma*), as per a citation from the Qur'an, al-Ṭahṭāwī also recognised that the West has the merit of "justice, truthfulness, equity", and above all, "the knowledge of various sciences, a knowledge which is both practiced and used in all fields from arts to artillery".[46]

In short, as one scholar puts it, the West appeared to al-Ṭahṭāwī "as less of a threat than a promise" which was always supported by Islamic references.[47] Al-Ṭahṭāwī's position reflects, in my view, both the ingenuity and the independence of this thinker's spirit. Above all, it reflects also the self-confidence which was to be found lacking in the latter part of the nineteenth century in Egypt where we witness, under Egypt's military occupation by Britain in 1882, the development of an intellectual trend whose adherents sought the good judgement of the West.

2. The Apologetics' Response to the Triumph of "Christian" Europe

In the last few years leading up to the end of the nineteenth century, the retreat and decline of Islam *vis-à-vis* "Christian" Europe was increasingly becoming too plain not to see. No less than a man such as al-Afghānī was to admit in his debate with Renan in 1883 that, just like Christendom, Islam's "Reformation" is yet to come. But for that Reformation to take place, al-Afghānī considered that Islam needed its very own Luther, perhaps, as Hourani suggests, seeing himself in the role.[48]

What is particularly interesting here is al-Afghānī's reference to Luther and his failure to invoke Muḥammad and any of the Muslim forefathers, revealing an acute sense of discontinuity with the Islamic past, and perhaps also an admission of the inadequacy of traditional Islamic thought to deal with the pertinent problems of the modern era. It is interesting in this respect to reflect on some of the associations and correspondences that began to be made by both al-Afghānī and 'Abduh in relation to Islam, and the East, as opposed to the West, as they outlined the aims of the first issue of their Paris-based secret society's periodical *al-'Urwa al-Wuthqa* (The Solid Bond) which was first published in 1884.[49]

One such aim of the said periodical warned Orientals against "failure to perform" which would result in "decline" and "weakness". Another of the periodical's aims sounded a call to hold fast to the principles of the forefathers which were depicted as being the same as those of "powerful" foreign nations. The periodical also refuted the accusations directed at the "East" in general, and at "Islam" in particular, seemingly responding to critics of Islam who argued that Muslims were held back, by the teachings of their faith, from joining in civilisation.[50]

Apart from the clear sense of failure and despair which underlies the above-mentioned correspondences in relation to both Islam and the East, there is obviously an awareness of western polemics against Islam as a force which was holding back Muslims from being effective contributors in the civilisation of the modern world. It is under such pressure that we begin to see what Choueiri refers to as a "re-arrangement of the priorities" within the Islamic reformist movement led by al-Afghānī and 'Abduh to respond to the problems faced by Muslims as a *political* community.[51]

Hourani notes that in 'Abduh's controversies with both the French historian Hanotaux and the Lebanese-Egyptian journalist, Faraḥ Anṭun, he was not concerned with the "truth" or "falsity" of Islam but rather with its compatibility with "the supposed requirements of the modern mind". In the process, he adds, 'Abduh's view of Islam may have itself been affected by his view of what the modern mind needs thus carrying further a process that was already at play, in the thought of al-Ṭahṭāwī, al-Afghānī and Khayr al-Din (d. 1889) of identifying certain traditional concepts of Islamic thought with the dominant ideas of modern Europe; thus, turning, for instance, *maṣlaḥa* into utility, *shūra* into parliamentary democracy and *ijmā'* into public opinion. Hourani argues that in this line of thought it is easy to see Islam becoming identical with civilisation and, in this way, it was also made easy "to distort if not destroy the precise meaning of the Islamic doctrines, and to lose that which distinguished Islam from other religions and even from non-religious humanism".[52]

In the face of the "actual humiliation' of Islam in the modern world, 'Abduh had devised what Jomier refers to as a "living exegesis" (*une exégèse vécue*) to respond to the challenges posed by the dominant West[53] and to recapture for Islam its "lost glory" (*sa gloire perdue*):[54]a great motif of modern Islam.[55] What is particularly interesting about 'Abduh's discourse against European civilisation is the emphasis that he placed on the "irrational" mind of the "Christian" European being seemingly in this regard particularly open to the criticism levelled by Renan, Blunt and Spencer against the Christian doctrine's inability to stand up to the scientific discoveries and the thought of the modern world.[56] 'Abduh insisted on the depiction of European Christianity as a "corrupted faith".[57]

McAuliffe observes, however, that when 'Abduh deals with "Qur'anic Christians", he seems to have followed in the footsteps of pre-modern commentators on the Qur'an by pitting Jesus' spirit and message as an "Apostle to humanity" against Jewish intractability;[58] thus, exhibiting like his predecessors of the classical age, no concern with the contemporary context under which he laboured.[59]

By unreservedly accepting the necessity of introducing much-needed reforms, such as the need to maintain equality before the law for Christians living in Muslim countries,[60] and some form of conditional equality between men and women and to abolish both polygamy and slavery,[61] in accordance with European modern ideals, 'Abduh was evidently acquiescing to the moral superiority of European civilisation even as he claims that it is up to Islam to rectify modern European thought and salvage it from its (moral) "filth".[62]

It was however up to the next generation of literati to come to grips with a world where Islam ceased to provide the social and moral norms befitting the humane bent of the new moral standards established in Europe at the time of "the Western Transmutation"[63] which was to give way to the "image of the man of humane civilisation".[64]

Hourani notes that, by and large, some of 'Abduh disciples, including both al-Azhar's '*ulama* and *élite* members of Egypt's intelligentsia, were to come to accept the moral judgement of a triumphant modern Europe.[65] Members of these two groups were, however, to take 'Abduh's thought in opposite directions with al-Azhar's '*ulama* adopting an apologetic approach while members of the second group, including Ṭaha Ḥusayn (1889-1973), taking 'Abduh's teachings in the direction of secularism, accepting as it were the truth of Islam while rejecting the notion of the superiority of Islamic civilisation over all other civilisations.[66]

By the 1920s, and throughout the 1930s, we come to a phase in Egypt's intellectual life when the supremacy of European civilisation was widely accepted by members of Egypt's intelligentsia including, apart from Ḥusayn, Ibrahim 'Abd al-Qādir al-Māzinī (1890-1949), (Quṭb's mentor), 'Abbās Maḥmūd al-'Aqqād (1889-1964), Tawfiq al-Ḥakīm (1899 or 1903-1987) and Aḥmad Amīn. All of these writers were solidly grounded in the traditional culture and had mastered Arabic and either French or English but they were, however, to grapple with the difficulty of using the Arabic language as a literary medium at a time when the colloquial and the classical Arabic were so far apart.[67] Arabic seemed to some all but inadequate as a vehicle of literary expression.

3. The Heyday of Liberalism in Egypt

In a review of the modernist phase in Egypt, published in an article entitled "Tendances Religieuses de la Littérature Egyptienne" in 1947,[68] Ḥusayn striked a triumphalist and optimistic note, asserting that the struggle of the 1920s culminated in an "assured victory" of "modern liberalism" over "orthodox traditionalism"; this ultimately allowed modernists to turn to rethinking Islamic history. Ḥusayn made sure, however, to clarify that the struggle was one which targeted prejudice and not religion as such.[69]

With no orthodox reaction being foreseeable at the time, Ḥusayn's above statement certainly conveys "a sense of self-confidence" which, Cachia observes, was to underlie the modernist project up till the late 1940s.[70] The following lengthy statement by al-'Aqqād in the early part of the 1920s seems to be typical of the liberal spirit which dominated the intellectual scene in Egypt in the early part of the twentieth century:

> You, O reformer of *ādāb*; you who want men to set life in verses inspired by a heavenly composition, to make it an art among the creative arts... what are you to do amidst those beings, creatures of playful fate which charges you, O reformer, with the price of its playfulness? Yours is the task to transport them from the buried world in which they live to the living world which is overflowing with ideals about which Aristotle mediated, which al-Ghazālī worshipped, Shakespeare put in verse, Wagner sang, Leonardo sculpted, to which Nietzsche aspired...and thousands and millions of their brethren in knowledge and consciousness have breathed.[71]

Beyond the unmistakable and complete openness to Western culture and civilisation reflected in the above statement, al-'Aqqād is also clearly indicating that he is open to universal ideals which he found reflected in a diverse and rich human heritage, developing as it were a "sense of comradeship" with a string of thinkers and artists including Aristotle, al-Ghazāli, Shakespeare, Wagner, Leonardo and Nietzsche. Equally interesting in the above statement is the reference made to a "brotherhood" binding humans together in matters of "knowledge and consciousness" which was probably unthinkable some three decades earlier under the auspices of 'Abduh who, unlike his predecessor al-Ṭahṭāwi, saw Christian Europe as more of a threat than a "promise".

It is noteworthy that the prejudicial views of the Christian European "other", which characterised 'Abduh's discourse, seem to have ultimately given rise to a literary "*salafiyya*" movement, not unlike its counterpart religious one, to revive Arabic classics.[72] It also becomes noticeable that there was a parallel movement to recoil from learning foreign languages for solely literary purposes. Jomier notes that both 'Abduh and his disciple, Rashid Riḍā, encouraged the learning of foreign languages for proselytizing purposes invoking prophetic traditions which encouraged the learning of Hebrew to achieve the same goal.[73]

Significantly, this turn of event came hand in hand with what Smith describes as "a newly-invigorated repudiation" of the two liberating forces from within the past Islamic tradition, namely: philosophy and Sufism. Smith adds that the intellectualism of philosophy and the humanism of Sufism "could provide important bases for reinterpretation". Although 'Abd al-Wahhāb, like all major Muslim reformers of the modern age – including Afghāni, 'Abduh, Gökalp, Iqbal – show "deep Sufi influence", mysticism was repudiated by the Wahhābī movement. Smith observes that

> the very flexibility of Sufism has meant that in the post-medieval decline its institutional degeneration has been outstanding, far outstripping that of other aspects of Muslim society. Sufism itself has sorely needed purgation.[74]

Rationalism was also repudiated by both the Wahhābī movement, and the Waliyullahi movement,[75] which was founded in India in the eighteenth century. Smith remarks that the vision of the founder of the Waliyullahi movement, Shāh Waliyallāh of Delhi (d.1762), retained a marked Sufi colouring, adding that he postulated "an interpretation of Islam that would coalesce a purified Sufism with a purified *Sunna*". His Islam was therefore more comprehensive and richer than the Wahhābīs.[76] Hartung notes that "Waliyallāh was styled the major point of reference for all the diverse reformist currents in the colonial period, ranging from the Deobandis* to Sir Muhammad Iqbal (d. 1938).[77] Unlike Quṭb, who repudiated all theology as he became particularly threatened by 'Abduh in 1962, as we shall see in chapter 5, Iqbal established a clear "sense of comradeship" with the founder of the Waliyullahi movement, Shāh Waliyallāh of Delhi, as he recognised him as "the last great theologian of Islam".[78]

It is in understanding the significance of these developments in Islam's modern history that one can appreciate the role played by Ṭaha Ḥusayn in his attempt at what Kreutz describes as "no less than a fusion between the classical age and modern times in the sphere of Arabic literature". Having advocated the view that "if there was no old, there would be no modern", Kreutz explains, Ḥusayn was no enemy of tradition and appreciated ancient Arabic literature as "a foothold of culture". To Ḥusayn, however, the "true past of Egypt" rested as well in Greek heritage which he found provided the roots of Western civilisation.[79] In 1921, Ḥusayn started his academic career with a chair of Roman and Greek History at Cairo University.[80]

In Hourani's view, Ḥusayn was the most systematic thinker, and perhaps the most considerable artist, among Egypt's men of letters in the first part of the twentieth century. The centrality of Ḥusayn's thought, Hourani argues, lies in being "the last great representative of a line of thought", and the writer who has given "the final statement of the system of ideas which underlay social thought and political action in the Arab countries for three generations." Significantly, Ḥusayn, who served as a Minister of Education in the last Wafdist government during the reign of King Farouk,[81] was replaced by an officer, Kamāl al-Din Ḥusayn, who altered the school curricula to build-up Nasser "as a regional anti-Western populist leader"[82] following the 1952 military coup d'état in Egypt.

Smith observes that much of the West came to the Muslim world "rearing indigenously a generation deeply exposed to Western modernity", who acquired a set of new ideas which were inculcated in educational ways. Broadly speaking, Smith considers that Islamic liberalism "has evinced many forms, taking on the individual quality of various persons" including Sir Sayyid Ahmad Khan (1817-98) and the 'Aligarh movement in India; the modernist Amir 'Ali (1849-1928); Shaykh Muḥammad 'Abduh, followed by Ṭaha Ḥusayn; Shinasi (1824-1871), Namik Kemal (1840-1888), Abdulhak Hâmid (1851-1937), Tevfik Fikret (1870-1915) among many others in Turkey.[83]

In 1900, a disciple of 'Abduh, French-educated Qāsim Amīn (1865-1908), published a book on the emancipation of women in which he questioned the very idea of Islamic civilisation providing the model for human perfection. Amīn was also to go as far as advocating the view that Islamic civilisation was not without its defects and that, in fact, it lacked moral originality, even in its great early age.[84] Hourani argues that the appeal in Amīn's book is no longer to Qur'an and *shari'a* "rightly interpreted", it is rather to the sciences and social thought of the modern West with Herbert Spencer being quoted on several occasions in the book.[85] Amīn argued further that "it is useless to hope to adopt the sciences of Europe, without coming within the radius of its moral principles; the two things are indissolubly connected".[86]

Throughout the early part of the twentieth century, comparisons were constantly being made by Egypt's literati to suggest, as Cachia puts it, "kinship in genius'" between Arab and Western authors when applying Western canons of literary criticism to Arabic literature.[87] Examples of these comparisons which he brings to light include Ḥusayn's description of al-Ma'arrī as "the Arab Lucretius".[88] In other instances, comparisons were also drawn between "the concordance of the senses", or the dependence of literary expression on cogency of thought as seen by Wordsworth and 'Abd al-Qāhir al-Jurjānī.[89] The latter topic was tackled in a 1947 study by Muḥammad

Khalaf-Allah[90] and was subsequently to attract Quṭb's attention, singling it out for one of his numerous attacks on academic works. Interestingly, al-Badawī observes, Quṭb seems to have been especially targeting studies which were favourably received by Ḥusayn in the course of the 1940s.[91]

Of particular significance to this study is the emergence of an intellectual trend which seemed to disregard differences of race or culture with Ḥusayn, for instance, going as far as claiming "kinship with the West" on account of a shared Mediterranean culture. Cachia finds that this trend came close to achieving an "all-embracing humanism" which went hand in hand with an awareness of the role of the West as both "forerunner" and "mentor".[92] In the same vein, Safran argues that there is a clear leaning to a form of "humanistic morality" in the works of both Ḥusayn and Hugo in view of the sympathy these two authors showed for human failure, and their ability to see moments of moral greatness even in sinful and corrupt lives.[93]

In Safran's discussion of the "progressive" phase in Egypt's modern thought, he finds that although Ḥusayn failed to present an explicit statement of his idea of ethics in his extensive works, his views on this particular matter were implicitly communicated in his summaries of, and comments on French novels and plays and in his biographical sketches of French authors. It seems to be the case too that in tackling the lives of French authors or classical Arabic poets, Ḥusayn's works tended to underlie "the dissent and deviation of his subjects from the real or alleged beliefs, norms and customs of their times". Safran further remarks that Ḥusayn's revision of the traditional view of the classical Islamic times, as the golden age of piety and greatness, aimed at once to make his poets more human while facilitating a wider acceptance of the "fluidity" and "permissiveness" of the time.[94]

Here again Ḥusayn's initiative seems to have unnerved Quṭb who accused Ḥusayn of a tendency "to portray deviant characters and to uncover the evil elements and lowly sentiments of the characters he tackles".[95] It was, however, rather Quṭb who had subscribed wholeheartedly to a school of thought which held derogatory views of the Arab Bedouins in favour of an Egyptian identity.[96]

As early as 1932, and throughout his literary career, Quṭb deprecated the desert poetry of the Arabs and stressed the impact of the environment in refining taste,[97] as we shall see in more detail in chapter 3. In 1946, Quṭb praised both al-Māzinī, and al-'Aqqād, for co-authoring the book entitled *al-Diwān* which, according to him, supplied the "axe of demolition" which he found was necessary before undertaking construction in the literary sphere.[98] It is noteworthy that al-Māzinī's work seems to have acquired a racialist tone against the Arabs. As revealed in an article he wrote on Ibn al-Rūmī in 1912,[99] al-Māzinī expressed the view that "of all Arab poets, writers and great men, the ones most deserving of being designated as geniuses were of non-Arab extraction".[100]

For all intents and purposes, it appears that Quṭb's anti-traditionist stance which went as far as dismantling the idea of the "sacredness" of the Arabic language, thus challenging in the process the regressive orientation underlying the whole edifice of Islamic and Arab tradition,[101] was more in tune with the modernist project than the position adopted by Ḥusayn who undertook the impossible task of attempting to revive classical Arabic while separating it from religion.[102] As Safran finds, Ḥusayn also recognised, at the same time, the possibility of conflict between the conclusions drawn by human reason and the content of the Qur'anic text.[103]

In Safran's view, it seems to be the case that the liberal trend was able to make great strides in the intellectual arena by "stretching" two principles established by 'Abduh with one of them limiting the confines of revelation and the other assuring that there was no contradiction between revelation and reason.[104] He finds further that the appearance of Ḥusayn's book *Fi al-Shi'r al-Jāhilī* dealing with pre-Islamic poetry in 1926 was to mark a 'turning point' in so far as the intellectual leaders were now faced with the problem of having to replace, in Safran's words, an "obsolescent" belief-system based on revelation with a worldview stressing human reason.[105]

It appears that the aforementioned work was also to create a great furore in Egypt on account of Ḥusayn's attempt to submit the Qur'anic text to scientific scrutiny which was especially to unnerve al-'Aqqād who went on to stress the idea of the limitation of the scientific techniques of the Orientalists and that the Qur'an was the "direct revelation of God to Muḥammad".[106] Quṭb was however to criticise Ḥusayn in 1947 for not going far enough in applying Cartesian methods to the study of the Qur'ān, as we shall see in chapter 3.

In his early Islamist writings, Quṭb's discourse did not centre on the contradiction between revelation and reason, but rather on Islam as an "idea" which stresses the social norms of Europe in general, and the egalitarian ethos of the French Revolution in particular. There is indeed something to be said about Quṭb's early Islamist writings reflecting a clear hint of what Cachia refers to as the "me-too-ism" which underlay 'Abduh's movement, whereby Islam is said to have assured the fullest equality between all men, and Muḥammad is also said to have appealed to reason.[107] Interestingly, Quṭb does not invoke in any of his writings the idea of "equity" (*inṣāf*), which is at the heart of English law, to affirm himself against the English. As discussed above, unlike the idea of equality, which has no pedigree in Islamic thought, the idea of "equity" has some remote roots in Islamic legal thought during the Umayyad period (661-750),[108] which is considered by Quṭb as being un-Islamic.[109]

To sum up, I consider that the downfall of the liberal movement in Egypt seems to have come about largely as a result of the moral compromises and the considerable loss of integrity of some modernist thinkers, including 'Abduh, who claimed for Islam the values they had found in the West. As Cachia points out, Muslim reformers "seemed to be belatedly claiming for Islam the values which had already come into currency in the West".[110]

Even more unsettling was the attempt by some intellectuals to defend Muḥammad in the face of mounting criticism in the West of some of his actions, and to adorn his personality with all kind of virtues.[111] Safran explains that

> The grafting of ethics onto the personality of Muḥammad involved a fundamental retreat from the position which the intellectual leaders had taken in the progressive phase, a retreat which handicapped the construction of any viable ethical outlook.[112]

For instance, Quṭb's mentor, al-'Aqqād, devised a theory whereby genius is seen to be an "inherent virtue in the soul" of Muḥammad in spite of his controversial actions,[113] which he defended in his series of studies on the genius of the Prophet and of other early Muslims.[114] Broadly speaking, Quṭb remained rather indifferent to the controversy around Muḥammad's persona during the literary stage of his life,[115]and did not support al-'Aqqād, who acted as Quṭb's mentor for over two decades from the mid-1920s.[116] In fact, as we shall see in chapter 4, Quṭb was particularly critical of the Prophet in the early stage of his Islamist career.

2

Historical Background II: The Life and Works of Sayyid Quṭb (1906-1966)

Born in 1906 in the Upper Egyptian village Musha of the Asyut province,[1] which was in rapid decline by the end of the 19th century mainly as a result of the loss of the Sudanese trade and the suppression of the slave trade,[2] into a reasonably well-off family[3] which was, on his father's side, six generations removed from an Indian ancestry,[4] it is perhaps no big surprise to see Quṭb exhibiting, throughout his literary career and well into the Islamist stage of his life, a marked attraction to the thought-world of India. As we shall see in chapter 4, Quṭb was especially to show a keen interest in the spirituality of the East, which he associated for the most part with India. Oddly enough, Quṭb was to take particular exception to deprecate the populist strand of Islam such as he experienced it as a child in his home village Musha, dedicating a whole chapter to the fearsome figure of *al-majdhūb*[5] in his memoirs *Ṭifl min al-Qarya* (A Child from the Village, 1946).

What is essential to pinpoint here is that Quṭb lived at a time of great turmoil, witnessing first hand the passing of the old and the advent of the modern world. Both traditional representatives of the faith, be it in its populist Sufi strand or its official al-Azhar variant with its affiliated *kuttāb* schooling, seemed to have failed abysmally to offer to Quṭb's generation of the early part of the twentieth century in Musha any degree of the essential "average expectable continuity" with the past, leaving it to the literati of the preceding generation, as we've seen in chapter 1 above, to grapple with the havoc caused by the advent of the modern world.

The effort by Egypt's literati seems to have gained particular urgency in light of the "dangers" posed by modernity to all theistic religions. As Gibb points out, the external pressure of secularism – be it in its seductive form of nationalism, or in its doctrines of scientific materialism and the economic interpretation of history – left a mark on various aspects of life in Muslim societies,[6] not excluding the Upper Egyptian village of Quṭb's childhood years, Musha, where nationalism and patriotism were certainly in the air in the early part of the twentieth century. With Quṭb's own father, Ḥajj Ibrahim, being seriously involved in the nationalist movement,[7] Quṭb was left fired up by the "sacred revolution" (*al-thawra al-muqaddasa*) which was led by the Egyptian nationalist leader Sa'd Zaghlūl (1857-1927).[8]

Quṭb recalls that barely aged ten, he was writing and delivering speeches in gatherings and mosques where the enthusiasm for the "sacred revolution" touched everyone, making them attentive to all those calling for revolution. "The new sacred name", he writes, "was that of Sa'd Zaghlūl".[9] Such was the strength of Quṭb's patriotic feelings that he also endeavoured to copy, and memorise in the process, an entire collection of poems which were banned by the authorities in Egypt for immortalising Khedive 'Abbās Ḥilmī II (1892-1914),[10] who was in Constantinople when the first World War broke out, and was subsequently deposed by the British authorities and replaced by his uncle, Ḥusayn Kāmil (1914-17), who was given the title of sulṭan. Increasingly, the British ran Egypt like a crown colony, after tightening their hold on Egypt and the Sudan.[11]

Reflecting the resentment which he must have harboured against the British, who severed Egypt's vestigial Turkish ties once the Ottoman Empire had formally entered the war on the German side,[12] Quṭb declares his allegiance to the Ottoman Empire which he accepted, at the time, as being "the state of Islam". In his memoirs, Quṭb writes that the "sentiments of the entire village were directed to the seat of the Caliphate in Turkey and against the Allies who represented 'the infidels' who were fighting the state of Islam".[13] It is important to point out here that the nationalist fervour in the National party, of which Quṭb's father was a member, was seriously compromised by a clear inclination to pan-Islamism, which placed an emphasis on strong ties with the Ottomans, while showing clear signs of animosity to Egyptian Copts. Both Copts and moderate Muslims are said to have left the party in droves.[14] One of the most celebrated members of the party, the Azharite Shaykh 'Abd al-'Aziz Jāwīsh, who wrote fiery editorials attacking the Copts,[15] deserves a mention in Quṭb's memoirs as one of the names being circulated in party meetings, along with other party leaders at the time such as Muḥammad Farid.[16]

In this chapter, I would like to address especially the section of Quṭb's memoirs entitled "Ḥaraka Thaqāfiyya" (cultural movement), in which Quṭb presents to the reader a somewhat detailed picture of the socio-cultural scene in Musha in the early part of the twentieth century. Through Quṭb's memoirs, we come to meet the central figure of 'Am Ṣāliḥ who was at the very centre of Musha's cultural life with his seasonal three to four day visits to the village, carrying over his shoulders a sack filled with some twenty or thirty books that he was to offer for sale in the village's marketplace.[17] Quṭb recalls 'Am Ṣāliḥ's visits as the most beautiful days of his life in the village, recounting that he spared no expense to purchase some of the books that 'Am Ṣāliḥ brought whatever the cost of these may be.[18]

The contents of the books of 'Am Ṣāliḥ's "library" varied to cover themes falling under the category of panegyrics and biographies,[19]with a number of other books covering a variety of topics ranging from ancient Arabic poetry telling heroic tales of Arab figures of the past such as Abu Zayd, al-Zanātī Khalīfa, Diyāb Ibn Ghanim and al-Zīr Salim and Kulayb,[20] while other books had a rather religious content with titles such as *Dalā'il al-Khayrāt,*[21] and two prayer books entitled *Du'ā' Niṣf Sha'bān* and *Du'ā' Laylat al-Qadr.*[22]

Other titles included in 'Am Ṣāliḥ's "library" fell under the rubric of detective stories such as *Sherlock Holmes*, *Sinclair* and *The Noble Thief*, while others dealt with general cultural themes covering subjects such as education, refinement and the benefit of the intellect selling alongside books dealing with Arabic grammar. One of the books dealing with Arabic grammar was entitled *al-Mawahib al-Fatḥiyya fī 'Ulūm al-Lūgha al-'Arabiyya*[23] (The Enlightening Talents in the Sciences of the Arabic Language)[24] was penned by an educator at Quṭb's future Cairo-based teachers' training college Dār al-'Ulūm, Ḥamza Fatḥ Allah.[25]

Included in 'Am Ṣāliḥ's "library" as well were some other books which are described by Quṭb as falling in the category of high-quality and what the villagers, and Quṭb, considered to be "dangerous" books which were used for dispelling magical spells or fortune-telling. These last books were reserved by 'Am Ṣāliḥ for the benefit of Quṭb,[26] and were to feed into Quṭb's own library. Quṭb tells us that these "dangerous books" won him fame in the circles of the "cultured" people in the village where he is said to have won a reputation for his reading habits and for the books which came into his possession. He also tells us that he was "elevated" in the eyes of the cultured people of Musha who predicted a bright future for the ten year old boy.[27]

Among the "dangerous" books in Quṭb's library which, according to him, won him great fame and reputation in the village, especially among many members of the village's womenfolk as well as some of its youth, is a work by Abu Ma'shar al-Falakī on astrology used for fortune-telling which, Quṭb writes, was based on certain mathematical equations which were derived from the old Hebrew language. Another book was that of Shamhūrish which contained many magical spells, incantations, iconography and charms and some recipes for incense which were said to bring good fortune, love and completion of one's needs and respectability.[28]

Both these two books were to be put to good use by Quṭb keeping him, as he recalls, quite busy with villagers' requests, especially in love-related matters and fortune-telling,[29] which filled him with "strange ecstasy" as he saw the requests pouring in with "all the doors being 'opened' to him", as he puts it.[30]

But for Quṭb's inability to procure copies of *Kitāb al-Kunūz* (The Book of Treasures)[31] and al-Bukhārī's *ḥadīth* collection,[32] Quṭb writes that he was "quite pleased with himself, happy with his library, taking delight in the 'breadth' of his culture and that of his reputation".[33] The acquisition of a copy of *Kitāb al-Kunūz* would have however guaranteed Quṭb "substantive and tempting wealth".[34] Being in possession of a copy of al-Bukhārī's *ḥadīth* collection, which was only readily available to the then highly-respected ten Azhar scholars and the two Qur'an reciters in the village, with the latter using their copies in sorcery-related matters and in what seemed to be a lucrative industry of spells, talismans and amulets,[35] which owes its origin in pagan customs,[36] would have presumably conferred on him the power he seems to have especially associated with Islam since his early childhood.

It is important to emphasise here that al-Bukhārī* (d. 870) was especially valued by Quṭb and Musha villagers for striking "terror" and "fear" in the hearts of those who were involved in organised and unbridled acts of theft and robberies in the village. Custom had it that some of these alleged robbers were, at times, made to endure taking an oath in al-Bukhārī's name.[37] Significantly, Quṭb accepts that al-Bukhārī seems to have superseded the place of the Qur'an in folk-beliefs in Musha in the early part of the twentieth century. He relates that al-Bukhārī's oath was placed in a higher echelon by villagers than taking a similar oath by placing one's hand on the Qur'an or taking one in the name of God or the Prophet of Islam.[38]

What is also made plainly evident in Quṭb's memoirs is the unfolding of an otherness process targeting the Arab Bedouins who are seen as outsiders by Quṭb. He recounts that the Arab Bedouins have introduced into the Egyptian environment "their" own traditions which confer heroism and courage on murderous acts and brigandage.[39] There is also a clear indication in Quṭb's recollections of his early childhood years that there was an apparent total discontinuity with the Arabic literary heritage. Even though 'Am Ṣāliḥ's "library" certainly never lacked copies of books on ancient Arab poetry, Quṭb did not seem to take an interest in that particular literary genre and espoused the view, seemingly shared by other villagers, that Arab poetry was a prerogative of the early Arabs of the peninsula. Quṭb recounts that upon sharing the news with his friends in the village that poets, such as Muḥammad Ibrāhim Ḥāfiẓ (d. 1932), and Aḥmad Shawqī (d. 1932), existed and lived in Cairo, none of them found the news even remotely credible.[40]

Significantly, the traditional chivalrous Sufi *futuwwa** (chivalry) institution,[41] which goes back to medieval times,[42] seems to have dwindled to being a "nocturnal base and ignoble activity" of brigandage in Quṭb's village. According to Quṭb, all the youth in the village, even those who belonged to rich families, engaged in acts of brigandage to seek an outlet for physical energy.[43] While there is some evidence that the *futuwwa* institution persisted in *dhikr* Sufi circles in other villages of Upper Egypt well into the mid-1990s,[44] the Muslim Brothers used the *futuwwa* institution at grass roots level to establish its Rover Scout units in the mid-1930s.[45] Those units played their first important role, as forces of "order and security"' in the late1930 s.[46]It is noteworthy that Naguib Maḥfouẓ (b.1911) wrote of the "*fatwana*" in *Malḥamat al-Ḥarāfīsh* (*Epic of the Ḥarāfīsh*,1977) in terms of a tradition which continued to be put in use in the alleys of old Cairo, as he witnessed it, for "the service of the people".[47]Often times, he expressed an "unconcealed admiration" about *futuwwa,* describing one of those that he witnessed as a "true Knight".[48]

Generally speaking, it appears that fewer of the *'ulama* and the educated élite class joined the Sufi orders which is particularly significant since, as Smith explains, the Sufi "*ṭarīqah* is to Islam as church is to Christianity".[49] According to Hourani, Sufi thought and practice were no longer held "within the restraints of the high urban culture".[50] The general decline of Sufism was such that none of the luminaries of the literati generation preceding that of Quṭb is known to have been an initiate of any of the existing Sufi orders, which came to be associated in Quṭb's early 1950s writings with sorcery and charlatanism.[51]

One also looks in vain in Quṭb's memoirs for a figure such as Ḥusayn's Shaykh in *Shajarat al Bu's* (The Tree of Misery, 1944). As Quṭb himself admitted in *Kutub wa Shakhṣiyyāt* (1946), the traditional deep "faith" (*imān*) of old of Ḥusayn's Shaykh in the work, a generation earlier, is worthy of portrayal as it was not likely to be found again in the modern age.[52] In 1951, Quṭb is said to have admitted to having been an atheist (*mulḥid*) for some eleven years to the Islamist Indian scholar Nadwi upon meeting him in Egypt.[53]

What we see unfolding in Quṭb's discourse instead, especially in the pre-Islamist stage of his life, is a systematic deprecation of the "traditional" which is almost always contrasted unfavourably with the "modern". This particular aspect of Quṭb's discourse becomes particularly discernible as Quṭb makes his way to the newly-opened local modern "sacred" school as he refers to it in his memoirs in favour of the traditional "repugnant" al-Azhar-affiliated *Kuttāb,* as we shall see in more detail in the next chapter.[54]

Except on occasions when Quṭb links men of the past to power and respectability in the same work, such as in the case of al-Bukhārī and that of al-Zamakhsharī (1074-1144),[55] there is hardly any quarter or deference given to any men of the Islamic past. In agreement with Goodman's analysis of Quṭb's writings, I find that

> Quṭb fails to rise above ideology. He does not draw from his own heritage that intellectual scope and catholicity of spirit that Ghazālī says made him "thirst from an early age to apprehend the true nature of things".[56]

Quṭb was also probably one of the first generation of Egyptian literati who were to bear the full brunt of the "hollowness" of the newly-introduced educational reforms in Egypt's countryside in the early part of the twentieth century.[57] For one thing, as Tibi points out, the deeply-rooted rote-learning methods used in Muslim societies rendered these somewhat semi-modern educational institutions unfit for the purpose of delivering modern content while allowing for the necessary cultural accommodation to introduce social change.[58] Tibi argues that these methods, which are traditionally applied to teaching the Qur'an, fail to deliver the content of European positive sciences.[59]

This particular problem becomes especially discernible during Quṭb's literary career in which he demonstrates great discomfort, and inability, to grasp the essentials of the "modern" in view of the linguistic disabilities from which he suffered throughout his life.[60] Al-Badawī points out that Quṭb has been a "hanger-on" in his total dependence on al-'Aqqād's appraisal and translations of English poetry in the course of his literary career.[61] Even following Quṭb's rift with his mentor in the late 1940s, Quṭb's critics caught on his total dependence on translated works in writing *al-Naqd al-Adabī: Uṣūluhu wa Manāhijahū* (1947), and accused him of plainly committing plagiarism by copying the terminology of the so-called "integral Psychology" group and its affiliated magazine.[62]

As Lord Cromer once remarked, emphasis on recitation and memorisation in Egyptian schooling was merely "loading the memory without exercising the mind".[63] It is hence no surprise to see Quṭb marvelling in his memoirs about the ability of one of Dār al-'Ulūm's students to deliver speeches which were written by himself and not derived from a book. He writes additionally that he had been sceptical about the possibility of this happening even as relatives of the said student swore that this "miracle" had taken place and that they had seen him "creating off-the-cuff [speeches] that he did not copy from a book!"[64] Quṭb was to boast about his ability to memorise the Qur'an in addition to other unspecified materials that he was taught at school.[65]

Safran remarks that, under British rule, public education in Egypt expanded extremely slowly and continued to be "purposely geared toward producing government officials". Apart from the traditional *kuttāb*, there were only sixty-eight government-supported primary and secondary schools in 1914 at a time when the population was much more than nine million. Private and missionary schools were, however, to mushroom, offering a parallel system of education at the same time. According to Safran, there were 739 private Egyptian schools with an attendance of 99,000, and 328 communal and missionary schools with 48,000 pupils in 1914.[66]

Apart from the slow expansion of schooling in Egypt, there was another serious weakness which was already leaving its deep mark on Egyptian society at the time of 'Abduh. As Hourani points out, behind the division of educational institutions in Egypt, there lays a "division of spirits" which was such that the parallel systems of education, at the time, had produced two different educated classes in Egypt, each with a spirit of its own and hardly sharing anything in common: the traditional Islamic spirit, which resisted all change, and the spirit of the younger generation, which was especially open to all modern European ideas, especially those of the French Enlightenment.[67] In the late 1930s, Ḥusayn caught on this particular weakness when he referred to the "social discord" created by the lack of harmony between the religious, foreign and public schooling.[68]

New modern state schools, (such as that attended by Quṭb), were to suffer from what Hourani describes as "the vices" of both forms of modern schooling. While they were imitations of the modern missionary schools, government schools taught no religion except in a formal way, and therefore "no social or political morality", while missionary schools taught Christianity.[69] Quṭb was, in fact, the one to initiate an effort to memorise the Qur'an in his modern school to compete with the village's *Kuttāb* children, as we shall see in the next chapter.

In the whole previous history of student missions in the early part of the twentieth century, eighty per cent had studied in France with some ninety six per cent of these taking up subjects related to the humanities and the social sciences. Besides these governmental missions, hundreds of students studied on their own in Europe, particularly in France.[70] Hourani notes that it was Ḥusayn's four-year study tour in France, beginning in 1915, which in fact "decided the destiny of his mind", as a similar study tour affected Ṭahṭāwī before him.[71] It is ultimately against the backdrop of the humanist trends of thought that those who obtained a French education were to form, especially Shawqī and Ḥusayn, that we see Quṭb's animosity to the West firstly unfolding.

As we shall see with more detail in the next chapter, Ḥusayn acted as the essential "other" to Quṭb as he seems to have harboured an ambition to replace his mentor, al-'Aqqād, as the leading poet in Egypt following the death of Shawqī in 1932. Although Quṭb was ill-equipped for joining the ranks of the leading members of Egypt's literati, who were shaping the future of Egypt in the early part of the twentieth century, due primarily to the poor quality of education he received. Yūnus points out that Quṭb's job at the Ministry of Education, between 1933 and 1952, hardly satisfied his ambition to achieve the "grandeur" to which he aspired.[72]

It is appropriate here to shed some light on the tremendous impact of Quṭb's mother, Fatima, in tracing the road that he was to tread in life. Perhaps nothing elucidates better the place of Quṭb's mother, and the role she played in his life, than a lengthy quote from his memoirs as he recollects a poignant scene that seemingly shook him and left a great mark on his life. One can only feel sympathy for Quṭb as he gives a detailed account of a day when, barely aged ten, his "small heart knew the bitterness of sadness" before the time it was ready to capture it, as he puts it, when he caught his mother profusely sobbing and grieving out loud. Recollecting the events of that day in the chapter he dedicates to the "Sorrows of the Countryside", Quṭb writes,

> His small heart knew the bitterness of sadness before it was time...this was a day when he returned from school and entered the house to find his mother, as usual, only to find her grieving out loud, repeating in a soft voice one of those numerous compositions to which villagers have recourse [habitually on occasions of sorrow, especially in funerals in Egypt's countryside] with tears

> pouring out abundantly from her eyes while she was fighting them, without success, when she saw him. He was barely aged ten when he saw her crying for the first time. He had seen her disheartened before but as soon as he would ask her 'what is wrong mother?' she would put on a happy face and answer him as she embraces him affectionately: Nothing! Nothing...just a bit tired..[73]

As it transpires, Quṭb's father had sold a piece of their fast dwindling land on that day as his mother confided in him making him promise to be a "man",[74] and commanding him to regain whatever was lost by his father.[75] Quṭb was made aware on that day that the sale was one in a series of sales over the years which would mean that eventually, if things continued this way, the family would face the prospect of not having any of its land left. That would mean that there would be "no field, no home, no animals and none of all the things that you see", his mother explained.[76]

Quṭb understood this to mean that there was a great catastrophe hanging over his head; one which, he thought, threatened him on a very personal level. Not only would he lose that "field" which he visited every Friday to run and jump around. He recounts that he had wondered whether he would lose a particular cow of which he was particularly fond, recalling the close friendship that had come to bind him, as well as his two sisters and his mother, to that particular cow.[77]

At the time, Quṭb had two sisters with one of them being thirteen and the other seven. His mother was yet to give birth to his younger brother, Muḥammad, and another sister as he tells us.[78] Quṭb's father married twice and by his first wife he fathered a son who did not seem to be close to Quṭb.[79] By his second wife, Fatima, he fathered three daughters, Nafisa, Amīna and Ḥamida, and three sons: Sayyid, Muḥammad and a third one who died soon after birth.[80] Interestingly, with the exception of Nafisa, all of Quṭb's other siblings became actively involved in the Islamist movement starting in the 1950s.[81] However, Quṭb seems to have been much closer to his younger brother, Muḥammad, which is clear in dedicating his mid-1930s anthology, *al-Shaṭi' al-Majhūl,* to the latter whom he considers to be the "unfulfilled hopes", a "consolation" and an "extension" to his life and a "son".[82]

1. Quṭb's Early Years in Cairo & the Emergence of a Poet and a Literary Critic

On that eventful day, when Quṭb's mother confided in him, he had become aware of the "reality of the responsibility" that was laid on his shoulders.[83] A few years later, Quṭb left for Cairo in fulfilment of the promise he had made to his mother to restore the family's lost fortune. For the next four years he was to live with his maternal uncle, Aḥmad Ḥusayn 'Uthmān, in the North Cairo district of Zaytūn[84] as his mother had planned so that he can get an education and become a salaried "effendi". He recalls that she then told him that he was to remember that the land in the village was being sold because of his father's extravagance, asking him to be careful with money, and to spend only on essentials so as to be in a position to buy back the lands that the family was losing.[85]

In the early 1920s, Quṭb met his future mentor, al-'Aqqād, through his uncle, and is said to have been highly impressed by his personality and thought. Under the influence of al-'Aqqād and his uncle, who were both members of the Wafd party, Quṭb became an active member of the same party and began to compose poetry and write articles attacking British policies and defending Sa'd Zaghlūl.[86] Over the next two decades or so, nationalist themes become a foremost concern in Quṭb's discourse against the West, with motifs such as the "conscience" of the West being often invoked in his writings of the 1940s, in relation to the issue of Palestine,[87] which seemed to have troubled him as early as 1931.[88] Having witnessed the British imposing a Wafdist cabinet on King Faruq by force of arms on February 4, 1942,[89] when British armour surrounded the palace,[90] Qutb was increasingly becoming disillusioned with the prevailing political situation by the mid-1940s.[91]

Given his own father's remoteness,[92] Quṭb seems to have found in al-'Aqqād a warm and affectionate father figure,[93] with whom he had forged such a strong bond that al-Khaldi finds it fitting to qualify it as no less than an "extinction [of Quṭb] in al-'Aqqād" (*al-fanā' fī al-'Aqqād*);[94] Badawī dedicates a whole section to the formative period of Quṭb's literary career, spanning the period between the mid-1920s and the late 1930s, to a discussion of Quṭb's life *Fī Ẓilāl al-'Aqqād* (in the shade of al-'Aqqād),[95] clearly drawing a parallel with the later Islamist period in Quṭb's life when the latter wrote his commentary on the Qur'an under the title *Fī Ẓilāl al-Qur'ān* (In the Shade of the Qur'an).

According to Badawī, Quṭb seems to have also sought to be an extension of al-'Aqqād in this early stage of his literary career, engaging in fierce battles to defend his mentor.[96] It is in this light that Badawī sees Quṭb's attacks of the period on the conservative Musṭafa Ṣadiq al-Rafi'ī (1880-1937),[97] the neo-classicist Shawqī and the founder of the Apollo group Aḥmad Zaki Abu Shādī,[98] to champion the case of al-'Aqqād[99] (and ultimately his own). Judging by the "extreme hatred" Quṭb seems to have harboured for the so-called "poets of occasions", especially Shawqī,[100] and the emotionalism and the total lack of any objectivity in Quṭb's "fanatic" feud with the latter in support of al-'Aqqād, Badawī concludes that Quṭb seems to have been even "more Christian than the Pope", in his fierce battles in defence of al-'Aqqād, and to have given up in the process all pretence of objectivity in studying Shawqī's poetic output.[101]

At this early stage of his life, Quṭb seems to have seen his literary career unfolding especially in defiance of Ḥusayn who seems to act as his essential "other", as well as a role model for Quṭb to emulate on a literary level well into the 1940s.[102] As early as

1932, Quṭb seems to have been particularly incensed by Ḥusayn's assessment of the literary aptitude of the younger generation of poets (to which he belonged), quoting the latter as stating that he could hardly find in the new generation of poets the likes of Shawqī, Ḥāfiẓ and Khalīl Muṭrān (1872-1949), and in prose any youth who had introduced a "creed" (*madhhab*) to rival Haykal, al-Mazinī and al-'Aqqād.[103]

In response to Ḥusayn's statement, Quṭb defies Ḥusayn and retorts in a lecture at the teachers college Dār al-'Ulūm, of which he was a student between 1929 and 1933, that the younger generation would excel even more than the older one, adding that the future would prove what he proposes.[104] Aged only twenty six at the time, Quṭb has already been on the job market for some seven years,[105] with apparently nothing to show for it. As the material situation of Quṭb's family in Musha began to deteriorate, Musallam contends that Quṭb came to be more concerned about saving his family from total ruin, and gave up on the more ambitious goal of restoring his family's wealth.[106] It seems that the circumstances of Quṭb's life in Cairo were rather difficult, and that his pay, as a teacher, hardly covered his needs and those of his family.[107]

What is important to pinpoint here is Ḥusayn's use of the word *madhhab* in reference to literary "creeds", or literary schools of thought,[108] and his expectation that the younger generation of literati (Quṭb's generation that is) should introduce a (literary) *madhhab* to be accepted as new entrants in Egypt's literary scene. More importantly, Quṭb speaks of his own full conviction in the "literary creed" (*al-'aqīda al-adabiyya*) to which he belongs even though he acknowledges that the credit does not go to him for disseminating "the message" (*al-risala*). "This is part of my convictions. I will defend it as any person of faith would defend his creed, even if the credit is not mine (to claim) for this message".[109]

Throughout Quṭb's literary career, however, he seems to have failed to commit to any of the existing literary schools, and to have come under severe criticism for failing to do so. In a later edition of his book on literary criticism *al-Naqd al-Adabī* (1947), Quṭb seems to have been made acutely aware of the criticism that was levelled against him by some members of the literati in relation to the "disturbance" in his "methodology" (*manhaj*) or the lack thereof to which he responded by detracting his critics and claiming that, unlike them who use "borrowed [literary] standards/ principles" (*qawa'id muqtabasa*) and "established/fixed forms" (*qawalib muqarara*), he knows his way and that a "creative critic has his own way"((*li-kul naqid mubtakir ṭarīqatahū*).[110]

Clearly, Quṭb shows in his early writings deference to al-'Aqqād as the carrier of *the* "message", citing here one of al-'Aqqād's poems which, he explains, he felt "compelled" to choose as he found nothing to match it in *all* Arabic poetry, be it modern or ancient.[111] The said poem represents to him, as he explains, an ideal type leading to "the high ideal" (*al-mathal al-a'la*).[112] Reflecting, however, an early dislike for philosophy and making a case for his "mission in life", Quṭb goes on to explain that the poet is more in tune with "the truth" than the philosopher, stating that "those who feel are more truthful than those who observe".[113]

In Quṭb's anthology of poems of the mid-1930s, *al-Shaṭi' al-Majhūl,* however, one begins to see clearly that the defiance and the optimism which were the hallmarks of his mission statement above have somewhat dissipated giving way, on some occasions, to a clear sense of acute despair and estrangement which seem to have accompanied him following his father's death in the same year he graduated from Dār al-'Ulūm in 1933.[114] Good examples in this respect are provided in some of the poems of the said anthology such as the one entitled *al-Insān al-Akhīr* (The Last Man) in which he writes of feelings of "despair" and indicates a clear longing for death,[115] and in his other poem *al-Gharīb* (The Stranger) in which he writes of the "death of hope" and "extinction".[116]

Although there is certainly no lack of self-aggrandisement and self-glorification which, Shalash observes, begin to be visibly discernible starting 1932 when he delivered his lecture in college,[117] there is also a clear hint that Quṭb's dreams of recuperating his family's wealth and of achieving the grandeur for which he and his mother believed he was meant, have been dashed.[118] Eventually, Quṭb's family moved in with him in Cairo in 1936[119] after selling both the family house and (whatever bit of) land they had left in Musha.[120]

In *al-Aṭyāf al-Arba'a* (The Four Phantoms, 1945) which was co-authored by Quṭb, his two sisters Ḥamida and Amīna and his younger brother Muḥammad as a tribute to their mother, who died in 1940, Quṭb is quoted as saying that his mother had instilled in him, since early boyhood, the idea that he was made of a "unique fabric" (*nasij farid*) to fulfil her hopes, leaving him with an impression of himself as being "great", and that he was required to pay the "dues of this greatness".[121]

Throughout the 1940s, Quṭb continues to be actively engaged in literary activity, publishing a novel under the title *al-Madīna al-Masḥūra* (The Bewitched City, 1946) which appears to be inspired by the Persian legendary tale of Scheherazade who seems to have seized Quṭb's imagination especially as depicted by Ḥusayn in *Aḥlam Scheherazade* (The Dreams of Scheherazade, 1942).[122] Quṭb also published a number of works which were later denounced by him as "un-Islamic".[123] These include: *al-Aṭyāf al-Arba'a* (1945), mentioned above, Quṭb's autobiography *Ṭifl min al-Qarya* (1946), and his other work *Ashwāk* (Thorns, 1947)[124] which was published only once.

At this stage of Quṭb's life, I tend to agree with Abu Rabi' that there are signs of great confusion in Quṭb's thought[125] which casts serious doubt on the unsubstantiated suggestion made by al-Khaldi that Quṭb's "voyage of loss" had nearly come to an end in 1940, giving way to the first Islamist stage of his life between 1940 and 1945.[126] Naguib Maḥfouz writes that he had doubts about Quṭb's integrity and that he was "disturbed" by an "opportunistic side" in Quṭb as he depicts the latter's "blind attitude" toward a

Coptic writer.[127] In a series of vignettes of Egyptian characters,[128] published under the title *al-Marayā* (*Mirrors*) in 1972,[129] Maḥfouz describes Quṭb as someone who

> never spoke about religion, pretended modernity in his ideas and dress and adopted European habits in food and going to the cinema, yet the effect religion had on him, his belief, even fanaticism, were not a secret to me.[130]

For example, Quṭb shows total openness to the decadent movement in Europe as late as 1947,[131] and is even said to have advocated nudity in the 1940s.[132] In the novel, *Ashwāk,* of the same year, the main character Sami (who is supposed to be Quṭb in real life) emerges as someone who is somewhat confused, and free of any moral or social grounding even as he mentions that his upbringing in the countryside impressed on him that people there were made of "a better stock, and were more magnanimous, and in possession of a purer conscience".[133]Quṭb tells us of an incident when Sami walks in, unannounced, on his fiancée, Samira, in her bedroom, and talks of seeing her in her underwear.[134] While admitting that he had only known women on paper, Sami, however, talks of hot embraces and kisses between him and Samira,[135] and takes exception to tell the reader about his fiancée's "seductive breasts".[136]

I note here that it is very doubtful that the character Samira existed in real life in Egypt of the 1940s when women had just been emancipated in the early part of the twentieth century to conform with the egalitarian ideals of modern Europe. Cachia explains that the process of "*iqtibās*" in modern Egyptian literature involved "transferring the [literary] topic from one milieu to another, and changing the foreign characters into Egyptians or Orientals. As an example, he quotes al-Ḥakīm as explaining that in the sex-segregated Egyptian society of the early part of the twentieth century, before women abandoned the veil, the literati got around this situation by making all men and women related in all of the plays of the period.[137]

Although Quṭb did not advocate the seclusion of women, his discourse starting the late 1940s is replete with suggestions that women are no more than sex objects. Thus, in his review of al-Ḥakim's novel *Al-Ribāṭ al-Muqadas* (The Sacred Bond), for instance, Quṭb commands the idea of medieval chastity belts, as a copycat of "the natural and special seal" (of virginity). He claims that "eternal nature" (not God) meant to convey a special meaning when it presented only female humans, and not animal females, "sealed" (*makhtūma*) and "locked" (*muqfala*), adding that he is talking about cases of "precious" and "upright" female humans.[138]

Generally speaking, Calvert observes that Cairo's watchful literary critics commented on "the effusive quality" of Quṭb's poetry, and criticised him for his "weird mental images", and "the lack of a moral vision and a philosophical outlook". Quṭb is also said to have been criticised for "the excessive praise" that he tended to heap upon himself.[139]

In my view, the one consistency which I have seen in Quṭb's works is his insistence on his pioneering role firstly, as a poet and a literary critic, and then as an Islamist ideologue. One of the most interesting views which Quṭb brings to the fore, in the late 1940s, is the one relating to the role of the "*grand littérateur*" as one which is on a par with that of the Prophet.[140] Cachia remarks on the "heroic dimension" in modern Arabic literature with its emphasis on the exalted function of literature with its ascription of a prophetic function to the poet. He observes further that, as early as 1876, poetry came to be seen as a matter of inspiration – as in *ilhām* rather than the Qur'anic-related word *waḥy.*[141] It is in the same sense that Quṭb uses the word *ilhām,* even as early as 1932, when he claims that the "true poet" is endowed with "genuine *ilhām*" together with "deep *waḥy*".[142]

It is worth mentioning that Quṭb claimed that he was in a state of *ilhām* when he wrote *al-Taṣwīr al-Fannī fī al-Qur'ān* (Artistic Portrayal in the Qur'an, 1945)[143] which received a poor reception by Egypt's older literati generation. In his other anthology of articles of the period *Kutub wa Shakhṣiyyat* (1946), which offers a good overview of the literature which has come to Quṭb's attention at the time,[144] Quṭb articulates his understanding of his function as a literary critic even as he lashes out at senior members of Egypt's literati.

The last main work which belongs to this period is *al-Naqd al-Adabī: Uṣūluhu wa Manāhijahū* (Literary Criticism: its Sources and Methods, 1947) which seems to have failed to attract the attention of scholars who have done work on Quṭb[145] even though it is crucial in illuminating the vital period leading up to the Islamist stage of Quṭb's life. As will be discussed in chapter 3 and 4, this work marks the beginning of the disruption of Quṭb's literary career, especially as he was accused of plagiarism in relation to this particular work in 1952. I consider the work to be an extension of *al-Taṣwīr al-Fannī fī al-Qur'ān* in which Quṭb spells out his leaning to an "emotive logic" (*manṭiq wijdāni*) in dealing with texts even as he deals with the Qur'an which he considers to be a book of literary excellence irrespective of its sacred content, thus weakening the argument of some scholars who argued that Quṭb had received the Qur'an as a religious text at this early stage of his life.[146]

2. The Early Islamist Stage of Quṭb's Life (1949-1958)

Starting with 'Abduh, there appears to have been a strong trend to discount, to a great extent, the value of the whole Sunna tradition in accordance with 'Abduh's conception of prophecy which, according to Safran, tended to restrict the notion of the infallibility of the Prophet to the sole activity of transmitting the divine message. Emphasis was placed instead on his activity as a great social reformer, notwithstanding that he was subject to human failures and errors which largely translated in 'Abduh's discourse in a *de facto* detraction from the authoritative character of prophetic traditions.[147]

As Cachia remarks, a marked feature of post 1930s literature is the greater emphasis which was placed on what religion can do for man's social good rather than on what man can do to glorify God.[148] A good illustration of this kind of literary genre is found in the work of the Azharite Khalid M. Khalid (b. 1920), whose collection of works under the title *Religion in the Service of the People* (1953) conveys a modernist approach, stressing that "the rights of man are of the rights of God".[149]

Cachia further notes a conjoining of Muḥammad and Christ, best exemplified by another of Khalid's works,[150] towards a common cause stressing the triumph of love and peace in line with the modern view of religion as a guardian of man's social good.

Although, according to Musallam, Quṭb and a number of other Egyptian intellectuals "saw a need to base social justice on the comprehensive Islamic way of life" as they set up the journal *al-Fikr al-Jadid* (*Modern thought*) in 1947,[151] it is particularly interesting to note that Quṭb was quite sceptical and critical of 'Adil Kamil's novel *Millīm al-Akbar* (1944) which he qualifies as falling under the rubric of "social awareness" literature for his call to tax all artists. In a review of the work, Quṭb notes that the novel is one which deals with class struggles and falls under the category of "social awareness" literature within a worldwide intellectual movement. He notes further that the call was particularly led by communism and socialism and that, while he values this particular literary genre at that particular juncture of world history, he criticises the excessiveness in the attempt of some to impose it on all artists as a "human tax".[152]

Two years later, Quṭb develops the idea of "social justice" as the main theme of his first Islamist work al-*'Adāla al-Ijtimā'iyya fī al-Islām* (1949) which was penned by him in 1948 before his two-year journey to the United States. As indicated in the Introduction, al-*'Adāla* represents the central work I will be relying on in my analysis and appraisal of Quṭb's thought. In my view, the work reflects an excessive degree of intellectualism, with the emphasis placed on Islam being an "idea" (or a "concept" in later editions of the work), as we shall see in chapter 3.

For the purpose of this study, I will be analysing the second edition of the work (1950), its fifth edition (1958), and the work's last edition (1964) which reflects a clear departure from Quṭb's earlier thought especially in relation to his openness to Christianity, which is confirmed in his other work of the early 1950s *Ma'rakat al-Islām wa al-Ra'simāliyya* (The Struggle between Islam and Capitalism, 1951). Quṭb reveals also in the last edition of *al-'Adāla* a heightened level of anxiety in relation to Wilfred C. Smith's *Islam in Modern History* (1957), which seemingly prompted him to radicalise his views on the Christian West which he finally dismisses, along with the rest of the world, as a "*jāhiliyya*" in his later works, as we shall see in chapter 5.

In the course of Quṭb's two-year visit to America between 1948 and 1950, he wrote a number of articles and letters which were collected and edited by al-Khaldi under the title *Amrīka min Al-Dakhil bi-Minẓār Sayyid Quṭb* (America from within as seen by Sayyid Quṭb). This collection of Quṭb's writings on America is particularly interesting in relation to the otherness formulations touching the "American" who is essentialised in a brutal manner on a par with that relating to the "Jew" in the 1960s. The reader of this collection should be warned about al-Khaldi's own antagonistic attitude towards America.[153]

Of less significance, for the purpose of this study, is a collection of early 1950s articles which were first published in Saudi Arabia in 1967 under the title *Fī al-Tarīkh Fikra wa Minhaj* (In History, [there is] an Idea and a Method)[154] by the same Saudi publishing house, al-Dār al-Sa'ūdiyya, which published Quṭb's other rather controversial anthology of articles entitled *Ma'rakatuna ma'a al-Yahūd*. The initial anthology is said to have included two pieces of research which were published in *Majallat al-Muslimīn* in Cairo under the same title in 1951. Two additional undated research papers dealing with art and literature, which were referenced in later editions of *al-Naqd al-Adabī* (1947), were added to the collection later on.[155] For the purpose of this study, I deemed it necessary to disregard these last undated articles.

Quṭb's other anthology *Ma'rakatuna ma'a al-Yahūd* (Our Battle with the Jews) includes an undated article bearing the same title, which was at the centre of Nettler's study *Past Trials and Present Tribulations: A Muslim Fundamentalist's View of the Jews*. This article reflects a more extreme position which somewhat contradicts Quṭb's own views in *Ma'ālim*. The reader of this anthology should be warned that references inserted in the work are rather a reflection of the views of the collection's Saudi editor and publisher, who also published Quṭb's 1939 anti-Christian polemical work *al-Rad 'ala Mustaqbal al-Thaqāfa fī Misr*, and the views of his younger brother, Muḥammad,[156] who is said to have been entrusted by his older brother to review his works before his execution in 1966.[157] (Shepard makes no reference to this anthology which is not included in the bibliographies supplied by Musallam and Abu-Rabi'.)

Other anthologies of the period which vary in the degree of their importance include *Naḥw Mujtama' Islāmī* (Toward an Islamic Society): a collection of early 1950s articles published posthumously in 1969. Another anthology, *Dirāsāt Islāmiyya* (Islamic Studies), supposedly belongs to the early 1950s.[158] The copy I am using is a Dār al-Shurūq (Cairo) publication of 1995 which shows signs of revision,[159] but seems to belong, on the whole, to the early 1950s as Quṭb's concerns in the work converge with those he expressed in other works at the time.[160]

Lastly, *al-Salām al-'Alamī wa al-Islām* (World Peace and Islam, 1951) is another anthology belonging to the early 1950s which was subject to revision, possibly by Quṭb, to accommodate it to his later Islamist radicalised thought.[161] According to al-Ristūnī, a whole chapter aiming to expose American policy had been removed from all editions of the work following its 1954 edition.[162]

3. The Radical Islamist Stage of Quṭb's Life (1959-1966)

In 1957, Quṭb was a witness to a serious episode involving the death of twenty one of the Brotherhood members and the injury of approximately the same number of members in Cairo's Ṭura prison[163] where he was to spend the last twelve years of his life leading up to his execution in 1966, which was only briefly interrupted in 1964 when Quṭb was released for a few months.[164]

In the same year, Quṭb is said to have composed some poems against the Nasserite regime which were smuggled out of prison and published by Islamists in Jordan in the periodical *al-Kifāḥ al-Islāmī* in 1957 and in an anthology under the title *Laḥn al-Kifāḥ*. In one such poem which was published under the title "Hubalon, Hubal", Nasser is compared to the pre-Islamic pagan idol chief deity of Mecca Hubal.[165] In addition, Quṭb makes reference to "Uncle Sam's dollars" which were meant to bestow respectability on the Nasserite regime:

Hubalon, Hubal
Hubalon...Hubal
It is the symbol of stupidity, ignorance and deception,
Don't ask, O! My friend, those throngs
To whom belong worship, reward and submission,
Leave them, they are only the sheep of the flock,
Her worshipped one is an idol which
Uncle Sam sees,
The dollar guaranteed to bestow on it respect
And the flock moved around in dumbness...O! hero
Hubalon...Hubal
It is the symbol of treason, treachery and deception,
Fake glories were formulated for him,
And the dumb one believed them to be true,
The free and proud one denounced
The explicit lie and refuted it;
But free men in this time are few in number,
So let them enter the terrible prison
And have good patience,
And let them see the most cruel novel
For every tyrant has an end,
And for every creature there is death,
Hubalon...Hubal
Hubalon...Hubal[166]

According to Zollner, the years 1957-1958 constituted "a turning point within the Muslim Brotherhood's trajectory". As she puts it, "it was then that signs of revival began to replace disillusionment" when younger members of the Brotherhood at Qanāṭir prison were particularly attracted to Quṭbian ideas.[167] Following the above incident in Cairo's Ṭura prison, Quṭb reveals that he set out to revise and undertake a lengthy study of the Brotherhood movement with the help of another member of the movement, Muḥammad Yusuf Huwāsh, who was a prison inmate in Ṭura at the same time. According to Quṭb, Huwāsh and himself came to the conclusion that the Islamic movement, at the time, was confronting a situation which was similar to that which prevailed in human societies in the early days of Islam, not only in terms of departing from the Islamic system and *sharī'a*, but also in terms of "ignorance of the truth of the Islamic creed and [in terms of] the drift away from Islamic values and ethics".[168]

Although Quṭb makes use of the dehumanising doctrine of "*jāhiliyya*" in both *Khaṣṣā'iṣ al-Taṣawwur al-Islāmī wa Muqawwimatu* (Characteristics of the Islamic Concept and its Essentials, 1962), and in its second part, which was left in draft form, *Muqawwimat al-Taṣawwur al-Islāmī* (The Essential Components of the Islamic Concept, 1963?) which was published posthumously in 1969, and in a*l-Islām wa Mushkilat al-Ḥaḍāra* (Islam and the Problems of Civilization, 1962), I find that Quṭb's most radical views unravel in *Ma'ālim fi al-Ṭarīq* (Milestones on the Road, 1964) in which he openly confronts Nasser and in the revised sections of *Ẓilāl.*

Shepard's analysis of Quṭb's works reveals that he seemed to have undertaken a revision in 1965 of his commentary on the first thirteen parts of the Qur'an [corresponding to Q1-14] in *Fī Ẓilāl al-Qur'ān* (In the Shade of the Qur'an).[169] I note, however, that Quṭb's commentary on the first chapter of the Qur'an, *al-Fātiḥa*, reflects the antagonistic stance he expressed, starting the late 1940s, towards the Greeks. According to al-Khaldi, Quṭb had not been able to review his commentary on the remaining parts of the Qur'an, including parts 14 to 27 [Q15-57].[170] It is evidently safe to assume that these latter parts do not reflect Quṭb's later extreme and radicalised views. As discussed above, Quṭb's commentary on the Meccan *sura* XXI, *al-Anbiyya'*, in *Ẓilāl* reveals an open admiration for both Solomon and David, and for the Jewish tradition, as a living tradition, in general.[171]

Other less important works in illuminating Quṭb's thought of the period include his revised two works *Hadha al-Dīn* (This Religion, 1963?), *al-Mustaqbal li-Hadha al-Dīn* (The Future belongs to this Religion, 1963?) & *Limadha A'damūnī* (Why Did They Execute Me?) a publication of the Saudi Company for Research and Marketing based on a statement made by Quṭb in 1965 prior to his execution in 1966.

3

Quṭb's Early Encounter with Western Modern Civilisation

In this chapter I aim to illuminate Quṭb's early views as he first encountered the modern West with the view, at least in part, to respond to Buruma's and Margalit's claim that all forms of Occidentalism fit into a "chain of hostility" which targets the "city" and the "mind of the West" as manifested in science and "reason".[1] For one thing, as Hodgson argues, Islamic culture bears the influence of a long urban tradition and it is "as city-oriented as any variant of that tradition".[2]

As will be argued below, Quṭb's discourse reflects no particular "hostility to the City" per se. Much like 'Abduh,[3] Quṭb does not waver, even in his early Islamist discourse, from the view he expressed in the late 1930s when he made a clear distinction between civilisation as in "settled urban life" (*madaniyya*), which includes the realms of sciences and applied arts, which he maintains can be adopted unreservedly from the West, and "culture" (*thaqāfa*) which includes religion, art, ethical norms, traditions and myths, which should be "preserved" albeit "renewed".[4]

Far from targeting the Western "Mind", as manifested in its sciences and reason, Quṭb makes a rather pragmatic distinction between the Western "Mind" which produced material by-products, which he was happy to consume, and the Western "Mind", which he aimed to challenge, which gave rise to the ideological underpinnings of Western civilisation which were assimilated by the Westernised Egyptian luminaries of the day.

In dealing with the so-called "Mind" of the West, Quṭb, in fact, reveals a marked attraction to some of the most controversial elements in the thought-world of modern Western civilisation in the literary stage of his life. Beginning in the mid-1940s, however, Quṭb creates an "imaginary category" which serves him to demarcate a clear-cut "space" in dealing with the Western "Mind".[5] Included under the category of the "Mind" of the West is Quṭb's use of various Arabic words such as "*'aql*", "*'aqliyya*" or "*dhihn*", translated, depending on the context, as mind, intellect, reason, mentality or mind-set. I also include under the rubric "Mind" of the West, Quṭb's use of the expression "*ḍamīr al-Gharb*" (conscience of the West) which is contrasted to the imaginary construct of the "conscience" of Muslims that he creates.

In the discussion below, I will attempt to analyse how Quṭb deals with Western content, stressing continuities and discontinuities in his discourse in relation to his later radical writings. In the first part of the discussion, I will be looking at Quṭb's early encounter with the modern world by paying special attention to his schooling years in Musha. I will then dedicate a section to analyse Quṭb's works in the crucial literary stage of his life leading to his turn to Islamism in 1948. The third and fourth sections of this chapter will cover the early Islamist phase of Quṭb's life, including a discussion of Quṭb's two-year stay in America (1948-1950), which sees him dehumanising the American "other" in very similar terms that those he reserved for the "Jew" in the mid-1960s, as we shall see in chapter 5 later.

1. Quṭb's Schooling Years in Musha, and the Clash between the "Modern" and the Traditional Worlds

Barely aged six, Quṭb was made aware of a division in his family that was, ultimately, to affect the course of his life and the direction of his thought. In his memoirs, Quṭb recounts how members of his family had a difference of opinion as to whether he should pursue a "traditional", or a "modern" type of schooling.

Those members of Quṭb's family, who supported the view that Quṭb should go to the traditional *kuttāb*, argued that he would be able to "memorise" the Qur'an there, and obtain the "blessing" afforded to "those who carry the Book of God on [not in] their hearts".[6] They probably also wanted Quṭb to follow in the footsteps of two of his maternal uncles, who had been sent off to al-Azhar in Cairo to study like most wealthy families of rural background and, upon graduating, conferred, on this side of the family, a kind of "scientific refinement".[7]

Quṭb does not miss the opportunity to tell us that this "scientific refinement" went, hand in hand, with the "rural eminence" that his maternal side of the family enjoyed, stressing that although his family did not have great wealth, it stood out as enjoying "manifest excellence". He adds further that both sides of his family (maternal and paternal that is) were of similar backgrounds, but that his maternal side of the family might even be of "better stock".[8]

The other group of his family supported the view that Quṭb should enrol in the newly-opened primary school, arguing that it was "cleaner" and "more refined", (especially) considering that the Qur'an was taught there as well, along with the other "modern" sciences.[9] At the end, it was, ultimately, those members of his family who favoured modern schooling who won the day.[10]

A few days later, Quṭb was prepared to go to the modern school, geared with a new pair of shoes, and a small tailored *Quftān*, instead of the traditional *jalābiyya*.[11] Apparently, all it took to join modern schooling was a change of headgear, as well, out with the *ṭaqiyya* (traditional close-fitting peakless cap), and in with the *ṭarbūsh* (fez).[12] The symbolism behind this change of headgear to achieve social mobility cannot be under-estimated, for it goes to show the superficiality, and the shallowness, of the process of social change and modernisation in Egypt in the early part of the twentieth century.[13]

Quṭb was now on the threshold of becoming an *Effendi*,[14] like the *Effendis* of his village he nearly "worshipped", as he tells us, in his memoirs.[15] It is known that the Muslim Brotherhood came to define itself as a movement of *Effendiyya* in the early 1950s, seemingly in an effort to dissociate itself from what Mitchell refers to as the "dervishism" of Sufism.[16]

For all of the flaws of the traditional *kuttāb* schooling, especially in terms of intellectual training, Quṭb still missed out on an important social function which was performed by the institution throughout a big part of Islamic history. As Gibb and Bowen point out, it was the *kuttāb* which completely succeeded in "imposing uniformity throughout the length and breadth of [Islamic] territories" during the early centuries of Islam. Thus, the traditional subjects and methods of elementary education were pursued alike by Niger, Nile, and Indus populations in Qur'anic schools which remained in existence till modern times. Gibb and Bowen give the example here of Ḥusayn's account of his schooling years in his memoirs *An Egyptian Childhood* (1932).[17]

Gibb and Bowen further remark that, in Arabic-speaking provinces of the Empire, the *kuttāb* fulfilled the added task of familiarising its students with the classical Arabic language, and gave them some grounding in religious culture and ethic which "prepared them to take their place in the Muslim community in accordance to their station in life". In most cases, students of the *kuttāb* passed into the guilds and corporations where they would have received the teachings of the great mystics of Islam.[18]

Remarkably, there is scant reference in Quṭb's memoirs to his school curriculum, apart from a passing mention of a particular distaste he harboured for Arabic lessons, and his inability to grasp Arabic grammatical constructs,[19] reflecting an early dislike for the Arabic language which becomes evident in the course of his literary career. We learn, however, that, whatever modern content the school curriculum might have included, it was still up to two Qur'an reciters, a *faqīh*[20] and a *'arīf*, to manage the modern school until such time that enough primary school teachers would graduate to replace them.[21] Lord Cromer, who acted as Britain's Consul-General in Egypt between 1888 and 1907,[22] writes that the demand for qualified Egyptians who have received a European training and grasped the spirit of European civilisation was "greatly in excess of the supply" at the time.[23]

Until the time Quṭb joined the newly-opened "modern" school in his village Musha, the *kuttāb* provided the only form of schooling in the village. It seems to be the case that the opening of the new modern school hardly affected the attendance in the *kuttāb*. Quṭb recounts that only children who would "fail" in memorising the Qur'an would opt to go to the new modern school.[24]

For the first year that Quṭb attended the new modern school, therefore, the position of the *faqīh, shaykh* Aḥmad, seemed to have remained unshaken. In the second year, however, there seems to have been a big upheaval as the school attempted to replace *shaykh* Aḥmad with some more learned teachers, who had some sort of training and degrees in mathematics and other (unspecified) cultural subjects. These new teachers were, however, still recruited from the *faqīh* social strata.[25] Quṭb tells us that rumours circulated in the village that the government wanted to "erase" the Qur'an, by not making the children memorise it in the modern school, which saw a great number of the school children leaving it to preserve their religion from "the school of unbelief and perversity" (*madrasat al-kufr wa al-ḍalāl*).[26]

Under the pressure of *shaykh* Aḥmad, Quṭb's father sent Quṭb to the *kuttāb,* but the young Quṭb was filled with such a distinct revulsion in relation to the *kuttāb* that he escaped, after spending just one day there, to go back to the modern school.[27] Quṭb's loathing of the traditional *kuttāb* was particularly exacerbated as he drew comparisons between it and the modern elementary school for which he reserved much awe: an attitude which set him off on a life-journey of estrangement, and violent dislocation, in the realms of both the "modern" and the "traditional", which was acutely, and especially, felt throughout his literary career.[28]

In Quṭb's memoirs, we note the opposed associations which are made in relation to the "modern" school and the "traditional" *kuttāb* to the detriment of the latter. Thus, we see Quṭb recounting that, at the age of six, he was to seek safe haven in the modern "beloved place" that is school, which he describes fondly as the "strongly fortified fortress" (*ḥiṣn ḥaṣīn 'aṣīb*), and refers to it in his adulthood, as the "sacred school" (*al-madrassa al-muqaddasa*).[29] The traditional *kuttāb*, however, was to fill him with feelings of "repugnance" (*ishmi'zāz*), and "bitter and demeaning estrangement" (*ghurba marīra dhalīla*), which was to strengthen his resolve to never return to that "filthy place" (*al-makān al-qadhir*) again, whatever rebuke and threats were to be inflicted on him.[30]

For all of Quṭb's enthusiasm for the modern, however, its lure was crucially to fall short of grasping, let alone embracing the essential intellectual foundations of Western civilisation, and its modern sciences, and rather centred on its externals: an attitude which was to be distinctly felt when he leaned to radical Islamism later. In a detailed recollection of his early school years, Quṭb gives pride of place to the "cleanliness and elegance" of the school's building, which he finds stood in contrast to the "old and filthy" building of the *kuttāb*.[31]

Quṭb's recollections of his "sacred school" included other externals, in contrast to the essentials of modernity, such as the school's spacious yard, with its two shady trees and beautiful flowers, and other minute details including the school's chairs, desks and yearly supplies for students, including notebooks and pens which were made of red reed, and especially the school sign in which Quṭb took special pride for its similarity to those in the capital which, according to him, gave the school its "unique characteristic" in the village.[32] Typically, and perhaps, to compensate for his dwindling fortunes as an adult, Quṭb does not miss the opportunity to boast about his large contribution towards purchasing the said sign, noting that he endeavoured to pay five times as much as the students who belonged to the richest families of Musha did.[33]

At some level, however, one can detect that Quṭb's enthusiasm for the modern was not all that it was made out to be. For all of Quṭb's "repugnance", and "bitter and demeaning estrangement" *vis-à-vis* the traditional *kuttāb*, his move to modernity was, seemingly, skin-deep. We would recall here Quṭb's use of the two "dangerous" books in his library, that of Shamhūrish and al-Falakī, on fortune-telling, and the industry of magical spells and amulets in his childhood years. We also learn that Quṭb was to form a "front", and lead an effort in his "modern" school to compete with the *kuttāb* in memorising the Qur'an.[34]

Quṭb's memoirs also reveal the special lure of city-life to him and to members of his own family. He recalls, for instance, that he was not allowed to play on the streets of the village, or to roam its alleys, to keep his "clean clothes" from the "filth" (*al-qadhāra*), and to shield him from the "pollution" (*talawuth*) of the village children morality and their "obscene words" (*alfāẓuhum al-badhī'a*).[35]

Elsewhere, Quṭb recounts that his maternal grandfather (together with his wife), spent a great deal of his life in Cairo, building on his return to the village a house which is nearly like those of Cairo houses in its "order", its "arrangement", its "usages", and its "standards". Once again, Quṭb stresses here that he grew up in a (family) environment with everything around him making him feel that he is from a "different" milieu to that of the village.[36] In short, Quṭb kept himself on the "outside" of the essential "outside-inside" division in his own home town Musha.

For all of Quṭb's later expression of feelings of estrangement in Cairo, which become particularly discernible in his mid-1930s anthology of poems *al-Shaṭi' al-Majhūl*, Quṭb seems to have been only too happy to leave Musha when he did. In the words of Musallam, Quṭb arrived to Cairo with the dream to "conquer Acre",[37] by completing his studies and, ultimately, restoring his family's fortune.

Quṭb's dreams were, however, to come crashing down as he encountered financial difficulties in Cairo, after his family became nearly destitute around the mid-1920s,[38] forcing him to work and to join, albeit perhaps reluctantly,[39] Dār al-'Ulūm in 1929.[40] The aforementioned institution is said to have offered modest monthly stipends to those who were "needy or exceptionally qualified".[41] It may be the case that Quṭb was dependent on such a stipend for survival, given his reduced circumstances. Be that as it may be, it is noteworthy that Quṭb insisted that his younger brother, Muḥammad, should take advantage of English language studies on offer at Cairo University in the late 1930s. As Calvert puts it, Quṭb "did not want monolingualism to hamper his brother's intellectual development".[42]

It goes without saying that Quṭb was only too aware of his own disability to fully attain modern knowledge, and had come to accept that his own intellectual development was hampered by the limitation of his linguistic skills.[43] In response to Ḥusayn's labelling of Dār al-'Ulūm's graduates as ignorant of foreign languages, Quṭb does not hesitate to admit that graduates of the said institution are unable to follow "advances" in the world:

> There is no doubt that the *jahl* (ignorance) in foreign languages decreases, not only, the teaching capability of its graduates, but also hinders them in upgrading themselves by following, and being aware of the development and intellectual advances in the world.[44]

It is to be known that Dār al-'Ulūm was, on the whole, of a "conservative bent",[45] being founded in 1872 with the view of bridging the gap between the traditional education provided by the *kuttāb* and that provided by the newly-founded modern schools. The institution was, however, to prove disastrously inadequate to fill the purpose for which it was created.[46]

As Krämer observes, Dār al-'Ulūm was "modern" only in so far as it was patterned on Western models in both its "outward form" and teaching methods. In as far as content was concerned, higher education was provided in traditional religious subjects, whereas "modern" subjects were taught at an elementary level, with the result that the institution was not fully recognised by either al-Azhar, or modern institutions, such as Cairo University.[47] Ḥusayn is said to have been particularly critical of the "scholastic" approach which was applied in government schools, and in Dār al-'Ulūm, as early as 1927 when he wrote *Fī al-Adab al-Jahilī*, especially as it had displaced the ancient method adopted by al-Azhar.[48] Krämer quotes Ḥusayn as remarking that Dār al-'Ulūm's alumni stood "uncomfortably suspended" between the old knowledge and the new, "ill-prepared to teach either"[49]: a comment which must have unnerved Quṭb particularly as Ḥusayn came to represent the essential "other" whose stature, and extensive knowledge, Quṭb could have hardly attained.[50]

It seems to be the case that Quṭb was apparently ill-prepared for what Calvert refers to as the "soft landing", into the world of Cairo, afforded to "would-be *effendis*" at Dār al-'Ulūm by its "hybrid type" of education.[51] For one thing, it took Quṭb a journey of some thirteen years to complete his studies at Dār al-'Ulūm in 1933, enrolling firstly for three years at a state secondary school, Madrassa 'Abd al-'Azīz,[52] which would have normally allowed him to pursue a university education had it not been for the financial difficulties he encountered. In an obvious disruption of the "proper [educational] sequence",[53] Quṭb then went on to study at Tajhīziyya Dār al-'Ulūm, which was created in 1920 to prepare students to proceed to Dār al-'Ulūm, until graduating in 1929 to join Dār al-'Ulūm.[54]

It is to be noted that al-Banna, who shared the same birth date as Quṭb (1906), had completed his studies in the same institution in 1927.[55] The gap between al-Banna and Quṭb may be explained in terms of the elementary education they both received, in their respective villages, with the latter shunning the "traditional" *kuttāb*, while al-Banna received a combination of *kuttāb* and government schooling, which gave him both a good grounding in the traditional spheres[56] and, unlike Quṭb, a "proper [educational] sequence".

What is certain is that the curriculum on offer in Dār al-'Ulūm,[57] was not to the liking of Quṭb who described it as one which was "loaded with old, difficult, exhausting and dry subjects".[58] Suffice it to note here that students were expected, upon admission to Dār al-'Ulūm, to recite the Qur'an from memory, and to have a thorough knowledge of the thousand-verse grammatical poem *Alfiyya* composed by the Damascene scholar, Ibn Mālik (d. 1274),[59] which must have posed a real challenge to Quṭb given the clear distaste he held for the topic since his early childhood.

2. The Literary Stage in Quṭb's Life and his Early Attitude towards the Civilisation of the West

Given the hybrid education Quṭb had received and the linguistic impairment from which he had suffered, it should come as no surprise to the reader that Quṭb's career, as a teacher and a littérateur, was somewhat marred by a marked sense of confusion which saw him, as Ḥusayn remarked, "uncomfortably suspended" between the old knowledge and the new. As discussed in chapter 2 above, Quṭb seems to have come under fire by his critics for the "disturbance" in his methodology, or the lack thereof, as he indicates in the revised edition of his work *al-Naqd al-Adabī*.[60]

Perhaps nothing better elucidates the extent of the confusion in Quṭb's thought than the following statement, which he made some three years after graduating from Dār al-'Ulūm in the Introduction of his anthology *al-Shāṭi' al-Majhūl* (1935):

> The spiritual powers of the poet are what link him with the grand unity of the Universe...whereas, the powers of the intellect fall short [of fulfilling this function]; and he [speaking of himself in the third person singular] sees that feeling time is a result of the existence of the body and the conscious powers, and that the soul feels the infinite existence, [which is] not tied down by time, and a priori not tied down by place. Thus, when he took off the body and scrapped off the outside layer of his body in the 'Unknown Shore', he has seen that there was no 'since', and no 'yesterday', and no 'today', and no 'tomorrow',

> and no 'other', and no 'self'...etc. But, he has seen the 'times as a big circle', and has seen 'the unity which has been concealed'...he has seen no imprint or vestige [left by] the times, and has seen that everything was a symbol of eternity. This sentiment may have a connection with Einstein's theory of relativity, as it may have a connection with Islamic Sufi *theories*.[61]

Apart from the apparent confusion and clear nihilistic inclinations in the above statement, it is clear that Quṭb confers on himself, as a poet, a degree of distinction which sets him apart, with his spiritual powers, from those endowed with the (limited) powers of the intellect. Even before graduating from Dār al-'Ulūm in 1933, Quṭb tended to aggrandise the role of the poet in society to near prophetic dimensions, claiming that the function of "the imagination" of the poet is to provide a "link" between "incapacitated humans" (*al-insān al-qāṣir*) and the "concealed truth",[62] stating, elsewhere, that the poet had been moulded by life to act as an intermediary between it and other beings, for he is an "excellent" human.[63]

Having been under the tutelage of al-'Aqqād for some fifteen years, when he composed *al-Shāṭi' al-Majhūl*, it is clearly the case that, unlike the emerging educated Egyptian youth,[64] Quṭb failed to appreciate his mentor's efforts to fill the younger generation's "need for a re-synthesis of the prevalent world image" which is crucial to establish an "average expectable continuity" with the past.[65] To attempt a synthesis of Einstein's *theory* of relativity and, as Quṭb puts it, "Islamic Sufi *theories*" is, however, indicative of the impact that al-'Aqqād exerted on his disciple with regard to seeing the world in terms of "theories" at this stage of his life. Interestingly, as Karen Armstrong argues, Einstein was one of a handful of "secularised Jews" – the others being Wittgenstein [and Muḥammad Quṭb's "three Jews"] Marx, Freud, Durkheim – who had a profound impact on modernism in the West.[66] Charles Smith observes that the furore over ether and Einstein's theory, in general, lasted throughout the 1920s in Europe and America and was dealt with at length in Egyptian journals at the time.[67]

Quṭb's above reference to Einstein's theory as a possible intellectual antecedent for his thought, along with Sufi "theories", gives us at least some inkling as to the extent of the confusion in his thought in the mid-1930s, which is especially made evident when he introduces another poem, "Al-Insān al-Akhīr" (The Last Man), in the aforementioned anthology. In this poem, there is clearly a hint of Shelley's apocalyptic vision in his "Last Man" (1826), in so far as Quṭb describes his "Last Man" as waking up in a universe which was emptied of any living creatures.[68] There is also clearly an allusion to Nietzsche's "Last Man" [69] in Quṭb's poem with the latter's "Last Man" also waking up to a "confused [Nietzschean] universe",[70] where there is only "despair" and "misery",[71] and, above all, no meaning following Nietzsche's proclamation of the "death of God".

As Armstrong observes, Nietzsche was writing at a time when "a profound terror, a sense of meaningless and annihilation, would be part of the modern experience" which was beginning to give way to "a nameless dread" which affected, not only Christians of Europe, but Jews and Muslims as well.[72] The "death of God" in the modern West, she argues, had given way to "individualism as "a new form of idolatry" which placed a stress on "the genius of the individual" which could be dangerous if allowed absolute free rein.[73]

> A breed of Supermen who regarded themselves as Gods, as envisaged by Nietzsche, was a frightening prospect: people needed the challenge of a norm that transcended the whims and notions of the moment. It was the mission of Islam to uphold the nature of true individualism against the Western corruption of the ideal. They had their Sufi ideal of the Perfect Man. Unlike the Superman, who saw himself as supreme and despised the rabble, the Perfect Man was characterised by his total receptivity to the Absolute and would carry the masses along with him.[74]

Unlike Iqbal, who counters Nietzsche's idea of the "Superman" in *The Reconstruction of Religious Thought in Islam* by invoking "the ideal of Perfect Manhood in Islam" which, he finds, is embodied in the "Prophet's experience of Divine illumination" in reliance on Q53:17 and Persian poetry,[75] Quṭb finds much in favour of the idea of "genius". In *al-Naqd al-Adabī* (1947), and its later revised edition, Quṭb quotes rather approvingly, and at great length, from one article which expanded on psychoanalytic theories put forward by Freud, Adler and Jung on the issue of "genius" (*nibūgh* and *ʿabqariyya* are used here) and its link to the "collective unconscious" (*al-lashiʿūr al-jamʿī*).[76]

Specific reference is also made elsewhere in the same work to Freud's study of Leonardo da Vinci to make the point that psychoanalysis, as per Freud's findings, cannot enlighten the nature of artistic (creative) work,[77] confirming again here his firm belief in the pioneering role of creative artists and intellectuals in society.

Significantly, Quṭb quotes also from the same article a detailed exposition of Nietzschean idea, as expressed in *Thus Spoke Zarathustra* (1883), as signifying the "collapse of the old symbol" (God) and the need for a "new reformer" (the superman), with the "superman" being described in the same article as someone who responds to the "collective unconscious" at a given time in a society's history.[78] Quṭb demonstrates, however, a degree of superficiality in his acquaintance with Western modern thought, never recognising, for instance, the ethical component in Nietzsche's thought as al-Aqqād did.[79]

Nor does Quṭb also seem to move past Freud's idea of the "unconscious" in the course of his literary career, earning him the rebuke of al-ʿAqqād who described those who clung to the idea of "unconscious", and were not aware that Freud moved on to the idea of the Id, instead, as belonging to the category of "*al-mutafayqihūn*" (those pretending to be in the know) who mingle in the circles of "*al-juhalā*'" (the ignorant).[80]

What is clear is that there is certainly a strong Freudian impulse in Quṭb's thought until, at least, the late 1950s which is particularly interesting given the unwarranted othering of Freud, as one of "Three Jews: Marx, Freud and Durkheim" for the "sexual and animalistic inclinations" underlying his thought which occurs in his commentary on Q5:82 in *Ẓilāl*, discussed earlier. Interestingly, Quṭb seems to have been in tune with Freud's idea of "incestuous desire for the mother",[81] quoting Suwif's article referred to above on Freud's analysis of Da Vinci's painting "Saint John the Baptist" (1515), which portrays him as an androgyne,[82] as reflecting the artist's association of sexual desire with his own mother which reflected negatively on his own love life.[83]

Apart from Quṭb's clear attraction to certain aspects of Freudian thought, which unambiguously shows that he succumbed to what his younger brother Muḥammad describes in the late 1960s as the most violent "strife" in the West brought about by his own three "others" Freud, as well as Marx and Durkheim,[84] he also seemed to owe a big part of his thought to Darwin, in the course of his literary career, and in the early Islamist stage of his life as we shall see in chapter 5. This is particularly remarkable given the upheaval occasioned by Darwin's work *The Origin of Species* (1858) in shaking the foundations of the religious mythical world-views.[85]

Under the influence of al-Aqqād, Quṭb is said to have taken an interest in Darwinism,[86] although he seemed to have rather placed an emphasis on the idea of evolution, without delving deeper into the ethical component in Darwin's thought. In contrast, al-Aqqād worked out a theory whereby he placed al-Mutanabbī at a higher echelon than both Nietzsche and Darwin, by crediting him with offering a "beautiful reconciliation", and finding a middle course, between Darwin's "will to life", or self-preservation, and Nietzsche's "will to power", and quest for victory and nobility, in their individual quests to find causes for eliciting ethics, and virtues.[87]

In contrast to Ṭaha Ḥusayn, who believed in the "purity of the Arabic language",[88] as Abu-Rabi' finds, Quṭb did not believe in the notion of the "sacredness of the Golden Age of the Arabic language and literature", and rather adhered to the Darwinist school of evolution, by regarding language to be a "continuously evolving organism".[89] Under the possible influence of al-'Aqqād, who was an exponent of ideas stressing the "racial characteristics" of thinkers which owe their origin in the thought-world of the English essayist and critic William Hazlitt (1778-1830),[90] Quṭb clearly held disparaging views of the "desert Arabs".[91] Even as late as perhaps the mid-1960s, Quṭb continues to hold the same dehumanising views of the Arabs, arguing that the Arabs amount to nothing without the "idea" of Islam. As he puts it, "what is the 'idea' that they [the Arabs] can offer to humanity if they give up this idea?"[92]

Carrying the Darwinist approach, which was applied by Quṭb to the Arabic language to its logical conclusion, he was to go on deprecating the poetry of the "desert

Arabs", stressing the impact of the environment in refining taste as early as 1932[93] and through the mid-1940s.[94] In line with the Diwān* Group, which drew its inspiration largely from a number of 'Abbasid poets,[95] Quṭb held the view in *Muhimmat al-Sha'ir fī al-Ḥayya wa Shi'r al-Jīl al-Ḥaḍir* (1932) that the Arab (desert) environment is not to be compared with the more complex environments, which include a variety of interrelated life forms, such as that found in Europe, Egypt, and even at the time of the Abbasid caliphate. According to Quṭb, the "florescence" which was seen in the Abbasid state was not only due to the natural environment, but to the "refinement of the intellectual faculties" (*irtiqā' al-malakat al-fikriyya*) of the Arabs.[96] In the mid-1940s, Quṭb continues to express open admiration for the Abbasid "civilisation of the intellect" (*al-ḥaḍara al-'aqliyya*).[97]

Oddly enough, Quṭb went as far as claiming in the mid-1940s that, except on rare occasions, Arabic forms of expression, especially in poetry, fail to impress on the reader that there was a human being behind the texts.[98] To illustrate this last point, Quṭb draws a comparison between a poem by Alice Meynell and another by the Andalusian poet Ibn Zahr on the process of ageing, to the detriment of the latter. According to Quṭb, Ibn Zahr stopped at addressing "senses", and not the "inner depth of the soul" (*aghwār al-nafs*).[99] Quṭb found, however, "the face of a human" (*wajh al-insān*) in a translated text of Meynell's poem.[100] (This comes as a bit of a surprise since there is a clear leaning in Quṭb's writings to objectify women, which suggests an inconsistency in his thought regarding gender issues.)

The oddity in Quṭb's thought is that he goes on to find, through translated texts of English poetry provided by his mentor al-'Aqqād,[101] all of what he found lacking in Arabic forms of expression and imagery. In *Kutub wa Shakhṣiyyāt*, Quṭb stresses that he is not looking for a "meaning" or an "idea" at this stage, and rather wants to share in the particulars of the human experience conveyed by the poets, giving the example in this context of a poem by the English poet Housman (d.1936) in which the latter describes his experience of going to the market with insufficient funds to pay for what he needed to buy.[102] Quṭb was equally to bestow lavish praise on a poem by Thomas Hardy (d. 1928) which deals with nature for the "imagery" and "shadings" which characterise his poetic expressions.[103]

Quṭb was also to advocate the view that in the modern age, one was "under obligation" to "renew" the method of literary diction, by drawing from "international wellsprings",[104] such as he found these in the poems of Housman,[105]and those of Tagore.[106] He also did not fail to point out the "sublime horizon" of the method used by the Qur'an in its "imagery and (in throwing) shadings" (*taṣwwīr wa takhyyīl*).[107] Elsewhere, Quṭb makes a point of criticising Ḥusayn for claiming that the language of the Qur'an is neither in prose, or poetic, form, but plainly Qur'anic.[108]

At the height of his animosity to 'Abduh in the 1960s, Quṭb reveals that his ambition is to help people who "drifted away from the Qur'an" to appreciate the

Qur'anic "*manhaj*" (way/method) by providing an interpretation of the Qur'an in human expressions.[109] Perhaps seeing himself as filling Luther's role, with whom he developed a degree of affinity in the later stage of his life, Quṭb sought to emulate Luther who, as Armstrong puts it, "had wiped the sacred page clean, erasing the traditional gloss in order to start again".[110] By that time, Quṭb almost lost interest in affirming himself against the Francophile, Ṭaha Ḥusayn, who emerged as Quṭb's main "other" in his refutation of the former in *Muhimmat al-Sha'ir fī al-Ḥayya wa Shi'r al-Jīl al-Ḥaḍir* (1932).

Although Quṭb challenged Ḥusayn in 1932 by promising that "the younger generation would excel even more than the older one," he did not spend much energy in pointing out the excellence of the younger generation in the 1930s, as he eventually did in the mid-1940s.[111] Instead, Quṭb became rather embroiled in 1938 in a feud to defend al-'Aqqād against his detractors, the followers of al-Rafi'ī (d.1937).[112] In a campaign which was described later by Quṭb as "ignoble", he hailed his mentor as the "imām" of the new school whose "psychological capacity" and "artistic vision" far surpassed that of al-Rafi'ī's "limited propensities".[113] In Quṭb's view, it was fitting that al-'Aqqād should have been nominated "Prince of Poets" by Ṭaha Ḥusayn following Aḥmad Shawqī's death in 1932.[114]

Soon thereafter Quṭb was to clash, yet again, with Ḥusayn following the publication of *Mustaqbal al-Thaqāfa fī Miṣr* (1938), perhaps being particularly threatened by Ḥusayn's incisive analysis of the existing "silent, but nonetheless dangerous and violent enmity" in the Ministry of Education between those, (like Quṭb), who did not receive a university education, on the one hand, and graduates of the newly-founded Egyptian University, and European universities', on the other.[115]

In his rebuttal of Ḥusayn in *al-Rad 'ala Mustaqbal al-Thaqāfa fī Misr* (1939), Quṭb disregards Ḥusayn's criticism of Dār al-'Ulūm's graduates. Instead, he addresses Ḥusayn's premise which, according to Cachia, seems to have been inspired by Duhamel, that "Egypt's culture had always been not so much Oriental as essentially Mediterranean".[116] In the chapter "The Impact of Islam and Christianity on Mediterranean Nations", Quṭb concedes that "Greek philosophy did undoubtedly influence Islam". He, however, questions the validity of the argument that religions impact peoples with their respective philosophies.

In an argument revealing a marked attraction to the Torah, as a legal text, Quṭb makes the argument that philosophy affects only "*al-khaṣṣa*" (the elect few),[117] clearly making reference to Ḥusayn), adding that it is rather "the spiritual 'system' [*niẓām*] of 'religions', which is the prime influence" on people. In addition, he argues, it is laws, economic-socio-political 'systems' [*anẓima*, pl. of *niẓām*], such as those found in the Qur'an and the Torah which affect people.[118] "Had the Torah, instead of the *Injīl*, crossed the sea to Europe", he argues,

> it would have undoubtedly had a great impact in changing 'the nature of its *practical* and *realistic* mind' [*ṭabī'at 'aqluha al-'amaliyya al-wāqi'iyya*]; for it has 'legislation' [*tashrī'*], a 'penal code' [*ḥudūd*, plural of *ḥad*], an 'economic system' [*niẓām iqtiṣādī*], which lack in the *Injīl*.[119]

Obviously, in presupposing that the Torah did not cross the sea to Europe, Quṭb is negating the Jewish religio-cultural component in European history. As Wilfred C. Smith explains, Christians are "participants in an overt tradition that has become rich and varied".[120] The history that Quṭb is assuming is the early Christian "community's history before a New Testament had yet been added to the Old to make a Christian Bible".[121] As Wilfred C. Smith points out, the concept of "*religio*" was introduced by St. Jerome (c. 342-420) at a few places in his Latin translation of the bible, in the sense of "a rite" rendering in the New Testament "the Greek *thrēskeia*, religious observance, ritual practice, way of worshiping", and in the Old Testament various terms for "ordinance" and "ritual prescription". In St. Augustine's title *De Vera Religione*, the argument is made that "*vera religio* means the worship of the one true God; it hardly mentions 'Christianity'".[122]

Clearly, St. Jerome did not read into the Old Testament, which Quṭb assumes is made up of only the Torah, a "legislation, a penal code, or an 'economic system', as Quṭb does. As Smith explains, the Old Testament is "innocent" of the concept of "religion", it rather makes reference to the phrase "the fear of the Lord" (*yir'ath Yahweh*) in the sense of "personal piety" which clearly does not designate a "system, sociological or ideological".[123] In the same vein, Chittick argues, Ibn 'Arabi certainly did not consider that the Torah designates "a system". He rather considered that "all the messengers came with Speech, such as the Qur'an, the Torah, the Gospels, the Psalms, and the Scriptures" which is meant to give "knowledge" of God "through listening to His Speech".[124]

It is important to point out here that, in refuting Ḥusayn's premise that Egypt's culture is essentially Mediterranean, Quṭb accepts that emulating European civilisation is an "inevitable necessity" given that Europe is well ahead on the "scale of refinement" (*madarij al-ruqiy*). Here, he creates an imaginary construct of "nations of the East", which are emulating Western civilisation, including three blocs which, he accepts, are of "different mindsets" (*ikhtilāf 'aqliyatuhā*): Japan and China in the far East, Iran and Turkey in the Middle East, and Egypt and Syria in the Near East.[125]

Interestingly, although Quṭb makes reference to Japan as the main example of a country of the "East" that was able to preserve its culture -including *religion*, art, ethical norms and traditions- while adopting the latest in European civilisation – including sciences and applied arts –[126] he failed to appreciate, as W. C. Smith observes, that the Japanese Imperial government took the position, following the introduction, under Westernising pressure, of a clause in the Meiji Constitution in

1889, which guaranteed "freedom of religion", that "(state) *Shinto is not a religion*".[127] (my italics)

Significantly, Quṭb demonstrates a great deal of openness in relation specifically to the Cartesian methodology followed by Ḥusayn in his work *al-Adab al-Jāhilī* (1927) in 1947. In *al-Naqd al-Adabī: Uṣūluhu wa Manāhijahū* (1947), he criticises Ḥusayn for failing to adhere faithfully to Descartes' methodology,[128] even at the risk of putting in question the Qur'anic account of *jāhiliyya* life.[129] Quṭb was specifically critical of Ḥusayn for relying on the accuracy of the Qur'anic depiction of *jāhiliyya* life and for favouring it over that of the early Arab historians, and was, furthermore, to cast doubt on the results of Ḥusayn's research by stating that these results were inconclusive and subject to further discussion.[130]

Although it is clear that Quṭb seems to have developed a heightened level of anxiety in relation to the rationalist literati luminaries of the day, especially as he came to realise that Plato's *Republic* was free of poets and artists, and that "poetry is despicable work, and does not need to exist in the Utopian city",[131] he nonetheless refers approvingly to Plato's notion of "high ideals" (*al-muthul*), i.e. "archetypal forms", commending it as a "beautiful literary concept" in both editions of *al-Naqd al-Adabī* (1947).[132]

One cannot fail to discern a degree of confusion and anxiety in Quṭb's thought when he contradicts himself in the same work, by criticising Plato's theory of "high ideals" for placing a stress on (archetypal) "ideas",[133] seemingly not realising that these "high ideals" and (archetypal) "ideas" are one and the same in Platonic thought, as expounded by Ḥusayn in his work *Qadat al-Fikr*,[134] with which Quṭb seems to have been acquainted. Unlike Ḥusayn, Quṭb fails to appreciate Aristotle as 'a kind of patron saint of individual freedom'. Kreutz argues that Ḥusayn extends this line of thought to the era of French enlightenment, in which 'he attributes to Descartes the role of a modern incarnation of Aristotle'. Despotism, Ḥusayn argues, was "alien" to both Greeks and Romans in ancient times.[135]

3. Quṭb's Feud with Egypt's Literati, and the Lure of Islamism

The mid-1940s saw Quṭb becoming "greatly embittered" for several years by al-'Aqqād's indifference to his works. According to Musallam, Quṭb's embitterment was such that it helped to speed Quṭb's eventual "departure from al-'Aqqād's orbit".[136] Shalash observes that in the spring of 1947 Quṭb unleashed fits of anger which turned to sheer (rhetorical) violence, targeting al-'Aqqād, following the latter's glowing endorsement of Saudi national 'Abdullah al-Qaṣimī's book *Hadhihī Hiya al-Aghlāl* (These are the Shackles, 1946).[137]

In a newspaper article under the same title, which was published in *al-Risāla*[138] on October 28, 1946[139] al-'Aqqād praised al-Qaṣimī's work as:

> A 'revolution in understanding the mind, religion and life' as it strikes at the tyrannical authority of ignorance, and the fortified bastion of habit together with the oppressive legion of the mob, and demi-demagogues.[140]

Al-'Aqqād went on to praise al-Qaṣimī for going on the assault against "ignorance" and "feeble-mindedness", and for recognising the role played by both Aristotle and Plato in laying the foundations for civilisation,[141] (a proposition which must have unnerved Quṭb). Not only did al-Qaṣimī recognise the contributions of these two Greek philosophers, but he also accepted that all Muslims are visibly "backward" in comparison with modern Western nations,[142] in both the "material" and the "immaterial" realms.[143]

In an argument which runs diametrically opposed to views advanced by Quṭb,[144] al-Qaṣimī argues that the strength of nations such as Germany, Japan and the US lies, not in their faith in God or their religious and spiritual ethics, but in the "industrial-material-secular" norms of these nations.[145]

According to Shalash, al-'Aqqād's article aroused the jealousy and indignation of Quṭb, especially as al-Qaṣimī (1903-1995) was roughly the same age as him, prompting Quṭb to retort in a newspaper article published in *al-Risāla* on December 16, 1946, under the title "The Recklessness of Literature" (*Ghaflat al-Adab*) that the book was "dubious". In the same article, Quṭb accused some of the important writers, i.e. al-'Aqqād, of having been "deceived" by the work, and of giving it "superfluous value".[146]

Although it is not for the first time that Quṭb's literary battles in the 1940s developed into "violence, cruelty and defamation",[147] he seemed to have developed a heightened level of anxiety in relation to al-Qaṣimī's work. Thus, in a clear effort to discredit al-Qaṣimī, Quṭb accused the former of plagiarism from Abd al-Mun'im Khalāf's work *U'min bi al-Insān* (I Believe in Humans).[148]

Khalāf's work, which consists of articles that were published between 1940-1945, was favourably reviewed by Quṭb in the same year that al-Qaṣimī's work was published. Quṭb commended *U'min bi al-Insān* for "calling on the tortured humanity... not to drown in the noisy clatter of [Western] machines, and to attempt to make way in its sentiments for other spiritual wellsprings".[149] In a passage quoted approvingly by Quṭb from the work, Khalāf states that "the Westerners presented to us the "genius of matter", we seek to present to them the "genius of the soul"; to give comfort to their souls as they gave comfort to our bodies".[150]

Quṭb was, however, to reprimand Khalāf for falling under the "overwhelming spell" of the "material" civilisation of the West[151] which, according to him, is a mere by-product of the "material spirit of the West".[152] In absolute Manichean terms, Quṭb emphasises a spirit-matter duality of East against West, arguing that the way forward is to believe in the "unadulterated spiritual inclinations" and the "spiritual accumulated energy" of the East which, if rightly channelled and purified of legends and ignorance, can lead to "certitude" in the "greatness of the human spirit".[153]

Such a simplistic view involving the spiritual East and the materialistic West duality, as expressed by Quṭb above, was ridiculed by Ṭaha Ḥusayn in the late 1930s. Ḥusayn was especially baffled by those Egyptians (like Quṭb) who considered themselves "Easterners", arguing that "the Egyptian mind's real ties were with the Near East and the Greeks, and insofar as it was affected by outside influences, these influences were Mediterranean".[154] He further argued that European civilisation possessed great spiritual content, and put in question the presupposition of some Egyptians who consider that religion is "spirit" in the East and "matter" in the West.[155]

As we shall see in the course of this study, Quṭb became open to influences of Pakistani-Indian Islam beginning in the late 1940s. By that time, the rift between al-ʿAqqād and Quṭb reached a new climax as the latter rejected his mentor's vision of poetry.[156] In a newspaper article which was published in February 1948,[157]Quṭb criticised al-ʿAqqād for placing an emphasis on "the idea", which stresses "abstraction, and does not touch the heart".[158]

Clearly, the above negative view of al-ʿAqqād's poetry marks an unambiguous departure from Quṭb's earlier unrestrained adulation toward his mentor. According to Yūnus, Quṭb admitted in the mid 1940s that he bowed to no one except al-ʿAqqād, accepting, at that stage of his life, which is described by Yūnus as one of "grandiose romantic dreams", no one except for al-ʿAqqād as the "one god" on Egypt's literary scene.[159] Yūnus notes further that upon losing his "one god", al-ʿAqqād, Quṭb switched the centre of his worship to Tagore, even as he turned to Islamism.[160]

In the same 1948 newspaper article, Quṭb now opines that poetry is in crisis, explaining that poetry ought to be understood in a *new way* (my italics), away from the school of Shawqī, Ḥāfiẓ and al-Manfaluṭī, and that of al-Aqqād, Shukrī, and al-Māzinī.[161] Evidently, Quṭb had by that time been totally detached from the existing literary schools, both that of al-ʿAqqād with its stress on rationalism, and the school of craftsmanship to which Shawqī belonged. (It is noteworthy that a similar detached position was to be taken by Quṭb, especially in the later Islamist stage of his life, when he announces his detachment from, and denounces, all human thought which is in conflict with his own thought. In *Khaṣā'iṣ*, for instance, Quṭb announces that his is a "new" and "clean" concept which is derived straight from the Qur'an, and is thus free from "all accretions of *jāhiliyya*",[162]which at this point he saw had engulfed the whole world.)

As Quṭb drifts away from al-ʿAqqād's orbit, he seems to have developed a clear distaste for the rationalism of his mentor's literary school, arguing well into the 1950s in *al-Naqd al-Adabī* that poetry is "an expression of the strongest moments, and those which are more filled with emotive energy in life", adding further that the attempts made by some men of letters to introduce "abstract ideas", "intellectual experiences", and "everyday occurrences" into poetry failed in both the modern era and the past: "Thought should not be allowed into the world of poetry, unless it comes concealed... and not motionless, cold, and abstract".[163]

Even in the radical Islamist stage of Quṭb's life, he continues to express an open aversion to the "abstract mind", developing an argument in *Khaṣṣā'iṣ* against the conceptions of the "abstract mind", and its "idealism" which, according to him, do not exist in the world of reality, and furthermore do not agree with one of the characteristics of the Islamic "concept" of "realism".[164] Instead, Quṭb proposes ambiguously what he refers to as an "idealist realism" as he takes on the abstract "Mind" of the Greeks deriving content solely from al-Aqqād's work *Allah* (1947),[165]and seemingly appropriating Socrates' idea of "an axis of goodness", as interpreted by Ḥusayn,[166] in developing the idea of "*thabat*" (fixity) as one of the characteristics of the Islamic "*taṣawwur*" in the same work.[167]

The essential point to reiterate here is that stepping out of the shadow of al-Aqqād who, for some twenty five odd years, provided a level of anchorage for Quṭb, together with being shunned by the senior members of the literary community of Egypt, posed the greatest challenge yet to Quṭb in the course of his literary career. As discussed in the Introduction, in such instances, as Erikson finds, when a given individual comes to develop "a deep sense of the inadequacy of one's general equipment" due to "the fact that the immediate social environment does not have a niche for the individual's true gifts", one may experience a situation of "extreme work paralysis", leading to destructive tendencies as one's "ego ideal" would settle for nothing less than making the unrealistic demand of commanding "omnipotence".[168]

Thus, instead of delivering on his promise to set up a "*new way*" for the appraisal of poetry, which is to say that Quṭb aims to destroy the old ways, he assumes the role of the litterateur-Prophet, starting in the late 1940s. It is arguably the case that the assumption of such a role was largely dictated by the imminent challenge which was posed by the senior literati, especially as al-Aqqād's "mind" seems to have represented a major threat to Quṭb starting in the mid-1940s.[169] In fact, one of al-Aqqād's works of the late 1940s implicitly, but firmly, placed his former disciple in the class of the "ignorant". In *Al-Falsafa al-Qur'āniyya* (1947), al-Aqqād argues that there are two categories of people: "the elect few" (*al-khawās*), including philosophers and Sufis, and "the ignorant" who are, according to al-'Aqqād, (just like Quṭb), limited to a sensory perception of the afterlife, and unable to attain abstract meanings, and feel "the love of truth" (*ḥub al-ḥaqīqa*) and the "worship of perfection".[170]

In effect, I surmise here that Quṭb's claim that he was endowed with the power of *ilhām* in *al-Naqd al-Adabī* (1947),[171] together with his clear leaning to the idea of unbridled "genius",[172] give impetus to my conjecture that Quṭb is likely to have been making the claim of placing himself in the category of "*al-khawāṣṣ*", most probably, in response to the challenge posed especially by al-'Aqqād at this stage of his life.

Aged forty-one in 1947, Quṭb was totally dependent on translated texts, especially those provided by al-Aqqād, for the very basic knowledge of European literature he acquired in the course of his literary career through the mid 1940s. In contrast to the encyclopaedic erudition of his mentor,[173] Quṭb seemed to have developed very little interest in literary content, Arab or European for that matter, actually taking a hostile attitude to the very notion of an "idea", or a "meaning", that one might derive from texts even when he read the Qur'an in the course of his literary career, as discussed above. By the mid-1940s, Quṭb seems to have steadily moved away from the direction of al-Aqqād's world-view which placed an emphasis on the necessity of reconciling all religious texts with the requirements of the "Mind"(*al-'aql*), by going beyond the literalist and sensory meaning of texts.[174]

Although Quṭb penned his first Islamist work, *al-'Adāla*, in the late part of 1948,[175] before departing to the US, there is, however, some clear indication that he was keen to pursue his literary career up till at least 1953.[176] It is evidently the case that Quṭb continued to revise his literary works throughout the early 1950s when he clashed with Nasser.

Having spread the word, through his admirers, that he was the "Voltaire" of Egypt's July, 1952, Revolution, and that it was, furthermore, his own work, *al-'Adāla*, which inspired the military revolutionaries,[177]and his call to muzzle all opponents from within the ranks of intellectuals and litterateurs,[178]Quṭb's fiery inciting articles were to unleash a wave of harsh criticism against him by different writers who put in question Quṭb's very integrity, and accused him openly of harbouring much "poisonous venom", and of holding a grudge against the deposed King Farouk.[179]

By far the most serious criticism that was levelled against Quṭb is the article which was published in the prestigious literary magazine, *al-Thaqāfa,* by 'Izz al-Dīn Ismā'īl, who pointed out the "deceptive halo" which conceals Quṭb's "shallowness", and that he was, in fact, a "great sham". Open charges of plagiarism were also made by Ismā'īl against Quṭb who was accused by the former of passing off ideas, as his own, in *al-Naqd al-Adabī*[180] from translations into Arabic of works[181] by the Georgian Laureate, Lascelles Abercrombie,[182] H. B. Charlton,[183] and the French literary critic, Gustave Lanson (d. 1934).[184]

Having freely admitted in 1947 to having recourse to "borrowing" from Adham's work, *Naẓarāt fī al-Ḥayat wa al-Mujtama'*,[185] Quṭb was probably not too distraught by Ismā'īl's criticism. He must, however, have been particularly unnerved by Ismā'īl's rejection of Quṭb's claim that he was the "Voltaire" of Egypt's revolution, and by the former's methodical critical scrutiny of *al-Taṣwīr al-Fannī and Mashāhid al-Qiyāma* which, he claimed, lack in originality and expand on ideas which were originally put forward by al-'Aqqād; and of his criticism of *al-'Adāla* as being made up of lengthy quotes from various works without assimilating the idea of social justice in Islam even as he quotes, at some length, from al-Guindī's work *Abu Ḥanīfa: the Paragon of Freedom and Tolerance in Islam.*[186]

Nothing less than a sea change seems to have occurred in the orientation of Quṭb's thought when he penned his first Islamist work *al-'Adāla* in 1948. Not only do we see Quṭb insisting on objectifying Islam as an "idea" of social justice (though to a certain extent this is a process that was already in progress starting 1947[187]), but we also see him essentialising the European "Mind", as he accuses the Europeans of being naturally, not even remotely receptive to the very religious idea, and being additionally unable to recognise, and incorporate, any ethical elements in their thought.

Thus, in spite of the near revulsion Quṭb came to harbour in relation to "the poetry [which conveys] ideas", as he called it,[188] and his increased criticism of the modern literary "rationalist school" in Egypt, which he claimed exceeded all bounds in its "intellect-bent orientation" to the detriment of "emotive ethos", well into the 1950s,[189] Quṭb insists, in all six editions of his first Islamist work *al-'Adāla* (1949-1964), on reducing Islam to being a mere "idea", invariably using the words "concept" (*taṣawwur*), and "philosophy", in connection with Islam.[190] However, Quṭb sets a limitation on human thought – other than his - by claiming a Divine source for what he refers to as the Islamic "idea", thus, turning it, and his own thought, in the process into a primordial (uncreated) idea of God.[191]

Quṭb then goes on to ascertain, in all editions of the work, that: "the European 'mentality' (*'aqliyya*) is deeply-rooted in material foundations, with the spiritual idea having slight impact on it, since the time of the Roman civilisation to the modern era".[192] Pushing this line of argument further, Quṭb equally maintains in all editions of the same work that Europe had *never* been at any point (truly) Christian,[193] seemingly owing these disparaging views of Europe to the Jewish convert to Islam Leopold Weiss (Muḥammad Asad), whose book *Islam at the Crossroads* (1934) is quoted at great length in the work.[194] It is worthy of note that W. C. Smith includes Asad, as he does Mawdudi, in the reactionary movement in India, noting that Asad's popular writings form part of a literary genre in modern India which offers "strict orthopraxy as the only salvation" against the "inhumanity, haste and mechanism of modern Europe".[195]

Interestingly, the above mentioned work by Asad features in a list of eighty-one Arabic books' titles which was compiled by Smith in 1958 to mark "the historical development" of the "concept of Islam" in the Arabic-speaking world between 1888 and 1952.[196] I note here that, according to my estimate, some 78% of these works (63 titles) were published in Egypt. This suggests that Egypt contributed more than its fair share in what Smith refers to as the "mundane process" of "religious reification" which occurred in the modern period whereby "men come to substitute, for a vivid personal faith in direct commerce with transcendence, a human and limited conceptualisation". Smith observes that the Islamic instance in the modern age best illustrates this process of "reification" in an "unusually intricate and yet revealing way".[197]

At this level of essentialisation of the European "Mind", and its civilisation, it is evidently clear that the intellectual might of Europe, as interpreted by Egypt's senior literati, came to pose a much greater level of threat to Quṭb in 1948, when he penned his first Islamist work,[198] than a year earlier even as he had come to realise, probably through the writings of Ḥusayn,[199] that he was facing a situation of "extreme work paralysis" as a litterateur.

In contrast to the stance Quṭb took in 1939, when he revealed a clear leaning to Darwinism by accepting that European civilisation is well ahead on the "scale of refinement", Quṭb now develops a line of argument which deprecates Western modern thought for not having an ethical dimension. In this line of thought, Quṭb creates an imaginary category of an Islamic "mind", and one of a Western "mind", which are bound to clash, arguing that the way of Islamic thinking, which is founded on ethical goals guiding human acts, and modern Western thought, which is founded on utilitarian goals for ethics, are not able to meet.[200]

Paradoxically, Quṭb argues in all six editions of *al-'Adāla* that the rejection, or acceptance, of any ramification of Western thought, is conditional on whether it agrees with the "basic idea", and the "spirit" of Islam. In such instances of agreement, Quṭb advances the view, rather pragmatically, in the first five editions of the work, that Muslims are allowed "to take advantage of all the fruits of human efforts", within the limits of the "basic [Islamic] idea" of the universe, people and life, adding further that "no barrier is to be erected between Muslims and human efforts", and that Muslims should not stand in isolation from "the ever moving procession of the world".[201]

Obviously, the idea of an "ever moving procession of the world" in the above quote might suggest that Quṭb is in agreement with the general tendency in the modern thought of the West to believe in progress as "the law of human history".[202] In its fullest form, Shepard finds, the "myth of progress", i.e. "the modern religion" (of the West), which arose in eighteenth century Europe, involves "not only physical progress, but also moral, social and spiritual conditions".[203]

However, Shepard observes, Quṭb seems to have steadily moved in the direction of rejecting the "myth of progress". Thus, he argues, in his more radical Islamist writings, Quṭb continues "to accept the reality and qualified value of material progress, but the idea of social and moral progress becomes increasingly problematic".[204]

I find, however, that by claiming a divine origin for the Islamic "idea", there is no latitude in Quṭb's writings to allow for any progress on the plane of social and moral norms especially on gender issues. In fact, Quṭb uses the same method which was used in the early part of the twentieth century by some Indian Muslims who claimed the supremacy of Islam in feminist-related issues. As Smith observes:

> One of the methods used to inculcate the superiority of Islam, in this [the position of women], as in other regards, is to picture the modern West as a den of unrelieved vice. It is supposed that there exists in Europe and America a situation of total moral depravity, sexual perversity, rank libertinism, wrecked

marriages, a *de facto* polygamy, and general foulness from which one might well revert.[205]

Smith makes explicit reference to Iqbal specifically, pointing out that the latter never wished that the new values should apply to women. He imagined European women heartless, hating maternity, love and life. He wanted to keep women 'pure' and in subjection. He kept his own wives in seclusion (*purdah*).[206] Clearly, although Iqbal made use of the Sufi doctrine of "The Perfect Man" (*al-insān al-Kāmil*), this "reformist" did not, like Ibn 'Arabī, understand it to be "a universal cosmology of the self larger than gender, history or culture".[207]

In all editions of al-*'Adāla*, Quṭb creates a rigid dichotomy between the West of "matter" and Islam on matters of gender in the chapter entitled "*Usus al-'Adāla al-Ijtimā'iyya fi al-Islām*" (The Foundations of Social Justice in Islam). In a line of argument that will become a main element of Quṭb's *jāhiliyya* discourse against the animalistic-beastly West in the 1960s, Quṭb argues that "when Islam granted women their spiritual and material rights, it was looking upon them as humans and acting in accordance with its view of human unity". In this context, he quotes Q7:189 "It is He who created you out of one living soul, and made of it its spouse that it might rest in her".[208]

Quṭb then goes on to criticise the "material" West when he claims that "the freedom that the materialistic West has granted to women does not arise from this honourable source [of Islam] nor were its motives the innocent motives of Islam".[209] In all editions of al-*'Adāla,* Quṭb argues that when France offered equality to women, it granted them "the total right of harlotry" which is "the only right that Islam forbids to women and men alike".[210]

Given that the stress is on the "idea" of equality on gender issues being a foundational component of social justice in Islam in Quṭb's Islamist discourse, it is easy to infer that Quṭb is implying, against historical facts,[211] that Islam in history maintained its superiority over the West in its social norms. Moreover, Quṭb argues in all editions of *al-'Adāla*, that "Islam is not antagonistic to science, and does not harbour hatred towards scientists".[212] To the contrary, he argues, Islam makes (seeking) scientific knowledge "a sacred duty" falling under the rubric of obedience to religion", citing a saying attributed to Ibn Māja to the effect that "seeking science is a duty which is incumbent on every Muslim".[213] In line with 'Abduh's reform school,[214] Quṭb adds in the early editions of the work that seeking science is a duty which should be upheld by every Muslim woman, as well.[215]

In the first five editions of *al-'Adāla*, Quṭb quotes also a ḥadīth commanding Muslims to seek scientific knowledge from places as far afield as China,[216] which, along with Quṭb's reference to the duty of every Muslim woman to seek knowledge, was removed in the fifth and last editions (1958 & 1964) of the work,[217] reflecting a clear bias against women in his later writings.

Interestingly, al-Banna seems to have alluded to the same ḥadīth quoted by Quṭb above, when he remarks on the dilemma and the hesitation he experienced upon graduating from Dār al-'Ulūm, in the late 1920s, when he considered furthering his education abroad.[218] Al-Banna writes in his memoirs (1940s?), that he experienced a "violent struggle" when he reflected on al-Ghazālī's views on sciences and knowledge,[219] finding himself torn between the love of sciences, and his desire to acquire more of these sciences, even if it meant going as far as China, or Europe, and his other desire to dedicate himself to *al-da'wa* (missionary activity), to call for

> going back to the teachings of Islam, and a disaffection with the blind imitation (*taqlīd)* of the West, and the corrupting [effects] of the 'husk' of Western civilisation (*madaniyya*).[220]

No such qualms were, however, known to have seized Quṭb, who failed to establish any "comradeship" with al- Ghazālī, and actually showed an unequivocal desire to adopt the very external "husk" of Western civilisation, as al-Banna puts it. To put Quṭb's position into perspective, I would like to emphasise here that Quṭb made seeking "pure sciences", leading to material comfort, "a sacred duty", arguing rather pragmatically that "there is no 'pure goodness', nor 'pure evil' in life".[221]

Al-'Aqqād, however, came to the conclusion that *all* kinds of thought are considered to be an Islamic "duty"(*farīḍa*), which are sanctioned by the Qur'an, in a way which he considers to have been unprecedented in all other religious books.[222] It is worth mentioning here that, unlike Quṭb, al-'Aqqād established "comradeship" with al-Ghazālī. Furthermore, al-'Aqqād found parallelism in the last's thought and that of Descartes, Newton, and the Scottish philosopher David Hume (d. 1776) in his work *Al-Falsafa al-Qur'āniyya* (The Qur'anic Philosophy, 1947).[223]

As expected, Hume is not tackled in Quṭb's Islamist discourse, nor does Quṭb seem to show any interest in addressing himself to any modern Western literary content, for that matter, in the first five editions of *al-'Adāla*. Quṭb, in fact, seems to be struggling in the course of this period to provide any substance to validate the argument he makes against the Western "mind" although, as Calvert argues, he "evinced intellectual airs throughout his life".[224]

4. Repudiation of the Great Humanist Philosophers of Islam: al-Fārābī (d. 950), Ibn Sinā (Avicenna, d.1037) and Ibn Rushd (Averroes, d. 1198)

In contrast to Ḥusayn who recognised the great reception that Aristotle has obtained during the Abbasid era and the considerable impact of his works on Muslim philosophers like al-Farabī, Ibn Sinā and Ibn Rushd,[225] Quṭb points out that "true

Islamic philosophy" is not to be sought in the works of Ibn-Sinā, or Ibn-Rushd, or any other so-called philosophers of Islam in the first five editions of *al-'Adāla*). He further explains that the philosophy of these men is nothing but "a shadow of Greek philosophy, which, in reality, is unrelated to the philosophy of Islam".[226]

At a later stage, Quṭb added al-Fārābī[227]without explaining why he placed these three Muslim philosophers on the outside of the crucial outside-inside division that he drew. It is also unclear what elements of Greek philosophy he found wanting, or alien, in comparison to Islam's "true philosophy". Nor does one get any sense of what Quṭb meant precisely by referring to "true Islamic philosophy". To be certain, Quṭb never came even remotely close to the subtlety and depth of al-'Aqqād's thought, who not only acknowledged, and established "comradeship" with, Ibn-Sinā, Ibn-Rushd, and al-Fārābī, as "the most acclaimed philosophers of Islam,[228] but pointed out, as well, that Greeks in ancient times made a clear distinction between "logic" (*al-mantiq*), which they held in high esteem, and "polemical, or dialectical disputations" (*al-jadal*), which they viewed with suspicion. al-'Aqqād argued further that the Greeks disproved of "sophistry" (*al-safsaṭa*), or "rhetoric", as in "the science of rhetorical [persuasion] by evidence" (*'ilm al-barāhīn al-khitābiyya*).[229]

For someone who "evinced intellectual airs throughout his life", as Calvert puts it, Quṭb certainly demonstrates a remarkable inability to take on Western modern thought in the first five editions of *al-'Adāla*. He, however, takes exception in criticising American educational programs and pedagogic methods, for what he sees to be an inclination to "practical training", rather than to "scientific knowledge", and giving precedence to "practical skilfulness" over "theoretical assumptions", which he puts down to the philosophy of "pragmatism".[230] In developing this argument, Quṭb relies solely on a single article entitled "Pragmatism or the Philosophy of Expediency" (*al-brajmatizm or falsafat al-dharā'i'*) by Dr. Ya'qūb Fam.[231]

Although Quṭb is critical of the "empirical philosophy" (*al-falsafa al-tajrībiyya*)", and the "empirical method" (*al-ṭariqa al-tajrībiyya*), and finds that these permeated "the materialistic Western mentality" at the time, he singles out the Americans for his attack against the "philosophy of pragmatism" (clearly projecting his own pragmatism onto the American "other") for introducing a "method" which he considers to be a "reversal" (*inqilāb*) in ways of thought and research, and a "total drift away" from "abstract ideas", and "theoretical meanings", as well as a drift away from the "nature and truth of things", to limit research to the "practical" sphere and its implications.[232]

Obviously, Quṭb's stress on abstraction and meanings in the above statement is in clear opposition to the near revulsion he seems to have harboured toward both meaning and abstraction in the earlier course of his life, which seems to suggest that he evidently became aware of his impending expedition to the US, seemingly to acquaint himself with American pedagogic methods, in the course of writing his first Islamist work in 1948.

Although Quṭb seems to have developed a heightened level of anxiety in relation to the aggressive stances of European colonialism, specifically France and England, towards Islam,[233] singling out the latter for its attempts to create a "general mentality" which derides the fundamentals of Islamic and Eastern life in Egypt, by infiltrating Egypt's educational institutions,[234] he nonetheless appears to hold the American "other" at a lower echelon of sophistication than the European, especially the French, when he claims that the philosophy of pragmatism directed American life to "practical production", and "turned it away, to a great extent, from [attaining] an artistic and theoretical culture".[235]

In the course of Quṭb's two-year sojourn in the US (1948-1950), he seems to have engaged in a process of self-assertion, by claiming for himself the sophistication of the French (associated with Ḥusayn), in othering the American. Thus, in his recollections of his visit in the United States, Quṭb writes in 1951 that the Americans "must import their *high culture* from Europe".[236] In his comments on the "artistic primitiveness" of the Americans, Quṭb reveals an admiration for the French. He writes that the Americans lack in "artistic taste" to appreciate "precious human heritage", recounting that he noticed during his tenth visit to the San Francisco Museum of Modern Art that only one person, out of one hundred and nine he counted, stopped for a couple of minutes to look at Jean-Baptiste Huet's painting "The Elder or Younger Fox in the Chicken Yard" (1766) that he particularly admired. Unlike the primitive Americans, Quṭb writes that he appreciated the splendid "genius" of Huet's painting. [237]

The ambivalence in Quṭb's position towards the European "other" is only too apparent when we see him quoting in all six editions of *al-'Adāla* an article summarising Haykal's book *Ḥayāt Muḥammad* in which there is reference to Bernard Shaw's prediction that Europe is turning to Islam. In the same quoted passage from that article, reference is also made to the impartiality of some nineteenth century European thinkers, such as Carlyle, Goethe, and Gibbon, who are praised for recognising the "intrinsic value" in the religion of Muḥammad.[238] In all editions of *al-'Adāla*, however, Quṭb insists that there is an "inherited enmity" towards Islam in the "depth of the European nature".[239] Only in the last edition of *al-'Adāla* does Quṭb make reference to the "inherited enmity" towards Islam which is found in "the depth of the European and American natures".[240]

5. Quṭb's Sojourn in America (1948-1950) and Encountering the American "Other"

Given his linguistic disabilities, and his dark complexion, It was not initially clear why the Egyptian authorities decided to send Quṭb to the United States at the peak of racism in the US, which certainly placed Quṭb in a disadvantaged position during his stay. As one journalist pointed out,

> America in 1949 was not a natural place for Quṭb. He was a man of colour, and the United States was still largely segregated. He was an "Arab", and American public opinion favoured Israel.[241]

During his two-year stay in America, Quṭb is said to have particularly suffered because of his dark skin,[242] which helps to explain why the United States remains an epitome of abominable racism in Quṭb's later Islamist writings with Quṭb even going as far as comparing the US unfavourably to the Nazis in their treatment of the Jews in his commentary on *Sura* 6, *al-In'ām*, in *Ẓilāl*.[243] Calvert remarks that the racism, then rampant in America, appears to have provided Quṭb with a degree of "racial consciousness".[244] The impact of such a newly-found "racial consciousness" was certainly to be immediately discernible in Quṭb's writings of the early 1950s upon his return to Egypt.[245]

In a 1951 article, for instance, Quṭb identifies the "White Man", in Europe and the US, as the "prime enemy" (of Islam), when he launches an attack targeting the "slaves of the White Man" in the Ministry of Education.

> Colonialism does not emerge victorious today by fire and iron, it wins above all with these men whose souls and ideas have been colonised...in the Ministry of Education, in newspapers, in books, it wins us with these pens which are steeped in the ink of spiritual 'humiliation' (*dhul*) and 'ignominy' (*hawān*) to write about the victories of France, Britain and the United States.[246]

Perhaps the most adverse impact of Quṭb's sojourn in the United States was the severe estrangement and loneliness he felt during his two-year journey which must have been aggravated by his linguistic limitations.[247] Quṭb is said "to have aggrandised his loneliness into heroic solitude", seeing himself as being "the secret, lone agent of God's Will" as he walked the streets of Greeley.[248]

In a letter dated March 6th, 1950, Quṭb wrote to his friend the literary critic, Anwar al-Ma'adawī, indicating implicitly that he wanted to emulate the role of a prophet or a saint to give (enduring) life to (his) "ideas".

> The warmth of faith belongs to the one who gives life to "ideas" and opens the windows of souls and hearts to them. This is why the words of the prophets and saints live, while the words of philosophers and thinkers have died.[249]

An analysis of a series of articles and some correspondence which recorded Quṭb's impressions of America, posthumously collected and published by al-Khaldī, reveals that America came to represent to Quṭb a strange dichotomy of spirit-human and matter-animalistic which places it simultaneously at the summit of material progress, and at the lowest ebb on the scale of human values.

> I fear that there is no correspondence between the greatness of the material civilisation in America, and the greatness of the 'human' who creates this civilisation, I further fear that the wheel of life will turn, and the record of times will fold sway, with America not adding any, or making slight, contribution to humanity's stock of values, which distinguish between a human and a thing, or an animal.[250]

Quṭb expresses an especially acute revulsion against the inhabitants of New York, and the city itself which he dubbed the "gigantic workshop". In an article entitled "Ḥamā'im fī New York" (Doves in New York, 1949), he describes a flock of "meek doves" that he saw landing on a side-walk in that city, which appears to have struck a chord in him, seemingly finding that the meekness of the doves is at odds with the nature of that city, and its inhabitants whom he denigrated and described as "a frantic and unbridled herd" (*qaṭī' hā'ij maḥmūm*).[251]

He writes in the same aforementioned article that he had spent a whole year in this "gigantic workshop", moving from New York to Washington, Greeley and Denver, without seeing – except on rare occasions – "the face of a human" which expresses the meaning of (being) human, or a human look which reflects (any) human meanings. The Americans are "slaves of lust" (*'abīd al-shahawāt*) who feel beauty only as "beasts and monsters" in the jungle.[252]

In all of his later writings on his recollections and impressions of his visit to the United States, America comes across as an epitome of a mechanical and abhorrent modern Western civilisation which suffers the ills of moral depravity, profanity, sexual promiscuity, savagery and materialism. Writing in retrospect in *Signposts on the Road* (1964), for instance, Quṭb reveals that, throughout his stay in the United States, he came to see himself as "one of a few (real) adherents to Islam in America", and took it upon himself to go on the assault against the American society which was held by him to be the epitome of Western *jāhiliyya* with its "flimsy" religious beliefs, and its "harmful" moral and socio-economic conditions.[253]

Quṭb's recollections of his visit includes as well a particular scene of a ball which he claims he witnessed in 1950, after a service at a church in Greeley, Colorado, which seems to have haunted him for the rest of his days, as he relays to us in *al-Islām wa Mushkilāt al-Ḥaḍāra* (1962):

> After the 'religious service' ended in the Church, with member youngsters participating in hymns and prayers...we passed from a side door to the dancing

> floor which was adjacent to the 'prayer' hall'...in the heat of dancing to the tunes of the 'gramophone', the dancing floor was filled with feet and legs, with arms wrapped around waists, and lips and breasts meeting...the air was fully filled with amorousness, when the pastor came down from his office...it's as if he noticed that the [bright] white lanterns...spoilt this 'romantic' dreamy atmosphere...so he endeavoured to switch them off avoiding [at the same time] interrupting the dancing...He then proceeded to the 'gramophone' to pick a record to suit this atmosphere. And he picked one famous American song: 'But Baby its Cold Outside'...And the pastor waited until he saw the steps of his 'daughters and sons' gliding to the [tune of the] music of this exciting song. He seemed joyful and content and left the dance floor for his home.[254]

Calvert remarks, however, that the city of Greeley was established as a Utopian community in 1870, and, at the time, Quṭb enrolled at the Colorado State College of Education in the late 1940s, the city still maintained "the moral rigour, temperance and civic mindedness of its founding fathers". He notes further that during Quṭb's stay in the city, a total ban on alcohol, which was imposed by the first American settlers, was still in effect. As Calvert puts it, "Greeley's highly touted civic virtue made little impression on Quṭb", whose assessment of the inhabitants of Greeley as carrying within themselves the same moral flaws of materialism that characterised Western civilisation "fitted well with Quṭb's overall picture of the world".[255]

As Quṭb was to recount later, he had already made the decision, as he set out on his journey to New York, to adhere to Islam and to guard against the American society which, to him, stood for "lust", "pleasure" and "sin".[256] Musallam argues that when Quṭb arrived in the United States, he was looking for things to reinforce his preconceived ideas about Western civilisation and the United States.[257]

It is arguably the case that whatever the Americans did or did not do, might have been beside the point. Calvert relays that when Quṭb left for New York in early 1948, the voyage "elicited in him a heightened sense of destiny and moral purpose."[258] The "American" seems to have confirmed to Quṭb what he already *knew* about America before he actually visited the United States, primarily through the prism provided by Asad's work *Islam at the Crossroads*.[259]

One particular passage from Asad's work, which is quoted by Quṭb in all editions of *al-ʿAdāla*, reveals that Quṭb had adopted Asad's views of the West as irreligious, materialistic and pragmatic:

> The average Occidental [Quṭb uses European instead but that might be an error by the translator] – be he a Democrat or a Fascist, a Capitalist or a Bolshevik, a manual worker or an intellectual – knows only one positive 'religion', and that is the worship of material progress, the belief that there is no other goal in life

> than to make that very life continually easier or, as the current expression goes, 'independent of Nature'. The temples of this 'religion' are the gigantic factories, cinemas, chemical laboratories, dancing halls; and its priests are bankers, engineers, film stars, captains of industry...The unavoidable result of this craving after power and pleasure is the creation of hostile groups armed to the teeth and determined to destroy each other. And on the cultural side, the result is the creation of a human type whose morality is confined to the question of practical utility alone, and whose highest criterion of good and evil is material success.[260]

On the whole, however, Quṭb was certainly to go much further in demonising the American "other" than he did in othering the "European", actually he makes out the American to be the worst version of the European. In a 1951 article, for instance, Quṭb pushes the theme of demonising the Americans to an extreme by claiming that they lack in compassion for one another giving caricatured, and highly unlikely, examples of life in America to prove his point. In this context, he recounts a scene of American patients in George Washington hospital, where he was receiving treatment, laughing upon hearing the news that one of the hospitals' employees was gravely injured, and on the brink of death.[261]

Another example is given of a woman whose husband had just died, and who showed no feelings of sorrow for his death. Quṭb recounts that he overheard a conversation between a woman who helped him with English when he arrived in America, and the woman who had just lost her husband, in which the latter expressed feelings of joy that she was lucky enough to have taken out life insurance on her dead husband, and that treatment did not cost her much as he was covered by medical insurance.[262] Quṭb was to conclude that creatures such as crows and chickens are much more advanced than the Americans in showing respect and awe for the sanctity of death.[263]

Having probably never read Thoreau, as Calvert suggests,[264] Quṭb develops a line of argument which presupposes an innate "disfigurement" of the "character of the Americans" which he links to the circumstances surrounding the birth of America, when their forefathers first encountered nature:

> They [the American forefathers] encountered nature [armed with] the weapon of science and the power of muscles; it excited nothing in them but the power of the "dry intellect" and the power of "overwhelming senses". Nature did not open to them windows into the soul, the heart, and sentiments as it did in the soul of early humanity.[265]

What is especially interesting in Quṭb's discourse against the American, is that he recognises that the birth of America marks a clear departure from the Ancient World which gave rise to a "balanced formation of humans".[266] The "American" in Quṭb's discourse, however, is taken out of the history of humanity altogether, for being of low stock, with their forefathers being invariably depicted by Quṭb as "criminals", who were brought to America by the English Empire for construction and production works, or merely "adventurers seeking wealth, adventures and pleasure".[267] Reflecting on ideas which he seems to owe to Henry Nash Smith's *Virgin Land: the American West as Symbol and Myth* (1950),[268] Quṭb deduces that the Americans are war-mongers by instinct, with the idea of war and struggle running in their blood-streams throughout their (entire) history.[269]

Apart from Quṭb's reference to Nash in the above statement which was made in 1951, following his return to Egypt in 1950, it is to be noted here that Quṭb seems to have been unable, and perhaps also unwilling, to acquaint himself with American literature, or any literature of man for that matter, in the course of his two-year stay in America, having been denied access to translated material as he was throughout his literary career in Egypt.

In a letter to Tawfīq al-Ḥakīm dated May 9th, 1949, Quṭb thanks the former for sending him a copy of his newly-released book touching on the story of Oedipus (*al-Malik Udīb*, 1949), noting that he had found in al-Ḥakīm's dedication to him "the friendly spirit of the East" and its "soft breeze", especially as he found himself living in a huge "workshop" which is called "the New World". Quṭb writes to al-Ḥakīm that the Americans have everything except for a "soul", adding that he was in need of a conversation which has nothing to do with "dollars, movie stars and cars' brands...a conversation in affairs of humans, thought and spirit".[270]

From what Quṭb has conveyed to us in his writings on his sojourn in America, one can see that the Americans were kind and open to him, sharing with him moments of sadness and vulnerability in funerals and hospitals which seemingly left him disturbingly immunised to their suffering and sadness. It is also in America that Quṭb was to receive some recognition when the American Council of Learned Societies (ACLS) commissioned the Arabist John B. Hardie to translate *al-'Adāla*.[271] The founders of ACLS, who represented thirteen American learned societies, created it in 1919 to represent the United States in the Union Académique Internationale with the belief that such a federation of scholarly organizations stood for America's democratic ethos.[272] Quṭb's work was one of twenty-two books which were translated as part of a translation programme which was initiated in 1948 by ACLS with the aim of acquainting the American reader with "modern" thought in the Near Eastern world.[273] Members of ACLS were obviously unaware of the animosity that Quṭb harboured against the Americans.

It is arguably the case that Quṭb endowed the American "other", and later on the "Jew", "with the evil which is actually in him", as Erikson would put it,[274] thus projecting onto the "American" at this stage of his life attributes of racism,[275] and their obsessiveness with sexuality.[276] Interestingly, Quṭb recounts, without giving any details, that he reflected on the Old Testaments' account of God's creation of males and females, obviously making reference to Genesis, when he witnessed the "sexual primitiveness" of the Americans.[277]

To be certain, Quṭb never budged from the earlier position he had taken in 1948 of seeing the American as the quintessence of pragmatism, throughout the 1950s,[278] depending for this view on a single article, as discussed earlier. In all the first five editions of *al-'Adāla*, Quṭb quotes the said article in tracing the history of pragmatism to its founder the American philosopher Charles Peirce (d. 1914), and crediting William James (d. 1910) with putting together the philosophy of pragmatism, and John Dewey (d.1952) with modifying it in modern times. In the first five editions of *al-'Adāla,* he expressed a particular aversion to the emphasis placed on the "practical" aspect of research in American pedagogic methods as developed by Charles Pierce.[279]

In none of Quṭb's writings do we ever see him recognising the fact that Dewey actually made ceaseless attempts, in his essays on pragmatism, to settle metaphysical disputes, and was able in his writings "to support much of religion, including the hypothesis of God".[280] Nor do we ever see Quṭb even venturing into the idea that the philosophy of pragmatism bears influences from the thought-worlds of men such as one of the founding fathers of America, Thomas Jefferson (d.1826), and the principal author of The Declaration of Independence (1776), and the education reformer, otherwise known as "The Father of the Common School Movement", Horace Mann (d.1859). None of these men are ever invoked in Quṭb's discourse. Nor do we see Quṭb recognising that the philosophy of pragmatism had actually come into prominence to fulfil an obvious need in the educational thought of America which was against "the elitist philosophies of education, and in search of a view of education to make it available to all men".[281]

6. Conclusion

In problematising Quṭb's attitude to the "Mind" and the civilisation of the West, I have argued in the above discussion that Quṭb never stepped back from his unequivocal appreciation of the "material" civilisation of Europe, and argued rather pragmatically that this should be adopted wholeheartedly from Europe. There is, however, some clear ambivalence in relation to the thought-world of Europe, when he seems to reject the ideological underpinnings of European civilisation in favour of the Islamic "idea", or "philosophy", without however establishing comradeship with men and women of the Islamic past. In fact, we have seen him placing on the outside the "three greatest philosophers of Islam": al-Fārābī, Ibn Sinā, and Ibn Rushd who contributed much to

Islamic ethics and humanist traditions by developing the ethics of Aristotle and the politics of Plato.[282]

Instead, Quṭb rather resorts to modern content, especially to Asad's work, in making a case against the Westernised senior members of Egypt's literati in the latter part of the 1940s. As Smith remarks in his observations on Muslims' apologist discourse in the modern age:

> The spirit of the defence against the West was strikingly westernising in so far as Islam is defended not only against Western disparagement [but] also by means of Western approval...[in a] simultaneous repulsion and attraction in relation to the West.[283]

According to Smith, this "simultaneous repulsion and attraction in relation to the West" indicates both a lack of confidence, and that "the good opinion of Europe is a matter of deep concern" to Muslim apologists.[284] Indeed, as discussed above, Quṭb claims the sophistication of the European in asserting himself against the "desert Arab", and the high culture of the French especially against the soulless essentialised American "other" later. What is also made plainly clear in the discussion above is that whatever merit the American has, Quṭb did not want, and was, additionally, ill-equipped to acquaint himself with Western modern thought. Additionally, he relied totally for his superficial knowledge of Western content on translated, and somewhat abridged studies, as the gulf between him and Egypt's senior literati steadily widened. Although Quṭb quoted Goethe (d. 1832), for instance, to affirm the triumph of Islam, as an idea in history, he failed to appreciate that the great German humanist had come to the conclusion that "Orient and Occident should no longer be separated".[285]

4

The "West-East" Duality & Quṭb's Early Views on "Islam" in Relation to "Christianity" and "Judaism"

In this chapter, I address "the spiritual East" and "material West" duality in Quṭb's mid-1940s writings leading to the early Islamist stage of his life. In the discussion below, I will attempt primarily to analyse how Quṭb deals with religious content, looking especially to find the crucial "average expectable continuity" with the past, and whether Quṭb establishes any "sense of comradeship" with men and women of the Islamic past in formulating the vital self-other, or outside-inside, divisions in relation to both Jews and Christians.

In the first part of the discussion, I will be looking at Quṭb's early views of folk-beliefs and his early encounter with Christians in his home town Musha. In the second section, I will analyse Quṭb's views of Christianity and Judaism in the course of his literary career, especially during the key period of the late 1940s leading to his turn to Islamism. The third section of this discussion will centre on an analysis of the first editions of *al-'Adāla*, with the view of illuminating Quṭb's views on the place of Islam in history, in comparison to both Christianity and Judaism. The fourth section deals primarily with Quṭb's radicalised views of "the People of the Book" in the period leading to the later stage of his life.

1. First Views of Religious Traditions and Folk-beliefs in Musha

At the age of seven, Quṭb attended the first funeral procession in his lifetime. It was that of his childhood friend, Gom'aa, who was believed to have been possessed by an *'ifrīt* (demon/evil spirit). Under the heading of "al-'Afārīt" (pl. of *'ifrīt*) in his memoirs, Quṭb recounts that he walked in his friend's funeral procession, crying. The whole event, he writes, remained "etched in his mind and its memory cannot be erased."[1]

In recollecting the events leading up to Gom'aa's death, Quṭb writes that one day as the youth, including himself and Gom'aa, gathered to listen to a story which was related by one of them, a black tomcat jumped from the window of the small mill, leading the youth to run away "in terror at this sudden and terrifying apparition". Gom'aa, however, lost his balance and "fell down in a dead faint". He was convinced that the *'ifrīt* was talking to him. Confronted by the body of her grandson, Gom'aa's grandmother attempted, to no avail, to restore the health of her son. The amulets and the talismans of the *awliya'* of the village, and the *zār* ceremony that she arranged for him, (to exorcise the demon), had no effect. Three months later Gom'aa was dead.[2]

The tales of the miracles of the *awliya'*, Quṭb tells us, were widespread in Musha, including examples of their ability to burn or bind the *'afarīt*.[3] Indeed, in drawing a comparison between the respective memoirs of Quṭb and al-Banna, Krämer observes that, unlike al-Banna, who fought "the illicit", Quṭb encountered "the eerie and the unsettling." Thus, the latter portrays in his memoirs "a world of magic, sorcery pervading each and every thing".[4] In the course of Quṭb's literary career, Calvert finds, scattered references in the former's works suggest that Quṭb remained "anchored in the cultural universe of village Egypt", with the presence of *jinn* and *'afārīt* being made felt in his imagination throughout his adult years.[5]

In the opening passage of a chapter in Quṭb's memoirs which is dedicated to a description of his encounter with the fearsome figure *al-majdhūb*,[6] when he was barely aged six, he writes of feeling a "shudder" in his body which "silently penetrates his bones" upon recalling the events surrounding his encounter with *al-majdhūb* some quarter of a century before.[7]

> It was this man with dishevelled hair and torn clothing, sometimes naked with nothing to cover his body, wandering about the streets and alleys of the village with a stick in his hand that struck at everything and everybody. He would let out a confused but terrifying growl or guffaw in a high dreadful voice.[8]

Quṭb recounts that folk beliefs (in the first part of the twentieth century) in Musha have it that *al-majdhūb*, Shaykh Naqīb, was given "*al-sharba*",[9] which is known as "*sharbat al-wilāya*".[10] Following drinking "*sharbat al-wilāya*", he turned into "a fearsome wandering devil, out of his mind, staring blankly and behaving strangely...tearing his clothes, and then rolling in the mud, or pouring dust over his head and naked body."[11]

The figure of *al-majdhūb*, as depicted by Quṭb, is what Hoffman explains to be one of the personalities which are considered in Sufi milieus in twentieth-century Egypt to be "social anomalies".[12] For one thing, it seems to be the case that the idea of "*sharbat al-wilāya*" owes its origin in India where the idea of "*sharaab*"' in Sufi parlance refers literally to a "wine not well fermented [which is] the states overtaking the [Sufi] seeker in the beginning" of his journey.[13] In Egypt,

> Sufi experience appears to entail a certain amount of loss of control over one's mind and behaviour [which] appears most dramatically in the case of *gazb*

> (*jadhb* in classical Arabic), which literally means "attraction" or "pulling", that is, a divine attraction that strips people of their normal mental faculties. One might say that it is losing one's mind in God. The first vision of the light of God is a shock to the mental faculties...the Qur'an itself, according to Sufi interpretation, indicates that the Law (i.e. *Shari'a*) may be transcended by those who access to esoteric knowledge: for Khiḍr baffled Moses by the apparent immorality of his acts, which nonetheless had a hidden purpose and were performed at the command of God (Q18:65-82).[14]

It appears to be the case that *mūlid(s),* which are "an important place for Sufis to meet and attract new members into the life of an Order",[15] provided an important space which allowed for a process of initiation of *al-majāzīb* (pl. of *majdhūb*).[16] Interestingly, the *mūlid* in the popular dimension of the Coptic faith attracted Coptic pilgrims in so far as the festivities, which usually celebrated a "saint's feast day" (*mūlid*), "were a time when boundaries of prevailing social norms could be overstepped or redefined". In the decades following the Ottoman conquest of 1517, "Egyptians [Copts and Muslims] engaged in a kind of spiritual introspection, as seen by the noticeable popularity of Sufism and interest in commemorating *mawālid(s)*".[17]

It is noteworthy that the major Coptic pilgrimage destinations since the fourth century included the ancient monasteries in Wadī al-Naṭrūn, along the Red Sea, as well as Upper Egypt[18]- of which Minya and (Quṭb's) province, Asyut, are the two main provinces – which offer the best representation of Copts.[19]

As Calvert and Shepard point out, Quṭb's village, Musha, stood nearby a Coptic monastery, which had been prominent enough in its medieval heyday to merit a mention by the fifteenth-century historian Taqi al-Dīn al-Maqrīzī (d. 1442). Although Quṭb makes no mention of the monastery, they note that

> it must have been a tangible reminder for Musha's Muslim populace that even after centuries of indigenous conversion and Arab-Muslim settlement, Coptic Christians, with whom Muslims shared much in the way of culture, continued to comprise a significant portion of Southern Egypt's population.[20]

By the beginning of the twentieth century, Baer observes that a new class of educated Muslims had emerged, and attempted to enter many of the occupations formerly monopolised by the Copts, especially certain branches of government employment. This development is said to have created "a sharp antagonism between the two communities, culminating in the rival congresses of Copts and Muslims held in 1911".[21]

Interestingly, Quṭb fails to associate any of the local churches in Egypt, including the Coptic Orthodox Church, which begins its calendar from the rule of the Roman Emperor Diocletian (284-305), when thousands of Egyptians were killed for their faith,[22] with the spirituality of "the East". And there is equally some evidence to suggest that he felt a degree of anxiety in relation to the Copts as his immediate "others".[23] Instead of identifying with the Copts, Quṭb comes to recognise in Tolstoy's works in his anthology *Kutub wa Shakhṣiyyat* (1946), without seemingly being acquainted with the Russian author's oeuvre, the "transparent Eastern spirit" he came to associate with the Christianity of the East before, as he puts it, it came to be "inspissated" by the "thick materialism of the West".[24]

In his memoirs, Quṭb disregards the three monasteries which are within the hinterland of Asyut- Deir al-Gabrawi, Deir al-Muḥarraq (known as the second Bethlehem for falling on the path of The Holy Family during their sojourn in Egypt which ended in Asyut), and Deir Dronka (otherwise known as the Monastery of the Virgin).[25] He also makes no mention of any of the *mawālid*(s), or pilgrimages to the tombs of martyrs and saints such as that to Deir Dronka mentioned above.[26]

Quṭb's lack of interest in the Coptic component of Egyptian culture, which was confirmed by the discovery of the Rosetta stone by Jean-François Champollion (1790-1832), which brought to light the link between the Pharaonic and the Coptic eras, extends also to Egypt's Jews who appear to have made a claim in 1942 of a link to Asyut since the time of Moses.[27] As Beinin argues, the dubious evidence supporting such claims does not diminish their significance in the construction of the identity and self-presentation of Egyptian Jews.[28]

Significantly, unlike al-Banna, who at the age of twelve became a disciple of the leading shaykh of the mystic Ḥaṣaflyya Order for twenty years after witnessing, and becoming impressed by its circle of "*dhikr*"[29] (recital of chants in a communal ceremony/ act of remembrance of God), Quṭb seems to have not watched, or participated in an act of devotional "*dhikr*". Instead, he claimed to have been particularly impressed by (al-'Aqqād favourite), Strauss, as he indicated in a newspaper article that he contributed to *al-Risāla* in 1941.[30] Following his dispute with al-'Aqqād, he also revealed in an article in *al-Thaqāfa* in 1951, that he considered himself a "*murīd*" (disciple in Sufi parlance) of the last.[31] Calvert and Shepard note that Quṭb does not give a description of the tomb of Musha's Muslim saint (*wālī*), who is identified in Quṭb's memoirs as Shaykh 'Abd al-Fattāḥ. They remark that the tomb served as "the focus of popular religious devotion and festivities, including the practice of praying for the saint's intercession with God". They note further that once a year, Musha would have come alive in "raucous celebrations" of Shaykh 'Abd al-Fattāḥ's *mulid*.[32]

What is particularly important to stress here is that the great fear which was incited by "the eerie and the unsettling" in Quṭb's childhood was shared by Christian and Muslim children alike in Musha. As Quṭb recounts, the legendary tales of the "*'afārīt*", and those of the *awliya,* mixed, and met, with an *accumulation of inherited beliefs* in the "miraculous supernatural" and the "paranormal" permeating the inner-beings of the naive villagers.[33]

Most probably, assuming a highly sophisticated readership, especially from within the ranks of Egypt's academia,[34] Quṭb reflects in his memoirs a relatively high degree of openness to Coptic Christianity, and its iconography. In a passage, which was ultimately altered in subsequent editions of Quṭb's memoirs, he gives us an account of the great tribulation which befell the villagers when a child tripped and fell in Musha. In such instances, according to folk-beliefs, a child risked to be possessed, or worse yet, to meet sudden death. Quṭb recounts that to ward off such a fate all villagers would resort "to invoking the name of Allah, if the child was a Muslim, or the name of "the Pure Virgin", and "the Great Cross", if the child was a Christian".[35]

Clearly, Quṭb shows here that he developed a degree of understanding of the symbolism of the Cross to the Copts in Musha, although he did not go on to explicitly articulate this first impression of Christianity in any of his works (as Muḥammad Kāmil Ḥusayn notably did in the late 1950s[36]). It is probably the case that Quṭb is reflecting in writing his memoirs a degree of awareness of 'Abduh's effort to bring about a rapprochement between Islam and Christianity on matters of doctrine.[37]

For the purpose of this study, I find it particularly noteworthy that, when Quṭb penned his memoirs in 1946, he was writing against a long-standing Islamic polemical tradition which associated Christians' use of icons and the cross with idolatry.[38] (As early as 38/658-9, there seems to be a clear indication that Christian Arabs were referred to as "*mushrikūn*".[39] Under the rule of the Umayyad Caliph al-Walid (705-15), the chief of the Banu Taghlib tribe was tortured and martyred on the grounds that it was "shameful that the chief of the Arabs should venerate the cross".[40])

As discussed earlier, Quṭb was an eager enthusiast for nationalism until the late 1940s which may explain why he chose to ignore, at this point in his life, some of the polemical material targeting Christianity that he will eventually quote in *Ẓilāl*.[41] And there is certainly no trace as well in his memoirs of the anxiety which seized al-Banna in his childhood in relation to missionary activities in his home town al-Maḥmūdiyya.[42] As Krämer notes, the challenge posed by the missionary activities in al-Maḥmūdiyya was such that it came to be seen as "a Christian plot to weaken Muslim society, and Islam at large, by corrupting its weakest members: women and children."[43]

In contrast to al-Banna, who relied solely on the Qur'an and some apocalyptic Ḥadīth[44] in his knowledge of Christianity and Judaism, and perception of Christians and Jews, often to the detriment of the last,[45] Quṭb bypassed both the Qur'an and Ḥadīth, and relied mostly on translated texts of biblical Scripture in his knowledge of Christianity and Judaism in the mid-1940s. As we shall see below, Quṭb begins to show a special attraction to *Christianity* in the late 1940s, and well into the early Islamist stage of his life through the late 1950s.

2.1 Quṭb's Views on "Religion", and the East-West Dichotomy in the Early Literary Stage of his Life

As Quṭb recounts in his memoirs, when he left his village life in Musha behind him, and headed to the city, his culture was "broadened", and consequently the legendary myths which were woven around the *'afārīt* became a matter of "humour" and "joke" to him. However, it appears to be the case, as he admits, that the *'afārīt* still haunted him in his dreams and visions. Speaking of himself in the third person, he writes

> This reveals that the myth of the *'afārīt* is deeper in his soul than culture, and that the *'afārīt* of his childhood and boyhood, will haunt his imagination for the rest of his life.[46]

To appreciate the significance of this last statement, one must place it within the intellectual milieu of the mid-twentieth century in Egypt, which was totally inhospitable to Quṭb's mythical world-view. Aḥmad Amīn, for instance, partly in response to De Lacy O'Leary's criticism of the Arab "mind" in his work *Arabia before Muḥammad* (1927),[47] developed the view in his work *Fajr Al-Islām* (The Dawn of Islam, 1929),[48] that the prevalence of legends and fables in pre-Islamic Arabic works of literature is symptomatic of a weakness in the Arab mental makeup. According to Amīn, this weakness in the Arab mental makeup is due to the Bedouin mode of life which precedes the later stage of civilisation in all nations.[49]

Quṭb seems to have been especially drawn to a section in Amīn's work which was dedicated to a discussion of "Poetry as an Indication of the Life of the Mind" (*Dalālit al-Shi'r 'ala al-Ḥaya al-'Aqliyya*), quoting from it at great length in his work on literary criticism *al-Naqd al-Adabī* (1947).[50] This particular theme seems to have gripped the senior members of Egypt's literati fairly early on in the twentieth century. Cachia notes that figures such as Ibn al-Rūmī (d.896) and Abu Nuwās (d. c. 803) invited studies which placed an emphasis on a psychological approach by two of the founders of al-Dīwān* school, al-Māzinī as early as in 1913, and particularly by al-'Aqqād.[51]

Reflecting a clear influence by the Nietzschean paradigm, which put in question "the frozen structures of the past" in the realm of values,[52] al-'Aqqād shows himself to be particularly concerned about the question of "good" and "evil", and went on to develop a philosophy in 1916 which was founded on combining reason, senses and spiritual consciousness, in an "integrated pattern" which he called the "Universal Consciousness".[53] Clearly, al-'Aqqād went beyond Emile Durkheim's idea of "collective consciousness" which was firstly coined by the French sociologist/theorist in *Les Règles de la Méthode Sociologique* (1895).[54]

As discussed in chapter 1, al-'Aqqād seemed to have found in the early 1920s much in favour of Aristotelian ideals which, he finds, were shared by al-Ghazālī,

Shakespeare, Wagner, and Leonardo. He was also aware then of Nietzsche's aspiration to achieve such ideals, and of the idea of a brotherhood in knowledge and consciousness which united millions of thinkers[55] in the history of mankind. In 1924, however, there seems to have been a slight change in his outlook as he showed himself to be particularly drawn to al-Mutanabbī, in comparison to both Darwin and Nietzsche, in the realm of ethics and virtues.[56]

Although Quṭb ends up developing a keen interest in Nietzsche in 1947, it is clearly the case that he did not share his mentor's "vision quest", nor did the last, who assumed a highly-educated readership, articulate his ideas in a manner that allowed his disciple to grasp ideas which have become current in the West. Generally speaking, as W. C. Smith argues, the liberalised Muslim reformers "fell short of producing an effective, transmissible synthesis of Islamic and liberal loyalties". He adds further that although the spirit of Muḥammad 'Abduh and of his teachings is "inherently liberal...the finished product of his work transmitted to others incorporates this only very partially".[57]

From the perspective of this study, I find it particularly significant that, as Western scholars, such as E. H. Whinfield, J. Redhouse, and J. R. A. Nicholson, took an interest in translating the works of Jalal al-Dīn al-Rūmī into English,[58] it was al-'Aqqād who repudiated this great 13th century humanist Sufi in the mid-1940s. And Quṭb followed suit, thus placing on the "outside" this important Sufi humanist of the "cumulative tradition" of the Islamic age of old piety.[59] As we shall see below, Quṭb reveals that he has been particularly drawn to a spiritual "East" imaginary construct which he associates mostly with the traditions of India, while he makes no mention in any of his writings to the preaching and the lives of Muslim saints who, Wilfred C. Smith argues, "knew and expressed a profound and universalist theistic humanism" in the course of the history of Mughul India (1526-1858). As Smith observes, it is arguably the case that there were "two facets of one single movement in India during these centuries: called *Bhakti* in its Hindu form and Sufi in its Islamic".[60]

2.2 The Discovery of India, and the "Spiritual" East and the "Material" West Dichotomy in Quṭb's 1940s Discourse

Sometime, perhaps in the early 1940s, following the confusion which permeated his thought in the mid-1930s,[61] and his dispute with Ṭaha Ḥusayn over the culture of the "East", Quṭb seems to have taken a degree of interest in the late 19th-century "spiritual Asia" paradigm which was adopted by the Theosophical Society[62] which had eight branches in Egypt in the late 1920s.[63]

The Theosophical Society was formed upon the basis of "a universal brotherhood of humanity",[64] which seemed to have appealed to Haykal in the late 1920s when he developed the idea of a "universal brotherhood combining Eastern wisdom and

Western activity and material productivity" which, according to Charles D. Smith, was probably inspired by the writings of the Hindu poet-philosopher Rabindranath Tagore (1861-1941).[65]

Such a social norm, whether it is the brainchild of the French revolution's "*fraternité*", or the theosophical version of "universal brotherhood", fails to preoccupy Quṭb in either the literary or the Islamist stages of his life. Instead, Quṭb rather subscribed to a world-view which, Bonnett argues, seems to have been inspired by Tagore, in setting up a "soulless" Occident against a "spiritual" Asia.[66] However, although Rabindranath, who was the grandson of the co-founder of the Brahmo Samāj movement,[67] identified strongly with Hindu India against the West,[68] Kopf warns against reducing his thought to "a simplistic spiritual East notion".[69]

It is noteworthy that Tagore is said to have written what Kopf considers to be "one of the most devastating attacks in the English language on the sources of Western nationalism".[70] However, unlike Quṭb (especially in the 1960s), Tagore considered history, in that case that of India, to be "a process of creation" to which various races of the world contributed including: the Dravidians, the Aryans, the ancient Greeks, the Persians, the Mohammedans of the West and those of central Asia, and finally the English.[71] Furthermore, the Indian poet-philosopher, who became the first Hindu Nobel laureate in 1913,[72] avowed his "deep love" and "great respect for the British race as human beings", and expressed a clear admiration of their "chivalrous humanity".[73]

In analysing *Kutub wa Shakhṣiyyāt* (1946), it becomes plainly apparent that Quṭb was particularly attracted to the aforementioned Bengali poet. Quoting from a translation of Tagore's poem "The Gardner" (1915), which was provided by Luṭfī Shalash, he finds in that specific poem "a deep and transparent tolerant Sufism" (*al-ṣūfiyya al-ʿamīqa al-samiḥa al-shafīfa*):[74]

> I hold her hands and press her to my breast
> I try to fill my arms with her loveliness, to plunder
> her sweet
> smile with kisses, to drink her dark glances with my
> eyes.
> Ah, but, where is it? Who can strain the blue from the
> sky?
> I try to grasp the beauty, it eludes me, leaving only
> the body in
> my hands.
> Baffled and weary I come back.
> How can the body touch the flower which only the
> spirit may
> touch?[75]

For all of Quṭb's open admiration for the transparent Sufism of the Bengali-Hindu Tagore (which, at times,[76] may have almost verged on, or been construed to be what Kopf qualifies as an "idolatrous veneration" for Tagore[77]) which went unabated well into the Islamist stage of his life,[78] he remained unable to place the Brahmo Samāj movement within the broader context of what Flood describes as "The Hindu Renaissance".[79] To be certain, Quṭb was also, perhaps, unaware that "The Hindu Renaissance" developed a tendency "to relegate ritual to a 'popular', below the ethical spirituality of the Upaniṣads and the Gitā",[80] when he reviewed Ḥusayn Fawzī's work *Sindbād al-ʿAṣrī* (Modern-day Sinbad).

In analysing Quṭb's review of Fawzī's 338-page work in which the latter gives an account of his visit to the Red Sea and Indian Ocean regions,[81] it becomes all too evident that Quṭb took a special interest, and found meaning, in certain aspects of Buddhist and Hindu religious "cumulative traditions" and rituals. Paradoxically, as Quṭb showed much openness to Hindu and Buddhist traditions in the mid-1940s, he showed, in equal measure, an open admiration for the Wahhābī sect which he defends as being part of "a religious reform awakening" (*nahḍa dīniyya iṣlāḥiyya*) in response to an onslaught of a "complete idolatrous degeneration" (*naksa wathaniyya kāmila*) which touched Islam.[82]

Unlike Abu'l-A'la Mawdūdī*(1903-79) who, Hartung finds, seems to have been particularly averse to "Buddhism" as well as "Sufism",[83] Quṭb recognised in Fawzī the mark of a "free thinker" for standing before a statue of the Buddha, and finding in "Buddhism" (*al-būdhiyya*)

> the "scent of freedom, simplicity, and tolerance" in spite of having nearly suffocated in a nightmare of "restrictions, complications, and extremism" [which is] attached to "Hinduism" which frightens, and terrifies him, making him at times disgruntled with all that is of the East![84]

Quṭb was, however, particularly opposed to Fawzī for expressing his "faith in all that is Western" and for despising the "East", its customs, legends, and religions.[85] He also declares that he parts company with Sinbad (Fawzī),[86] criticising the latter for failing to be in deeper empathy with the "tolerant and luminous Sufi Spirit" (*al-ruḥ al-ṣūfiyya al-mutasamiḥa, al-mushriqa)* of the "Spirit of the East", and for mocking the creed of "Nirvana", as his (unnamed) English co-traveller did, by misinterpreting it, and looking at it with the "Eye of the Westerners", thus equating it with "annihilation" (*al-fanā'*) because, as Quṭb sees it, the Westerner is in constant struggle with nature and lives in isolation from it.[87]

Reflecting a possible influence by Tagore's *Sādhanā*,[88] which is a collection of the Bengali poet's lectures in which he placed an emphasis on the philosophy of "oneness of Being" which allows the soul to achieve "union with the Brahman",[89] Quṭb asserts that as far as the Indian is concerned, he feels himself to be

> an atom which is in harmony with nature and considers it to be an "affectionate mother", [thus] he sees that "his extinction" in the *great power* (*al-quwa al-'uẓma*) represents life, perpetuity and immortality."[90]

Quṭb then goes on to call on the reader to stand in awe before the divine loftiness which he finds to be depicted in its highest form in Tagore's *Sādhanā*, and to bypass appearances and sociological conditions (in the East) to fathom the "heart of the East", which he describes as having within it:

> [the hidden] spiritual treasures which would save us from the "cruelty of the mechanical civilisation" which has no heart, and no conscience, and is in total harmony in its fundamentals with the spirit of the West.[91]

These "spiritual treasures" of the East include, according to Quṭb, the "Sacred King Portrait",[92] which is the famous sculptured portrait of the sage-King Parākramabāhu The Great (1123-1186) of medieval Buddhism in Sri Lanka,[93] who united the island under his rule (1153-86), and reformed Buddhist practices.[94] The sculptured portrait is especially appreciated by Quṭb for symbolising the "sacredness" which is attached to the "Great Unknown Power" in the East.[95] (With Buddhist traditions being silent about God, Quṭb is clearly making reference here to the teaching of "*pratityasamutpada*" (the "unknown reality", which is comparable to the notion of the Father in Christian theology[96]).

Included also in the list of the "spiritual treasures" of the East, which were seemingly not appreciated by Fawzī to the dismay of Quṭb, is the sculptured giant rock bas-relief monument known as the "Descent of the Ganges", or "Arjuna Penance", which is found in the 7th-century Mahabalipuram Indian religious centre in the Tamil Nadu state in India. The rock-cut monument, which represents an ascetic practicing austerity (*tapas*),[97] seems to have been especially appreciated by Quṭb for symbolising the rebirth of the "sacred wellspring". As he puts it, "all sorts of peoples and animals come from every corner to witness the birth of the sacred wellspring in [total] Sufism and reverence."[98]

Here, Quṭb reveals that, although he had come to accept Plato whom he associated with Ḥusayn's elite culture, he had harboured much animosity towards the ancient Greeks. Not only does he admonish Fawzī for not recognising the meaningfulness of Mahabalipuram, but he seems, above all, to be particularly incensed by the author's expressed open admiration for the Greek mystical hero of Thrace, Orpheus, who, (like Gandhi in the modern age), provided the inspiration for the non-violence ideal which was upheld by the sixth-century Orphic sect movement of ancient Greece.[99]

Fawzī, in fact, fails to appreciate the significance of the rock monument in Mahabalipuram, writing that had the rock been in Attica, a Greek artist would have sculpted, not a "sacred wellspring", but a statue of Orpheus mesmerising men and *jinn* to the tune of his harp.[100]

It is worth stressing the point here that it is arguably the case that Quṭb was perhaps especially drawn to the Mahabalipuram Dravidian-styled monument in Tamil Nadu as it falls in an area of the Indus valley, where the presence of Dravidian languages provides a strong evidence for the existence of a pan-Indian Dravidian culture,[101]before the predominance of the Indo-European linguistic group including: Greek, Latin, Indo-Iranian, Sanskrit, and the north Indian vernaculars of Gujarati, Hindi, Kashmiri, Oriya, Bengali and Urdu.[102]

Interestingly, the state of Tamil Nadu was dominated by the Dravidian movement which was committed to a Dravidian homeland consisting of the whole of southern India in the late 1940s.[103] Although the state is known as the "land of temples", which were mostly built in Dravidian style – with Mahabalipuram temples, being the oldest, representing a Dravidian art movement – there are, as well, a variety of places of worship which cater to the needs of minority groups including Christians, Jews, Jains, Sikhs and Muslims.[104] Except for some friction due to what Venkatachalapathy describes as "the avowed atheism of the Dravidian movement", Tamil Muslims remained, until being exposed to the Wahhābī doctrine during the Gulf oil boom of the 1970s, committed to a Tamil identity, adhering to a syncretic form of Islam in practice.[105]

Although Quṭb, rather than identifying with Tamil Muslims, or Mughul India, associated Tagore with the Sufism of the East, it is plainly evident that he failed to recognise that the Brahmo Samāj movement was aligned with the Unitarian association in the United States which bears the influence of the New England Transcendentalists, Ralph W. Emerson (1803-82) and Henri D. Thoreau (1817-62).[106] Had Quṭb been acquainted with Thoreau's thought-world, he would have, perhaps, learnt that, far from being a "primitive American savage", the American author found himself "suddenly neighbour to, rather than a hunter of birds".[107]

However, as we shall see in chapter 5, Quṭb becomes acutely aware of an imaginary construct which includes the Buddhist-Hindu traditions, on the one hand, and the Christian tradition of the West, on the other. Although, by the mid-1940s, Quṭb was certainly aware of an existing movement which drew "the material West" to the "spirituality of the East" in modern times, he appears to be inclined to consider that there are existing boundaries between the above three traditions, and that, furthermore, these traditions have an imaginary point of origin. In recognising, for instance, that Tolstoy's works "drew from the Christianity of the transparent spirit of the East,"[108] Quṭb seems unaware of the fact that, to a great extent, these works were inspired by a mythical fable which affected millions of others across the spiritual divides in the spiritual history of humanity. As Smith observes, the "unity of humankind's religious history"[109] is such that Tolstoy found his way to ascetic piety by finding in a particular fable from Christian hagiography "a real unanswerable truth".[110] The central theme of the fable is

> The renunciation of worldly power and wealth by a young prince, Josaphat, who, under the influence of the preaching of an otherworldly hermit, Barlaam, is baptised a Christian, abdicates his throne, and goes off into the wilderness in ascetic piety...Although the story, as presented, is explicitly Christian, the scene is set in India. Josaphat is portrayed as an Indian prince, converted by Barlaam, a Sinai desert monk...The Greek version...have been produced in the eleventh century on Mt Athos by a Georgian monk...It was the Georgians who had turned the story into a Christian tale. Their original, however, was Islamic...the story was not, however, original with the Muslims...they had got it in central Asia from the Manichees...the legend is indeed a Buddhist one... It was fundamentally the story of "the Buddha"...this word appears then in the Manichee versions as Bodisaf, in the Arabic version as Yudasaf, in the Georgian as Ioasaph, in the Greek as Ioasaph, and in the Latin as Josaphat.[111]

It is noteworthy that 'Abduh admired Tolstoy and wrote to him on the occasion of the latter's excommunication from the Russian Church.[112] Hourani observes that Tolstoy, along with Strauss, Renan and Spencer, helped 'Abduh in crystallising his thought on the "real Jesus" and his teachings, as opposed to the Christianity which was developed by St. Paul and the Catholic Church, and found to be, unlike Islam, "irreconcilable" with modern sciences and reason.[113] As we shall see below, Quṭb comes to identify, only some two years later, St. Paul as a "messenger"/founder of Christianity in the West, as he attempts to construct a history which obliterates "the Jew" from the history of both the "East" and the "West" in the year leading to the partition of Palestine in 1948.

3. Quṭb's Early Studies of the Qur'an and Reflections on Islam in Comparison with "Other" *Religions*

Almost immediately following writing a review of Ḥusayn Fawzī's work *Sindbād 'Aṣrī wa Sindbād Qadīm* in February 1944,[114] Quṭb appears to have been experiencing a critical situation of "work paralysis" after being briefly demoted to the rank of school inspector in the same year.[115] It was perhaps this situation of "work paralysis" which pushed him, once again, to study the Qur'an with the view of uncovering the "artistic imagery" (*al-taswīr al-fannī*) of the Qur'anic text,[116] especially as he appears to have been particularly threatened by the competition posed by the highly-educated Francophile Muḥammad Mandūr* in the field of literary criticism.[117]

Although, Boullata criticises *al-Taṣwīr al-Fannī* for suffering from some "unnecessary repetition, and avoidable overlapping", which he considers to be probably due to the fact that its chapters were written on separate occasions and over a period of several years,[118] I find the work to be particularly interesting in so far as it reveals a clear destructive tendency in Quṭb's writings which becomes more visible in the 1960s as he adopts the doctrine of *jāhiliyya*.

Having been made aware of the centrality of 'Abd al-Qāhir al-Jurjānī* (d. 1079) in the domain of literary criticism, and of comparisons which were drawn within Egypt's academia circles between the former and the English poet laureate Wordsworth (1850),[119] Quṭb develops an argument which sees him aggrandising, and affirming himself against al-Jurjānī, instead of developing "comradeship" with this man of the Islamic past. In much the same way that he comes to call for establishing a "new" school to appraise poetry, as discussed previously, Quṭb calls in *al-Taṣwīr al-Fannī fī al-Qur'ān* (1945), for applying a "new methodology" (*manhaj jadīd*) to study the Qur'an, to uncover "the general fundamentals" (*al-uṣūl al-'amma*) of the artistic beauty of the Qur'anic style. According to Quṭb, there is a need for devising a "unified method" to uncover "the artistic imagery" which, evaded all past philologists throughout Islam's entire history.[120]

It is worth mentioning here that two works on rhetoric by al-Jurjānī, who is renowned for "the brilliance" of his scholarship,[121] were edited under 'Abduh's auspices when he presided over The Society for the Revival of the Arabic Sciences which was founded in 1900.[122] As Gibb observes, al-Jurjānī belongs to the circle of Saif al-Dawla in the Golden Age of Arabic literature (750-1055) for supplementing the excessively formal analysis of his predecessors in literary criticism – al-Jāḥiẓ (d. 869), Ibn al-Mu'tazz (d.908), and Qudāma b. Ja'far (d. 922), and Abu Hilāl al-'Askarī (d. 1005) – by a system of logical and psychological analysis, "giving equal consideration to form and ideas" expressed in poetry. Additionally, attention was given to the argument on literary aesthetics by its bearing on "the doctrine of the incomparability of the Qur'an; the prevailing concentration of criticism upon form tended to emphasise unduly its supreme verbal qualities in terms of the current stylistic theories".[123]

One may surmise that the favourable comparison which was drawn by Egypt's literati between Wordsworth and al-Jurjānī might have contributed, at least partially, to providing Quṭb with a new "niche" for his equipment, as Erikson would put it. For not only did Quṭb offer himself as an improvement on the highly-acclaimed powerful figure al-Zamakhsharī* (d. 1143) of his childhood years,[124] who was renowned in Europe for his handbook of grammar, *al-Mufaṣṣal*, and the collection of moral apophthegms in polished rhymed prose called *The Golden Necklaces*,[125]but he also explicitly states in *al-Taṣwīr al-Fannī fī al-Qur'ān* that he can improve on al-Jurjānī's efforts to attain an appraisal of the Qur'anic style.

Quoting from Amīn's *Fajr Al-Islām,* yet again, in the chapter entitled "Kayfa Fuhima al-Qur'ān" (How was the Qur'an Understood), on the history of, and the hurdles involved in the "interpretation" (*tafsīr*) of the Qur'an, Quṭb makes the argument that the Qur'an should be read as a mere literary text; he puts forward the view that, starting from the second century of the Islamic calendar, the interpretation of the Qur'an was increasingly submerged in research which was "jurisprudential and dialectical" (*fiqhiyya wa jadaliyya*), "grammatical and morphological" (*naḥawiyya wa ṣirafiyya*), and "historical and legendary" (*tarikhiyya wa isṭūriyya*), instead of researching the "artistic beauty" and its harmony with the "beauty of the substance" (*al-jamal al-mawḍū'ī*) of the Qur'an, which he describes as reaching "perfection".[126]

Quṭb then goes on to discredit these two men of the Islamic "cumulative tradition" by claiming that al-Zamakhsharī reached a "degree of success" in attaining some aspects of the artistic beauty of the Qur'an only on some occasions. He then goes on to criticize al-Zamakhsharī for lacking both "clarity" and "crystallisation" in his thought.[127] When Quṭb discusses al-Jurjānī, he accepts that the latter attained some success, making sure, however, to detract from al-Jurjānī's success by adding that the latter's success was somewhat relative as it was only relating to the period in which he lived. Quṭb then argues that the eleventh-century philologist, al-Jurjānī, would have "almost reached something" in his book, *Dalā'il al-I'jāz,* but for his pursuit of researching "the meanings and words" (*al-ma'ānī wa al-ālfāẓ*) of the Qur'an, which caused him to drift away from what he "almost attained".[128] As he puts it, al-Jurjānī was "on the verge of reaching something critical...but for the method of '*al-kalām*' and logic which permeated the language of literature at the time".[129]

What is important to stress here is that Quṭb goes on to criticise all the efforts that were made in the history of Islam in the area of research into "rhetoric" (*al-balāgha*), by putting forward the view that these efforts stopped at "the *limit* of the ancient Arab mind of old". Not only does he stress the limitation of the Arab mind, but he also claims that this limitation went hand in hand with the "*primitive*" and "*inadequate*" level of awareness of the Arabs which made them look at texts in a "partial manner without attaining the general characteristics of the artistic work in its entirety...neither in [studying] literature nor in [studying] the Qur'an".[130]

This last criticism is particularly interesting on account of similar accusations having been made against Quṭb himself as discussed in chapter 3 above,[131]which suggests that Quṭb was probably projecting onto the Arab the accusations that were made against himself. In any case, apart from the fact that neither al-Jurjānī nor al-Zamakhsharī were of Arab extraction, these two men of Islam's past were hardly of "limited", "primitive", or "inadequate" intellectual dispositions. One can hardly dismiss altogether the efforts of these two thinkers in the history of Islamic thought, nor in all fairness claim, as Quṭb did, that they exhibited an inability to grasp the general characteristics of the Qur'anic text.

It is also important to emphasise here that these two Muslim thinkers made a large contribution in making the Islamic past meaningful to modern Egyptians, and thus helped towards preserving the crucial "average expectable continuity" with the Islamic past, with al-Jurjānī's *Dalā'il al-I'jāz*, for instance, being quoted by thinkers like 'Abduh, Riḍā, al-Shanqitī, and al-Marāghī in their respective commentaries on the Qur'an.[132] Quṭb must have also known (at least to a certain extent) about some of al-Jurjānī's thirty-one extant scholarly works and commentaries, which were mostly written in Arabic, including the latter's best-known work *Kitāb at-Ta'rīfāt* (Book of Definitions).[133]

I note here that, although Quṭb appears to be conversant with the twelfth-century Mu'tazilite al-Zamakhsharī's contribution to Islamic theology and spirituality,[134] he does not make reference in his commentary on Q109 (*al-Kafirūn*)[135] to al-Zamakhsharī, or any of the other exegeses, who contributed to the body of literature which expanded on the "excellences" (*faḍā'il*) of the holy book in their respective reflections on the 6-verse *sura* Q109,[136] which frequently figures in modern-day discussions of interreligious relations.[137] (Quṭb uses Q: 109 *a priori* in *Ẓilāl* to accuse *Ahl al-Kitāb* of *shirk*[138] while accusing all of humanity of falling into a state of "*jāhiliyya*" (ignorance).[139])

Significantly, Quṭb makes *no* reference in any of his writings, as well, to any of the early humanist grammarians such as the two eminent Baṣra scholars, Abu 'Ubayda (d. 825) and al-Aṣma'ī (d. 831), of what Gibb qualifies as the "Golden Age" (750-1055) of Arabic literature.[140] Gibb observes that, although Arabic philology arose out of the Qur'an, there is clear evidence that it was systematised principally in Baṣra on the basis of Aristotelian logic.[141]

Reflecting an early distaste for Aristotelian logic, Quṭb shows himself particularly impervious to the ethico-humanist tendencies in "the cumulative traditions" of Islamic philology which are associated by him to both Aristotle and the Alexandrian physicist-philosopher Galen (d. 199). It is noteworthy that Galen was first translated by Ḥunayn Ibn Isḥāq (d. 873), who was also the translator of Plato.[142] Goodman observes in *Islamic Humanism* that the great Christian translator and Galenist, Ibn Isḥāq, is credited with a genre of universal history of the world, which "will find enduring monuments in the works of Ya'qūbī (d. 897), and Mas'ūdī.[143]

Following his feud with the Aristotelian al-'Aqqād in 1946, Quṭb condemned specifically in *al-Naqd al-Adabī* (1947) the rhetorician Qudāma Ibn Ja'far (d. 922), who is chiefly known for his contribution to systematic criticism in the early days of Islam,[144] for being influenced by Aristotle's theory on "virtue" (*al-faḍīla*) and Galen's opinions on "ethics" (*al-akhlāq*). According to Quṭb, Ibn Ja'far's attempt to apply to poetry the "dry standards of the intellect" was doomed to failure precisely as he ended up pursuing ethico-philosophical research.[145]

Significantly, Quṭb avers in the chapter under the heading "Story-telling in the Qur'an" in *al-Taṣwīr al-Fannī fī al-Qur'ān*, his conviction that "one of the functions of story-telling" in the Qur'an was to provide proof of the authenticity of the revealed message that was brought by Muḥammad. In an argument revealing his belief in the authenticity of the two previous monotheistic religions, as practiced by Jews and Christians who were encountered by the early Muslims (probably in the early Medinan period), Quṭb adds that, although Muḥammad was not known to have mixed with "the Jewish and Christian learned men" (*aḥbār al-yahūd wa al-naṣāra*), the detailed accounts of Qur'anic stories - such as those of Abraham, Joseph, Moses and Jesus – were considered "proof" (*dalīl*) that Muḥammad was receiving Revelation.[146]

Furthermore, Quṭb affirms, once again, his belief in an existing affinity between Islam and Judaism, based primarily on the argument that both the Qur'an and the Torah are described as "*al-furqān*" in Q21:48.[147] Elsewhere, Quṭb argues that one of the functions of story-telling in the Qur'an is "to provide evidence" (*bayān*) of "God's Grace" (*ni'mat Allah*) on His "prophets and favourites" (*ānbiyā'uhu wa āṣfiyā'uhu*). Here, he gives the examples of Qur'anic stories which deal with Solomon, David, Job, Abraham, Mary, Jesus, Zechariah, Jonah, and Moses,[148] while making no reference to Ismā'īl (Ishmael).

In *Mashāhid al-Qiyāma fi al-Qur'ān* (1947), which is introduced by Quṭb in 1946 as the second instalment in a series of works that he intended to write on the Qur'an,[149] he continues to hold deprecating views of the Arabs. In the chapter "al-'Alām al-Akhar fī al-Ḍamīr al-Basharī" (The Afterlife in Human Conscience), where he reveals a clear influence of ideas which, W. C. Smith argues, are associated with Zarathustra, such as "notions of cosmic conflict dualism and Heaven and Hell",[150] Quṭb makes the claim that "in spite of the existence of Jews and Christians in the Arab Peninsula...the idea of resurrection was alien to the Arabs when Muḥammad brought about the Qur'an". According to Quṭb , it is the Qur'an's depiction of an afterlife, which originated in the conscience of Ancient Egypt, which brought the Arabs to the fold of human conscience as they developed faith in "an afterlife, heaven and hell, absolute justice, and great clemency." [151]

Given Quṭb's clear affinity with the Buddhist and Hindu cumulative spiritual traditions – especially the Dravidian – south-east Asian religio-cultural complex, it comes as no big surprise to see him fully incorporating both the Hindu and Buddhist traditions in the history of human conscience in the two editions of *Mashāhid al-Qiyāma* well into the early Islamist stage of his life.[152]

Against some qur'anic injunctions such as Q2:62,[153]which makes no reference to either the Buddhist or the Hindu traditions,[154] and further stipulates that belief in God and the Last Day are essential components of faith, Quṭb argues that, although both the Hindu "religions" – (note the use of the plural in relation to the Hindu religions, which becomes singular in *al-'Adāla*) – and the Buddhist "religion" which, he explains, is "the creed of some Indians, the majority of Japanese, many Chinese and the people of Ceylon (now Sri Lanka)", did not develop the idea of an afterlife, these religions offer instead "Nirvana" which, he explains, allows for "extinction in the Great Spirit (*al-fanā' fī al-ruḥ al-a'ẓam*)".[155] In revealing a noticeable attraction to the Buddhist and Hindu "*religions*" for allowing their respective initiates to reach "Nirvana", Quṭb is inadvertently repeating here one of the ideas which have gained currency in the nineteenth century by the Theosophical Society in the West before reaching Egypt, probably through its branches in Egypt, sometime in the early part of the twentieth century.[156]

It is probably the case that Quṭb was emulating the Theosophical movement enthusiasts in the West when he made the claim that he experienced a moment of "*shuhūd*" (not used here as an act of witnessing God in Sufi Muslim parlance which is normally a state attained only by prophets) on a couple of occasions, once on top of a mountain, and another time on a boat in the ocean (presumably invoking here his sea voyage to New York in 1948). These experiences, he finds, are akin to a moment of "Nirvana", or what he also describes to be a moment of "*ishrāq*" (enlightenment), such as the one experienced by the Buddha under the sacred tree".[157] Quoting, yet again, from Fawzī travelogue in *Mashāhid al-Qiyāma*, Quṭb makes reference to Buddha's final words to his disciple, Ananda,[158] without, however, identifying the last as "'The Keeper of the *Dharma* Store' (*Dharmabhandagarika*);"[159] *dharma* being used in Buddhist conception in reference to "the one absolute in an evanescent universe".[160]

Interestingly enough, Quṭb appears more amenable in *Mashāhid* to accept the erudition of Aḥmad Amīn than he did a year earlier in *Kutub wa Shakhṣiyyāt,*[161] following the latter's retirement in 1946.[162] In discussing the Hindu and Buddhist *religions*, for instance, Quṭb quotes (albeit rather eclectically, and with some conciseness), from a twenty-seven page section dedicated to a discussion of Indian ancient literature in the first of a three-volume work which was co-authored by Aḥmad Amīn and Zakī Najīb Maḥmūd (d. 1993), *Qiṣṣat al-Adab fī al-'Ālam* (The Story of World Literature, 1943)[163] with the view of introducing Egyptians to Western heritage.[164]

In reading *Mashāhid* contrapuntally, it becomes, however, only too apparent that Quṭb chooses to overlook the explanation provided by Amīn and Maḥmūd who make reference to the "*qiyam*" (virtues or values) of Nirvana which, to them, entail that "a human being becomes endowed with mercy, as his heart is purified and filled with love".[165] Unlike Amīn, Quṭb does not explicitly equate between Buddhist Nirvana with Sufi *fanā'* (as put in practice by Buddhists and Sufis) nor does he recognise that "a Sufi may be a Muslim, Christian, Jew, or Buddhist", as Amīn did in his four-volume work *Ẓuhr al-Islām* (1945-1955).[166]

Instead, Quṭb quotes only two paragraphs from the section dedicated to Indian ancient literature in the work where reference is made to the Hindu sacred texts - the Vedas, the Upanishads, the Brahma-Mimamsa (in the text referred to as Brāhmānā) - which, Amīn and Maḥmūd explain, allow for an array of orientations, including a multiplicity of gods and goddesses, monism, "*wiḥdat al-wujūd*" (unity of existence), and "*ḥilūl*" (incarnation).[167] As discussed above, Quṭb was particularly drawn to the Vedanta, perhaps because, as he notes, it was "the most modern". He, however, seems to have remained unaware that the Brahmo Samāj established a Vedanta college in 1825 for the teaching of the monotheistic doctrines of the Upanishads.[168]

Most probably, Quṭb was also attracted to the Vedanta for allowing "unity between God and man"[169] considering the strong element of pantheism which permeates his thought[170] even as he becomes aware of the heavy criticism which was levelled by al-'Aqqād in his work *al-falsafa al-Qur'āniyya* (The Qur'anic Philosophy,1947) in relation to some Sufi doctrines which he considers to be alien to Islam: the one which places an emphasis on "*ḥilūl*", and the other which places an emphasis on "*wiḥdat al-wujūd*". Al-'Aqqād identifies these doctrines with ascetics and philosophers who lived near India and in the frontier fringes of Persian territories.[171]

4. Rethinking the Christian and the Jewish Traditions in Quṭb's Discourse (1947-1948)

Considering Quṭb's avowed attraction to the Torah, it comes as a bit of an oddity that he makes no reference to the first five books of the Bible (Genesis, Exodus, Leviticus, Numbers, and Deuteronomy),[172] in the chapter "The Afterlife in Human Conscience" in *Mashāhid al-Qiyāma fī al-Qur'ān*.[173]

To put this seemingly purposeful omission of the Torah from the history of human conscience in *Mashāhid* in perspective, I would like to emphasise here that Quṭb has become acutely aware, probably as early as 1947, of the threat posed by Sanskrit studies undertaken by German-born Max Müller (d.1900), who is praised by al-'Aqqād as being the "imām of philologists" in his work *Allah* (1947).[174]In the aforementioned work, al-'Aqqād argues that Müller's translation of Sanskrit texts indicates the existence of some parallelism in the myths of the "Flood" in Genesis, on the one hand, and similar mythologies in ancient Greece, Mexico, Babylonia, and Asia minor, on the other.[175]

Although, as we shall see in chapter 5, the creation of the essentialist "Jew", as Quṭb's primary "other", is of a fairly late occurrence in his discourse of the 1960s,[176] one can discern, beginning in *Mashāhid*, that Quṭb begins to make a concerted effort to demote Judaism, in favour of Christianity. In contrast to the view expressed by Quṭb in 1939, which found in favour of the Torah's weltanschauung (which he found was close to that of the Qur'an), as opposed to that of the Gospel in his refutation of Ṭaha Ḥusayn's *Mustaqbal al-Thaqāfa fī Miṣr*, Quṭb becomes almost totally dismissive of the Old Testament from the history of human conscience in *Mashāhid*.

Interestingly, on the one rare occasion when Quṭb accepts that modern European poets have been influenced, albeit only in diction, by "their sacred Book" in *Kutub wa Shakhṣiyyāt*, he draws parallelism between the pessimism that *he detects* in an unidentified translated poem by Hardy and Ecclesiastes which he assumes is written by al-Jāmi'a Ibn Dawūd.[177] Most importantly, against the explicit background information given by al-Aqqād on the Indian influences permeating the English poetess Laurence Hope's poetry,[178] Quṭb seems to reject Hope as representative of the idealised spiritual India of the East construct that he created. Instead, he finds parallelism between the depiction of Shulammite in *The Song of Songs* (4: 1-5), and the following lines from a translation by al-'Aqqād of Laurence Hope's poem "Nay, not To-night" from *The Book of Indian Love* (1905)[179]

When thou desirest Love's supreme surrender,
Come while the morning revels in the light,
Bulbuls around us, passionately tender,
Singing among the roses red and white.

In choosing a poem by Hardy[180] (who in fact abandoned Christianity[181]) or Hope's highly controversial poetry,[182] as exemplary texts reflecting Old Testament influences, Quṭb is clearly showing, not only how little he actually knew of modern European literature, but also a resolute unwillingness to understand European, let alone American, Christians, or Jews, on their own terms. It is especially noteworthy that Quṭb purposefully omits any mention of metaphysical poets such as John Donne (1573-1631),[183]and John Milton (1608-74),[184] who were reviewed by Egypt's senior literati in the 1940s.[185]

Evidently, there is no acceptance on Quṭb's part of the Bible as "a timeless book...a living, life-giving source of the religious life of the continuing community,"[186] even as he probably knew of the renewed interest in the Bible in the West, especially in the United States (which was coincidental with his visit), following the Second World War.[187]

In the two editions of *Mashāhid*, Quṭb indicates that he researched the Old Testament with the view of unravelling the idea of an afterlife in the "creeds" of the "sons of Israel" (that is both Jews and Christians), only to discover that no reference whatsoever was made to the idea of an afterlife.[188] He, however, accepts that a "struggle" ensued in the "Israeli conscience" between (this) "naive creed" and the reality of life which sometimes allows for evil to go unpunished, while goodness may meet an opposite fate, adding that this struggle becomes only too apparent in the Book of Job.[189]

Here, Quṭb quotes selectively, and rather with some brevity (two paragraphs out of a total of twenty),[190] from the chapter "al-'Adāla al-Ilahiyya" (Divine Justice) in a work by a senior member of the literati, 'Ali Adham (1897-1981), *Naẓarāt fi al-Ḥayāt wa al-Mujtama'* (Views on Life and Society, 1945),[191] highlighting Job 13:15:

> Though he slay me, yet will I trust in him: but I will maintain mine own ways before him [192]

It is important to stress here that, not only does Quṭb reduce the entire 42-chapter and 1070-verse Book of Job to one verse but, unlike Adham, he avoids recognising that the Book of Job, which is based on an old folklore, may have been written during the exile of the Jews in Babylon in the 6th century,[193] and gives expression, not only to Job's, and the Israelite's longing for justice,[194] but touches *all* of humankind.[195]

Having become increasingly challenged, sometime in the mid-1940s, by the conflict in Palestine,[196] and the Zionist claim over the land of Palestine which, Woolfson observes, was based on a promise made by God to Abraham granting the land of Canaan to "Abraham's seeds" (Genesis 17:8),[197] Quṭb begins to depict the conflict in Palestine as being "the pivot in the struggle between the resurgent East and the barbaric West, between God's law for mankind and the law of the jungle."[198] Henceforth, one begins to discern in Quṭb's discourse, beginning in *Mashāhid,* a deliberate effort on his part to minimise the role of the Jews in biblical historiography,[199] though he did not join in the ranks of the Egyptian-Arab nationalist movement of the late 1930s.[200]

In an argument revealing that Quṭb clearly subscribed to the idea of an evolution in the thought-world of the "sons of Israel" pre-dating Islam, which is almost a verbatim reproduction of one made by al-'Aqqād in his work *Allah,*[201] Quṭb puts forward the view, in the two editions that I analysed of *Mashāhid,* that the idea of an afterlife must have "developed" in the long history of the "Sons of Israel" following the writing of the Old Testament. In this context, Quṭb quotes Matthew 22:23 "The same day came to him [Christ] the Sadducees, which say that there is no resurrection...". He adds further that one cannot ascertain with any precision the exact period when the idea of an afterlife made its way to the "Sons of Israel", and that the first indication of the existence of such a belief is found in the Book of Isaiah.[202]

Interestingly, Quṭb appears to be knowingly making a concerted effort in *Mashāhid* to minimise the importance of the Book of Isaiah in Hebrew historiography.[203] For one thing, Quṭb opts to keep from the text any quotes from the Book of Isaiah,[204] perhaps being especially threatened by Isaiah's prophecy that "the Lord of hosts shall reign in mount Zion and in Jerusalem" (Isaiah 24:23). Additionally, Quṭb makes the erroneous assumption, like al-'Aqqād, that "Isaiah of Jerusalem" (ca. 740 BCE205) lived around the third century BCE,[206] and stresses that there is a clearer indication in chapter 12 of the Book of Daniel of the idea of an afterlife than that which is found in the Book of Isaiah.[207] (Wilfred C. Smith notes that the concept "religion" is sometimes read into Daniel 6:6 reflecting "the impingement on Jewish religious life at this time of Iranian religious influences...in the direction of a closed and boundaried community."[208])

In contrast to Quṭb's noticeable lack of interest in the Old Testament in *Mashāhid*, it is apparent that he has taken much interest in the New Testament's account of the early history of Christianity which either lacks, or contradicts, at times, that which is found in the Qur'an. In what seems to be an act of open defiance to al-'Aqqād, who was particularly critical of Paul's epistles for introducing into Christianity "the philosophy of incarnation" (*falsafat al-ḥilūl*),[209] Quṭb accepts Paul, who is not mentioned in the Qur'an, as "the messenger [of God]" (*al-rasūl**).[210]

In accepting Paul as "the messenger [of God]", Quṭb does not only confirm a clear attraction to the pantheistic doctrine of *ḥilūl*, which was vehemently attacked by al-'Aqqād, but he now confirms, yet again, a revulsion he appears to reserve for the ancient Greeks. In reliance on the Acts of the Apostles, Quṭb gives an account of the arrest of Paul in Jerusalem, quoting Acts 23:6 in his description of Paul pleading his case before the governor of Caesarea, and confirming that he is a Pharisee who believes in the resurrection of the dead.[211]

In accordance with Acts 21:28, Quṭb gives an account of Paul's arrest on charges of sedition and corruption at the instigation of the Jews.[212] Interestingly, Quṭb purposefully omits from the text here that Acts 21:28, which he does not reference, states that "the Hellenized Jew",[213] Paul, was accused by some Jewish pilgrims of polluting the Temple in Jerusalem by bringing Greeks into it, and of teaching against the people, and the Law, which was kept by "(Jewish) Christians".[214] As Wilfred C. Smith notes in *The Meaning and End of Religion*, in Acts 26:5, St. Paul is reported as saying "I lived as a Pharisee according to the strictest school of our *thrēskeia*", clearly using "our" as referring back to an earlier time "when he was still within the Jewish religion".[215] Smith observes further that there is no evidence in the New Testament that "the early Christians were conscious of being involved in a new religion".[216]

As Quṭb braces himself for his two-year sojourn in the US, a year later, he depicts Christianity as crossing the sea to Europe with all of its "forbearance, all of its purity, and all of its renunciation of the material world".[217] Obviously, Quṭb alludes here to Paul's last sea journey on his way to Rome in 59-62, seemingly being, most probably, unaware of the role played by Peter, according to Roman Catholic tradition, in founding the papal seat in Rome.[218] (Unlike the tenth-century humanist polymath al-Mas'ūdī (d.956), Quṭb fails to identify in *Ẓilāl* the three unnamed messengers in Q36: 13-14,*219* as Peter, Thomas and Paul.[220])

Interestingly, Quṭb disregards, as well, the fact that Paul's first church in Europe was founded in about 49 CE in Philippi, which fell in the then Roman province of Macedonia (Acts 16: 9-11 & 13-15221). Nor does Quṭb make any mention of Paul's letter (Romans 1:16-17), which was written almost certainly from the Greek city, Corinth, sometime between 55 and 57CE, to explain his aim "to expound the gospel... as an obligation to Jews first, but also to Greek gentiles".[222]

According to Quṭb's account, Christianity crossed the sea, (from the East), to Europe where it

> found the Romans, heirs to the materialistic and pagan Greek civilisation, as it found other peoples across Europe who have just come out of barbarism... *religion* remained in isolation in hearts and conscience there, and in the sacred temple and the confessional seat! And thus came about a separation between religion and worldly affairs in the life of Europeans. In point of fact, Europe was never at any time Christian.[223]

Evidently, Quṭb's simplistic historiography of the foundation of the Christian tradition in Europe, fails not only to recognise that "Christianity probably took root in Rome by the conversion of Jews and God-fearers, [Hellenised or not], associated with the synagogues",[224] but it also fails to demonstrate, as al-Mas'ūdī did some ten centuries earlier, any familiarity with the Christian tradition as "a 'living rather than simply an historical phenomenon".[225]

Having now finally fallen out of al-'Aqqād's orbit, following the publication of *Mashāhid*,[226] Quṭb seems to have felt at liberty to remove what little content he derived from the Old Testament in the above work when he wrote *al-'Adāla* just a year later. In an argument which is made in all editions of *al-'Adāla*, Quṭb seems to render Judaism obsolete by advancing the view that Christianity in Rome "originated in the shadow of the Roman Empire, at a time when the Jewish *religion* had become ossified and its rituals had turned rigid, lifeless, and empty in appearances".[227]

Evidently, Quṭb's projection of a quality of ossification unto Judaism, which was actually an accusation made against modern-day Islam,[228]reveals that he has probably become severely challenged by the successful Zionist campaign towards partitioning Palestine, which was certainly made more palpable by what Nettler describes as "Islam's long slide into unprecedented eclipse" in the modern age.[229] In the same line of argument, Quṭb departs also starkly from the views he held in 1939 when he found in favour of the legalistic aspect of the Torah and the Qur'an, which he juxtaposed to the Gospel, quoting at length from Matthew (5: 21-41).[230]

In keeping with the same level of openness to the New Testament, Quṭb uses the same verses from The Sermon on the Mount from the Gospel of Matthew in the first five editions of *al-'Adāla* (1949-1958),[231] to lavish praise on the figure of Christ for breaking with the harsh penal code imposed by Moses, and describes Christ as a preacher who called for "spiritual purity (*ṣafā' ruḥī*), compassion (*raḥma*), leniency (*layn*), forbearance (*tasāmuḥ*), chastity (*'ifa*) and asceticism (*zuhd*)".[232]

In reliance on the same verses from Matthew 5:38-41 which he used in 1939 to criticise the inefficacy of the Christian tradition in regulating life in Christian Europe, Quṭb finds in favour of Christ's leniency. As he puts it,

> He [Christ] was not at ease with restrictions of customs imposed by priests, Levites and scribes, because these addressed outward actions, while he was sent

> to deal with inward spiritual matters which touch the soul. Thus, he allowed his disciples to break the Sabbath of the sons of Israel, and made it lawful for them to eat anything that enters the mouth provided it does not defile, and break the fast on Jewish fast days, and did not stone the adulteress who confessed to her sin and was brought to him, because those who were supposed to stone her – in accordance to the *shari'a* of Moses - were not themselves free of sin. [Quoting and referencing Matthew 5:38-41, Quṭb adds here] He (Christ) said: You have heard that it has been said, an eye for an eye and a tooth for a tooth, but I say to you do not resist evil, but whoever strikes you on the right cheek, turn to him the other also, and if someone wants to sue you and take your coat, let him take your cloak also. And whoever compels you to go one mile, go with him two.[233]

Here, as elsewhere, Quṭb clashes with the views of al-'Aqqād who, not only argued that "the Messiah offered a complete constitution for the pious human" in his "Sermon on the Mount",[234] but also recognised the "ingenuity" ingrained in the philosophy of government provided in St. Augustine's *De Civitate Dei Contra Paganos* (The City of God, 1475),[235] Thomas Aquinas' unfinished work on Aristotle's *Politics*,[236] and John of Salisbury's *Policraticus* (1159).[237]

Similarly, Quṭb fails to appreciate in any of his writings that it was only after the recovery of the ancient Greek Christian tradition, which had been all but completely abandoned in the thirteenth century, by humanists, such as Ambrogio Traversari (d. 1439), that humanist biblical scholarship got underway in the West.[238]

For all of Quṭb's deprecation of an imaginary "ossified" Judaism, there is evidence in *al-'Adāla* that there is much confusion in his thought as he insists on corporal punishment being a means to achieving purification in all editions of the work.[239] All at once, Quṭb praises the Prophet for showing "the mercy of Islam" in dealing with a confessed adulteress while admonishing him by relaying how he was accused of not taking *his religion* seriously in exacting the un-Qur'anic penalty of stoning on her in the first five editions of the work.[240]

Although Quṭb seems to have become acutely aware of the danger posed by Zionism,[241] it is important to stress here that he appears to have been left positively impressed by the success which was achieved by the extremist Zionist militias, the Irgun Zvi and LEHL.[242] Some two years earlier, Quṭb writes that "Britain received a bloody nose from these violent groups", adding that there is a lesson to be learnt from the Zionists: "the only language the modern world understands is the one used by the Jews [in Palestine], namely, force."[243]

Significantly, Quṭb is said to have been in accord with Britain's 1939 White Paper which guaranteed a majority Arab population in Palestine[244] which is to say that he did not necessarily negate the right of the Arab Jews to belong to a Palestinian "*patrie*", alongside Arab Muslims and Christians.[245] In fact, Quṭb reveals in his commentary on *sura al-Anbiyā'* (Q21: 71-3) in *Ẓilāl* which, I conjecture, was probably written in the late 1950s, or the early 1960s,[246] that he had come to accept that the Jews of the Levant, since the time of Abraham, had been privileged with what Erikson refers to as a "God-given" identity.[247] The gist of Quṭb's argument in *Ẓilāl* is that God granted Abraham, following immigrating from Iraq, with his nephew Lot,[248] a "homeland" (*waṭan*) in the "sacred land" in the Levant; one in which his offspring, in the line of Isaac and Jacob, were to become a great "*umma*" (people/community) including "*imāms* who guided people in accordance to God's commands."[249]

Having made the claim that Islamic history demonstrates that it is the epitome of "human equality, liberation of the soul, and absolute justice" in the chapter "From the Historical Reality in Islam" in *al-'Adāla*[250] and that, unlike previous *religions*, it is one which is free of any form of "coercion" (*qahr*),[251] it is particularly interesting that Quṭb finds no qualms in claiming that *all* non-Muslims, (in accordance to the oppressive social norms of the *dhimma* pact), should pay *jizya* and submit to Muslims in a relationship of "submissive subjection" (*khuḍū'*).[252]

In a clear borrowing from the Beveridge Report (1942), which provided the foundation of the modern Welfare State in England in 1945,[253] Quṭb alleges that the second caliph 'Umar I (634-44) introduced the principle of "social insurance" (*al-tā'mīn al-ijtimā'ī*) for all of those incapacitated and in need.[254] Quṭb gives the example here of 'Umar I who extended financial help to a needy Jew and to some Christians that he encountered on his way to Damascus who suffered from leprosy.[255] He, however, makes no reference in any of his writings to the oppressive decree which was enforced against the Jews in Yemen in 1905 in accordance to what is known as the "Pact of 'Umar".[256]

Quṭb rather goes on the offensive against the West for keeping its colonies from sharing in the benefits of Western civilisation in areas of education and economic development; in addition to stripping those colonised of all human dignity, and being subject to "thievery, plundering and pillage." [257] "As for the religious freedom of which some boast at this time", Quṭb writes, "it was preceded by the horrors of the inquisition in Spain and the Crusades in the East."[258] According to Quṭb, the English commander Allenby (d. 1936), who captured Jerusalem in 1917, speaks for "every European soul" when he said, "only now have the crusades ended."[259] In the third edition of *al-'Adāla* (1951),[260] Quṭb makes reference as well to the French general Catroux who declared in Damascus during its revolt in 1940, "we are the descendants of the Crusaders", adding that a colleague of his repeated the same thing in Algeria in 1945.[261]

Conveniently, Quṭb makes no reference in any of his writings to the Crémieux decree which granted some 30,000 Jews living in the three northern departments of Algeria French citizenship in 1870.[262] Algerian Jews are said to have been the *only* Jews who enjoyed the benefits of real "equality" in Arab/Muslim lands. Adolphe Crémieux is said to have been shocked by the backward state of Jewish education in

Egypt during his visit there with Sir Moses Montefiore in 1840 on behalf of the Jews accused in the Damascus Blood Libel.[263]

5. Conclusion

In the discussion above, we have seen Quṭb clearly shifting his attention from the cultural component of Western civilisation, which he identified in 1939 with the Platonic-Francophile, Ṭaha Ḥusayn, to amplifying, to an excess, an Eastern "spirit" and Western "matter" duality only some five years later.

In the process of developing such a dichotomous world-view to the detriment of the materialist Western "other", it is apparent that the imaginary idealised construct of the "East", which included Japan and China in the far East in 1939, has been expanded to allow for India to represent the quintessential spiritual "East" to the detriment of both Japan and China. Clearly, as Quṭb seems to have been particularly drawn to the Hindu and the Buddhist traditions, he did not assert himself as a Muslim in deprecating Christian Europe. In fact, as discussed above, Quṭb had plainly considered Islam to be more of an Arab religion which was authenticated by the Jewish and Christian learnt men who were encountered by Muḥammad presumably in the early Medinese period.

By 1947, it is also clearly the case that Quṭb departs from his deprecating views in 1939 of the Christian tradition, as it developed in Europe, as he was particularly drawn to the Torah, and ends up attaching a quality of spirituality to Pauline Christianity, albeit confined within the walls of the Church. Concurrently, he attempted to minimise the role of the Jewish tradition in the history of salvation as he seems to have become particularly threatened by the ascendency of the Jews in Palestine. In a clear departure from the critical and inimical stance that he adopted in 1939 specifically in relation to Matthew, it is clearly the case that Quṭb developed an apparent attraction to Matthew, even accepting the latter's account in 16: 27-8 in relation to the prediction of the return of "the Son of man (Jesus) in the glory of his Father" as proof that Jesus was resurrected three days following crucifixion[264] even as it contradicts "the traditional Muslim view that Jesus was somehow miraculously saved from death on the Cross"[265] in accordance to the Qur'an.

For all of his clear leaning to the spirituality of the East, it is evidently the case that Quṭb was unaware, as Wilfred C. Smith argues in *The Meaning and End of Religion*, that in the "Orient" men have on the whole not used the concept "religion" for their own faith, and not even in the Christian West until "the rise of unbelief".[266] As discussed above, Quṭb uses the term "religion" not only in relation to the Jewish and Christian traditions, but equally in relation to the Hindu and Buddhist traditions. It is obviously the case, as discussed in chapter 3, that Quṭb was captivated by Nietzsche's idea of "the need for a 'new reformer' (the superman)" following "the death of God", even as he continues to avow his admiration for the Sufi Tagore of the "East", while repudiating Rūmī. He, however, failed to understand the humanist component of Nietzsche's thought, nor of other Atheist humanists such as Comte, Feuerbach and Marx[267] even as he seems to accept the last in the 1950s as one of three prophets (the two others being Stalin and Lenin) of the modern world, as we shall see in the next chapter.

5

The Westerner as the "Other" in Quṭb's 1960s Writings, with Special Emphasis on the Doctrine of *Jāhiliyya*

One of, if not the most serious challenge posed by political Islamism in modern times is the formulation of the dehumanising concept of *jāhiliyya,* in its most extreme form, firstly by Abu al-'Ala' al- Mawdūdī in India starting 1939, and subsequently by Quṭb in Egypt in the 1960s.[1] Shepard observes, however, that, although the idea of modern *jāhiliyya* was already in circulation by the time Quṭb fully adopted it in his writings of the 1960s, it was Quṭb who took the idea much further than other thinkers in his later writings starting in 1964.[2]

To fully appreciate the serious implications that are derived from the incorporation of the concept of *jāhiliyya* into the world-view of radical Islamists, I would like to stress the point here that this concept is certainly to be seen within the context of some very destructive/dehumanising twentieth-century modern ideologies which have ended in massacre and genocide. As Karen Armstrong observes, the modern age saw the formulation of some very destructive mythologies which have been "narrowly racial, ethnic, denominational and egotistic, an attempt to exalt the self by demonising the other."[3]

To be certain, Quṭb's dehumanising otherness formulations, especially targeting the "Jew", in the radical Islamist stage of his life, places his thought within the gamut of totalitarian ideologies which were expounded in the West by both Hitler and Marx.[4] Beyond the clear totalitarian overtones in Quṭb's discourse, it is clear that his "ferocious anti-Semitism", as Buruma and Margalit put it,[5] emerges as he develops what Erikson refers to as "an age old awareness of man's division into pseudo-species".[6] In the chapter "Race and the Wider Identity", Erikson explains that an awareness of one's own "pseudo-species" becomes particularly problematic when man bypasses a certain degree of "identity-consciousness", and becomes aware of man's division into "pseudo-species", as he did before in tribal life. The example of national-socialist Germany is given here as "the most flagrant manifestation of the murderous mass 'pseudologia' (a form of lying) which can befall a modern nation" in realising its own "pseudo-species".[7]

An important distinction is made by Erikson between the "murderous mass pseudologia" which besieged national-socialist Germany, and forms of "artistic creation" which were expressed by revolutionary writers and writers from national and ethnic minority groups (like Irish expatriates or Negro and Jewish writers) who have become "the artistic spokesmen and prophets of identity confusion" in the modern age. Beyond complaint and exposure, these writers made

> the moral decision that a certain painful identity consciousness may have to be tolerated in order to provide the conscience of man with a critique of conditions, with the insight and the conceptions necessary to heal himself of what most deeply divides and threatens him, namely, his division into what we have called *pseudo-species*...namely, man's deep-seated conviction that some providence has made his tribe or race or caste, and, yes, even his religion 'naturally' superior to others...He becomes indoctrinated, then, with the conviction that his 'species' alone was planned by an all-wise deity, created in a special cosmic event, and appointed by history to guard the only genuine version of humanity under the leadership of elect elites and leaders...illusions and prejudices no longer deserving of the name mythology [are then developed] which make *hominem hominis lupum* far exceeding anything typical for wolves among wolves.[8]

In this chapter, I would like to emphasise the point that the doctrine of *jāhiliyya*, as formulated by Quṭb, brings to the fore how far removed this Islamist ideologue is from the rich Islamic humanist "cumulative traditions".[9] As Reichmuth points out, though medieval Islamic humanism was "nourished by a synthesis of Hellenist philosophy and Arab literary culture",[10] there is a consensus in Western scholarly circles that it was the strong influence of the Arabic literary culture of the Middle Ages which exerted a strong influence upon the development of European humanism.[11]

It is noteworthy that the concept of *jāhiliyya*, as developed by Quṭb (as an antonym of humanism), is entirely unknown to great humanists, such as the historian/philosopher Miskawayh (d. 1030),[12] and the Sufi Ibn 'Arabī (d. 1240);[13] and to Rifā'a al-Ṭahṭāwī, Aḥmad Luṭfī al-Sayyid, and Ṭaha Ḥusayn in the modern age.[14] In *The Encyclopedia of Islam*, the word *jāhiliyya* is defined as being used in almost all of its occurrences, as the opposite of the word Islam, in reference to "the state of affairs in Arabia before the mission of the Prophet, to paganism (sometimes even that of non-Arab lands), the pre-Islamic period and the men of that time".[15]

In modern times, 'Abduh made use of the word *jāhiliyya* in 1901 in relation to an undefined pre-Islamic epoch, as he found cause to write of the "*jāhiliyya*" of contemporary Muslims in Egypt which, he finds, "is more 'inveterate in ignorance' (*aʿraq fī al-jahl*) than that of *al-jāhiliyya al-ūla*" in his expanded exegesis on *al-Fātiḥa*.[16] In this context, he observes that children in Egypt, (as in Musha), know nothing about "the exalted place of the Qur'an" except in two areas known more to the "commoners" (*al-ʿamma*) than to the "select elite" (*al-khāṣṣa*): in the treatment of illnesses, and in warding-off Satan and *jinn* by the use of amulets and talismans in which are inscribed spells and foreign incantational inscriptions which owe their origin in pagan nations.[17]

Unlike the "big-bang outlook", which was adopted by Quṭb, especially as he first makes use of the doctrine of *jāhiliyya* in 1950,[18] Krämer observes that the Renaissance of Islam was perceived by early Muslims as "a conscious continuation of the cultural legacy of the Hellenistic and Greco-Roman epoch". In other words, Islamic culture was "linked from its inception with the cultural sphere of classical antiquity", and "directly affiliated with Hellenism and Roman civilisation". Early Arabs and Muslims, for instance, usually referred to the sciences of the Greeks, with whom they felt "affiliated", as "*ʿulūm al-awāʾil*" or (*ʿulūm*) "*al-qudamā*" (the sciences of the ancients).[19] Paintings of Socrates, Plato, and Aristotle dressed in Arab garb attest to the fact that early Arabs and Muslims did not regard (Greek) science and philosophy as "alien".[20]

Against the view espoused by Goldziher,[21] and expanded by Izutsu,[22] that the word *jāhiliyya* was used as an antonym of "*ḥilm*"* to denote "barbarism", Wilfred C. Smith points out that it is rather words for "knowing" which are frequent and emphatic in the Qur'an.[23] These words place an emphasis on the close correlation between knowledge given by God and faith which stands in opposition to the idea of "*ẓann* (doubt) *al-jāhiliyya*" as in Q3:154.[24] (It is indeed in this last sense that ʿAbduh explains the term *jāhiliyya* in his exegesis on Q3:154 which he considers to have been occasioned by the defeat of the Muslims in *Uḥud*. He explains that "*ẓann al-jāhiliyya*" makes reference to those believers, who are found in every *umma*, who demonstrate a weakness in their faith (in God).[25]

Rosenthal argues that the word *jāhiliyya* was used in the early days of Islam to denote "ignorance" of, or opposition to Muḥammad's message as opposed to both "knowledge and religion".[26] In both classical Arabic dictionaries and al-Bukhārī *ḥadīth* collection, the use of the word *jāhiliyya* was made in reference to the pre-Islamic epoch in Arabia to denote "ignorance" as an opposite of *ʿilm*.[27] Similarly, in Lane's lexicon, the word *jāhiliyya* came to be used in reference to pagan Arabs who are described as being of "*jahilī*" dispositions; the word *ʿjahl* being put in use in reference to one who acted in "an ignorant or a silly or foolish manner towards another".[28]

In the discussion below, I will offer firstly a background section in an attempt to contextualise Quṭb's *jāhiliyya* discourse within twentieth century Egypt's milieu, including Quṭb's first formulation of the doctrine of *jāhiliyya* in 1950. In the second section of this chapter, I will cover the period of the 1950s culminating in the development of the idea of *jāhiliyya* in Quṭb's thought in the early 1960s as denoting "ignorance" of the (un-Qur'anic) "characteristics of the Islamic *concept*" in *Khaṣāʾiṣ*.

Lastly, I will pay special attention to the culmination of Quṭb's thought on the "the Jew" in section three of this chapter. Throughout, I will stress as I go along continuities and discontinuities in Quṭb's thought as he constructs "the Jew" as his main "other" beginning in *Ma'ālim* in his later 1960s works.

1.1 Historical Background & Quṭb's First Use of the Doctrine of Jāhiliyya to Condemn the "Material Spirit" of Modern-day Jāhiliyya

Having returned to Egypt on August 20th, 1950,[29] without acquiring a mastery of the English language, or completing his mission to study pedagogic methods in the United States, much criticism was levelled against a high ranking official in Egypt's Ministry of Education, Ibrāhīm al-Qabbānī, and the historian Shafīq Ghurbāl, for supporting Quṭb's candidacy for the generous bursary awarded to him[30] as part of Truman's post-war aid "Point Four Program".[31]

Undeterred by the criticism that was levelled against him, Quṭb wrote in *al-Risāla* on July 28th, 1952, just five days following the military coup d'état in Egypt, that he attempted, to no avail, to found a *new* department to assess methods of education and schools' curricula following his return from the United States.[32] At that time, Quṭb is said to have confided to his Azharite friend and colleague at the Ministry of education, 'Abbās Khiḍr,[33]that he harboured an ambition to fill the portfolio of Minister of Education in the first ministry which was formed by the new military regime in Egypt in 1952.[34] Quṭb's ambition to become a minister of education was, however, dashed by Nasser's refusal to offer him the ministerial post.[35] According to one version of events, Quṭb is said to have resigned from the Liberation Rally, which was created on 23 January, 1953, as a "'people's movement' to replace the parties",[36] because Nasser withdrew Quṭb's appointment as minister of education in the first cabinet which was formed by the Free Officers and headed by Muḥammad Naguib. Quṭb seemed to have expected this ministerial portfolio, following his resignation from the Ministry of Education on October 18, 1952, as "a reward for supporting the Revolution and promoting it". [37] Obviously, Quṭb had experienced, yet again, a situation of "extreme work paralysis" which must have contributed to his decision to join the Muslim Brothers in February 1953.[38]

1.2 An Early Encounter with the Lucknow Nadwat al-'Ulamā Scholar Abu al-Ḥasan al-Nadwi and Quṭb's First Use of the Term Jāhiliyya*

Shunned by his peers, it was probably becoming increasingly apparent to Quṭb that his work environment is failing to offer him a "niche [for his] true gifts."[39] Not before long, a meeting with the Indian scholar al-Nadwi (d.1999) in the course of performing the pilgrimage to Mecca in November 1950,[40] must have helped towards alleviating, at least in part, what Erikson refers to as "an extreme work paralysis", which inevitably leads to identity confusion, and destructive tendencies.

During that meeting with the Indian scholar which was, most probably, organised by members of Egypt's Brotherhood[41] in support of King Saud's bid "to seize Islam,"[42] Quṭb offered al-Nadwi, who was fluent in Arabic, a copy of *al-'Adāla* which is said to have left the latter favourably impressed by "the clarity and decisiveness of the work."[43] Subsequently, al-Nadwi invited Quṭb to write an introduction for the first publication of his work *Madha Khasira al-'Alam bi Inḥiṭāṭ al-Muslimīn?*" (*What did the World Lose with the Decline of the Muslims?*) which was published in Cairo in 1950 by *Lajnat al-Ta'līf wa al-Nashr*.[44]

According to Choueiri, the Indian author published this book in Arabic in Egypt firstly in 1950, before it was translated four years later into Urdu.[45] Obviously, al-Nadwi eyed Egyptians primarily in writing the work which, Choueiri observes, became immediately a best-seller across the Arabic-speaking region with writers, especially in Egypt, giving it a very warm reception though the main theme of the work is a depiction of "Christian Europe" as a "materialistic *jāhiliyya*".[46]

Evidently, the decision of the chair of *Lajnat al-Ta'līf wa al-Nashr*, Aḥmad Amīn, to publish al-Nadwi's work, which depicts "Christian Europe" as being a "materialistic *jāhiliyya*," marks a turning point, to the negative, in Egypt's modern history in the context of attempts which were made by senior members of Egypt's literati, and Amīn himself, towards understanding the Western "other" in the early part of the twentieth century.[47] In a short introduction to al-Nadwi's work, Amīn writes that he finds it to be particularly praiseworthy for its attempt to wrestle with some Muslims' "inferiority complex" *vis-à-vis* a much revered Western civilisation which, he finds, to be unworthy of such aggrandisement.[48] (To put this turn of event in perspective, W. C. Smith notes the publication in *al-Manār* in Cairo, in 1930, of a series of articles by al-Amīr Shakīb Arslān which accepted that while the Muslims become "backward", "others" progressed.[49])

Although al-Nadwi's endorsement of Quṭb, as an "*Islāmī* researcher",[50] must have been a significant boost to the latter's ego, he seems to have been left initially unimpressed by the Lucknow Nadwat al-'Ulama scholar.[51] It is noteworthy that it is not till perhaps the late 1950s that Quṭb quotes, at some length (8 paragraphs), in his seven-page commentary on the eight-verse Medinan *sura* 98, al-Bayina,[52] for instance, from the first chapter of al-Nadwi's work, "al-Aṣr al-Jahilī," *without*, however, making use of the word *jāhiliyya*. Quṭb, in fact, makes the argument in his commentary on *sura al-Bayina* that the divisions amongst *ahl al-Kitāb* did not emanate from "ignorance" (*jahala*), accusing instead some members of *ahl al-Kitāb*, and polytheists, to have succumbed to "deviation" (*ḍalāl*) at the advent of Islam, as he discusses the "symptoms of unbelief" which prevailed in the world before Muḥammad's mission.[53]

Reflecting an early awareness of his own "pseudo-species", Quṭb exalts himself at the expense of abasing *all* "others" by putting forward the view that Islam is a "creed of haughtiness" (*ʿaqīdat istiʿla*ʾ), which instils in the Muslims the feeling of "responsibility" for (obviously a lowly) humanity. This responsibility, he argues, requires Muslims to assume the role of "custodianship" (*wiṣāya*) entrusted to them,[54] (clearly by divine decree[55]). In an unambiguous allusion to Jesus' parable of the "lost sheep" (Matthew 15:24), Quṭb makes the claim that Muslims have "the responsibility of leadership" to guide the "lost [human] flock" (*al-qiṭʿān al-ḍāla*) to "the worthy religion [Islam] and the straight path".[56] (Clearly, Quṭb is ignoring here the ban imposed by the Ottoman empire in 1856 of the use of derogatory terms such as "*raʿāya*" (grazing cattle), when referring to non-Muslims.[57])

I find it particularly important to emphasise here that, although Quṭb refers to al-Nadwi's depiction of the world as one which was "dominated by the spirit of *jāhiliyya*" before the advent of Islam,[58] he disregards in his own writings the Indian scholar's accusation against Paul to the effect that he led single-handedly to "the eclipse of the light of Christianity, and introduced into it the fictitious legends of *jāhiliyya*."[59] However, against his own convictions, as outlined in *al-Adāla*, Quṭb states in his review of al-Nadwi's work that the Indian scholar finds that all religions, especially Christianity (*not* Judaism), became "rigid" and "lifeless."[60]

In a line of argument that he continues to pursue in *Ẓilāl*, when he makes reference to "the new *jāhiliyya*",[61] Quṭb goes on to reprimand Muslims for being nominal Muslims who "ignore the [very] nature" of Islam.[62] Elsewhere, in the Introduction to al-Al-Nadwi's work, Quṭb confirms, yet again, an unequivocal attraction to Darwinism as he first formulates his doctrine of *jāhiliyya*, by stating plainly that

> It is worthy of note that the writer [al-Nadwi] uses constantly the word *jāhiliyya* in relation to the degeneration [*naksa*] which touched humanity since the Muslims failed [to assume the responsibility of] leadership. This is an accurate expression which shows that the writer understands the fundamental difference between the 'spirit' of Islam and the 'material' spirit which was prevalent in the world before the advent of Islam, as it is today when Islam relinquished [its responsibility of] leadership. This is *jāhiliyya* in its original nature. *Jāhiliyya* is not limited to a time period. It is one which has a specific spiritual and mental peculiarity; one which gains prominence when the fundamental values, which are ordained by God, are dropped and come to be replaced by values which are steeped in temporary longings. This is what humanity is undergoing today in its 'first evolution/refinement condition' (*ḥalat al-irtiqāʾ al-ūla*); [it is the same condition] that it endured previously in the days of 'first barbarism' (*al-barbariya al-ūla*).[63]

It is clear from the above line of argument that Quṭb's interpretation of history, which reflects a plain Darwinist imprint, sees him depicting it in terms of two main cycles:

one of original "first barbarism" (*al-barbariya al-ūla*), and the modern one of a "first evolution/refinement condition" (*ḥalat al-irtiqā' al-ūla*) which, according to him, eluded especially the Americans. In one of the three-part series of articles which were published in *al-Risāla* in 1951 under the title "Amrīka alatī Rā'ayt fī Mizān al-Qiyam al-Insāniyya", Quṭb, in fact, makes reference to the "primitiveness" of the Americans to demonstrate that the stage of "*irtiqā*" is reached by humans in all civilisations as they bypass "the stages of first feral savagery/brutishness" (*madarij al-ḥayawaniyya al-ūla*) in their sentiments and behaviour.[64]

In suggesting an opposition between the "spirit" of Islam and the "material" spirit of modern-day *jāhiliyya*, it is also clearly the case that Quṭb is not, like al-Nadwi, principally targeting the Christian West as such. In *Ma'rakat al-Islām wa al-Ra'simaliyya* (1951), it becomes apparent that Quṭb attaches a quality of refinement in the process involving the evolution of Western Christianity, arguing that Western Crusaders, as he encountered them in America, are aware that Islam is the only religion which represents a "threat" to them. In a plain contradiction to his own positive views in relation to the Buddhist and Hindu "religions" in the 1940s, and his negative impressions of Christianity, as practiced in America, Quṭb states that

> Crusaders do not fear Buddhism, Hinduism, or Judaism, as these are all nationalist religions which do not seek to spread out of their respective localities, and peoples; [these religions] are also less refined than Christianity (*aqal min al-Masiḥiyya ruqiyan*).[65]

It is worth noting here that the adjective "*ruqiy*" used above by Quṭb in connection to Western Christianity denotes a quality of refinement which goes beyond the mere notion of evolution conveyed by the use of the word "*irtiqā*".[66] As noted by Shepard, the word "*irtiqā*", which is the most common rendition in Arabic of the word "progress", "may refer in Quṭb's usage in the early 1950s to moral or spiritual advancement".[67]

To be certain, Quṭb's acceptance of the idea of a progressive evolution towards refinement in the Christian West is a stepping-stone in his discourse of the early 1950s towards some sort of a recognition that the Christian tradition in the West was hardly the lifeless object, which is described in *al-'Adāla*, as having been confined within the walls of the Church in Rome.[68] To admit, as well, that "Buddhism"(*būdhiyya*), "Hinduism"(*hindūkiyya*), and "Judaism" (*yahūdiyya*) are all "religions" which are "less refined" than Western Christianity is also a form of acceptance that all these traditions underwent a process of "progressive evolution", albeit all these traditions are now described by Quṭb, as Wilfred C. Smith would put it, as mere "reified" objects.[69]

Quṭb reveals, however, that, unlike the *Ikhwān*, who were particularly averse to Protestant missionary activities in Egypt,[70] he developed an acute level of anxiety in relation to Catholic missionary activities, not only in Egypt,[71] but in the Congo and the Tibet.[72] Identifying himself, still, as an "Easterner", Quṭb argues that, unbeknown to people in the East, "colossal missionary efforts are made by Europe and America to spread Christianity across the world".[73] In Egypt, where the largest number of Catholic missionaries came from France,[74] Quṭb warns specifically against "two important missionary messengers" who, according to him, work closely with foreign Catholic missionaries: Naguib Maḥfouz's mentor, the journalist Salāma Musa, and the founder of *Dār al-Hilāl*, Jurjī Zidān.[75]

Interestingly, in spite of Quṭb's apparent mistrust of indigenous Christians, he relies on translations into Arabic of works by the two pioneering British Orientalists, Sir T. W. Arnold's *The Preaching of Islam* (1896), to confirm the "toleration" of Islam in comparison to Christian Europe,[76] and Sir Hamilton Gibb's *Whither Islam?* (1932), to stress the egalitarian norms of Islam.[77]

Quoting Sir T. W. Arnold's and Sir Hamilton Gibb's aforementioned works to affirm the superiority of Islamic social norms in comparison to those of Christian Europe is all the more significant considering that Quṭb does not make reference in *Ma'rakat al-Islām wa al-Ra'simaliyya,* as he does in *al-'Adāla*, to "the Paragon of Freedom and Tolerance in Islam", Abu Ḥanīfa,[78] and the Prophet's contemporary, "the ascetic socialist", Abu Dhirr al-Ghafārī. (Note that, in line with the clear leaning to destruction that we observed previously, Quṭb dismisses the school of Abu Ḥanīfa, as well as those of al-Shāfi 'ī, *Māliki,* and Ibn Ḥanbal as irrelevant in *al-Islām wa Mushkilāt al-Ḥaḍāra.*[79])

No mention is made by Quṭb, as well, of al-Nadwi's work *Madha Khasira al-'Alam bi Inḥiṭāṭ al-Muslimīn* which was praised by him in 1950 as providing a model of historiography which depicts the transfer of leadership from *jāhiliyya* powers to that of Islam. Quṭb was particularly critical then of European historians whose works, he writes, are a reflection of their "material" culture and philosophy.[80] Only a year later, although Quṭb criticises Orientalists for "providing scientific support for colonialism",[81] he nonetheless reveals an open admiration for Sir T. W. Arnold's and Sir Hamilton Gibb's integrity, as two "*Christian European men*". As he puts it, "I have quoted these two *Christian European men*, because their respective testimonies in favour of Islam's absolute tolerance and justice (in dealing with non-Muslims) is beyond 'suspicion'".[82]

It is noteworthy that Quṭb continues to demonstrate much identity-confusion in his writings of the early 1950s as is evident in his contributions in 1951 to three publications with different ideological orientations, earning him much rebuke from his friends: *al-Da'wah* of the *Ikhwān*, *al-Ishtirākiyya*, which was published by the socialist Aḥmad Ḥusayn, and *al-Liwa al-Jadīd*, which was published by the nationalist Fatḥī Raḍwān. Defiant, Quṭb responded to the criticism which was levelled against him in 1952 by defending that he is contributing to all three publications "under the banner of Islam".[83]

Having developed in 1951 a heightened level of anxiety in relation to al-Azhar as representing the main impediment to his ambition to dominate the scene as an Islamist ideologue, Quṭb denounces al-Azhar in an article published in *al-Risāla* for its failure to fulfil its "constructive and creative message" to resurrect "the Islamic *idea*" with the view of preparing it for "*practical* application in light of present realities".[84] (Obviously, Quṭb is contradicting here his former self in 1939 when he criticised 'the nature of [Europe's] *practical* and *realistic* mind' [*ṭabī'at 'aqluha al-'amaliyya al-wāqi'iyya*] in refuting Ṭaha Ḥusayn's *Mustaqbal al-Thaqāfa fī Miṣr*,[85] not to mention that the word "practical" *wāqi'ī* is un-Qur'anic.)

Confirming a clear attraction to Christianity, as an abstract, and a newly-found open admiration for Communism, Quṭb argues in *Ma'rakat al-Islām wa al-Ra'simaliyya* (1951) that Islam can create "a total blend out of Christianity and communism". As he puts it,

> Islam must rule because it is the 'only positive and constructive creed' (*al-'aqīda al-waḥīda al-ijabiyya al-insha'iyya*) which can form a total blend out of Christianity and Communism, which reflects their respective goals, and adds [to these goals] balance (*tawazun*), harmony (*tanasuq*), and moderation (*i'tidal*). The world does not do without a positive creed. Christianity fulfilled its role, and is no longer a positive element in the reality of humankind's state of affairs. [At the present time], it is the public which leads the Church, and the Church continues to follow the public without any discomfiture, and without even defending what it holds sacred and its most honourable goals [to touch] the heart and the conscience![86]

Exactly what Quṭb meant by suggesting that Islamic rule can bring about "a total blend out of Christianity and Communism",[87] and how he intended to go about to create a *new* Islam, as an 'idea', out of blending Christianity and Communism, is unclear to me. I can only speculate, given Quṭb's clear attraction to modern European thought, and his continuous expressed admiration for Tagore in 1951,[88] that he probably envisaged the creation of a movement modelled after the Brahmo Samaj in India which was, at its inception, a "quasi-Protestant theistic movement within Hinduism" bearing also Islamic influences.[89]

Interestingly, it was within the ranks of the younger generation, which followed the one including the "intellectual giants" of Swadeshi modernist thinkers, such as Tagore,[90] that we see the emergence of the anti-colonial cosmopolitan avant-garde thinker, Manabendranath Roy (1887-1954), as one of the premier international communists of the colonial world in the 1920s.[91] Roy's world-view is seen in the context of an anti-colonial response to the British colonial project which "resolved Christian notions about redemption in history (eschatology) within a secular discourse about progress in history."[92]

Significantly, Quṭb does not affirm himself against the "evangelical zeal" of English and French colonialist powers, which pushed the idea of redemption,[93] by countering in any of his writings the Islamic doctrine of "intercession" (*shafāʿa*) which is considered as being offered to *all* prophets and the faithful to intercede on behalf of humanity on the day of resurrection in traditional and Sufi Islam.[94] Instead, just like Roy, Quṭb appropriates the Christian notion of redemption beginning in *Maʿrakat al-Islām wa al-Raʾsimaliyya*, arguing in the chapter "*Fī al-Islām Khalāṣṣ*" (In Islam, There is Redemption) that Islam, (as a blend of communism and Christianity), "is more *effective* [obviously as a power tool to guide the "lost [human] flock"] in an Egyptian environment than communism".[95]

In analysing the revised section of *Ẓilāl*, I find that, unlike Mawdūdī and al-Nadwi, who both wrote of the modern world as *jāhiliyya*, finding it in the Western and the Communist worlds alike,[96] Quṭb's commentary on *sura* six, *al-Anʿām*, reveals that he felt much disquiet that Marx's prediction of "the inevitability of communism" holding sway in England failed to materialise. Rather than denouncing Marx, like his younger Brother Muḥammad, as one of "the three Jews",[97] Quṭb appears to be rather disappointed that Marx, Lenin, and Stalin, turned out to be three false prophets. In his commentary on *al-Anʿām*, Quṭb expresses much consternation that Stalin's and Lenin's successor, Nikita Khrushchev, was calling (in 1956) for "peaceful co-existence", thus going against these two men's prophecies predicting the "inevitability of war" between the capitalist and the communist worlds. Additionally, Quṭb argues that communism is to be found in "the most backward" (*akthar takhaluf*) industrial countries, such as Russia and China [of the former East], but not in the "advanced/refined" (*rāqiyya*) industrial countries (such as England).[98]

In *Khaṣṣāʾiṣ* (1962), it becomes apparent that Quṭb developed a degree of anxiety in relation to Ezra, probably a culmination of the fear he must have experienced as he first heard of "Operation Ezra and Nehemiah" organised in 1951 to airlift 85, 893 Iraqi Jews as part of a mass "*ʿaliyah*" (meaning exalted in Arabic and English) to Israel from a number of Arab countries including Iraq, Libya, and Yemen.[99] Although both Christians and Jews are thrown by Quṭb into a state of *jāhiliyya* in his later work *Khaṣṣāʾiṣ* (1962) for deviating from "*tawḥīd*" (monism, or unity of God) which, he claims, is the *sui generis* of the Islamic "*taṣawwur*" which distinguishes it from all other conceptions of *jāhiliyya*,[100] Quṭb accuses "the Sons of Israel" of distorting "*tawḥīd*" by claiming to themselves a "national god", and claiming that "Ezra is the Son of God"[101] (as per Q9:30).[102] In reliance on Q9:31, Quṭb argues further that "The People of the Book", obviously encountered by the early Muslims, mentioned in that verse deified their rabbis and pontiffs by accepting legislation from them.[103]

However, as we shall see in section three below, it is not till 1964 that Ezra, otherwise known as "The Second Moses" for rekindling the hope for a renewal of God's covenant with David,[104] seems to have become a more serious threat to Quṭb as he openly challenges Nasser in *Ma'ālim*, and becomes acutely aware of the Jews, as a competing 'other' 'chosen' 'pseudo-species'. In the process, he would finally relinquish all claim for spirituality and insist more on a rigid interpretation of *shari'a* to make Islam more of an imaginary "ossified" Judaism.

2.1 The Otherness Formulations Targeting the West in Quṭb's Early 1960s Discourse with Special Emphasis on the Doctrine of Jāhiliyya

Having asserted himself, as the "founder" of a new Islam blending communism and Christianity (of the West), against the materialist modern-day *jāhiliyya* in the capitalist West, Quṭb appears to have been particularly anxious in the early 1950s to appropriate or, as Shepard puts it, "Islamise" the western presupposition of "the myth of progress".[105] In the process of "Islamising" the mythical idea of "progress", Quṭb reveals an acute level of apprehension in relation to the Roman component of Western culture which becomes a main part of his *jāhiliyya* discourse in the early 1960s, as we shall see below.

In what seems to be a rebuttal of al-'Aqqād's argument in his work *Allah* (1947), in which he accepts the progress achieved by modern-day Western philosophers, in general, and those made by the anti-fascist humanist historian/philosopher Benedetto Croce (d. 1952), in particular, towards the foundation of a "humanist religion",[106] Quṭb makes the argument in one of his early 1950s articles published posthumously in *Naḥw Mujtama' Islāmī* (1969) that Europe came out of its "ignorance" (*jahalatuha*) in Andalusia when it encountered Islam which provided the basis for its civilisation.[107] In reliance on mythical tales which were in circulation in medieval times in Europe,[108] Quṭb makes the argument that, under the rule of the feudal-terrorist Roman Empire, doubt has been cast about whether a "white woman had a human soul at all", adding that the French Revolution's ideas of "liberty, equality and fraternity" originated from the Islamic "idea" in Andalusia.[109]

Quoting a statement by the Nobel Laureate Bertrand Russell in which he predicted that "the rule of the 'White Man' has come to an end",[110] Quṭb makes the claim that the civilisation of "the White Man" exhausted its purposes, adding that it has nothing more to offer to humanity in terms of principles and ideas which allow for new "development" (*numuw*), or new "progress" (*taṭawwur*).[111] In September 1951, Quṭb reinforces the argument that "the rule of the 'White Man' has come to an end", as he indicates in another article which was published in *al-Risāla* that he finds much in favour of the leader of Egypt's Socialist Party, Aḥmad Ḥusayn's call on the Iranian religious leader, Ayat Allah Kashani, and Iranian Prime Minister, Musaddiq, to nationalise Iranian oil, and end Britain's monopoly of oil resources in Iran.[112]

Soon thereafter, especially following the CIA's direct involvement in overthrowing Musaddiq in 1953,[113] to secure Washington's interest in Iranian oil,[114] and the CIA's open support of Egypt's military regime,[115] Quṭb seems to have developed a heightened level of anxiety, amounting to what Calvert describes as a "paranoia" in relation to the infiltration of the Revolutionary Command Council (RCC) in Egypt by the CIA.[116]

Even as early as 30 July, 1951, Quṭb reveals in a newspaper article in *al-Risāla* that he was acutely made aware of American and British intelligence activities in Egypt, especially in directing the media to serve "international capitalism" (*al-ra'simaliyya al-'alamiyya*).[117] Under the headline, "Islām Amrikanī", Quṭb writes in another article published in *al-Risāla* on 30 June, 1952, that Americans, and their allies, need Islam only to ward off the danger posed by communism in the Middle East.[118]

As discussed earlier, following his two-year sojourn in the US, Quṭb developed an awareness of a system of representation in America which exalts "the White Man" as a "demigod", as he notes that in America they talk of "the coloured people", like "us", Egyptians and Arabs, as if they were talking of "sub-humans".[119]Douglas Little observes that, as early as the 1920s, "the images of Muslims and Jews, as represented in US popular culture began to diverge sharply". Whereas Arabs continued to be depicted as "primitive, untrustworthy, and malevolent figures", American anti-Semitism dwindled.[120] In 1953, Quṭb appears to have removed himself from the ranks of Muslims who, Smith observes, read Western books on Islam "not in order to see how illuminating they may be, but how laudatory."[121] Instead, Mitchell observes that Quṭb became particularly concerned about the danger posed by the missionaries, the Orientalists, and social researchers,[122] seemingly contributing to the Brotherhood's "increased awareness of, and sensitivity to what Westerners were saying about Islam and Muslims". Concern was voiced specifically about critical studies conducted by Western scholars, such as Gibb's *Modern Trends in Islam* (1947), which may "destroy Islam's sacredness".[123]

Following his arrest, and trial in July 1955, in relation to the failed attempt to assassinate Nasser on October 26, 1954, Quṭb seems to have developed the conviction that both "Zionism" and "imperialist Crusaders" aim to destroy the Muslim Brothers' movement in order to realise their mutual schemes.[124] In 1962, when Quṭb makes use again of the doctrine of *jāhiliyya* in *Khaṣṣā'iṣ,* it becomes particularly evident that he developed a heightened level of anxiety in relation specifically to Gibb's work *Modern Trends in Islam,* probably as he became aware of the British scholar's endorsement of 'Abduh's and Iqbal's reformist thought.

Khaṣṣā'iṣ also marks a paradigmatic change in Quṭb's position which sees him associating the Roman Church with corruption, amounting to paganism, as he attempts to shake the Greco-Roman foundations of modern European thought ultimately to discredit Nasser and his primary "others" 'Abduh and Iqbal. In so doing Quṭb effectively uses the doctrine of *jāhiliyya* in the work to bring out the "deviation" (*inḥirāf*) of these two prominent Muslim thinkers from his own conception of the so-called Islamic "*taṣawwur*", enumerating in the process seven characteristics of the Islamic "*taṣawwur*".[125]

2.2 The Doctrine of Jāhiliyya as a Deviation from Quṭb's Own Conceptualisation of the Islamic Taṣawwur in Khaṣṣā'iṣ

In the first instance when Quṭb offers us a definition of the term *jāhiliyya* in *Khaṣṣā'iṣ,* he affirms himself as the new founder of an objectified "Islam" which is free of all of its "cumulative traditions",[126] even of the Prophet's *sunna.*[127] Reflecting a clear leaning to what Wilfred C. Smith refers to as the "big-bang outlook",[128] Quṭb argues that

> The Qur'anic text was initially aiming to offer 'sound foundations' for human *concepts*, and life, as willed by God. The least [that one can do] to deserve this Grace from the High and Mighty, is to receive it with hearts and minds which are free from the dark blur [of any] intrusion, so that the new concept comes clean from all [cumulative] sediments of ancient and modern *jāhiliyya* as well.[129]

In an argument contradicting the claim he makes only two years later in the 1964 edition of *al-'Adāla*, when he *begins* to stress the role played by the primordial "Jew" in plotting against Islam since the time of the revolt against the third Caliph 'Uthmān (d. 656),[130] Quṭb traces here the beginning of the "deviations" (*inḥirafat*) away from "the 'pristine' (*aṣṣīl*) Islamic 'concept'" all the way as far back as the early days of Islam in the immediate aftermath of the dispute which erupted between the fourth Caliph 'Ali and Mu'āwiya in the mid-7th century.[131]

According to Quṭb, it is following the age of conquest that the early Muslims encountered different cultures in conquered territories and, having freed themselves from the strain of *jihad*, preoccupied themselves - particularly in Andalusia, and under the Abbasids - with Greek philosophy and Christian "speculative/scholastic theology" (*al-mabaḥith al-lahūtiyya*). The end result, he claims, saw the emergence of "deviations" from the "pristine Islamic concept" which came to "salvage humanity...and bring it back to the 'activist' (*ijabī*) and 'realist' (*waqi'ī*) Islamic *taṣawwur* ".[132] (obviously, the Qur'an makes no mention of a concept, let alone the adjectives 'activist' and 'realist'.)

Clearly, the incorporation of "speculative/scholastic theology", along with Greek philosophy, into the narrative of Islam's early encounter with "outsiders" is an important event in Quṭb's early 1960s' *jāhiliyya* discourse. Oddly enough, Quṭb does not develop an argument in any of his writings of the period against the Christian theologians encountered by the early Muslims.[133] Instead, like 'Abduh and Iqbal,[134] Quṭb makes the claim in his commentary in *Ẓilāl* on *Sura* four, *al-Nisa'*, that Luther's, Calvin's, and Zwingli's Reformation movements were all influenced by Islam in the course of the Crusades.[135]

Evidently, Quṭb failed to appreciate that "Luther's great concept (and word in Latin *fides* and German *Glaube*) is 'faith'";[136] As Wilfred C. Smith observes, both Zwingli and Calvin were leaders in a movement in the history of ideas, who, even as they made use of the word "*religio*", were making reference to something "personal, inner, and transcendentally oriented" ("*religio*" thus denoted "piety" in modern English).[137] Furthermore, Armstrong remarks that both Calvin and Zwingli were "ardent Pauline Christians", and that it was indeed during the lectures that Luther gave on the Psalms and Paul's epistles at the University of Wittenberg between 1513 and 1518 that he experienced "a spiritual breakthrough".[138]

In analysing Quṭb's discourse in *Khaṣṣā'iṣ*, it becomes only too apparent that he was, most probably, particularly distressed by Gibb's laudatory comments in relation to both 'Abduh's and Iqbal's modernist outlooks, especially in light of al-'Aqqād's positive review of Western studies which praised 'Abduh's and Iqbal's respective reform efforts.[139] In the chapter entitled "al-*Rabbaniyya*", which he dedicates to refuting the "deviation" introduced to Islam by 'Abduh's *Risālat al-Tawḥid* (1897) and Iqbal's lectures on *The Reconstruction of Religious Thought in Islam* (translated into Arabic as *Tajdīd al-Fikr al-Dīnī fī al-Islām*),[140]he, in effect, places these two Muslim reformists on the outside in the crucial "outside-inside" division by going as far as accusing them of "deviation" from the so-called Islamic concept, and thus falling into *jāhiliyya*.

To understand Quṭb's position, in relation to 'Abduh, I can only speculate that, as an Islamist ideologue, Quṭb was at least partially challenged by the enactment of the 1961 Reform Law which touched al-Azhar and is said to have been inspired by 'Abduh's ideas.[141] Additionally, Quṭb must have also been distressed by Nasser's proclamation of a "National Charter" in 1962[142] which referred to Muḥammad 'Abduh's "untiring efforts to bring about religious reform."[143] There is also some evidence to suggest that Quṭb may have gained some superficial knowledge about Smith's work *Islam in Modern History*, which was favourably reviewed by al-'Aqqād who refers approvingly to the agreement between Smith and Gibb on the last's assertion in *Modern Trends in Islam* "that the future of Islam lies in the hands of its original custodians the '*ulama*".[144]

Although Quṭb stresses in *al-Islām wa Mushkilat al-Ḥaḍāra* that the Roman era provided "the real foundation" of modern European civilisation, as he criticises Church conceptions of Christianity which amplify the "ignorance" (*jahala*) of man,[145]and makes the claim in *Khaṣṣā'iṣ* that the Roman state corrupted Christianity with "residues of Roman paganism,[146] he does not develop a thought-out argument against "real Christianity". Instead, he argues, that "real Christianity" was never represented by "Church conceptions" in the West.[147]

The main argument being made in *Khaṣṣā'iṣ* is that "Muslim thinkers have fallen under the 'spell' (*fitna*) of Greek philosophy – especially that of Aristotle [obviously making reference here to al-'Aqqād, as well] – and ecclesiastical theology in metaphysics."[148] Quṭb then proceeds to make an open accusation of "ignorance" (*jahl*) of the nature of Greek philosophy" against those who link it to the Islamic "*taṣawwur*" without realising that it owes its roots in "pagan and legendary elements".[149]

Although the thrust of Quṭb's argument in *Khaṣṣā'iṣ* is to discredit theology and Greek Philosophy, he nonetheless reveals that he developed a level of anxiety in relation to the Jews. In a clear departure from the views he expressed in the course of his literary career, and beyond, when he dissociated Christian Europe from Judaism, Quṭb now stresses that Greco-Hebrew legends left an "'ugly' (*qabīḥ*) and 'trifling' (*tafih*) concept in the minds of the Europeans which continued to dominate their conceptions even as they adopted Christianity".[150] Quṭb has much to say about the legends and concepts of the ancient Greeks, and those of the Jews, associating both with paganism and the latter additionally with "deranged nationalistic lunacy" (*lawtha qawmiyya*).[151] As he puts it,

> They [the Jews] have inserted in their sacred books, and in the New Testament, legends and concepts on God – Glory to Him – which are not very far from the 'most debased' (*aḥaṭ*) pagan concepts of the Greeks and other pagans.[152]

Considering the evidence that, by the time he wrote *Khaṣṣā'iṣ*, Quṭb developed some familiarity with Gibb's work *Modern Trends in Islam*, it seems to be the case that he was particularly threatened by Gibb's work which was complimentary of Iqbal's work *The Reconstruction of Religious Thought in Islam*. I conjecture that Quṭb must have been particularly incensed that Gibb praised Iqbal's attempt to introduce into Islam, in line with Bergson's anti-rational philosophy, the same tendencies in thought which "have been gradually transforming Christianity into a religion of humanism" in the West.[153]

In what is evidently a refutation of Iqbal's statement, which is quoted by Gibb, that "there is no such thing as eternal damnation in Islam," and that "Hell, as conceived by the Qur'an, is not a pit of everlasting torture inflicted by a revengeful God,"[154] Quṭb retorts, in his attempt to emphasise Iqbal's "deviation" from the so-called Islamic "*taṣawwur*", that Iqbal interpreted the Qur'anic text against its nature, and that of the Islamic "concept", to prove that "death, and the afterlife, are not the end of [human] experience," in accordance with Hegel's philosophy.[155]

In his later work, *Muqawwimat al-Taṣawwur al-Islāmī*, where Quṭb accepts that he developed the theme of "complex ignorance" (*al-jāhiliyyat al-mu'aqada*)- including "the *jāhiliyya* of cultured ignorance" (*jāhiliyyat al-jahl al-muthaqaf*), in reliance on Will Durant's (d.1981) development of the idea of "ignorance" in *The Story of Philosophy* (1926),[156] he appears to obsess about the contribution of the French philosopher, the Nobel laureate Henri Bergson (d. 1941), who was popular in both Egypt[157] and the US[158] in the early part of the Twentieth century, to what he considers to be a pro-Jewish campaign in the West.

In one instance, Quṭb criticises Will Durant for his pro-Jews writings which he considers to be part of "a plan by the Jews to dissolve the acrimony which built against them in the world of Christendom, due to their spiteful position in relation to Jesus", adding that the American philosopher depicts a character called Esther who accepts Jesus as "a great Jew".[159] In another instance, Quṭb quotes Bergson, whom he identifies as "a Jew", as stating that "Jesus was an Israelite Prophet". He then goes on to make the claim that (modern-day Western) philosophy plays a role in what he considers to be a pro-Jewish "scientific propaganda" which deceived *some* advocates of Islamic movements (Iqbal not doubt), into hailing the French philosopher as an anti-materialist "philosopher of spirituality".[160]

Although Quṭb has no qualms about quoting from Durant's work *The Story of Philosophy* in *al-Islām wa Mushkilat al-Ḥaḍāra* to highlight the superficial and licentious nature of modern-day American civilisation,[161] he makes use mostly of the French-American Catholic Christian eugenicist, Alexis Carrel's work *L'Homme Cet Inconnu* (1935)[162] to emphasise both the "ignorance" and the "barbarity" of modern-day Western civilisation. Choueiri observes that Quṭb was to read into the Qur'an, and quoted some of its verses, to confirm some of Carrel's views,[163] remarking further that the latter himself talked of Western civilisation as "*la barbarie*".[164]

In one instance when Quṭb invokes the word *jāhiliyya* in the section he dedicates to a discussion of the gender leitmotif in his discourse, he takes exception to mention specifically "ancient Greek *jāhiliyya*" as he goes on to criticise both ancient and modern "*jāhiliyya* methods" (*manāhij al-jāhiliyya*) alike for failing to recognise that the relation between sexes is one which is

> a means for the service of humankind by way of creating 'a safe, clean, aware, and specialised nursery' (*al-mahḍan al-amīn al-naẓīf al-wa'ī al-mutakhaṣiṣ*) in the industry of man...And to consider that 'duty' (*al-wajib*) – not 'pleasure' (*al-ladha*) - is the 'mainstay' (*'imad*) of the relation between sexes.[165]

Under the heading "Women and Relations between Sexes",[166] Quṭb recounts his own experiences in the US,[167] and quotes from Asad's work *Islam at the Crossroads* to support his critical views of the "material" West,[168]and Nadwi's work *What has the World Lost by the Decline of the Muslims*? On Europe's "religion of matter".[169] For the most part, however, Quṭb quotes rather extensively from al-Mawdūdī's work *Purdah* (seclusion, translated into Arabic as *al-Ḥijāb*) on the emergence of the Romans on the scene of history for the first time from a state of "savagery" (*waḥshiyya*) and "injustice of ignorance" (*ẓulm al-jāhiliyya*),[170]and on "Church conceptions" in relation to women and relations between sexes.[171]

It is noteworthy that Quṭb drops all of the above sources when he tackles the gender topos in the chapter entitled *Al-Islām Huwa al-Ḥaḍāra* (Islam is Civilisation) in *Ma'ālim.* In that work, he maintains the view that gender relations and family-related issues are "decisive factors in delineating whether a society is backward or civilised, *jahilī* or Islamic."[172] Quṭb highlights here scandals in the American Senate, and those involving British and American spies fleeing to Russia and the scandalous affair between the English minister Profumo and Christine Keeler in 1963,[173] while conveniently omitting any reference to the uproar and denunciations which followed the scandal and the call for a re-examination of values in English society at the time.[174]

> In modern *jāhiliyya* societies the conception of morality (*al-mafhūm al-akhlākī*) retreats to a level which no longer allows one to differentiate between what characterises humans and animals. In these societies illicit sexual intercourse – and even abnormal sexual relations – is no longer viewed as morally sinful (*radhīla akhlākiyya*).[175]

Although the American society is used by Quṭb to epitomise the animalistic nature of Western modern-day *jāhiliyya* societies in his writings of the 1960s, the American is hardly the main "other" at this stage of his life. In fact, as Binder puts it, Quṭb makes in *Ma'ālim* "a pilgrimage from idealism to pragmatism" that he attacked previously in the first five editions of *al-'Adāla.*[176] Suffice it to emphasise here that Quṭb is more in tune with the American-French Carrel's formulation of "*la barbarie*" of the West in formulating his own doctrine of *jāhiliyya* than he is with Mawdūdī's derogatory views of Christianity.

Interestingly enough, Quṭb seems to have been so enthralled by Alexis Carrel's ideas and works, that he goes on imparting a quality of "faith" (*imān*) to the French-American Catholic Christian eugenicist in the revised edition of *al-Islām wa Mushkilat al-Ḥaḍāra.*[177] Furthermore, he even describes Carrel as someone who "breathed in an environment which knew religion at its best in its Sufi 'buoyant' (*murafrif*), 'transparent' (*shafīf*) spiritual strand,"[178] (probably making reference to Lourdes[179]). At some level, Quṭb reveals in *Ma'ālim*, as well, a degree of admiration for "European genius" in areas of science, *culture*, systems, and material products, and accepts that humanity cannot relinquish these by-products of "European *genius*" which, he finds, lack in the Islamic world.[180]

Although Quṭb's reliance on Mawdūdī in *Ma'ālim* is such that Binder poses the question "if we subtract Mawdūdī from Quṭb is there anything of importance left?",[181] there is nothing in Quṭb's writings to indicate that he accepted the Pakistani ideologue as the "Rightly-Guided saviour" or the awaited "*Mahdī*".[182] In one instance, when he invokes the idea of the "saviour" in the chapter under the heading "*al-Mukhaliṣ*" (saviour/redeemer) in the last edition of *al-Mustaqbal li-Hadha al-Dīn* (1963),[183] he makes no reference to Mawdūdī. Clearly, seeing himself more, like Jesus, as "a saviour/redeemer" of mankind, rather than a "*mahdī*", he calls on both

Carrel and Dulles to adopt Islam as a "*manhaj*" (system) to rid humankind of both "the barbarity (*al-barbariyya*) of the industrial civilisation", as expressed by Carrel (in *L'homme Cet Inconnu*), and "the trap of communism", to which Dulles made reference (in *War or Peace*).[184]

Although Quṭb makes the claim that "Islam will salvage the human spirit from the humiliation which was inflicted on it by both Darwin and Marx",[185]he does not refer to Marx as one of "the Three Jews". In a statement which is very much in tune with the argument that he makes in the first five editions of *al-'Adāla*, Quṭb maintains the view elsewhere in the same work that Judaism, like all other religions, came as a "*manhaj*" for the Sons of Israel; Christianity followed as "*al-manhaj al-mu'adal*" (the modified/rectified system) for the Sons of Israel.[186] Only a year later, as we shall see below, as he challenges the Nasserite regime, Quṭb depicts the object Islam as a "*manhaj*" mostly in *Ma'ālim* (1964) and adopts Mawdūdī's concept of "*ḥakimiyya*" (governance), as he comes to identify 'the Jew' as the 'other' 'pseudo-species'.[187]

3. The Construction of 'the Jew' as the 'Other' 'Pseudo-Species' in Quṭb's Later 1960s Writings

Although it is clear that Quṭb developed an acute level of anxiety in relation to 'the Jew' as early as the late 1940s, I contend that it is only as he seems to have joined, albeit perhaps inadvertently, in a concerted effort, which was orchestrated mainly by the Wahhābī Saudi kingdom,[188] and its Western allies, to topple the Nasserite secular regime[189] that he dehumanises and produces the essentialist 'Jew' in *Ẓilāl*, and identifies 'the Jew' as the main 'other' 'pseudo-species' in *Ma'ālim*.

In the chapter entitled "The Muslim's Nationality and His Creed" (*Jinsiyat al-Muslim wa 'Aqīdatahū*) in *Ma'ālim*, Quṭb reveals that he is aware that 'the Jews' are the 'other' 'pseudo-species', even as he refutes the Jews' claim that they are 'God's chosen people' (*sha'b Allah al-Mukhtār*). In disproving the claim that 'the Jews' are 'God's chosen people', Quṭb argues that all forms of 'solidarity' (*'aṣabiyya*), which are based on affiliations with a clan, a tribe, a people, ethnicity, colour or land fall under the rubric of *jāhiliyya* which prevailed at times of 'spiritual degradation' (*inḥiṭāṭ ruḥī*) and was condemned by the Prophet as being 'putrid' (*minatina*).[190]

In his commentary in *Ẓilāl* on *sura* II, *al-Baqara* (the Cow), Quṭb explains that the *sura* revolves around 'one axis' (*miḥwar waḥid*), which pertains to the 'sons of Israel's' (inimical) position in relation to the call for Islam in Medina.[191] He adds further that the *sura* targets the Jews who claimed that they were 'the chosen people', and anticipated that 'the last messenger' will come from within their midst.[192] Consequently, he argues, "they became envious of the Prophet, Muḥammad, when

God chose him instead".[193] In his commentary on Q2:65, which represents one of two instances – the other being Q7:166 – when the Qur'an makes reference to "Jews who were changed into apes for profaning the Sabbath,"[194] Quṭb reads this verse literally.

Unlike 'Abduh, who relied on the exegesis of Mujāhid (d. 772) to offer an allegorical interpretation of Q2:65,[195] Quṭb argues that "they [the Jews] turned into apes in their souls and minds for forfeiting their covenant with God (*'ahd Allah*)" and reverted to the "world of animals and beasts".[196] In what seems to be a clear act of projection, Quṭb accuses the Jews of "extreme fanaticism" (*ta'aṣub shadīd*), and of not feeling a connection with humanity at large.[197] Here, he accuses, yet again, the Jews of deifying Ezra, as 'the son of God' as per Q2:116, and of adopting errant '*jāhiliyya* conceptions' (*taṣawwurāt al-jāhiliyya*).[198]

Paradoxically, Quṭb makes the claim in *Ma'ālim* that "God's real chosen people" is the Muslim *umma* which comes together under God's banner regardless of differences based on race, colour and homelands.[199] Here, Quṭb places an emphasis on the stark differences between *jāhiliyya* and Islam, stressing that the rule of Islam prevails only when *shari'a* is applied, and that 'the abode of Islam' (*dār al-Islām*) is where Islamic law and its '*manhaj*' are dominant.[200]

It is noteworthy that, rather than stressing faith in God, for whom he increasingly seems to presume to speak at this late stage of his life,[201] Quṭb lays emphasis in *Ma'ālim* on a this-worldly view of Islam, which he comes to objectify mostly as a revolutionary "method/system" (*manhaj*).[202] Interestingly, the word "*manhaj*" is of Hebrew origin (denoting a custom or conduct).[203] Additionally, as Robinson points out, it is rather the derivative from the word "*manhaj*", "*Minhaj*", which occurs only once in the Qur'an at 5:48, which is used in the Qur'an to denote that each of the religious communities has been given "an open path" (*Minhaj*).[204]

For the purpose of this study, I would like to make the point here that, apart from the above extreme dichotomous view of the world in *Ma'ālim*, I counted one hundred and eighty three instances when Quṭb made use of the word *jāhiliyya*, and its derivatives, such as *jahilī*.[205] In agreement with Hartung, I find that Quṭb's discussion of the doctrine of *jāhiliyya* in the work rarely gives a concrete definition of the word, except by negation.[206] Thus, *jāhiliyya* is defined as "an absence of Islam" with the stress being made on "man's domination over another" (*ḥakimiyyat al-bashar li al-bashar*), and on Mawdūdī's central dichotomies: God's absolute and unlimited sovereignty (*ḥakimiyya*) and man's servitude (*'ubūdiyya*).[207]

To appreciate the significance of Quṭb's adoption of the concept of "*ḥakimiyya*", which seems to be of *Kharijite** [*khawārij* in Arabic, for 'outsiders'] inspiration,[208] it is worth mentioning here that when disputes erupted between fellow Muslim Brothers inmates they habitually came to defer to Quṭb whom they came to recognise as "*al-ḥakim*"[209] (ruler/arbiter). Sometime, during the years he spent in prison, Quṭb came to compare his experience with that of the Prophet and the first Muslims.[210] According to Calvert, an analogy seems to have been drawn between "a tyrant Pharaoh", who imprisoned Joseph, and Nasser, who incarcerated Quṭb.[211]

Evidently, Quṭb's use of the concept of '*ḥakimiyya*', and the stress on Islam as a "*manhaj*", and a harsh penal code[212] in accordance with the rigid Wahhābī doctrine,[213]is directly linked to the effort to topple the Nasserite regime. This development necessarily entailed the obliteration of the "Jew" from the history of salvation, as Quṭb seems to affirm himself as "The Second Moses", instead of Ezra. Ultimately, this meant the demoting of Christianity from being a 'religion'(in accordance to modern parlance) in the first five editions of *al-'Adāla*[214]to being mere 'spiritual teachings' which are limited by their lack in *sharī'a* in the last edition of the work.[215]

The threat posed by Ezra to Quṭb appears to have been of such magnitude that he *knowingly* engages in a perversion of history by claiming in his commentary on *sura* XI, Hūd, in *Ẓilāl* that the Jewish scribe/priest lived at a time predating Moses as 'Azīz[216] (the pharaoh's guard in the Bible (Gen. 39), Potiphar,[217] whose wife is described in the Qur'an, *sura* Yusuf (XII: 30), as having attempted to seduce Joseph). Paradoxically, as he attempts to discredit both the Old and the New Testaments, in favour of the Qur'an, Quṭb accepts that Ezra amassed remnants of the Torah following the years of captivity of the Jews in Babylon. As he puts it,

> the so-called 'Sacred Book' – the Old Testament, which includes the Books of the Jews, or the New Testament which includes the Gospels of the Christians, is not what came down from God. The original copies of the Torah, which came down from God to Moses, were burnt by the Babylonians upon taking the Jews into captivity. It was rewritten several centuries later, five centuries before the birth of Jesus; it was written by Ezra, who may be 'Azīz, who collected remnants of the Torah; for the most part, [however], it is merely [his own] authorship! The same goes for the Gospels which all contain what was retained in the memories of the Messiah's disciples, and of their own disciples, about one century following the death of the Messiah – peace be upon him; many legends and tales were mixed in! It follows that no certainty can be obtained [by consulting] any of these Books in any matter![218]

It is noteworthy that Quṭb does not only break away from a long-standing "cumulative tradition", especially in Sufi Islam, which, Nettler argues, showed much openness to Judaism and incorporated figures such as Ezra ('Uzayr) in the "Islamic canon",[219]but he also brings to light that, unlike early mystics, such as Muqātil Ibn Sulaymān (d. 767), who did not hesitate to quote the Bible to illuminate the Qur'an, as Nwyia's study *Exégèse Coranique et Langage Mystique* indicates,[220] he actually reverses his own position in the 1940s-1950s by dismissing Judeo-Christian scriptures altogether.

In analysing *Ma'ālim*, I find it particularly important to emphasise here that Quṭb made no use of either the so-called *Protocols of the Elders of Zion*,[221] or Q5:82[222] which are both highlighted in the article "*Ma'rakatuna Ma'a al-Yahūd*" which is at the heart of Nettler's study *Past Trials and Present Tribulations*: *a Muslim Fundamentalist's View of the Jews* (1987). Most importantly, although Quṭb condemns all of humankind by defining *jāhiliyya* as "an aggression...against God's 'authority' [*sulṭān*], by entrusting to humans [obviously Nasser] the most particular characteristic of 'divinity' [*ulūhiyya*]: *ḥakimiyya*",[223] he appears to retain a degree of admiration for Marxism, arguing that

> Humanity stands today on the 'edge of an abyss' (*ḥafat al-hawiyya*)...because of its bankruptcy in the realm of 'values' (*qiyam*)...as is made amply obvious in the Western world...where 'democracy' has come close to bankruptcy. [The Western world] is now starting slowly to borrow "systems" (*anẓima*), especially economic ones, from the Eastern camp! These fall under the rubric of Socialism! The same condition applies in the Eastern camp...Theories about communities/ communalism (*al-naẓariyyāt al-jama'iyya*) with Marxism at their forefront, which appealed in its early days to many in the East [that would include Quṭb himself] - and even in the West – as a doctrine which carries the imprint of a creed" (*madhab yaḥmil ṭābi' al-'aqīda*), are on the retreat as well.[224]

Evidently, Marx is not identified as one of the "three Jews" in *Ma'ālim* as he is made out to be in both the article "Our Struggle with the Jews"[225] which, I conjecture, is an extract from Quṭb's commentary on Q5:82 in *Ẓilāl*,[226]albeit reflecting the views of Quṭb's Saudi editor and his younger brother Muḥammad. Even as he warns in the last edition of *al-'Adāla* that communism, like Freemasonry, is a "Jewish institution", and that "the first foundation of the Jewish plan to destroy the non-Jewish world is to divest it of religion,"[227] Quṭb does not incorporate Marxism into his *jāhiliyya* discourse in the last edition of the work.[228]

In *Ma'ālim*, however, Quṭb goes on the offensive against Nasser's '*ishtiraqiyya 'ilmiyya*' (scientific socialism)[229] as an 'order' (*niẓām*) of *jāhiliyya*, which clashes with Islam as a '*shari'a*' and an 'order' (*niẓām*).[230] In his commentary on *sura* XII, Yūsuf, where he makes reference to the "*jāhiliyya* which disfigures the human being in the name of artistic truth", Quṭb comes to associate Nasser's '*ishtirakiyya 'ilmiyya*' with Marxism which, he claims, together with "Freudianism" and "Darwinism" are in accord with the *Protocols of Zion* and "the terrifying Zionist schemes" (*al-mukhaṭaṭat al-ṣahyūniyya al-rahība*).[231] Rather than criticising Darwinism, (which Quṭb must have known was central in 'Abduh's Qur'anic exegesis[232]), Quṭb describes neo-Darwinism in *Ma'ālim*, as represented especially by Julian Huxley, as "*jahala 'ilmiyya*" (scientific ignorance), and criticises it for bringing out the animal-like dispositions of man in the modern-day *jāhiliyya* of the West.[233]

In a passage which he reproduces verbatim in the last edition of *al-ʿAdāla*,[234] as he draws a comparison between Islamic culture and '*jāhiliyya* culture' (*al-thaqāfa al-jāhiliyya*), Quṭb warns against the notion that culture is part of "human heritage" as being one of "the international entrapments set up by the Jews" (*maṣāyyid al-yahūd al-'alamiyya*)[235] (though he accepts European culture elsewhere in the same work). In the chapter entitled "*Al-Taṣawwur al-Islāmī wa al-Thaqāfa*" in *Ma'ālim*, Quṭb cautions that the Jews "aim to placate all creedal and conceptual obstacles to penetrate the relaxed and drugged body of the world so as to pursue their satanic activities".[236]

In a line of argument which is also pursued in the last edition of *al-ʿAdāla*,[237] Quṭb reveals in *Ma'ālim* that he developed an awareness of an existing alliance between Christians and Jews against Muslims. In reliance on verses Q2: 109, 120 and Q3:100, the argument is made in the aforementioned work that both Christians and Jews have a 'final [common] goal' against the Muslims.[238] To understand this important turn of event in Quṭb's 1960s discourse, it is important to point out here that Quṭb was probably influenced by ideas which were put in circulation by the Lebanese scholar, 'Umar Farrūkh, whose works included the translation into Arabic of Muḥammad Asad's work *Islam at the Crossroads* (1934), and who developed an awareness of "the improvement of relations between the Jews and the Vatican".[239]

According to 'Ali 'Ashmāwī, Quṭb seems to have developed the conviction that the Vatican is fully controlled by Portuguese Jews who converted to Christianity. Quṭb is said to have maintained the view that the Sephardic Jews of Spain, on the other hand, who immigrated to Turkey, converted to Islam with the aim of destroying it. Last, but not least, Quṭb made the claim that missionary activities were replaced by Orientalism. At the time, Quṭb seems to have also made the claim that Gibb is "a Jew", who, as "an Orientalist", launched a fierce war against Islam.[240]

By the time Quṭb revised the last edition of *al-ʿAdāla*, which was published a few months later than *Ma'ālim* in 1964 in the few-month period that Quṭb spent out of jail,[241] before his final arrest on the 9th of August 1965,[242] he seems to have acquired some detailed knowledge of Wilfred Cantwell Smith's critical analysis of *al-ʿAdāla*, and of modern-day Islamic movements in *Islam in Modern History*.[243] Quṭb appears to have been so unnerved by Smith's endorsement of Turkey that he re-orients his *jāhiliyya* doctrine in chapter 8 "The Present of Islam and its Future" (*Ḥāḍir al-Islām wa Mustaqbalahu*) to target Western scholarly works in the area of comparative religion in general, and Smith's work in particular.[244]

With Quṭb's works now being widely-read in the Islamic world,[245] he must have been particularly rattled by Smith's dismissal of the *Ikhwān*, along with Jama'at-i Islami of Pakistan, as mere "fanatical outbursts",[246] and his reference to Hardie's translated version of Quṭb's work *al-ʿAdāla* (1953) as an example of *Ikhwān* published literature which "shows no grappling with the more intricate responsibilities of modernity".[247] He must have also been challenged upon learning that Smith contributed a negative review of the work to *Middle Eastern Affairs* in 1954 on account of the "dullness of the work",[248]and that he recommended that the translation series must be "supplemented by translations of Islamic classics".[249]

Whereas Quṭb makes reference in *Ma'ālim* to the "defeatists" (*al-mahzūmūn*) who, under "the sly assault of Orientalists", depict *jihad* in Islam as defensive to prevent *jihad* against "present-day *jāhiliyya*" (*al-Jāhiliyya al-ḥāḍira*),[250] he makes use of the word *jāhiliyya*, and its derivatives, twenty one times altogether, mostly (12 times) in chapter 8 "The Present of Islam and its Future" (*Ḥāḍir al-Islām wa Mustaqbalahu*)[251] where he dismisses *all* Western thought as being "vestiges of *jahilī* activity", warning, however, specifically against all thought-orientations in Philosophy, history, psychology, ethical studies, comparative religion, and sociology.[252] Quṭb claims that "all of these tendencies in *jahilī* thought...are directly affected by *jāhiliyya* conceptions."[253]

Interestingly, Quṭb introduces into the text a paragraph where he reveals that he is in favour of reading European literature because it reflects "a spiritual view of life" and because it recognises "spiritual/moral values in life" (*qiyam ma'nawiyya l-al-ḥaya*).[254] In an argument reminiscent of the views he expressed in the course of his literary career, when he welcomed the demolition of all Arabic literature of the desert Arabs, Quṭb stresses, however, that Islamic history ought to be re-written in line with a "*manhaj*" (here used as a "methodology") which follows the "works of *demolition* and construction which were undertaken by Islam in the broad stretch of territory into which it spread".[255]

In a scathing attack on Smith and his work, *Islam in Modern History*, Quṭb accuses Smith of 'deceit' and 'wickedness', adding that the Orientalist, Wilfred Cantwell Smith, has written the whole book, *Islam in Modern History*, with the basic aim "to prove that Turkish secularism, which Ataturk advocated, is 'Islamic'; indeed, that it is the one successful 'Islamic movement' in the history of the modern period".[256]So abrasive is Quṭb's criticism of Smith that Carré rightly selects a quote in Quṭb's commentary on Q9:36-37 in *Ẓilāl* which describes the Canadian scholar as "an extremely cunning and profoundly evil Crusaderist [*sic.*] writer", and his work as an example of a text which links "modern *jāhiliyya*" and efforts by Jews and Christians to arrest Islamic revival.[257]

It is noteworthy that it is in his commentary in *Ẓilāl* on verses 29-35 of *sura* IX, *al-Tawba*, which is at the centre of Robinson's study of Quṭb's attitude towards Christianity, which, I contend, was probably revised before Quṭb's execution in 1966, that he targets Smith specifically. Rather than targeting Christianity, as such, I find that Quṭb is targeting Smith particularly as he stresses a stark opposition between "*manhaj* Allah" (the way/method of God) and "*manahij al-jāhiliyya*" (the way/methods of *jāhiliyya*) which aim "'to crush' (*tasḥaq*) the surging Islamic movement which is spreading '*manhaj Allah*' across the world".[258] In what I consider to be an unambiguous reference to Smith's *Islam in Modern History*, Quṭb warns against

> the enemies of that religion [Islam] who monitor the revivalist Islamic movements...who are keen to put up an Islamic signboard [to confer legitimacy on] conditions, movements, trends, values, traditions, and ideas which they put together and perpetuate to crush new revivalist movements across the globe.[259]

Giving the example of Turkey as an epitome of *jāhiliyya,* Quṭb argues that it is "Ataturk's non-Islamic infidel movement" in Turkey which fills the urgent need (of the enemies of Islam) to annul the caliphate which, he considers, to be "the last manifestation of an Islamic grouping which comes together under the banner of creed."[260] Although the juristic theory of the Islamic state was based on 'fiction', and emerged mainly when the caliphate, as an historical and political reality, was weakening,[261] Quṭb has no qualms to quote a ḥadīth by the Prophet, without *isnād* (chain of transmission), to the effect that the abolition of '*ḥukm*' (governance) and '*ṣalāt*' (prayer) signals the end of Islam.[262]

Although there is certainly much animosity directed at *Ahl al-Kitāb,* and Christians in particular, in Quṭb's commentary on Q9:29-35 in *Ẓilāl,*[263] it is important to emphasise here that Quṭb departs from the views that he expressed in *Ma'ālim* where he accuses Christian and Jewish societies of falling in *jāhiliyya* on account of their "deviant creedal concept" (*taṣawwur i'tiqādī muḥarraf*) in relation to the doctrines of "sonship and the trinity".[264] In what I consider to be largely a refutation of Smith's argument in favour of the Hindus' ability to go further than "the Semitic group", including Muslims, Christians and Jews, in interpreting religious diversity,[265] Quṭb makes the claim that pagan philosophy in India is "the source of the creed of the Christians".[266]

Quṭb draws the conclusion that the significance of Q9:30, which makes reference to the deification of Ezra by the Jews, and the deification of the Messiah by the Christians, became only too clear in modern times following research which revealed that "the corrupt creeds of *Ahl al-Kitāb*, especially the Christians", owe their origins in "the pagan creeds" of India, Ancient Egypt and those of the Greeks which all seeped into Paul's teachings, and those of the Sacred Councils later".[267]

Interestingly, Muslim exegetes of the age of piety seem to have disregarded Q9:29-35 in their exegesis.[268] However, as McAuliffe points out, when Quṭb adopted the idea of "the new *jāhiliyya*", just like Ibn Kathīr and Ibn Taymiyya before him, "he spends little time reproducing the exegetical insights that accumulated during the centuries of medieval *tafsīr*" in his commentary on the Qur'an.[269] Had he established an "average expectable continuity with Ibn 'Arabi, he would have read into 9:31 that God commanded "to worship but one God".[270] As Ibn 'Arabi puts it,

> The mistake of him who associates others with God is that he devises for himself an original form of worship which *God did not set down for him in a Law,* so *he worships something that he has created.*[271]

In ending this discussion, I find it particularly important to point out here that Quṭb came to associate Wilfred C. Smith with Nasser's "project to destroy Islam [i.e. Quṭb] by isolating the Muslim Brotherhood movement".[272] According to 'Alī 'Ashmāwī, Quṭb identified the Chief Rabbi in Egypt, Ḥayyim Nahum, (known for his anti-Zionist stance throughout his tenure in office (1924-60)[273]), as being part of the plan to destroy Islam which started, according to him, when Rabbi Nahum immigrated to Egypt at the end of the 19th century after supervising efforts to destroy Islam in Turkey and preparing the ground for the Ataturk movement.[274]

Egypt's revolution, according to Quṭb, was orchestrated by the Zionists and the Americans who both worked out an agreement with Nasser during the Fālūja siege in Palestine;[275] Nasser then followed Wilfred C. Smith's directives to turn Egypt to an industrial society which forfeits religion. The spread of socialism and industrialisation is part of an American-Zionist plan which is in accord with what the Jews state in the Talmud.[276] Reflecting possible influence by Martin Luther[277] and the German sociologist, Werner Sombart (1865-1941),[278] Quṭb makes the claim that the Talmud promises to corrupt the goyim (*al-umammiyūn*) so as to turn them into asses that they can ride...".[279]

Interestingly, Quṭb seems to have consulted the Old Testament to illuminate the word '*umiyyūn*' (illiterate) in his commentary on Q62:2 in *Ẓilāl*, as distinct from the word '*umammiyūn*' which, he explains, stands for the word 'goyim' which signifies the word '*umam*' (plural for *umma*, for nation in Hebrew). Although Quṭb argues that the Jews perceived of themselves as "the chosen people" (*sha'b Allah al-mukhtār*) in relation to 'other' '*umam*' (nations),[280]he did not make in his commentary on this verse reference to derogatory views expressed in the Talmud of '*al-umammiyūn*', as 'asses'. Like 'Abduh, and Mujāhid, Quṭb avoided, as well, a literal reading of Q62:5 which likens Jews to asses, while refraining, like 'Abduh, to establish "an average expectable continuity" with Mujāhid, or *any* exegetes of the Islamic age of piety.[281]

4. Conclusion

Although the idea of *jāhiliyya* is of a fairly late occurrence in Quṭb's discourse, Shepard rightly points out that "a path of development toward it can be traced earlier". According to Shepard, "the distinction East-West is a kind of precursor to the distinction Islam-*jāhiliyya*".[282] As discussed in chapters 3 and 4 above, however, Quṭb constructed two different sets of "East": one cultural in his encounter with the Francophile Ṭaha Ḥusayn in 1939, and one spiritual, five years later, as he deprecated Fawzī and his English co-traveller where we see him emphasising the matter-spirit duality.

In section 1 above, it is plainly the case that, in the first instance, when Quṭb made use of the word '*jāhiliyya*' in 1951, he highlighted the stark difference between the 'spirit' of Islam and the 'material' spirit of modern-day *jāhiliyya,* in the same way that he made use of 'the matter of the West' and 'the spirit of the East' duality in *Kutub wa Shakhṣiyyāt;* only in the last instance, Quṭb seemed to have been particularly drawn to Hindu and Buddhist traditions.

In 1951, however, one sees that the 'spirit' of Islam is depicted as an objectified idea in the making, which is detached from all of the Islamic 'cumulative traditions': one blending together Christianity, as formed by the Church in Rome, and communism/ Marxism with the view of perfecting them. Although Islam is considered in this instance as an antonym of *jāhiliyya,* Quṭb had clearly been attracted especially to Pauline Christianity and to communism/Marxism. It is also the case that he also accepted that all of humanity, except perhaps the primitive Americans, is undergoing a stage of "first evolution/refinement" (*ḥalat al-irtiqā' al-ūla*) and has moved away from the state of "first barbarism" (*al-barbariya al-ūla*). In creating a spectrum, which places Buddhism, Hinduism, and Judaism at a lesser level of refinement than Christianity which, he argues, did not "fear" these three "nationalist religions", while it feared Islam, it is arguably the case that Quṭb is revealing a heightened level of anxiety in relation to new movements in the Christian West, such as the Theosophical movement, which sought spirituality in the "East" while criticising Islam as an "ossified" religion of an alien "other/outsider".

As discussed in chapter 4, it is clearly the case that Quṭb was particularly threatened by the ascendency of the Jews in Palestine. To describe Islam as "a creed of haughtiness" (*'aqīdat isti'la'*), at a time when he was obviously made aware of what Nettler describes as "Islam's long slide into unprecedented eclipse" in the modern age,[283] is particularly indicative of the level of disquiet which he must have experienced following the partitioning of Palestine in 1948.

Although Quṭb had described the issue of Palestine in 1946 as being "the pivot in the struggle between the resurgent East and the barbaric West,[284] it is clearly the case that he depended on the impartiality of both Arnold and Gibb, as two "*Christian European men*", to affirm "Islam's absolute tolerance and justice (in dealing with non-Muslims)". One can certainly not underestimate the level of anxiety which was generated by Gibb's approval of Iqbal and 'Abduh, on the one hand, and of theology, on the other, in *Modern Trends in Islam* when Quṭb wrote *Khaṣṣā'iṣ* and accused both Iqbal and 'Abduh of falling in a state of *jāhiliyya.*

I, therefore, find it important to emphasise that Quṭb's commentary on Q9: 29-35 in *Ẓilāl* is hardly indicative of his attitude towards Christianity, as per Robinson's study, especially given the fact that he clearly admired Christianity in general, albeit it is the French Catholic scientist, Alexis Carrel, who becomes the quintessential Christian in the early 1960s, instead of Tolstoy of the 'East' in the mid-1940s.

Although Haddad's analysis of *Ẓilāl* reveals that Quṭb's interpretation of the Qur'an contains long sections on Christians and Jews with both peoples being treated in some sections as 'the West' that has striven for centuries to undermine Islam,[285] the examples that she gives betray a heightened level of anxiety on the part of Quṭb in relation to the Orientalists in particular, as he succumbs to the idea of a conspiracy involving Orientalists, on the one hand, as well as Christians, Jews and Communists, on the other. Haddad points out, for instance, that Quṭb sees in his commentary on *sura* II, *al-Baqara*, a warning that "the true goal of the People of the Book, whether Jews or Christians ...is to lead Muslims astray from their religion to the religion of the People of the Book," adding that Quṭb warned Muslims to guard against "the opinions of the Orientalists (of Jews, Christians and unbelieving communists) in the matters of our religion".[286]

As discussed above, it is clearly the case that one can discern that, only *after* becoming acquainted with Smith's work *Islam in Modern Trends,* Quṭb finally associates the Jews with Orientalism, and Christianity in the West, and launches an attack in his commentary on *al-Tawba* in *Ẓilāl* on "the corrupt creeds of *Ahl al-Kitāb*, especially the Christians", which, he claims, owe their origins in "the pagan creeds" of India, Ancient Egypt and those of the Greeks which all seeped into Paul's teachings". At this point, even India of the idealised spiritual 'East', has fallen in *jāhiliyya.*

One must not also disregard the fact that, it was in reading Will Durant that Quṭb seems to have been particularly threatened in *Muqawwimāt* by 'the Jew', Bergson, specifically, as he developed an acute awareness of a Jewish "plan to dissolve the acrimony which built against the Jews in the world of Christendom", and by the Jews' claim that Jesus was "a great Jew". It is my contention that, at least in part, in learning firstly of Gibb's, and later of Smith's approval of Bergson, and of Islamic theology, that Quṭb becomes finally aware of scholarship in the Christian West, which accepted 'Abduh, and Iqbal, but did not recognise his own omnipotence. Hence, I conjecture, the culmination of Quṭb's otherness formulations depicting the Christian West as a '*jāhiliyya*'.

Finally, it is my contention that Quṭb did not affirm himself against "the other" "Chosen" Jewish pseudo-species, despite his apparent expressed apprehension in relation to Ezra, until his open confrontation with Nasser in *Ma'ālim.* As discussed above, I find that Quṭb did not produce the essentialist Jew in any of his writings, except in *Ẓilāl* which suggests that Quṭb's younger brother, Muḥammad, was probably involved in the final revision of this work, as he assumed the role of being "the primary custodian and official interpreter of his older brother's legacy,"[287] even before relocating to Saudi Arabia one year following his release from prison in Egypt in 1973. According to Calvert, Muḥammad Quṭb was quick "to accommodate his brother's thought with the generally apolitical discourse of the Wahhābi shaykhs' upon relocating to Saudi Arabia in 1974.[288]

I surmise that it is evidently the case that Muḥammad's "three Jews" – Durkheim, Marx, and Freud – are hardly Sayyid's "three Jews". The argumentation in Quṭb's later writings is rather built against "two Jews": first Ezra and later Bergson, and to a certain extent Marx. Yet, from having a special affinity with the Jews, and the Jewish *religion* in 1939, Quṭb seems to have developed a phobia, not only in relation to the CIA, but also in relation to the "Jew", which must have been exasperated after becoming aware of Wilfred C. Smith's scholarship which dismissed him as an Islamist ideologue.

In conclusion, I find that Quṭb's perception of the challenge which was posed by Orientalism in general, and Wilfred C. Smith in particular, to his own 'omnipotence', as an ideologue, was of such magnitude that the otherness formulations targeting humanity at large in his commentary on Q9: 29-35 go much further than the views he expressed earlier on in the radical stage of his life. To be certain, the condemnation of *Ahl al-Kitāb*, especially the Christians", in *Ẓilāl* as corrupt creeds, which owe their origins in "the pagan creeds" of India, Ancient Egypt and those of the Greeks which all seeped into Paul's teachings, mark a serious departure from Quṭb's clear attraction to Western Christianity. Unlike Quṭb, who objectified Islam as an "idea" and a "*manhaj*", as Wilfred C. Smith points out in *The Meaning and End of Religion*,

> The classical Hindus developed religious ideals and practices in richer profusion and subtler intellectual depth with more insistent emphasis and more refined analysis earlier than any other people...the religious vocabulary of classical Sanskrit is probably the subtlest and most elaborate that man has ever devised... the ancient Egyptians and the medieval West, were well able to be religious without reifying.[289]

Quṭb's own ancestors, who probably converted to Islam from the Hindu traditions, adopted Islam, like many early Hindu converts to Islam, by being "presented Islam as the crowning phase of Hinduism: the Qur'an was presented as the final Veda, completing previous revelations".[290]

Conclusion: Quṭb's Islamism as a Drastic Discontinuity with the Islamic "Cumulative Traditions" of the Past

Throughout this study, I have made an attempt to illuminate Quṭb's otherness formulations targeting the West with the view of placing him in both his immediate cultural-historical context and the broader context of "the cumulative traditions" of the Islamic age of piety. In concluding this study, I find that Quṭb's works mark a severe disruption, and a drastic discontinuity with the Islamic age of piety. In fact, as discussed throughout this study, Quṭb had attempted, as early as the late 1920s, to purposefully deconstruct all vestiges of the Arab and Islamic past.

In many ways, I find that Quṭb's life and thought best exemplify the transition from what Wilfred C. Smith describes in *Islam in Modern History* as "the massive certainties of the nineteenth century" to "the bewildering complexity [and I might add the uncertainties] of the twentieth".[1] Perhaps it is fitting here to draw a comparison between the Azharite Rifa'a al-Ṭahṭāwi (1801-73), who recognised that the West has the merit of "justice, truthfulness, equity" in the first part of the nineteenth century, and the next generation of Muslim reformers – including Jamal al-Dīn al-Afghāni (1839-97) and Muḥammad 'Abduh (1849-1905) – who "borrowed eclectically" and claimed for Islam Western concepts – such as liberty, individualism, and social contract.[2]

As discussed in chapter 1, al-Ṭahṭāwi, like many of his generation, came into contact with Western civilisation through being a member of one of Muḥammad 'Ali's (r. 1805-48) first scholastic missions to Paris between 1826-31.[3] Dodge notes that during Muḥammad 'Ali's rule, the first group of a hundred young men to enter the medical school and many candidates for other forms of higher education were recruited from the student body of al-Azhar.[4]

During the rule of Khedive Ismā'īl (r. 1863-79), there was an attempt to revive some of the projects which were started by Muḥammad 'Ali. It was in this period that Dār al-'Ulūm was founded in 1872[5]with the view of modernising education. As discussed earlier, Dār al-'Ulūm was hardly a modern institution. It counted among its graduates both al-Banna and Quṭb. However, while the former appreciated the "soft landing", into the world of Cairo, afforded to "would-be *effendis*" at Dār al-'Ulūm by its "hybrid type" of education,[6] the latter was, as Ṭaha Ḥusayn put it, "uncomfortably suspended" between the old knowledge and the new, "ill-prepared to teach either".[7]

In 1879, the rule of Khedive Ismāʿīl came to an end as he was forced into exile by a despotic Sultan and a group of European creditors.[8] The European Debt Commission which was established then would take more than half of Egypt's government revenues in 1880. Government cutbacks for the army, schools, public works, and essential maintenance followed.[9] Following the occupation of Egypt by British troops in 1882, the British government appointed Sir Evelyn Baring, later called Lord Cromer, as its Consular General in Cairo. He remained in office for twenty-four years until 1907, and gradually became the de facto governor of Egypt.[10]

Although Quṭb conferred a quality of "scientific refinement" (*al-ruqay al-ʿilmī*) on al-Azhar in his memoirs in 1946,[11] it is clearly the case that he became particularly threatened in the early stage of his Islamist career by the then some one-thousand year old institution which was founded in 970,[12] especially as he became aware in June 1952 of America's attempt to manipulate Islam to ward off the danger of communism. He, however, remained silent about the covert US propaganda program, which was headed by the CIA during the presidency of President Eisenhower, and brought over three dozen Islamic scholars and civic leaders in 1953 for what was officially an academic conference at Princeton University to promote an anti-communist agenda in the Islamic world.

In *Khaṣāʾiṣ* (1962), it becomes only too apparent that Quṭb harboured an open animosity against all forms of theology as he became increasingly aware of the centrality of ʿAbduh's reform movement in Western studies, especially Gibb's, and probably associated ʿAbduh as well with the Nasserite project. Significantly, Cromer deserves a mention in Quṭb's commentary on *sura* IX, *al-Tawba*, in *Ẓilāl*, as one of "the Crusaders" who was in favour of ʿAbduh's libertarian school, and its disciples, who called for borrowing freely whatever they deemed suitable from European ideas, such as democracy and freedom, which, he argues, were alien ideas in relation to the Islamic "*manhaj*".[13]

Although Quṭb showed much antagonism to the ideas of democracy and freedom at this later stage of his life, it is clearly the case that in the early Islamist stage of his life, before his encounter with America as a neo-colonialist power in the early 1950s, and its lust for oil, he showed himself very much in favour of the liberal and egalitarian ethos of the French Revolution by claiming them to Islam. Quṭb even goes as far as alleging that the French Revolution's ideas of "liberty, equality and fraternity" originated from the Islamic "idea" in Andalusia,[14] although he had placed not only, the Andalusian Ibn Rushd (Averroes), but also Ibn Sinā (Avicenna) and al-Farābī on the outside of the crucial outside-inside division in his first Islamist work, *al-ʿAdāla*, following his dispute with the literati in general, and the Aristotelian al-ʿAqqād in particular in the late 1940s.[15]

As discussed in chapter 2, Quṭb's literary career, as a poet, unfolds in his dispute with Ṭaha Ḥusayn as early as 1932 when he was made aware of Ḥusayn's criticism of the literary aptitude of the younger generation of poets in comparison with the generation of poets - including the likes of the Francophile humanist Aḥmad Shawqī (d. 1932), Ḥāfiẓ (d. 1932), and Khalīl Muṭrān (1872-1949) - and in prose Haykal, al-Māzinī and al-'Aqqād.[16] It is, however, ultimately against the backdrop of the humanist trends of thought that those who obtained a French education were to form, especially Shawqī and Ḥusayn, that we see Quṭb's animosity to the West firstly unfolding.

Consequently, we have seen Quṭb engaging in the 1930s in fierce battles, not only against the conservative Musṭafa Ṣādiq al-Rāfi'ī (1880-1937), but also against Shawqī's neo-classicist School in his attempt to champion the case of his mentor, al-'Aqqād, and ultimately his own as he attempts to secure "a niche" for himself as a poet. In *Kutub wa Shakhṣiyyāt* (1946), it becomes only too apparent that Quṭb harboured an antagonistic attitude to the classical age of Islam as he welcomed the Diwān School's efforts to demolish classical Arabic literature. Following his fallout with al-'Aqqād, he went further by calling for establishing a *new* school to appraise poetry.

In his dispute with Ṭaha Ḥusayn over his work *Mustaqbal al-Thaqāfa fī Miṣr* (1938) in 1939, Quṭb, however, comes to accept the Greek component of the Mediterranean European culture, which he associated with Ḥusayn, as the culture of "*al-khāṣa*" (the elect few, as opposed to *al-'Āma* for the commoners/the laymen), while revealing an early admiration for the Torah over the Gospel, which he confirms in *al-Taṣwīr al-Fannī fī al-Qur'ān* (1945). In the same work, Quṭb accepts previous monotheistic traditions by making reference to "the Jewish and Christian learned men" (*aḥbār al-yahūd wa al-naṣāra*) who were encountered by Muḥammad. He, however, seems to be unaware that the word "*aḥbār*" is a loan word which was borrowed from Hebrew for "learned doctors",[17] and that, furthermore, no less than the Prophet's cousin and "the father of exegesis", 'Abd Allah ibn 'Abbās (d. ca. 68/686), and the early commentators of the second/eighth century, (who appear to have been particularly problematic for Quṭb as he adopts the *jāhiliyya* doctrine in *Ẓilāl*), recognised the presence of foreign words in the Qur'ān.[18]

As a literary critic, it is clearly the case that Quṭb affirmed himself in his wrangle with Egypt's academia, *against* both 'Abd al-Qāhir al-Jurjānī (d. 1079) and al-Zamakhsharī (d. 1143), and ended up calling in *al-Taṣwīr al-Fannī fī al-Qur'ān*, for applying a "*new* methodology" (*manhaj jadīd*) to study the Qur'an to uncover "the artistic imagery" (*al-taṣwīr al-fannī*) which, according to him, evaded all past philologists throughout Islam's entire history.[19] In *al-Naqd al-Adabī* (1947), following the culmination of his dispute with the literati, and the academic community, Quṭb shows himself to be particularly antagonistic to the rhetorician Qudāma Ibn Ja'far (d. 922), who is chiefly known for his contribution to systematic criticism in the early days of Islam, for being influenced by Aristotle's theory on "virtue" (*al-faḍīla*) and Galen's opinions on "ethics" (*al-akhlāq*).

In chapter 3, I made the argument that Quṭb showed himself to be particularly appreciative of the "material" civilisation of Europe, and argued rather pragmatically that this should be adopted wholeheartedly from Europe. There is, however, some clear ambivalence in relation to the thought-world of Europe, when he seems to reject the ideological underpinnings of European civilisation in favour of the Islamic "idea", or "philosophy", without, however, establishing comradeship with men and women of Islamic history. In making such an argument, I have placed Quṭb's thought within the category of what Wilfred C. Smith's identifies as an apologist trend in Islamic modern history. As Smith puts it,

> The spirit of the defence against the West was strikingly westernising in so far as Islam is defended not only against Western disparagement [but] also by means of Western approval...[in a] simultaneous repulsion and attraction in relation to the West.[20]

According to Smith, this "simultaneous repulsion and attraction in relation to the West" indicates both a lack of confidence, and that "the good opinion of Europe is a matter of deep concern" to Muslim apologists.[21] Indeed, Quṭb claims the sophistication of the European in asserting himself against the "desert Arab", and the high culture of the French especially against the soulless essentialised American "other" during his sojourn in America and in the early 1950s as he first makes use of the doctrine of *jāhiliyya* and reveals that he was particularly humiliated by Truman's four point plan designed to give handouts to deprived people of the third World.

In chapter 4, I made the argument that Quṭb clearly shifted his attention from the cultural component of Western civilisation, which he identified in 1939 with the Platonic-Francophile, Ṭaha Ḥusayn, to amplifying, to an excess, an Eastern "spirit" and Western "matter" duality only some five years later. In the process of developing such a dichotomous world-view to the detriment of the materialist Western "other", it is apparent that the imaginary idealised construct of the "East", which included Japan and China in the far East in 1939, has been expanded to allow for India to represent the quintessential spiritual "East" to the detriment of both Japan and China.

Additionally, Quṭb seems to have been particularly drawn to the Hindu and the Buddhist traditions while refraining from asserting himself as a Muslim as he deprecates the Christian Europe of "matter". It is also plainly the case that Quṭb considered Islam to be more of an Arab religion which was authenticated by the Jewish and Christian "learnt men" who were encountered by Muḥammad presumably in the early Medinese period.

By 1947, it is also clearly the case that Quṭb departs from his deprecating views in 1939 of the Christian European tradition, and ends up attaching a quality of spirituality to Pauline Christianity, albeit confined within the walls of the Church. Concurrently, he attempted to minimise the role of the Jewish tradition in the history of salvation as he seems to have become particularly threatened by the ascendency of the Jews in Palestine.

For all of his clear leaning to the spirituality of the East, it is evidently the case that Quṭb was unaware, as Wilfred C. Smith argues in *The Meaning and End of Religion*, that in the "Orient" men have on the whole not used the concept "religion" for their own faith, and not even in the Christian West until "the rise of unbelief".[22] Although Quṭb shows himself to be open to the meaningfulness of the Buddhist and Hindu traditions in South East Asia, he, however, comes to make use of the word "religion" not only in relation to the Jewish and Christian traditions, but equally in relation to the Hindu and Buddhist traditions.

It is also clearly the case, that Quṭb was captivated by Nietzsche's idea of "the need for a 'new reformer' (the superman)" following "the death of God", even as he continues to avow his admiration for the Sufi Tagore of the "East", while repudiating Rūmī. He, however, failed to understand the humanist component of Nietzsche's thought, and of other Atheist humanists such as Comte, Feuerbach and Marx[23] even as he seems to accept the last in the 1950s as one of three prophets (the two others being Stalin and Lenin) of the modern world, as discussed in chapter 5, when he adopts the dehumanising doctrine of *jāhiliyya*.

In chapter 5, I have attempted to bring to the fore the clear confusion in Quṭb's thought as he first made use of the word '*jāhiliyya*' in 1951. For, even as he highlighted the stark difference between the 'spirit' of Islam and the 'material' spirit of modern-day *jāhiliyya*, Quṭb goes as far as objectifying Islam as an idea in the making, which is detached from all of the Islamic 'cumulative traditions': one which he proposes blends together Christianity, as formed by the Church in Rome, and communism/Marxism with the view of perfecting them both. Although Islam is considered in this instance as an antonym of *jāhiliyya*, Quṭb had clearly been attracted especially to Pauline Christianity and to communism/Marxism.

It is also the case that Quṭb accepted that all of humanity, except perhaps the primitive Americans, is undergoing a stage of "first evolution/refinement" (*ḥalat al-irtiqā' al-ūla*) and has moved away from the state of "first barbarism" (*al-barbariya al-ūla*). He, however, creates a spectrum, which places Buddhism, Hinduism, and Judaism at a lesser level of refinement than Christianity which, he argues, did not "fear" these three "nationalist religions", while it feared Islam. Presumably, Quṭb is inferring that the object Islam is as refined as Christianity in the West. I have also argued that it is arguably the case that Quṭb is revealing a heightened level of anxiety in relation to new movements in the Christian West, such as the Theosophical movement, which sought spirituality in the "East" while criticising Islam as an "ossified" religion of an alien "other/outsider".

I have also argued that it is clearly the case that Quṭb was particularly threatened by the ascendency of the Jews in Palestine as he comes to describe Islam as "a creed of haughtiness" (*'aqīdat isti'la'*), at a time when he was obviously made aware of what Nettler describes as "Islam's long slide into unprecedented eclipse" in the modern age[24] especially following the partitioning of Palestine in 1948.

Although Quṭb is said to have been in accord with Britain's 1939 White Paper which guaranteed a majority Arab population in Palestine,[25] he clearly came to describe the issue of Palestine in 1946 as being "the pivot in the struggle between the resurgent East and the "barbaric West".[26] Regardless of his criticism of the "barbaric West" in relation to the issue of Palestine, it is clearly the case that he depended on the impartiality of both Arnold and Gibb, as two "*Christian European men*", to affirm "Islam's absolute tolerance and justice (in dealing with non-Muslims)". (Eventually, all four schools of Sunni jurisprudence, including that of Quṭb's favourite, the paragon of freedom and tolerance, Abu Ḥanīfa, are repudiated by Quṭb, as he switches the stress in his discourse from *Fiqh* to *shari'a* in his later writings.)

In making such an argument, I made the point that one can hardly underestimate the level of anxiety which was generated by Gibb's approval of Iqbal and 'Abduh, on the one hand, and of theology, on the other, in *Modern Trends in Islam* when Quṭb wrote *Khaṣṣā'iṣ* and accused both Iqbal and 'Abduh of falling in a state of *jāhiliyya.*

I also emphasised the point that Quṭb's commentary on Q9: 29-35 in *Ẓilāl* is hardly indicative of his attitude towards Christianity, as per Robinson's study, especially given the fact that he clearly admired Christianity in general, albeit it is the French Catholic scientist, Alexis Carrel, who becomes the quintessential Christian in the early 1960s, instead of Tolstoy of the 'East' in the mid-1940s.

I have also made the argument that Quṭb's discourse in the 1960s betrays a heightened level of anxiety in relation to the Orientalists in particular, as he succumbs to the idea of a conspiracy involving Orientalists, on the one hand, as well as Christians, Jews and Communists, on the other, especially as he familiarises himself with Smith's work *Islam in Modern Trends.* Finally, Quṭb deconstructs his own earlier thought in his commentary on *al-Tawba* in *Ẓilāl* on "the corrupt creeds of *Ahl al-Kitāb*, especially the Christians", which, he claims, owe their origins in "the pagan creeds" of India, Ancient Egypt and those of the Greeks which all seeped into Paul's teachings".

Additionally, I have made the argument that it was only in reading Will Durant that Quṭb seems to have developed a heightened level of anxiety in relation specifically to the modern-day "Jew", Henri Bergson, as he reveals in *Muqawwimāt.* It is in the aforementioned work that Quṭb reveals that he developed an acute awareness of a Jewish "plan to dissolve the acrimony which built against the Jews in the world of Christendom", and that he became threatened by the Jews' claim that Jesus was "a great Jew". It is further my contention that, at least in part, in learning firstly of Gibb's, and later of Smith's approval of Bergson, and of Islamic theology, that Quṭb becomes finally aware of scholarship in the Christian West, which accepted 'Abduh, and Iqbal, but did not recognise his own omnipotence. Hence, I conjecture, the culmination of Quṭb's otherness formulations depicting the Christian West as a '*jāhiliyya*'.

Finally, it is my contention that Quṭb did not affirm himself against "the other" "Chosen" Jewish pseudo-species, despite his apparent expressed apprehension in relation to Ezra, until his open confrontation with Nasser in *Ma'ālim*. As discussed in chapter 5, I find that Quṭb did not produce the essentialist Jew in any of his writings, except in *Ẓilāl* which suggests that Quṭb's younger brother, Muḥammad, was probably involved in the final revision of this work, as he assumed the role of being "the primary custodian and official interpreter of his older brother's legacy",[27] even before relocating to Saudi Arabia one year following his release from prison in Egypt in 1973.

It is also my contention that much of what is assumed to be Quṭb's thought, especially in *Ẓilāl*, is a reflection of the thought of his younger brother, Muḥammad, who, according to Calvert, was quick "to accommodate his brother's thought with the generally apolitical discourse of the Wahhābi shaykhs' upon relocating to Saudi Arabia in 1974.[28] In this line of argument, I surmise that it is evidently the case that Muḥammad's "three Jews" – Durkheim, Marx, and Freud – are hardly Sayyid's "three Jews". I further put forward the view that the argumentation in Quṭb's later writings is rather built against "two Jews": first Ezra and later Bergson, and, to a certain extent, Marx.

It is also the case that Quṭb seems to have developed a phobia, not only in relation to the CIA, but also in relation to the "Jew", which must have been exasperated after becoming aware of Wilfred C. Smith's scholarship which dismissed him as an Islamist ideologue. Furthermore, I find that Quṭb's perception of the challenge which was posed by Orientalism in general, and Wilfred C. Smith in particular, to his own 'omnipotence', as an ideologue, was of such magnitude that the otherness formulations targeting humanity at large in his commentary on Q9: 29-35 go much further than the views he expressed earlier on in the radical stage of his life. To be certain, the condemnation of *Ahl al-Kitāb*, especially the Christians", in *Ẓilāl* as corrupt creeds, which owe their origins in "the pagan creeds" of India, Ancient Egypt and those of the Greeks which all seeped into Paul's teachings, mark a serious departure from Quṭb's clear attraction to Western Christianity.

Clearly, as Wilfred C. Smith points out in *The Meaning and End of Religion*,

> The classical Hindus developed religious ideals and practices in richer profusion and subtler intellectual depth with more insistent emphasis and more refined analysis earlier than any other people...the religious vocabulary of classical Sanskrit is probably the subtlest and most elaborate that man has ever devised...

> the ancient Egyptians and the medieval West, were well able to be religious without reifying.[29]

Not only did Quṭb seem to be unaware that the early Hindu converts to Islam converted to Islam by being "presented Islam as the crowning phase of Hinduism", and that the Qur'an was presented as "the final Veda, completing previous revelations",[30] but he was also dismissive in his *jāhiliyya* discourse of the fact that the foreign vocabulary in the Qur'an reveals an assumption of previous cultures and revelations. In fact, as Quṭb was certainly aware, Müller's translation of Sanskrit texts clearly indicated the existence of some parallelism in the myths of the "Flood" in Genesis, on the one hand, and similar mythologies in ancient Greece, Mexico, Babylonia, and Asia minor, on the other.

Clearly, Quṭb subscribed to the "big-bang outlook" which, again, marks him out as an Islamist ideologue who was clearly on the outside of the crucial inside-outside division in relation to Islam's humanist traditions of the past.

Notes

Introduction

1 Fareed Zakaria. "The Politics of Rage: Why Do They Hate Us?" *Newsweek,* 22 August 2007 (accessed 17 December 2011), http://www.fareedzakaria.com/ARTICLES/newsweek/101501_why.html; Mohsin Hamid. "Why Do They Hate Us?" *The Washington Post,* 22 July 2007 (accessed 17 December 2011), http://www.washingtonpost.com/wp-dyn/content/article/2007/07/20/AR2007072001806.html?nav=rss_opinions/outlook?nav=slate; Peter Ford. "Why Do They Hate Us?" *The Christian Science Monitor,* 27 September 2001 (accessed 17 December 2011), http://www.csmonitor.com/2001/0927/p1s1-wogi.html; Jacob G. Hornberger. "Why do They Hate Us?" *Freedom Daily,* 9 August 2006 (accessed 17 December 2011), http://www.fff.org/comment/com0608c.asp

2 Bernard Lewis explains reports of the jubilation of the crowds on the streets of cities in both the Arab and the Islamic countries in the aftermath of the 9/11 attacks as one which was partially due to sheer "envy". See Bernard Lewis, 2003a. *The Crisis of Islam: Holy War and Unholy Terror.* London: Weidenfeld & Nicholson: 120.

3 All hijackers were in their mid-twenties with the exception of Wa'il al-Shehri, 33, and the Egyptian ring leader Muḥammad 'Aṭṭa who was aged thirty six at the time of the attacks. For further information on the hijackers' background, see Lawrence Wright, 2006. *The Looming Tower: Al-Qaeda and the Road to 9/11.* New York: Vintage Books, 394-6; Jason Burke, 2004. *Al-Qaeda.* London: Penguin Books, 237-253; see also http://news.bbc.co.uk/1/hi/world/americas/1567815.stm (accessed 17 December 2011).

4 The comment was made by Said in the course of a debate between him and Lewis which was organised by the American Middle East Studies Association in 1986 & cited in Robert Irwin, 2007 [2006]. *For Lust of Knowing; the Orientalists and their Enemies.* London: Penguin Books, 302.

5 http://www.military-quotes.com/george-bush.htm (accessed 17 December 2011).

6 http://www.quotationspage.com/quotes/George_W._Bush/ (accessed 17 December 2011).

7 Ibid (Bush committed to democratic values, liberty, and justice, admitting that the US had long tolerated oppression in the Middle East in the name of stability).

8 Ṭahir 'Abbās, 2007. *Islamic Political Radicalism: a European Perspective* in T. 'Abbās (ed.), Edinburgh: Edinburgh University Press, xiii.

9 Peter Baker. "Obama's War Over Terror". *The New York Times Magazine,* January 4, 2010, see http://www.nytimes.com/2010/01/17/magazine/17Terror-t.html?pagewanted=all&_r=0 (accessed 30 August, 2013).

10 Kan'an Makkia & Ḥasan Munaymina. "Ghazuwwat al-*Ḥādī ‹Ashr min Aylūl fi Qira›a li Wathīqa Tu›ahil Qurā'uha al-Khaṭ*iffīn li al-Mawt" (The September 11 Raid: a Reading of a Document Preparing its Readers, the Hijackers, for Death). *Al-Ḥayat,* January 4, 2002; See also http://www.guardian.co.uk/world/2001/sep/30/terrorism.september113 (accessed 17 December 2011).

11 Ziauddin Sardar. "Why do They Hate Us?" *New Statesman*, 4 October, 2004 (accessed 17 December 2011) http://www.newstatesman.com/200410040042.

12 Quṭb is credited by Ayman al-Ẓawahiri, al-Qa'ida's network second-in-command in 2001, for being behind the formation of the "nucleus of the *jihad* movement", see Ayman al-Ẓawāhiri, 2001, "Fursān taḥt Rayit al-Nabī" (Knights Under the Prophet's Banner), *Asharq al-Awsat*, (8407), December 4, 2001. He is also said to have inspired Bin Laden, see Robert Irwin. "Is this the Man who Inspired Bin Laden?" *The Guardian*, November 1, 2001 in http://www.guardian.co.uk/world/2001/nov/01/afghanistan.terrorism3 (accessed 17 December 2011).

13 Albert J. Bergesen, 2008. *The Sayyid Quṭb Reader: Selected Writings on Politics, Religion and Society*. New York: Routledge, 164n2.

14 Edward J. Lifton, 2007. "A Clinical Psychology Perspective on Radical Islamic Youth" in T. Abbās (ed.) *Islamic Political Radicalism: a European Perspective*. Edinburgh: Edinburgh University Press, 29.

15 Ibid: 29-30.

16 See http://www.youtube.com/watch?v=1mXnbgsg9DM (accessed April 8th, 2013); see also http://www.youtube.com/watch?v=KFyNPOstbhU (accessed 3 April, 2013).

17 *Ẓilāl*, I:77 & ibid II: 926.

18 Richard P. Mitchell, 1993 [1969]. *The Society of the Muslim Brothers*. New York: Oxford University Press, 23.

19 See http://www.waqfeya.com/book.php?bid=786 (accessed September 11, 2013).

20 Ian Buruma & Avishai Margalit, 2004. *Occidentalism: The West in the Eyes of its Enemies*. New York: the Penguin Press, 101-2.

21 Ibid: 122.

22 Smith remarks on the use of Islam as a "system of life" (Niẓām-l Ḥayat) by Mawdūdī as part of a modern trend towards systematization in the Islamic world in the early part of the twentieth century, see Wilfred C. Smith, 1964. *The Meaning and End of Religion*. New York: Mentor Books, 271n10.

23 Nazih Ayubi, 1991. *Political Islam: Religion and Politics in the Arab World*. London: Routledge, 123.

24 Of particular importance in this context is Lenn E. Goodman's study *Islamic Humanism* (2003); Moḥamed Arkoun's study *Humanisme et Islam: Combats et Propositions* (2005) and his article «The Vicissitudes of Ethics in Islamic Thought" in Stephan Reichmuth, Jörn Rüsen, Aladdin Sarhan (eds.) *Humanism and Muslim Culture: Historical Heritage and Contemporary Challenges*. National Taiwan University Press, 61-86; see also Joel Krämer 's study *Humanism in the Renaissance of Islam: the Cultural Revival during the Buyid Age* 1992 [1986]; George Makdisi's work *The Rise of Humanism in Classical Islam and the Christian West: with Special Reference to Scholasticism* (1990); see also works by Louis Gardet including *La Pensée Religieuse d'Avicenne*,(1951), *La Conaissance Mystique Chez Ibn Sinā et ses Présupposés Philosophiques* (1952),, *Expériences Mystiques en Terres non-Chrétienne* (1953), *Les Hommes de L'Islam, Approches des Mentalités* (1977).

25 Nettler, Ronald L, 1993. "Prophecy, Qur'an and Metaphysics" *in Ibn 'Arabī's Discussion of 'Uzayr (Ezra)* in Ronald L. Nettler (ed.) *Studies in Muslim-Jewish Relations*. Switzerland: Harwood Academic Publishers, 1993 , 94.

26 Stephan Reichmuth, Jörn Rüsen, Aladdin Sarhan, 2012. "Humanism and Muslim Culture: Historical Heritage and Contemporary Challenges". National Taiwan University Press, 17.

27 Arkoun, 2005: 74.

28 Renate Würsch, 2012. "Humanism and Mysticism – Inspirations from Islam" in Stephan Reichmuth, Jörn Rüsen, Aladdin Sarhan (eds.) *Humanism and Muslim Culture: Historical Heritage and Contemporary Challenges*. National Taiwan University Press, 90-1.

29 Ibid: 92-3 (for the quote from Schöller see Schöller "Zum Begriff des 'islamischen Humanismus'" in *Zeitschrift der Deutschen Morgenländischen Gesellschaft* (2001), pp 275-320 in ibid: 93 & 93n20).

30 The above information is based on a quotation from Schimmel's article "Mystik and Humanitāt:Aspekte der islamischen Mystik" in Geerk, Frank (ed.) *Kultur and Menschlichkeit. Neue Wege des Humanismus*, Basel: 1999, pp 261-272. See ibid: 93 & 93n21.

31 Abu al-Faḍl advocates the view that both Quṭb and the founder of the Wahhābī movement, Muḥammad Ibn 'Abdul Wahhāb (d. 1792) are to be considered ideologues of puritanical Islamic movements, see Khaled Abu al-Faḍl, 2007. *The Great Theft: Wrestling Islam from the Extremists.* New York: Harper San Francisco, 51.

32 Renate Würsch, 2012: 94-95 (there is no consensus on the humanist component in the doctrine of "the Perfect Man", see on this point Hinrich Biesterfeldt, 2012. "The Perfect Man- a Humanist?" in Reichmuth, Rüsen, Sarhan (eds.) *Humanism and Muslim Culture: Historical Heritage and Contemporary Challenges.* National Taiwan University Press, 101-113).

33 John Calvert, 2010. *Sayyid Quṭb and the Origins of Radical Islamism.* London: Hurst and Company: 295n17. Muḥammad Quṭb was offered the position of teacher of Islamic studies in Saudi Arabia in the early 1970s, see ibid: 230.

34 According to Calvert, Quṭb's younger brother was quick "to accommodate his brother's thought with the generally apolitical discourse of the Wahhābi shaykhs' upon relocating to Saudi Arabia one year following his release from prison in Egypt in 1973, see ibid: 276.

35 Nettler, 1993: 94.

36 Paul Nwyia, 1970. *Exégèse Coranique et Langage Mystique.* Beirut: Dar El-Machreq, 85.

37 On Mujāhid, otherwise known as Ibn Jabr al Makkī, and his exegesis, see Goldziher, 2006 [1920]. Schools of Koranic Commentators. Wiesbaden:Harrassowitz Verlag, 70.

38 Donald K. Swearer, 2011. "The Moral Imagination of Wilfred Cantwell Smith". *Harvard Divinity Bulletin.* Winter/spring, 39: 1 & 2 in http://www.hds.harvard.edu/news-events/harvard-divinity-bulletin/articles/the-moral-imagination-of-wilfred-cantwell-smith (accessed August 13th, 2012).

39 Angela Oswalt, "Erik Erikson and Self-Identity". http://www.sevencounties.org/poc/view_doc.php?type=doc&id=41163&cn=1310 (accessed September 6, 2013); see also Kendra Cherry, "Erik Erikson Biography (1902-1994)" . http://psychology.about.com/od/profilesofmajorthinkers/p/bio_erikson.htm (accessed September 6, 2013).

40 Sadiq J. Al-Azm makes the point that Islamist Occidentalism ,manifested itself in recent times in "the vulgar, barbarous, and spiteful Talibanish variety", see al-Azm. Orientalism, Occidenatlism, and Islamism: Keynote Address to "Orientalism and Fundamentalism in Islamic and Judaic Critique: a Conference Honouring Sadiq al-Azm" in *Comparative Studies of South Asia, Africa and the Middle East,* 2010, vol. 30, 1: 8.

41 It was the Egyptian philosopher Ḥasan Ḥanafī who first coined the term "*istighrāb*" as an Arabic equivalent for the word "Occidentalism" in 1981. See Carool Kersten, 2011. *Cosmopolitans and Heretics: New Muslin Intellectuals and the Study of Islam.* London: Hurst & Co, 156; Apart from the awkwardness of the word "*istighrāb*" which, al-Azm notes, denotes in its current usages "to find something strange, odd, queer, or far-fetched",(al-Azm, 2010, 6), it is the case, al-Azm argues, that Ḥanafī's call led to no tangible results in producing what he calls an "Orientalism in Reverse", see ibid; see also al-Azm's critique of Said's *Orientalism* in "Orientalism and Orientalism in Reverse" in A. L. Macfie (ed.) *Orientalism: a Reader.* Edinburgh University Press, 2000, 217-238.

42 Venn uses the term "Occidentalism", for instance, in relation to the coming together of the Occident. The credit goes to Foucault for picking up on the unfolding of a subjective process of opposition between the "Orient" and the "Occident" in the violent coming together of the "Occident" in Europe's Classical Age. See Couze Venn, 2000. *Occidentalism: Modernity and Subjectivity.* London: Sage Publications, 117.

43 Daniel M. Varisco, 2007. *Reading Orientalism: Said and the Unsaid.* Seattle: University of Washington, 265.

44 Ibid: 264.

45 Wilfred C. Smith, 1966 [1957]. *Islam in Modern History.* New Jersey: Princeton University Press, 116.

46 Ibid: 117.

47 Ibid: 141.

48 Ibid: 157-8.

49 Quoted in Cracknell, 2001: 16.
50 Smith, 1966 [1957]: 8n5.
51 Smith, 1964: 168.
52 Ibid: 168-9 (see on this point, Smith's *Patterns of Faith Around the World*, 1962).
53 Ibid: 175.
54 Erik H. Erikson, 1994 [1968]. *Identity, Youth and Crisis*. New York: Norton & Company: 221-2.
55 Ibid: 223-4.
56 Smith, 1966 [1957]: 60-1.
57 Ibid: 62-3 (Smith refers specifically to Haykal's *Ḥayat Muḥammad* (1935); Tawfīq al-Ḥakīm's *Muḥammad* (1936); al-'Aqqād's *'Abqariyyat Muḥammad* (ca. 1942); Ḥusayn's three-volume biography of the Prophet, *'Ala Hamish al-Sīra* (ca. 1934), see ibid: n42).
58 Erik H. Erikson, 1994 [1968]: 139.
59 Ibid: 182.
60 Ibid: 184-5.
61 Ibid.
62 Ibid: 192.
63 Arkoun, 2005: 83.
64 Erikson, 1994 [1968]: 298.
65 Ibid: 298-9.
66 Reichmuth, Rüsen, Sarhan , 2012: 14.
67 Smith, 1966 [1957]: 90.
68 Reichmuth, Rüsen, Sarhan , 2012: 22.
69 Smith, 1966 [1957]: 146.
70 Arkoun, 2005: 82.
71 Smith, 1997. *Modern Culture from a Comparative Perspective*. State University of New York Press, 130.

Chapter 1

1 Afaf L. al-Sayyid Marsot, 2007 [1984]. *A History of Egypt: from the Arab Conquest to the Present*. Cambridge: Cambridge University Press, 44.
2 Bernard Lewis, 1995b. *The Middle East: 2000 Years of History from the Rise of Christianity to the Present Day*. London: Orion Books, 276.
3 Ibid: 275.
4 Ibid: 277.
5 Ibid: 309.
6 Nasrin Rahimieh, 1990. *Oriental Responses to the West: Comparative Essays in Select Writers from the Muslim World*. Leiden: Brill, 3.
7 Bernard Lewis, 2000 [1982]. *The Muslim Discovery of Europe*. London: Phoenix Press, 172.
8 Ebrahim Moosa, 2000. "Introduction" in Fazlur Raḥman, 2000. *Revival and Reform in Islam: a Study of Islamic Fundamentalism* edited & with an introduction by Ebrahim Moosa. Oxford: One World, 26.
9 Ibid: 5.
10 Smith, 1966 [1957]: 35.
11 Ibid: 37.
12 Quṭb, 1969 [1939]. *al-Rad 'ala Mustaqbal al-Thaqāfa fī Misr*. Jeddah: al-Dār al-Sa'ūdiyya, 28.
13 Quṭb, 1993 [1964a]. *al-'Adāla al-Ijtimā'iyya fi al-Islām*. Cairo: Dār al-Shurūq, 184; see also Shepard, 1996. *Sayyid Quṭb and Islamic Activism: A translation and Critical Analysis of Social Justice in Islam*. Leiden: E.J. Brill, 281 (Note that Quṭb's use of the expression "the spirit of Islam" is reminiscent of India's Amīr 'Alī's *The Spirit of Islām* (1873), which is described by Smith as "the

greatest single work" in the liberal trend in the Muslim world, see Smith, 1966 [1957]: 62; Smith notes that the first version of this work was published as *A Critical Examination of the Life and Teachings of Mohammed*. London & Edinburgh.

14 Arkoun, 2012: 66.

15 Jacques Jomier, 1996. *Dieu et l'Homme dans le Coran*. Paris: Cerf, 33 (note that God is depicted as a ruler, in *Ma'ālim* as Quṭb adopts the doctrine of "*ḥākimiyya*" and makes reference to the "authority" (*sulṭān*) of God, see Quṭb, no date [1964b], 9).

16 Quṭb quotes in all editions of *al-'Adāla* a Ḥadīth by Muslim (d.875) and al-Nisā'ī (d.915-16) relaying the incident of Ma'iz Ibn Mālik asking the Prophet to "purify" him by stoning after committing adultery, and holds Ibn Mālik to be a symbol of the "constant alertness" of conscience, see Quṭb, 1993 [1964a]: 130-1; and see Shepard, 1996: 188 (Schacht dates the tradition of Ma'iz to the 2nd century of the Islamic calendar, see Joseph Schacht, 1979 [1950]. *The Origin of Muḥammadan Jurisprudence*. Oxford University Press, 74; this doctrine was confined to Iraq and was not adopted by the Medinese School of jurisprudence, see ibid: 106-7; on the whole, there was adherence to the maxim "restrict *ḥadd* punishments as much as possible", which was ascribed to the Prophet's Companions and "Successors", and finally to the Prophet, see ibid: 184; the general tendency to restrict *ḥadd* punishments as much as possible prevailed in Iraq from Abu Ḥanīfa onwards, see ibid: 285; Mitchell notes that the two legal minds of the Brothers' Society, Huḍaybī and 'Awda, observed in 1954 that the law imported into Egypt and Islamic societies, apart from a few exceptions, was in agreement with *shari'a*. See Mitchell, 1993 [1969]: 241 & ibid: n35; Italian law was directly adopted by Egypt in her Criminal Code of 1937, see N. J. Coulson, 1964. *A History of Islamic Law*. Edinburgh University Press, 152).

17 Arkoun, 2012: 78.

18 Ibid.

19 Würsch, 2012: 91.

20 Caroline Gaultier-Kurhan, 2005. *Mehemet Ali et la France : 1805-1849. Histoire Singulière du Napoléon de l'Orient*. Paris: Maisonneuve & Larose, 16.

21 Muḥammad Rifaat, 1964. *The Awakening of Modern Egypt*. Lahore: Premier Book House, 1.

22 Hamilton A. R. Gibb, 1926. *Arabic Literature: an Introduction*. London: Oxford University Press, 114.

23 Gaultier-Kurhan, 2005: 16.

24 Bernard Lewis, 1984a. *The Jews of Islam*. New Jersey: Princeton University Press, 64.

25 Albert Hourani, 1983 [1962]. *Arabic Thought in the Liberal Age 1798-1939*. Cambridge University Press: 51.

26 Lewis, 1984a: 64.

27 Ibid: 21.

28 Ronald L. Nettler, 1987. *Past Trials and Present Tribulations: A Muslim Fundamentalist's View of the Jews*. Oxford: Pergamon Press: 1.

29 Lewis, 1984a: 30.

30 Ibid: 14.

31 Jane D. McAuliffe, 1991. *Qur'anic Christians: An Analysis of Classical and Modern Exegesis*. Cambridge: Cambridge University Press, 127.

32 Lewis, 1984a: 65.

33 Hourani, 1983 [1962]: 68.

34 Dodge notes that Muḥammad's 'Ali's reform program included the founding of numerous secular schools and technical institutions, as well as the sending of students to Europe for study. The first group of a hundred men to enter the new medical school and many candidates for other forms of higher education were recruited from al-Azhar. It was al-Ṭahṭāwi who started the School of Languages and Translation Bureau of the government, see Bayard Dodge, 1961. *Al-Azhar: a Millennium of Muslim Learning*. Washington: The Middle East Institute, 113-4.

35 Hourani, 1983 [1962]: 75.

36 Ṭāriq al-Bishri, 1996. Al- Waḍ' *al-Qānūnī al-Mu'āṣir bayna al-Shari'a al-Islāmiyya wa al-Qānūn al-Waḍ'ī.* Cairo: Dār al-Shurūk, 43-44.
37 Bassam Tibi, 1991. *Islam and the Cultural Accommodation of Social Change.* Oxford: Westview Press, 87.
38 Lewis remarks that the rank of a full member of society in pre-modern Islamic societies was restricted to free male Muslims. Those who lacked any of these essential qualifications - that is, the slave, the woman, or the unbeliever - were not equal. See Lewis, 1984a:8 (Hurvitz provides some evidence that Ibn Ḥanbal adhered to egalitarian ethos in relation to gender. Referencing Laoust's article "Le Ḥanbalisme sous le Califat de Bagdad, 214/855-656/1258" (1959), Hurvitz argues that Ibn Ḥanbal had much respect for women, and bequeathed his granddaughters the same amount of money as he did his grandsons, see Nimrod Hurvitz,2002. *The Formation of Ḥanbalism: Piety into Power.* Oxon: Routledge, 35).
39 Pierre Cachia, 1990. *An Overview of Modern Arabic Literature.* Edinburgh University Press, 77.
40 Muḥammad A. Ḥamdūn, 1976. *Islamic Identity & the West in Contemporary Arabic Literature.* Michigan: The Temple University, 121.
41 Hourani, 1983 [1962]: 78.
42 Ayubi, 1991: 58.
43 Hourani, 1983 [1962]: 77.
44 Ibid: 82.
45 Ḥamdūn, 1976: 115.
46 Ibid: 120 (Based on an account provided by al-Kindī of Tawba Ibn Namir's term of office in Egypt (733-737) as a typical picture of the activities of the later Umayyad judges, Coulson observes that Ibn Namir's decisions, on the selling and buying of faulty slaves, embody principles of equity which are "remarkably parallel to certain notions of equity introduced into English law in late medieval times", See Coulson, 1964: 32-33; al-Ṭahṭāwī is probably invoking Q3:110 which makes reference to Muslims as being "*khayr umma*" (the best community) which was used by Quṭb. Unlike the latter, he didn't use the verse to infer that Muslims form a "pseudo-species" which distinguishes them from the rest of humankind).
47 Ibid: 131.
48 Hourani, 1983 [1962]: 122.
49 Ibid: 109 (note that al-Afghānī stayed in Egypt for eight years starting 1871 where he was secured a government pension by a minister of liberal views, Riaz Pasha. He taught a group of young men, mainly from al-Azhar, including 'Abduh and Sa'd Zaghlūl who, fifty years later was to become the leader of the Egyptian nation, what he conceived to be the true Islam: theology, jurisprudence, mysticism, and philosophy. But he taught them as well "the danger of European intervention" and the need to limit the ruler's power. Khedive Tawfiq (1879-92), perhaps under pressure from the British Consul-General, or because of fear of his influence over the educated class, deported him to India. By 1884, he was in Paris where he was joined by 'Abduh, see ibid).
50 Cachia, 1990: 3.
51 Youssef M. Choueiri, 2010 [1997]. *Islamic Fundamentalism: the Story of Islamist Movements.* London: The Tower Building 49.
52 Hourani, 1983 [1962]: 144.
53 Jacques Jomier, 1954. *Le Commentaire Coranique Du Manār: Tendances Modernes de L'Exégèse Coranique en Égypte.* Paris: Maisonneuve, 10.
54 Ibid: 44.
55 Smith, 1966 [1957]: 47 (Smith observes that, from the beginning of the eighteenth century, there was concern in Turkey about how to arrest the un-Islamic decadence of Islamic society, and how to resist the infidel encroachment on their domain. From Ibrahīm Müteferrika (1674-1745) to Namik Kemal (1840-1888) there have been representatives of the movement to proclaim that a true Islam demands a restored "glory for the empire". These two tendencies -internal reform, external defence- are "typified and fused" in al-Afghānī, see ibid).

56 Hourani, 1983 [1962]: 143.
57 Ibid: 144.
58 McAuliffe, 1991: 142.
59 McAuliffe remarks that, in the pre-modern period, commentators "exhibit virtually no concern with the contemporary context of their own work", ibid: 35.
60 Hourani, 1983 [1962]: 156.
61 Yvonne Y. Haddad, 1994. *Muḥammad 'Abduh: Pioneer of Islamic Reform* in Rahnema Ali (ed.) *Pioneers of Islamic Revival*, London: Zed Books, 30& 56-58.
62 Ibid: 44.
63 Hodgson explains that in the two centuries between the late sixteenth century and the late eighteenth century, a general cultural transformation took place in Western Europe. According to Hodgson, the convention that the beginning of modernity started a century earlier between 1450-1500 obscures certain crucial distinctions. As he sees it, the cultural transformation of Europe culminated in two more or less simultaneous events: the Industrial Revolution which transformed "the presuppositions of human production" and the kindred spirit of the French Revolution which established "unprecedented norms in human social relations". He explains further that these events did not constitute the broad transformation he had in mind but they were rather its most obvious early consequences which, along with the establishment of European world hegemony, had far-reaching consequences that were to be felt in Islamic societies. Furthermore, Hodgson took the position that the Western Transmutation, as a world event, has far-reaching effects not only among Europeans but in the world at large, see Marshall G.S. Hodgson, 1974 [1961]. *The Venture of Islam: Conscience and History in a World Civilisation: the Gunpowder Empires and Modern Times*. The University of Chicago Press, III: 176-7.
64 Ibid: 191.
65 Hourani, 1983 [1962]: 163.
66 Ibid: 324.
67 Ibid, 325 (As we shall see in chapter 5, Aḥmad Amīn became a staunch critic of European civilisation; Roded gives the example of al-'Aqqād's work *Women in the Qur'an* as an example of a tendency in modern-day Egypt to render a misogynistic interpretation of the Qur'an. See Ruth Roded, 2001-2006. "Women and the Qur'an" in *Encyclopaedia of the Qur'an*, J. D. McAuliffe (ed.), Leiden: E. J. Brill, 5: 537).
68 Cachia, 1990: 215n16.
69 Ibid: 207.
70 Ibid.
71 Nadav Safran, 1961. *Egypt in Search of Political Community: an Analysis of the Intellectual and Political Evolution of Egypt, 1804-1952*. Cambridge, Massachusetts: Harvard University Press, 161.
72 'Abduh is said to have found written Arabic in Egypt "abhorrent to good taste" and, under his patronage, Ḥusayn al-Marṣafī [ca. 1815-1890] was to take up a project to revive Arabic classics. Cachia notes the total lack of even a "veneer" of European-derived modern standards in favour of past ones in al-Marṣafī's work remarking, furthermore, that while al-Marṣafī reserved the same admiration for Arabic literary tradition spanning the pre-Islamic *jāhiliyya* era, and up till the Abbasid period, he was to treat the later taste as an "aberration" for its excessive verbal ornamentation, see Cachia, 1990: 81.
73 Jomier, 1954: 336.
74 Smith, 1966 [1957]: 55-6.
75 Ibid: 56.
76 Ibid: 45.
77 Jan-Peter Hartung, 2013. *A System of Life: Mawdūdī and the Ideologisation of Islam*. London: Hurst & Co, 77.
78 Muhammad Iqbal, 2012 [no date]. *The Reconstruction of Religious Thought in Islam* (translated as *Tajdīd al-Fikr al-Dīnī fī al-Islām*). New Delhi, Kitab Bhavan, 122 (both Iqbal's and Smith's

positive references to Waliyallāh must have unnerved Quṭb upon familiarising himself with Smith's work in 1964).

79 Michael Kreutz, 2012. "Understanding the Other: Ṭaha Ḥusayn on Reason and Individualism" in S. Reichmuth, J. Rüsen, A. Sarhan (eds.) *Humanism and Muslim Culture*. Taiwan: V & R Unipress, 131-2.

80 Ibid: 130.

81 Hourani, 1983 [1962]: 326.

82 Calvert, 2010: 195.

83 Smith, 1966 [1957]: 57-9.

84 Hourani, 1983 [1962]: 168.

85 Ibid: 167.

86 Ibid: 169.

87 Cachia, 1990: 10.

88 The comparison is made by Ḥusayn in the introduction section of his study *Étude Analytique et Critique de la Philosophie Sociale d'Ibn Khaldūn* (Paris, 1917). See Ibid & 26n29 (I find the parallelism that Ḥusayn drew between the Roman philosopher and poet Lucretius (d. ca. 50 BC) and the medieval Syrian poet al-Ma'arrī (d. 1057) most interesting on account of the former being branded an enemy of religion in the early days of Christianity, see http://plato.stanford.edu/entries/lucretius/ - accessed 10 July 2012); like al-Ma'arrī, Ḥusayn saw religion playing a positive role in society which does not necessarily contradict philosophy and reason, see Kreutz, 2012: 141).

89 Cachia, 1990: 10.

90 Ibid: 26n27.

91 For further details on Quṭb's feuds with academia, see Ahmad M. al-Badawī, 2002: *Sayyid Quṭb Naqidan* (Sayyid Quṭb the Critic). Cairo: Al-Dār al-Thaqāfiyya li al-Nashr, 127-8; On this occasion, however, Quṭb's violent attack against Khalaf Allah's study seems to be more of a lashing out at his opponents following the first publication of his study of the Qur'an *al-Taṣwwīr al-Fannī fi al-Qur'an* (1945) which received a negative reception by Cairo University's academia on account of its lack in originality. Quṭb's work is said to have been criticised by Bint al-Shāṭi', a rising literary figure at Cairo University, with the latter observing that research on the beauty of the Qur'an was covered by previous studies at the university which invited a response by Quṭb claiming that his own work was "unprecedented". Quṭb was later to launch an attack on Bint al-Shāṭi's husband, Amīn al-Khūli, who is said to have supported his wife in her criticism of Quṭb. Al-Khūli supervised and defended Khalaf Allah's controversial university dissertation *The Art of the Story in the Qur'an* (1947) in which he put forward the view that, beyond the artistic nature of the Qur'anic stories on a literary level, these lack on the side of "investigatory historical exposition". See Adnan A. Musallam, 2005. *From Secularism to Jihad: Sayyid Quṭb and the Foundations of Radical Islamism*. London: Praeger, 63.

92 Cachia, 1990: 10-11.

93 Safran, 1961: 158.

94 Ibid.

95 Quṭb's comments are made in a 1948 article and cited by al-Badawī, see al-Badawī, 2002: 127.

96 Hodgson notes that cultural revivalism in Egypt in the modern era was one which was primarily centring on an Egyptian identity which placed modernists far apart from the "Arab Bedouin". See Hodgson, 1974 [1961], III: 297; Smith remarks that "the core of Haykal's thought in the early 1920s was Pharaonism, his belief that the true 'spiritual heritage' of a modern Egyptian culture could be found in the Pharaonic era". See Charles D. Smith, 1983. *Islam and the Search for Social Order in Modern Egypt*. Albany: State University of New York Press, 89; As late as 1929, Haykal maintained views, (which bear some distinct similarities to those that Quṭb espoused), when he argued that "Islam and the Arabs were foreign elements, last of a line of invaders who had sought to erase the distinctive Egyptian Pharaonic spirit", ibid: 90.

97 Quṭb, 1996 [1932]. *Muhimmat al-Sha'ir fī al-Ḥayya wa Shi'r al-Jīl al-Ḥaḍir* (The Mission of the Poet in life and the Poetry of the Present Generation). Köln: al-Kamel, 49-50.
98 Quṭb, 1946b. *Kutub wa Shakhṣiyyat* (Books and Personalities). Cairo: Maṭba'it al-Risāla, 4.
99 Cachia, 1990: 100n43.
100 Ibid: 85.
101 Abu Rabi' argues that Quṭb did not believe in the idea of the sacredness of the so-called "Golden Age" of the Arabic language and literature, and was rather influenced by the Darwinian school of thought viewing language as a "continuously evolving organism". See Ibrahim M. Abu-Rabi', 1996. *Intellectual Origins of Islamic Resurgence in the Modern Arab World.* New York: State University of New York Press, 97.
102 Ḥusayn is said to have advocated the view in *Mustaqbal al-Thaqāfa fī Misr* (1938) of the need to submit Arabic to the natural laws of development by accepting changes in grammar and writing without however allowing for colloquial Arabic to replace its classical variant. Ḥamdūn argues that Ḥusayn's grounds were however shaken when he attempted to align Arabic with a number of dead languages including Syriac, Coptic, Latin and Greek. See Ḥamdūn, 1976: 252-3; Ḥusayn was to recognise later that the problem with attempting to introduce much-needed changes to modernise Arabic lies in the sacredness which is attached to it by theologians, Ibid: 254.
103 Safran, 1961: 166.
104 Ibid: 165.
105 Ibid (Kreutz finds that Ḥusayn's thought placed an emphasis on the "decay" of "spiritual life" in the Eastern Mediterranean in the aftermath of the failure of democracy and philosophy which he considers have been gradually replaced by autocracy and religion. See Kreutz, 2012: 140; Hourani offers a somewhat different interpretation of Ḥusayn's thought, arguing that, in spite of the religious element becoming more prominent in Ḥusayn's writings, starting the 1930s, his view of the place of religion, specifically Islam, in society remains unchanged. In Ḥusayn's words, "Religion exists to give comfort to the hearts of men, by teaching certain general 'truths' about the universe in powerful and moving symbols'... which "must be expressed anew" to conform with the change of men's minds from age to age. Hourani concludes that Ḥusayn's works must be seen as "attempts to re-tell the story of Islam in ways which will appeal to the modern Egyptian consciousness". See Hourani, 1983 [1962]: 333-34. In re-telling the story of Islam, Hourani argues, the religious symbols in Ḥusayn's works are not only restated in new terms, they are also "subtly (and perhaps not quite consciously) re-cast in order to make an appeal to minds formed by Western education. Thus, in *al-Fitna al-Kubra* (the Great Strife), Ḥusayn treats the caliphs as early revolutionaries, establishing a reign of social justice, "a middle way between socialism and capitalism, a system of social security rather like the Beveridge plan [which provided the basis for the post-World War II welfare state in the UK], a unique form of government uniting the advantages of all others, a daring and hazardous experiment which failed because it came too soon", ibid: 334).
106 Zahia R. Dajani, 1990. *Egypt and the Crisis of Islam.* New York: Peter Lang, 29.
107 Cachia, 1990: 6.
108 See n46 above.
109 The argument is made in the chapter "The Historical Reality of Islam" in all editions of *al-'Adāla* that the first two caliphs Abu Bakr and 'Umar illustrated the Islamic principles of government and that the weaknesses of 'Uthmān gave power to the Umayyads, under whom "the spirit of Islam was submerged, though it surfaced briefly under 'Umar Ibn 'Abd al-'Aziz (717-20). See Shepard, 1996: xxi.
110 Cachia, 1990: 205.
111 Safran, 1961: 211.
112 Ibid: 212.
113 Dajani, 1990: 96.

114 Safran argues that in al-'Aqqād's attempt to absolve Muḥammad of any use of violence, he was to claim that force was never used by the Prophet to impose the Islamic faith, while contradicting himself by alleging that wars against the Meccans were conducted to "eliminate obstacles in the way of spreading Islam". See Safran, 1961: 212; Al-'Aqqād, along with Haykal, was to even go further by sanctioning and defending the killing of the prisoners of war, contending that these were "notorious enemies of Islam" and that the rejoicing of Muḥammad at the sight of slaughtered enemies agrees with human nature and is, thus, "un-blameable" with al-'Aqqād having no qualms about the massacre of the Jews by Muḥammad and the enslavement of their womenfolk, see ibid.

115 In a section dedicated to biographies in *Kutub wa Shakhṣiyyāt, for i*nstance, Quṭb simply remarks that al-'Aqqād reaches a "maximum degree of maturity" in his series on genius (*'Abqariyyat*), see Quṭb, 1946b:315.

116 Musallam, 2005: 35.

Chapter 2

1 Musallam, 2005: 29.

2 Gabriel Baer, 1969. *Studies in the Social History of Modern Egypt.* The University of Chicago Press, 146 (the slave trade in Asyut continued as late as 1880; the railway line which reached Asyut in 1874 gave the development of the town further impetus. In times of famine fellahs from its vicinity flocked into it, ibid 142; in 1907 there lived in Cairo about thirty thousand people born in Asyut province; many of Cairo's porters came from Musha, ibid: 223).

3 Calvert, 2010: 298n10.

4 Quṭb is said to have revealed to the Indian scholar Abu al-Ḥasan Nadwi*(1913-99) that he owed his origin to India, and that he had wanted to visit India. See Ṣalāḥ A.al-Khaldi, 1994 [1989]. *Sayyid Quṭb min al-Milād ila al-Istishhād.* Damascus: Dār al-Qalam:29.

5 Hoffman renders the word *majdhūb* as referring to "one whose mind was taken up by God". She explains further that in Sufi circles in Egypt *al-majdhūb* is seen as someone who is more likely to perform miracles than an intellectually-oriented Gnostic, and often considered to have acquired a saintly status and to possess a strength of spirit to allow him to perform miracles, See Valerie J. Hoffman, 1995. *Sufism, Mystics, and Saints in Modern Egypt.* University of South Carolina Press: 100-1; some learned Sufi shaykhs, however, consider that these miracles, which people have come to expect, detract from sainthood, ibid, 100.

6 H. A. R. Gibb, 1970 [1949]. *Moḥammedanism.* London: Oxford University Press, 129.

7 Quṭb mentions that his father was a committee member of the National Party providing a meeting place for all the village nationalists at the family home. See Quṭb, no date [1946a]. *Ṭifl min al-Qarya* (A Child from the Village). Beirut: unknown publisher, 146.

8 Ibid: 151.

9 Ibid.

10 Ibid, 146 (Khedive 'Abbās, to whom Quṭb refers in endearing terms as "Our Effendi" in his memoirs, was known for posing a challenge to British authorities. See Calvert and Shepard (ed.), 2004. *A Child from the Village.* New York: Syracuse University Press: 145n12).

11 Arthur Goldschmidt Jr., 2004. *Modern Egypt: the Formation of a Nation-State.* Oxford: Westview Press, 64-5.

12 Ibid: 64.

13 Quṭb, no date [1946a]: 146.

14 Goldschmidt, 2004: 63.

15 Ibid.

16 Quṭb, no date [1946a]: 146.

17 Ibid: 127.

18 Ibid: 129.

19 These included, for instance, the devotional poem in praise of the Prophet *Qaṣidat al-Burda* by Muḥammad al-Buṣirī (d. 1294). See Calvert and Shepard, 2004: 143n2-3 & see Quṭb, no date [1946a]: 128. Another book which is mentioned by Quṭb relates to al-Sayyid al-Badawī (d. 1276) who is believed to be Egypt's most popular Sufi saint with his tomb in the Delta town Tanta being the focus of the largest and most celebrated Sufi *mulid* in Egypt. See Hoffman, 1995:9 & 60.

20 Quṭb, no date [1946a]: 127. (Abu Zayd, Zanātī Khalīfa, Diyab Ibn Ghanim are heroes of the romance and the tales that were built around the migration of the Banū Hilāl Bedouin Arab tribe from the Arabian desert to Tunisia via Egypt, in the tenth century; whereas, the story of al-Zīr Salim was a folk elaboration of pre-Islamic Arab battles celebrating the epic cycle of the Banū Hilāl tribe. *See* Calvert and Shepard, 2004: 143n1).

21 A handbook of prayers and invocations by al-Jazūlī (d. ca. 1465) invoking blessings over the Prophet, see Calvert and Shepard, 2004: 144n4.

22 Quṭb, no date [1946a]: 128.

23 The title of the book in question is supplied by Calvert and Shepard. See Calvert and Shepard, 2004: 144n5.

24 The translation of the title of the book is my own, with the rendition of "*al-Fatḥiyya*" as enlightening based on the root of the word *al-Fatḥ* denoting conquest normally in battle, but here it obviously indicates a literary conquest of sort.

25 Quṭb, no date [1946a]: 128.

26 Ibid: 129.

27 Ibid: 131.

28 Ibid: 140.

29 Ibid: 142.

30 Ibid: 141.

31 Ibid: 143 (according to Quṭb, this particular book was believed to have been hand-written by the Prophet (King) Solomon himself, ibid; Quṭb reveals in his commentary on the Meccan *sura* XXI, *al-Anbiyā'*, in *Ẓilāl* that he was particularly drawn to this biblical King, as well as to David, see Quṭb, 2009 [ca.1952-1965]. *Fī Ẓilāl al-Qur'ān,* IV , 2389; he also reveals a marked attraction to the Psalms of David which he must have overheard being recited in Arabic in one of Egypt's synagogues which catered to the spiritual needs of some 80,000 of Egypt's Jews, out of Egypt's population estimated at 19 million in the early 1940s. Quṭb makes reference to "moments of enlightenment" (*laḥaẓāt al-ishrāq*) which one feels in imagining David reciting his Psalms, see ibid: 2390; for information on the Jewish population see http://www.ipsnews.net/2014/04/erasure-exodus-forgotten-history-jews-egypt/ (March 5, 2014); note that David's Psalms were translated into Arabic from Hebrew by Dr Hillel Farhi (d.1940) in a book of prayers, *Siddur Farhi,* which was published in 1914 in Egypt so that his fellow Egyptian Jews can understand the text, as conveyed to me by personal email by Dr Farhi's grandson, Alain Farhi, on 8 October 2014); Dr Farhi translated also 'Umar al-Khayyām's *Rubā'iyāt* from Persian, and the Torah's six-hundred-thirteen-Commandments, in accordance to Maimonides interpretation, see Introduction in Hillel Farhi, 2003 [1914]. *Siddur Farhi*: *Daily Prayers.* New Jersey: The Farhi Foundation; on the role of Maimonides in formulating the articles of Jewish faith, see Samuel T. Lachs, 1993. *Humanism in Talmud and Midrash.* Ontario: Associated University Press, 27).

32 Ibid: 139.

33 Ibid: 142.

34 Ibid: 145.

35 Ibid: 131-2.

36 Pagan customs, such as the use of amulets, was traditionally justified by Q17:82 with many *ḥadīth* in al-Bukhārī collection, for instance, alluding to the proper use of amulets bearing Qur'anic verses, see Cathleen Malone O'Connor, 2001-2006. "Amulets" in Jane D. McAuliffe (ed.), *EOQ*, Leiden: E. J. Brill, 1: 77.

37 Ibid: 137.
38 Ibid: 136
39 Quṭb, no date [1946a]: 157.
40 Ibid: 149.
41 Hoffman renders the term *futuwwa* to designate Sufi chivalry explaining that "Sufi ethics came to be known as *futuwwa*" or "young manliness", which came to literally mean a "code of chivalry that demanded courage, self denial, and heroic generosity". See Hoffman, 1995: 229. According to Hitti, the *futuwwa* tradition flourished in the early part of the thirteenth century, when it took the form of sworn brotherhood orders, which was a sort of "knighthood of chivalry" including members known as *fityān*. See Philip. K. Hitti, 1970 [1937]. *History of the Arabs*. London: Macmillan Press, 481.
42 Calvert and Shepard relate that in the medieval period, *futuwwa* referred to brotherhoods practicing a kind of chivalry and often associated with Sufism. In modern times, the term is used to describe young men living "lives of delinquency" which, they argue, appears to be the sense used by Quṭb in the section of his memoirs which deals with "the law of the thieves". See Calvert and Shepard, 2004: 146n1.
43 Quṭb, no date [1946a]: 156-7.
44 Hoffman makes reference to Upper Egyptian songs which are recited in Sufi *dhikr* circles to celebrate the ability of "chosen young men" (as in *futuwwa*) to attain "the secret beyond the comprehension of human vision". See Hoffman, 1995: 176.
45 Calvert, 2010: 83.
46 Mitchell, 1993 [1969]: 16.
47 Rasheed El-Enany, 1993. *Naguib Maḥfouz: the Pursuit of Meaning*. London: Routledge, 149.
48 Ibid: 3.
49 Wilfred C. Smith, 2001 [1959b]. "Some Similarities and Some Differences between Christianity and Islam" in Kenneth Cracknell (ed.) *Wilfred Cantwell Smith: a Reader*. Oxford: Oneworld Publications, 61 (Smith bases this argument on the fact that a Christian is a member of a church however a Muslim is not a member of a mosque, see ibid).
50 Albert Hourani, 1991. *A History of the Arab Peoples*. London: Faber & Faber, 348.
51 See, for instance, Quṭb, 1952. "Al-Islām Niẓām Ijtimā'ī la Ta'wīdha" (Islam is a Social System, Not an Amulet, 1952) in *Ma'rakatuna ma'a al-Yahūd* (Our Battle with the Jews). Jeddah: al-Dār al-Sa'udiyya, 1970 [ca. 1965-66?], 68-70.
52 Quṭb, 1946b: 121.
53 al-Badawī, 2002: 9.
54 Quṭb dedicates a whole chapter to his "sacred" school in his memoirs. See Quṭb, no date [1946a]: 33-56.
55 Quṭb mentions in his memoirs that attending lessons on al-Zamakhsharī's exegesis by al-Azhar *'ulama* in the village was meant to make him feel "like a man", Ibid: 52.
56 Goodman, 2003: 13-14.
57 The credit goes to Hodgson for using the word "hollowness" to qualify the reforms introduced by Muḥammad 'Ali in the early part of the nineteenth century. See Hodgson, 1974 [1961], III: 218. I consider that the whole educational reforms introduced by the dynasty did not go far enough and rather centred on the form and not the core or the essence of modernity, hence the use of the word "hollowness" to qualify it.
58 Tibi, 1991: 107.
59 Ibid: 10.
60 Quṭb is said to have complained about the deficiency of foreign language instruction while he was studying in Dār al-'Ulūm, especially in relation to mastering English, which he deemed necessary for an understanding of the wider world. See Calvert, 2010: 60.
61 al-Badawī, 2002: 185.
62 Reference is made here to the group and its magazine which were founded by Dr. Yusuf Murād in the aftermath of WW II. See Shalash, 1994: 93-4. One of Quṭb's critics, the Egyptian academic

researcher Shawqī Ḍayf, lists a number of words which are verbatim reproductions of the said group's terminology. For details of these, see ibid: 94n16. Shalash, however, makes the point that the expression "the spirits of utterances" (*Arwāḥ al-alfāẓ*), which was used in Quṭb's said work, owes its origin to the French writer Guy de Maupassant (d. 1893) who is quoted by Aḥmad H. al-Zayyāt (d. 1968) in his book *Difā' 'an al-Balāgha* (In Defence of Rhetorical Style), Ibid; It is to be noted that al-Zayyāt's book was reviewed by Quṭb in 1946, and al-Zayyāt's reference to Maupassant is quoted approvingly by Quṭb, who comments that "it was high time to appreciate the value of the word in colouring artistic pictures", and went on to attack the "rationalistic school", i.e. al-'Aqqād's school), for stressing meaning, and *al-lafẓ al-dāl* (the utterance conveying significance), at the expense of neglecting the value of what he refers to as *al-lafẓ al-muṣawwir* (the utterance which gives vivid portrayals). See Quṭb, 1946b: 298.

63 Quoted in Gudrun Krämer, 2010: 12.
64 Quṭb, no date [1946a]: 150.
65 Ibid: 41.
66 Safran, 1961: 55.
67 Hourani, 1983 [1962]: 138.
68 Ibid: 336.
69 Ibid: 138.
70 Safran, 1961: 55-6.
71 Hourani, 1983 [1962]: 326.
72 Sharīf Yūnus, 1995. *Sayyid Quṭb wa al-Uṣūliyya al-Islāmiyya*. Cairo: Dār Ṭība, 26-7.
73 Quṭb, no date [1946a]: 201.
74 Ibid: 202.
75 Ibid: 206.
76 Ibid: 203.
77 Ibid.
78 Ibid: 202.
79 Quṭb recounts that his older brother was always making fun of him for running away from school, making sure to mention that he was only half a brother to him, Ibid: 33.
80 Calvert, 2010: 27.
81 Ibid: 298n14.
82 Quṭb, no date [ca.1935]. *al-Shaṭi' al-Majhūl.* Unknown publisher, 2.
83 Quṭb, no date [1946a]: 208.
84 Musallam, 2005: 35.
85 Quṭb, no date [1946a]: 207.
86 Musallam, 2005: 35 (Quṭb was ,however, to follow al-'Aqqād in distancing himself from the Wafd Party and began to support its rival, the Sa'dists (al-Sa'diyyīn) of Aḥmad Mahir and Nuqrāshī Pasha, seemingly sharing "the outrage of his countrymen" following the order given by the British ambassador, Sir Miles Lampson, which led to surrounding 'Abdīn Palace by tanks to force King Fārūq to appoint a compliant Wafdist cabinet on 4 February 1942, see Calvert, 2010: 104).
87 See, for instance, *al-Ḍamīr al-Amrikanī wa Qaḍiyyat Filisṭīn* published in 1946 in which Quṭb launches a scathing attack on the Western conscience in general, and the American conscience in particular, and makes the sweeping generalisation that all Westerners share a "putrid" conscience (*ḍamīr muta'affin*). See Quṭb, 1946. *Al-Ḍamīr al-Amrikanī wa Qaḍiyyat Filisṭīn* in *Amrīka min al-Dakhil bi-Minẓār Sayyid Quṭb*. Jeddah: Dār al-Manāra, 1987, 124-9.
88 In a poem entitled "Ila al-Bilad al-Shaqīqa", which was included in Quṭb's own mid-1930s anthology, *al-Shāṭi' al-Majhūl,* Quṭb writes that the poem was occasioned by the Palestinian revolution and its bloody events. See Quṭb, no date [ca.1935a], 195.
89 Musallam, 2005: 84.
90 Mitchell, 1993 [1969]: 22.
91 Musallam, 2005: 86.

92 Based on anecdotal evidence in Quṭb's writings, Calvert remarks that, in contrast to the close relationships Quṭb forged with his mother and siblings, his dealings with his father were mostly "formal'". See Calvert, 2010: 27. In Quṭb's dedication to his late father in *Mashahid al-Qiyama fī al-Qur'an,* Quṭb mentions that his father taught him "fear" of the Day of Judgement. See Quṭb, 1959 [1947c]. *Mashahid al-Qiyama fī al-Qur'ān.* Cairo: Dār al-Ma'ārif, 5; Quṭb also mentions in his memoirs that upon escaping from school on one occasion, his father did not even address one word to him, which left him with a feeling of "bitterness" which he felt was harder on him than the sarcasm of his older half brother, see Quṭb, no date [1946a]: 33.

93 In remarks on al-'Aqqād's eulogy of his dog Bijū in a poem under the same name, Quṭb comments on the great extent of al-'Aqqād's "paternal warm-hearted affection" which the latter feels for his dog. See Quṭb, 1946b: 102.

94 al-Khaldi, 1994 [1989]: 145.

95 Badawī, 1992: 9-29.

96 Ibid: 9.

97 Al-Rafi'ī is said to have been an "eloquent representative" of the conservative trend, engaging in bitter polemics with the modernist critics within academia, who seemed to have developed a taste for a direct, functional style in writing Arabic to agree with the modernist approach of the early part of the twentieth century, and sought to introduce changes to this end while "preserving the purity of the Arabic language and a keen interest in the literature which their forefathers had produced". See Cachia, 1990: 86.

98 One of the literary schools of the time with which al-'Aqqād's school al-Dīwan had collided, ibid: 90; both al-'Aqqād and Quṭb are said to have contributed to the journal of the Apollo group in the early 1930s. Quṭb was to champion, then, the case of al-"Aqqād against the poets of the said group, conferring on the latter the qualities of the "best poet" and the "most powerful" littérateur in Egypt and the entire East. See Aḥmad Badawī, 1992. *Sayyid Quṭb.* Cairo: al-Hay'a al-Miṣriyya al-'Āmma li al-Kitāb, 52.

99 Ibid: 67.

100 Ibid: 30.

101 Ibid: 34.

102 Quṭb's autobiography *Ṭifl min al-Qarya* (1946) is, in fact, dedicated to Ḥusayn and modelled after the latter's al-*Ayyām* (volume I, 1929). In the dedication of the work, Quṭb mentions that he hopes that "his days" will be like Ḥusayn's *Days.* Oddly enough, Quṭb fails to dedicate any of his works to al-"Aqqād.

103 Quṭb, 1996 [1932]: 6 (As early as 1900, the Lebanese poet Muṭrān is said to have espoused the view that the Arabs did not follow any known method in literary criticism. This view was to be taken up by Ḥusayn in *Ḥadīth al-Arbi'ā'* (the Wednesday Talk, 1937). See Cachia, 1990: 85 & 100n39-40; Quṭb is said to have been incensed by the Apollo group's suggestion that al-'Aqqād, among other writers, was a mere disciple of their patron Muṭrān. See Badawī, 1992: 56).

104 Ibid (Quṭb's speech in the lecture was subsequently published in book form under the title *Muhimmat al-Sha'ir fī al-Ḥayyā wa Shi'r al-Jīl al-Ḥaḍir* (The Mission of the Poet in Life and the Poetry of the Present Generation, 1932).

105 Quṭb had the opportunity to write, and get published, before he reached the age of twenty. He is also said to have worked at the Ministry of Education firstly as a teacher, and then as a cleric, before he graduated from Dār al-'Ulūm in 1933, to earn a living, see Shalash, 1994: 8.

106 Musallam, 2005: 40.

107 Ibid: 41.

108 Cachia observes that it has become common to speak of various literary schools, in the early part of the twentieth century in Egypt, giving the examples of the *Dīwan* school, which was led by al-'Aqqād and al-Māzinī, and its rival school the Apollo group. Certain standards that Western scholarship expected had to be respected by the literati. Writers were, for instance, expected to give attention to the socio-cultural background of their subjects. See Cachia, 1990: 90.

109 Quṭb, 1996 [1932]: 5.
110 Quṭb, 2003 [1947b], 9 (the adjective *muqtabasa* is used in reference to *iqtibās* (borrowing) which, according to Tawfīq al-Ḥakīm (d.1987), amounted almost to semi-authorship", quoted in Cachia, 1990: 37).
111 Quṭb, 1996 [1932]:5.
112 Ibid: 6.
113 Ibid: 13.
114 Calvert, 2010: 61.
115 Quṭb, ca.1935b: 32-7.
116 Quṭb, ca.1935c: 51-2.
117 Shalash, 1994: 98.
118 In the dedication to his brother Muḥammad in *al-Shaṭi' al-Majhūl,* Quṭb talks of his younger brother as the image of his unfulfilled hopes, see Quṭb, no date [ca.1935]: 2.
119 al-Khaldi, 1994 [1989]: 20.
120 Ibid: 28.
121 Quoted in ibid: 39.
122 Quṭb dedicates a whole section in his work *Kutub wa Shakhṣiyyat* to an appraisal of Scheherazade in Arab modern literature, comparing al-'Aqqād's poetic portrayal of Scheherazade in 1916, al-Ḥakīm's novel *Scheherazade* (1934), the depiction of Scheherazade by both Ḥusayn and al-Ḥakīm in *al-Qaṣr al-Masḥūr* (The Bewitched Palace, 1936) and Ḥusayn's novel *Aḥlam Scheherazade* (The Dreams of Scheherazade, 1942) which he compliments for its "extreme sensitivity", Quṭb, 1946b, 115-9.
123 Aḥmed S. Moussalli, 1992. *Radical Islamic Fundamentalism: the Ideological and Political Discourse of Sayyid Quṭb*. American University of Beirut, 45.
124 According to both Calvert and Musallam the novel *Ashwāk* is a reflection of a shattered love affair which was experienced by Quṭb sometime in the early part of the 1940s. See Musallam, 2005: 68 & Calvert, 2010: 108; (Based on an account by Aḥmad Amīn's son, Ḥusayn A. Amīn, who relays that Quṭb's proposal to marry a Cairene young lady, who belonged to a rich family, was rejected on account of him being "ugly", "unpleasant", and having no means or standing in society (Ḥussein A. Amin, 2007: 35), I find it more plausible that *Ashwāk* was written following this rejection; I note here that the main character in the novel, Sami, is described as someone with a distinguished standing in the literary and political circles in Cairo albeit with limited financial means, see Quṭb, 1947a: 20).
125 Abu-Rabi' argues that even though Quṭb is troubled by Ḥusayn's central thesis that the Egyptian mind has always been westernised because of the geographical proximity of Egypt to Europe in *Mustaqbal al-Thaqāfa fi Miṣr* (1938), he remains rather impressed with Ḥusayn's literary qualities and persuasive arguments concerning the state of education and culture in Egyptian society but he maintains that Greek philosophy influenced only the educated *élite* in Islam and thereafter. However, he still dismisses both Arabic and Islam while refusing, at the same time, to accept Ḥusayn's liberal orientation, see Abu-Rabi', 1996: 100-1.
126 al-Khaldi, 1994 [1989]: 215.
127 Naguib Maḥfouz, 1972 [1999]. *Mirrors* (*al-Marayā*) translated by Roger Allen. The American University in Cairo Press, 120.
128 According to El-Enany, the sketch of 'Abd al-Wahhāb Ismā'īl is the fictitious name given to Quṭb in Maḥfouz's novel al-Marayā, see El-Enany, 1993: 217n89.
129 Roger Allen, 1999. "Introduction" in Naguib Maḥfouz. *Mirrors* (translated by Roger Allen). The American University in Cairo Press: 9.
130 Maḥfouz, 1972 [1999]. 119-120.
131 In the first edition of *al-Naqd al-Adabī* (1947), Quṭb quotes approvingly a poem by the English poet E. C. Dowson (d. 1900), commemorating his love for Cynara, as an example of literary excellence. He points out that works, such as Dowson's poem, provide examples of the best ways of literary exposition, explaining further that literature which makes of other people's experiences

one's own are the most "luminous and suggestive". See Quṭb, 1947b: 57. (Reference to Dowson, and passages from his aforementioned poem, were to be subsequently removed in the 8th (2003) edition that I analysed of the work).

132 Moussalli, 1992: 23; Musallam confirms the incident and reports that al-Banna advised against a rebuttal on the grounds that it will give Quṭb's ideas more impetus. Musallam, 2005: 73-4.

133 Quṭb, 1947a: 54 (there is, however, an inconsistency in Quṭb's thought here as he talks of his "beloved Cairo" and of "beautiful life" elsewhere in the novel, see ibid: 70).

134 Ibid: 36.

135 Ibid: 39.

136 Ibid: 21.

137 Cachia, 1990: 37.

138 Quṭb, 1946b: 139-40.

139 Calvert , 2010: 69.

140 Quṭb, 1947b, 28-9 (Cachia finds that emphasis came to be placed on the significance of the poet's social and universal vision in the 1940s, with Adūnis (b. 1930), for instance, developing a view of poetry in which every innovation is tantamount to the creation of a new world. See Cachia, 1990: 103n105. Quṭb expresses similar views in the late 1940s, see Quṭb, 1947b, 16).

141 Cachia, 1990: 98.

142 Quṭb, 1996 [1932]: 49.

143 Quṭb, 1947b: 42.

144 The work reflects a striking special affinity that Quṭb seems to have developed with the literature of the East such as he found it especially in the poems of the Persian Ḥāfiẓ al-Shirazī (d. 1390) and those of the Hindu philosopher-poet Rabindrinah Tagore (1861-1941); Smith relates that Tagore visited Egypt in 1926 and that both Europeans and Egyptians were attracted to his writings at the time and points out that Haykal acknowledged Tagore's writings as influential, which might suggest that his own vision of a universal brotherhood combining Eastern "wisdom" and Western "activity" and "material" productivity may owe its origin to Tagore's writings. See Charles D. Smith, 1983, 100.

145 Calvert considers that Quṭb simply develops in the work the idea of an "integrative approach" to criticism encompassing the artistic, historical and psychological elements of the literary subject, see Calvert, 2010: 106; Musallam argues in the same vein that the work describes Quṭb's comprehensive and critical method in appraising literary works, see Musallam, 2005: 54.

146 Boullata, for instance, argues that Quṭb had gone back to the Qur'an to "understand its meaning" as early as the 1930s, see Issa J. Boullata, 2000. "Sayyid Quṭb's Literary Appreciation of the Qur'an" in Issa J. Boullata (ed.) *Literary Structures of Religious Meaning in the Qur'an*. London: Routledge, 355; Musallam also relies on a 1962 edition of the work to argue that Quṭb had inadvertently dealt with the religious qur'anic content when he wrote *al-Taṣwīr al-Fannī fī al-Qur'ān* in 1945, see Musallam, 2005: 62-3.

147 Safran, 1961: 65.

148 Cachia, 1990: 6.

149 Ibid & see ibid: 25n11.

150 Cachia makes reference here to Khālid's title *Ma'an 'ala al-Ṭarīq: Muḥammad wa al-Masīḥ* (Together on the Road: Muḥammad and the Messiah, 1958), see ibid:6 & 25n12.

151 Musallam, 2005: 95 (Musallam identifies, in addition to Quṭb, eight other founders of the journal including his younger brother, Muḥammad, Naguib Maḥfouz, Ṣādiq, Ibrāhim 'Arjun, Muḥammad al-Ghazālī, Fāyid al-'Amrusi, 'Imād al-Din 'Abd al-Ḥamid, 'Abd al-Mun'im Shumays, and Abd al-Ḥamid Juda al-Saḥḥār, see ibid: 94.

152 Quṭb, 1946b: 178.

153 See the introduction of the book for Al-Khaldi's comments about the "American danger" in Sayyid Quṭb, 1987 [late 1940s-early 50s]. *Amrīka min al-Dakhil bi-Minẓār Sayyid Quṭb*. 8.

154 Musallam 2005: 237.

155 Al-Raystūni, 1987. *Sayyid Quṭb wa Manhajuhu fi al-Tafsir*. Tit wān: Mat ba'at al-Nūr, 115.

156 Reference is made, for instance, to the 1967 war which took place one year following Quṭb's execution in 1966, see Quṭb, no date, 1970 [ca. mid-1960s?]. *"Ma'rakatuna ma'a al-Yahūd" in Ma'rakatuna ma'a al-Yahūd*. Jeddah: al-Dār al-Sa'ūdiyya, 56; reference is also made to "the three Jews: Marx, Freud and Durkheim" (page 58) which is seemingly copied from the revised last edition of *Ẓilāl* in which there is reference in the commentary on Q5:82 to a chapter entitled "The Three Jews: Marx, Freud and Durkheim" from Muḥammad Quṭb's undated work *Al-Taṭawwur wa al-Thabāt* which, I contend, was probably published following, or right before Sayyid's execution, see Quṭb, 2009 [ca. 1952]. *Fi-Ẓilāl al-Qur'ān*. Cairo: Dār al-Shurūq, II: 961n2. The editor of the work had no qualms in adding [the Christian] Sartre to the list of "The Three Jews" thus making them four instead! In fact, as we shall see later, Quṭb shows at different intervals of his life much admiration for Freud and Marx.

157 According to a leader of the Muslim Brothers' secret apparatus, 'Ali 'Ashmawī, Quṭb did not want to involve his younger brother in the militant activities of the Brothers in the final clash with Nasser in the 1960s, and told his disciples, including 'Ashmawī , that Muḥammad has another "mission" and that he was ill-equipped to carry out militant activities, see 'Ali 'Ashmawī, no date. *Al-Tarīkh al-Sirrī li-Jamā'at al-Ikhwan al-Muslimīn*. Cairo: Dār al-Hilāl, 109.

158 Musallam cites this anthology as a publication of Cairo's Maktabat Lajnat al-Shabāb al-Muslim which initially published the work in 1953, see Musallam, 2005:237.

159 See, for instance, Quṭb's reference to *ḥākimiyya* which is an idea first developed in *Ma'ālim fī al-Ṭarīq* (1964), see Quṭb, 1995 [no date]. "Muḥatim al-Ṭawaghīt" in *Dirāsāt Islāmiyya* (Islamic Studies). Cairo: Dār al-Shurūq, 17.

160 References are made, for instance, to "American Islam" in one article entitled "Islām Amrikanī" (pp. 119-123) in which there is particular concern about America as a colonialist power. In other parts of this collection, Quṭb expresses an acute anxiety relating to the dominance of the "White Man" in both Europe and America (see pp. 183-4).

161 References are made, for instance, to Quṭb's 1962 work *Khaṣṣā'iṣ al-Taṣawwur al-Islāmī wa Muqawwimatu* (page 13) and to Quṭb's more controversial 1964 work *Ma'ālim fī al-Ṭarīq* (page 35).

162 al-Raystūni, 1987:130.

163 Quṭb, 1965b. *Limādhā A'damūnī*. (Why Did They Execute Me?), 14.

164 Shepard, 1996: XVII.

165 Musallam, 2005: 162.

166 Ibid: 163 (according to Abu Rabi', Quṭb became aware of the "potential danger" of the United States as a leading world power in comparison to the waning imperialism of Western Europe following his two-year study tour in the US (1948-1950). See Abu Rabi', 1996: 133).

167 Barbara Zollner, 2007."Prison Talk: the Muslim Brotherhood's Internal Struggle during Gamal Abdel Nasser's Persecution, 1954 to 1971" in *IJMES*, 39:416.

168 Quṭb, 1965b: 17.

169 This work was initially partly serialised in the Muslim Brothers' periodical *al-Muslimūn* in the early 1950s. Quṭb is said to have completed his commentary on the Qur'an in 1959 in prison and it was then published in book form, and had gone into three editions by the late 1950s, see Shepard 1996: XVII.

170 al-Khaldi, 2000: 50-1.

171 See n31 above.

Chapter 3

1 Buruma & Margalit, 2004: 11.
2 Marshall G.S. Hodgson, 1999 [ca.1961]. "Cultural Patterning in Islamdom and the Occident" in E. Burke (ed.) *Rethinking World History: Essays on Europe, Islam and World History*. Cambridge University Press: 133.
3 'Abduh makes the argument that Islam is not against '*al-madaniyya*", but it aims to "purify it", see Muḥammad 'Abduh, no date [1993]. *al-Islām bayna al-'Ilm wa-l-Madaniyya*. Cairo: al-Hay'a al-Maṣriyya al-'Āma li-l-Kitāb, 170.
4 I am making reference here to Quṭb's rebuttal of Ḥusayn's *Mustaqbal al-Thaqāfa fī Miṣr* (1938), which was expressed in a lengthy article in the journal of *Ṣaḥifat Dār al-Ulūm* in 1939, see Musallam, 2005: 82.
5 The expression "imaginary category" is coined by Spencer in his study of Occidentalism in South Asian societies in reference to the delineation of a clear-cut "space" in dealing with the thought-world of the West. See Jonathan Spencer, 1995. "Occidentalism in the East: The Uses of the West in the Politics and Anthropology of South Asia" in James G. Carrier (ed.) *Occidentalism: Images of the West*. Oxford: Clarendon Press, 25.
6 Quṭb, no date [ca.1946a]: 22.
7 Ibid: 21.
8 Ibid.
9 Ibid.
10 Ibid: 22.
11 Ibid (the *Quftān* is a long-sleeved outer garment, open in front, whereas the *jalābiyya* is a long loose-fitting garment commonly worn by Egyptian men (normally in the countryside). See Calvert and Shepard (ed.), 2004: 141n4; there are, however, some distinctions between the undecorated *jalābiyya* of the labourer, servant, a craftsman, and the more formal *jalābiyya* of the class of prosperous merchants and the "status conscious" Azharite, see Mitchell, 1993 [1969]: 330).
12 Quṭb, no date [ca.1946a]: 22. (The fez was firstly introduced by one of the first major reformers of the nineteenth century, Sultan Maḥmud II (r. 1808-1839). Although it was first resented as an "infidel innovation", it was finally accepted and became a symbol of Islam. Eventually, the fez was abolished by Atatürk in 1925, and replaced by European headgear in his campaign to westernise the country, Lewis, 1995b: 5; Hodgson remarks that the fez had been adopted only by certain urban classes, apart from the officials in the Ottoman Empire, adding that the introduction of the Occidental brimmed hat caused a great outcry, considering that it was a common feature of all Islamic headgear that they had no brim which would keep the forehead from touching the ground during the prayers, Hodgson, 1974 [1961], III: 264.
13 In similar vein, Ḥusayn recounts in his memoirs that he was barely nine when he got to be called a shaykh, after memorising the Qur'an in the local *kuttāb*. See Ṭaha Ḥusayn, 1929. *Al-Ayyām*. Cairo: Dār al-Ma 'ārif, I: 37.
14 The term *Effendi* (plural *Effendiyya*) is a title of respect, of Turkish provenance, which may be used as an equivalent of Mr. & connected to urban, lower Middle, or middle classes. See Hamilton A. R. Gibb & Harold Bowen, 1957. *Islamic Society and the West: a Study of the Impact of Western Civilisation on Moslem Culture in the Near East*. London: Oxford University Press, II: 274.
15 Quṭb, no date [ca.1946a]: 44.
16 A random sample of the 1940s members of the Brotherhood revealed the predominance of urban, middle class, *effendi* among the activist members, and the leadership of the movement, see Mitchell, 1993 [1969]: 329.
17 Gibb & Bowen, 1957, II: 139.
18 Ibid: 141 (The decline of the guilds in Egypt followed the creation of a large industry by Muḥammad 'Alī, see Baer, 1969: 149; see also "Decline and Disappearance of the Guilds" ibid: 149-160).

19 Quṭb, no date [ca.1946a]: 51.
20 The average *faqīh* was normally found to be "ignorant and venal" and worked as a teacher in the *kuttāb*. His profession was despised by the higher *ulama,* although he still enjoyed a degree of respect by the general population, see Gibb & Bowen, 1957: 140; with the vast majority of the populations in the Ottoman empire being illiterate, especially in the countryside, those who could read or write, especially the *ulama,* are said to have enjoyed a degree of respect that they might not attain in a "more book-oriented" society, ibid: 142.
21 Quṭb, no date [ca.1946a]: 23.
22 The Earl of Cromer,1908. *Modern Egypt.* New York: the Macmillan Company, 574.
23 Ibid: 294.
24 Quṭb, no date [ca.1946a]: 23-4.
25 Ibid: 36-7.
26 Ibid: 37.
27 Quṭb gives a detailed account of that day writing, for instance, about the "filthy" method used by the *kuttāb* students, spitting on tin sheets, used to inscribe Qur'anic passages, to erase them and write new ones. Quṭb writes that he was equally horrified to see the shaykh licking the wrong words to replace them with the right ones, ibid: 39.
28 Abu-Rabiʿ notes that, in contrast to Ḥusayn's ideas which reflect "the established literary and professional position of a successful public figure immersed in Western culture and education", Quṭb's ideas reflect "the deep soul of a man in search of cultural identity and of intellectual certainty", see Abu-Rabi', 1996:103; Calvert argues in the same vein that he detects Quṭb's "apparent alienation" during the early phase of his literary career from the world around him, see Calvert, 2010: 69.
29 Quṭb, no date [ca.1946a]: 45.
30 Ibid: 39.
31 Ibid: 41.
32 Ibid: 41-2.
33 Ibid: 43.
34 Ibid: 41.
35 Ibid: 28.
36 Ibid: 21-22.
37 Musallam quotes an Egyptian proverb used to denote an endeavour to achieve greatness which is figuratively seen as a conquest of sort, see Musallam, 2005: 35.
38 Yūnus, 1995: 23.
39 Quṭb is said to have attempted to join Cairo University because of its most progressive curriculum, especially because of the variety of languages offered by its Faculty of Arts, including English, Hebrew and Syriac, see Calvert, 2010: 60.
40 Musallam, 2005: 36.
41 Calvert, 2010: 59.
42 Ibid: 61.
43 In the 1960s, Quṭb loses this integrity when he claims in the last edition of *al-ʿAdāla*, for instance, that he spent forty years of his life reading and acquainting himself with human knowledge in all fields only to come to know the reality of "*jāhiliyya*", see Quṭb, 1993 [1964]: 203.
44 Quoted in Sayed Khatab, 2006. *The Political Thought of Sayyid Quṭb: The Theory of Jāhiliyya.* London: Routledge, 49.
45 Calvert, 2010: 59 (In fact, the said institution was so conservative as to prompt al-Banna to write that it was a place which allowed youths of rural origin to disengage from their peasant backgrounds "with a minimum of psychological discomfort", ibid).
46 Ibid: 58-9.
47 Krämer, 2010: 18 (Dār al-Ulūm was recognised as a university faculty in 1945. However, it remained till the early 1980s among the smallest faculties of Cairo University, see Lois A. Aroian,

1983. *The Nationalisation of Arabic and Islamic Education in Egypt.* The American University in Cairo, 64).

48 Cachia, 1956. *Ṭaha Ḥusayn : His Place in the Egyptian Literary Renaissance.* London : Luzac & Company Ltd., 119.

49 Krämer, 2010: 18.

50 Much is said about the influence that al-"Aqqād exerted on Quṭb. It is, however, to be noted that Quṭb showed particular deference to Ḥusayn in the course of his literary career. Generally speaking, I agree with Shalash's observation that Quṭb sought the approval and the good opinion of what he refers to as Egypt's "literary government", including, beside al-"Aqqād, Ḥusayn, Amīn, Haykal and al-ZAyyat, who all remained silent about Quṭb's literary output, clearly not appreciating his contribution, which is said to have left Quṭb particularly "angry and embittered", see Shalash, 1994: 122-4.

51 Calvert, 2010: 58.

52 Ibid.

53 Erikson & J. M. Erikson, 1998. *The Life Cycle Completed.* London: W.W. Norton & Company, 28.

54 Calvert, 2010: 58.

55 Krämer, 2010: 24.

56 Ibid: 88.

57 Courses on offer at the said institution combined those which offered instruction in traditional religious sciences, such as jurisprudence (*Fiqh*) and Qur'anic exegesis, and "scientific-oriented" subjects such as history, economics and politics, see Calvert, 2010: 58.

58 Ibid: 60 (Boullata relays that Quṭb was particularly averse to reading books of exegesis in higher learning institutions, see Boullata, 2000: 355).

59 Calvert, 2010: 58.

60 Quṭb, 2003 [1947b]: 9.

61 Quṭb, no date [ca.1935], 7 (I used the expression "outside layer" as an approximation of the meaning of the term *al-jaḥāfī* used by Quṭb based on the root word being *jaḥaf* which could be rendered in a variety of ways denoting a removal of an outside layer, i.e. "scrapping off", or "scratching off"; all inverted commas are placed by Quṭb).

62 Quṭb, 1996 [1932]: 32.

63 Ibid: 14.

64 Roger Allen, 1998. "al-'Aqqād, 'Abbās Maḥmūd (1889-1964)" in Meisami, Julie Scott & Paul Starkey (eds.), *EAL*. London: Routledge, 98.

65 Erikson, 1994 [1968]: 222-4.

66 Armstrong, 2001a. *The Battle for God: Fundamentalism in Judaism, Christianity and Islam.* London: Harper Collins, 14.

67 Charles D. Smith, 1983: 100.

68 Quṭb, no date [ca.1935]: 8.

69 It is to be noted that it was Faraḥ Anṭun who undertook the first translations of Nietzsche's works in 1908. See Hishām Sharabi, 1970. *Arab Intellectuals and the West: the Formative Years, 1875-1914.* London: The Johns Hopkins Press, 70n12. Sharabi remarks that for Christian intellectuals – including Sarruf, Shumayyil and Anṭun – it was not quite a matter, as Nietzsche puts it, of sacrificing God to nothingness", but merely of "sacrificing an untenable old truth for a valid new one, adding that unconsciously they were advocating the same philosophy of man that the European humanists had preached on the eve of the Renaissance, see ibid: 74.

70 Quṭb, no date [ca.1935b]:34.

71 Ibid: 33.

72 Armstrong, 2001a: 97 (Naguib Maḥfouẓ's novel *Khān al-Khalilī* (1945), is a good example of literature in Egypt which gave expression to such a "dread" in the mid-1940s. El-Enany notes the friction between religion and modern science in *Khān al-Khalilī* with the advocate of religion, Aḥmad 'Ākif, being depicted as "so ignorant" that he has not heard of Marx, Freud or Nietzsche.

Maḥfouẓ's other character who is an advocate of modern science in the same novel, Aḥmad Rāshid, believes that the prophets of modern times are Marx and Freud, see El-Enany, 1993: 48).
73 Karen Armstrong, 1999. *A History of God*. London: Vintage Books, 428.
74 Ibid: 428-9.
75 Iqbal, 2012 [no date]: 118.
76 The long quotes are extracted from an article by Muṣṭafa Ismā'īl Suwif entitled "Al-Taḥlīl al-Nafsī wa al-Fanān" (Psychoanalysis and the Artist), see Quṭb, 2003 [1947b]: 211-2.
77 Ibid: 123.
78 Ibid: 211-2 (It is noteworthy that Quṭb condemns Nietzsche's ideas of the "Superman", and "the death of God", in *Khaṣṣā'iṣ al-Taṣawwur al-Islāmī* (1962) only as he associates the German thinker with Iqbal's reform movement, see Quṭb, 1962c. *Khaṣṣā'iṣ al-Taṣawwur al-Islāmī wa Muqawwimatu*. Syria: Dar Iḥyā' al-Kutub al-'Arabiyya, 21).
79 Al-'Aqqād actually drew a parallel between the philosophy of al-Mutanabbī and that of Nietzsche on ethical foundations and the purpose of life, See al-'Aqqād, 1924a. "Falsafit al-Mutanabbī wa Falsafit Nitsha" in *Muṭāla'āt fī al-Kutub wa al-Ḥayya*. Cairo: al-Maṭba'a al-Tujāriyya al-Kubra, 156.
80 Al-'Aqqād, 1958a. *Bayna al-'Ilm wa al-Falsafa wa al-Fann* in *Dīn wa Fann wa Falsafa*. Cairo: al-Hay'a al-'Āma li al-Kitāb, no date, 45-6.
81 Calvin S. Hall, 1954. *A Primer of Freudian Psychology*. New York: Mentor Book, 110.
82 http://objectiveart01.tripod.com/john_the_baptist.htm (accessed March 28, 2013); see also http://www.egs.edu/library/sigmund-freud/articles/leonardo-da-vinci-a-psychosexual-study-of-an-infantile-reminiscence/iii/ (accessed March 28, 2013).
83 Quṭb, 2003 [1947b]: 211.
84 Muḥammad Quṭb, no date [ca.1966?]. *Al-Taṭawwur wa al-Thabāt*. Cairo: Maktabit Wahba, 36.
85 Wild finds that starting in the nineteenth century, there was a tendency in Muslim exegesis, as reflected in *al-Manār*, to prove to a colonised public that there was no contradiction between human reason and Western-dominated science, on the one hand, and Islam, on the other. Allusions to inventions such as the telegraph, telephone and steamships were found in the Qur'an. The Indo-Pakistani Ghulām Aḥmad Parvez (b. 1903) discovered Darwin's evolutionary theory in the Qur'an. See Stefan Wild, 2011b [2006]. "Political Interpretation of the Qur'an" in Jane D. McAuliffe (ed.) *The Cambridge Companion to the Qur'ān*. New York: Cambridge University Press, 280-1; Al-Banna as well denied that some Qur'anic verses clash with Darwin's scientific views which, he claims, remain inconclusive. See al-Banna, 1999 [ca. 1930s]. *Fiqh al-Wāqi'* (A Jurisprudence of Realism) Cairo: Dār al-kalima, 73.
86 Musallam, 2005: 36.
87 Al-'Aqqād, 1924d. "Falsafit al-Mutanabbī, bayna Nitsha wa Darwin" in *Muṭāla'āt fī al-Kutub wa al-Ḥayya*. Cairo: al-Maṭba'a al-Tujāriyya al-Kubra, 165-6.
88 Cachia, 1998: 297.
89 Abu-Rabi', 1996: 97.
90 Toth, 2013: 260 (I find that there is also much parallelism in Quṭb's and Amin's thought in *Fajr al-Islām* (1929) on the impact of desert – as opposed to urban-settled (*ḥaḍar*) - environments on the mind-sets of different peoples, see Aḥmad Amin, 2005 [1929]. *Fajr al-Islām*. Tunis: Dār al-Ma'ārif, 58-9).
91 See al-Badawī, 2002: 30-1; Abu-Rabi', 1996: 96; Musallam, 2005: 52.
92 *Ẓilāl*, VI: 3981.
93 Quṭb, 1996 [1932]: 49-50.
94 Quṭb maintained the view that the desert environment in which the Arabic language originated deprived it of any "shading", (by this he probably means it lacked in delivering nuances) to allow for it to reach the soul with "nothing to read between the lines" (*rien à lire entre les lignes*), see Quṭb, 1946b: 52.
95 R. C. Ostle, 1998: 196.
96 Quṭb, 1996 [1932]: 55.

97 Quṭb, 1946b: 160 (By the 1960s, Quṭb drops this line of thought in his criticism of 'Abduh's "rationalist school" (*al-madrassa al-'iqlaniyya*) in his commentary on *sūra* 105, *al-Fīl* (the Elephant), in *Ẓilāl*, see *Ẓilāl*, VI: 3976 & 3978.

98 Quṭb, 1946b: 52.

99 Ibid: 55.

100 Ibid: 60.

101 Quṭb quotes extensively from an anthology of poems collected and translated by al-'Aqqād in *Kutub wa Shakhṣiyyāt* (1946).

102 Quṭb, 1946b: 54-5.

103 Ibid: 38 (Quṭb never came to appreciate that Hardy, as Armstrong finds, was one of the first people in Europe to move away from Nietzsche's "heroic atheism", to give expression to the "dry desolation" which developed due to "the growing blankness where God once existed in the human conscience", see Armstrong, 1999: 467).

104 Quṭb, 1946b: 29.

105 Ibid: 25.

106 Ibid: 27.

107 Ibid: 30.

108 Quṭb, 1959 [1945b]. *al-Taṣwīr al-Fannī fī al-Qur'ān*. Cairo: Dār al-Ma'ārif, 87n1.

109 Quṭb, 1997 [1969]. *Muqawwimat al-Taṣawwur al-Islāmī*. Cairo: Dār al-Shurūq, 39.

110 Karen Armstrong, 2007. *The Bible: the Biography*. London: Atlantic Books, 160.

111 Calvert notes that Quṭb "saluted the ethical, religious and nationalist contents of Naguib Maḥfouẓ's writings" in the 1940s. He makes reference to positive reviews which were contributed by Quṭb to *al-Risala* of three of Maḥfouẓ's novels: "*Kifaḥ Ṭība li Naguib Maḥfouẓ* " on 17 December 1945 on *Kifaḥ Ṭība* (The Struggle of Thebes, 1944); a review of *Khān al-Khalīlī* (1945) on 17 December 1945; "al-Qāhira al-Jadīda" on 30 December 1946 on *al-Qāhira al-Jadīda* (New Cairo, 1946), see Calvert, 2010: 106 & ibid: 313n13-15.

112 These are designated by Calvert as "partisans of the heritage" including al-Rafi'ī's biographer, the historical novelist Muḥammad Sa'īd 'Aryan, the editor of Dār al-'Uṣur (1930), Ismā'īl Mazar, and the conservative religious writer Aḥmad al-Ghamrawī, see Calvert, 2010: 307n71.

113 These comments are made in two articles which were published in *al-Risala* "Bayna al-'Aqqād wa al-Rāfi'ī" (25 April, 1938) and "al-'Aqqād" (29 August, 1938), see ibid: 72 & ibid: 307n73-4.

114 Quoted in ibid: 72 and see ibid: 307n72 for reference "Bayna al-'Aqqād wa al-Rafi'ī" (6 June, 1938).

115 Ḥusayn, 1993 [1938]: 178 (note that Ḥusayn points out specifically that Dār al-'Ulūm graduates are jealous of university graduates, see ibid: 137).

116 Cachia, 1998: 297.

117 Quṭb, 1969 [1939]: 19.

118 Quṭb, 1969 [1939]: 19-20.

119 Ibid: 24 (note that Quṭb identifies "realism" (*al-Waqi'iyya*) as one of the components of the Islamic "concept" (*taṣawwur*) in *Khaṣṣā'iṣ* (1962), see n173 below; I note further that I did not translate the word *Injīl* as Bible or Gospel for, as Musallam points out, Quṭb makes use only of Matthew (5:21-41) to illustrate that "Christianity is spiritually oriented and has little to do with the enactment of laws, the statutes, or religious duties", see Musallam, 2005: 81; I note further that, although Quṭb criticises Christianity in Europe, he nonetheless associates it with "ethical purity" (*taṭahur khuluki*), citing Matthew 5: 27-8 to confirm this point (Ye have heard that it was said by them of old time, Thou shalt not commit adultery; But I say unto you, That whosoever looketh on a woman to lust after her hath committed adultery with her already in his heart), see Quṭb, 1969 [1939]: 23; it is not an association he makes with Islam or Judaism).

120 Smith, 1964, 150.

121 Ibid.

122 Ibid: 30-31.

123 Ibid: 57.

124 William C. Chittick, 1989. *Ibn al-'Arabī's Metaphysics of Imagination: the Sufi Path of Knowledge*. State University of New York: 213.
125 Qutb, 1969 [1939]: 28.
126 Ibid: 46.
127 Smith, 1964: 258n75.
128 Quṭb, 1947b: 111.
129 To put Quṭb's position in perspective, it is important to note that al-Banna vehemently criticised Ḥusayn for submitting the Qur'an to scientific scrutiny, see Ḥasan al-Banna, 1999 [ca. 1930s]: 186.
130 Quṭb, 1947b: 183 (Note that in *Ẓilāl*, Quṭb was to reverse his position in relation to Descartes when he criticises the methodology of 'Abduh's school for its excessive stress on the role of "reason" (*'aql*) in matters of creed, and for being influenced by Cartesian philosophy which, he argues, is "alien" (*gharība*) to Islam, perhaps not realising that he himself had attempted to make Islam equivalent to "reason" throughout the 1950s, as discussed above. In his criticism of 'Abduh's school, Quṭb argues that one might add to "the proofs" (*al-barāhīn*) provided by reason and science those "proofs" which are provided in the Islamic religion by "innate instinct and intuition" (*al-barāhīn al-fiṭriyya al-badīhiyya*) with the latter being considered by Quṭb at the radical Islamist stage of his life as more in tune with "human nature", see *Ẓilāl*, III: 1588n1).
131 Quṭb, 1947b: 112.
132 Ibid: 13.
133 Ibid: 112.
134 Ṭaha Ḥusayn, 1932 [1925]: 70.
135 Kreutz, 2012: 136-7.
136 Musallam, 2005: 88.
137 Shalash, 1994: 117.
138 *Al-Risāla* (The Message) is one of a few literary-political journals – including *al-Thaqāfa* (*Culture*), *Ṣaḥīfat Dār al-'Ulūm*, and *Majallat al-Shu'un al-Ijtimā'iyya* (*The Journal of Social Affairs*) which provided a platform for writers in Egypt to voice their views on culture-related subjects. Quṭb contributed articles which were published in all of these journals, see Calvert, 2010: 87-8 (the most exhaustive bibliography of Quṭb's articles is offered in Muḥammad Ḥāfiẓ Diyāb's work *Sayyid Quṭb: al-Khitāb wa al-Āydulujiyyā* (1987); Yūnus observes that Quṭb contributed on a regular basis for some fifteen years to *al-Risāla*, see Yūnus, 1995: 27).
139 Shalash, 1994:117.
140 'Abbās M. Al-'Aqqād, (1946a). "Hadhihī Hiya al-Aghlāl" (These are the Shackles) in al-Ḥasanī Ḥasan 'Abdullah (ed.) *al-Islām wa al-Ḥaḍāra al-Insāniyya wa Maqalat Ukhra*. Beirut: Manshūrāt al-Maktaba al-'Aṣriyya, 28.
141 Ibid: 29.
142 'Abdullah al-Qaṣimī, 2000 [1946]. *Hadhihī Hiya al-Aghlāl* (These are the Shackles). Köln: al-Kamal, 8.
143 Ibid: 14.
144 I refer here to Quṭb's views on the spirit of the East and the matter of the West duality which constitute a major part in his otherness formulations targeting the West in the 1940s, as we shall see below.
145 al-Qaṣimī, 2000 [1946]: 16.
146 Quoted in Shalash, 1994:117.
147 Musallam, 2005: 54 (Musallam quotes 'Abd al-Bāqī M. Ḥusayn here, see ibid:213n10; on this occasion, Quṭb's battle was with the literary critic Dr. Muḥammad Mandur* in 1943, and revolved around the so-called "whispered poetry" of the inner soul which was composed by the diaspora literati such as Mikhā'īl Nu'ayma and Nasib 'Arida. Quṭb is said to have rejected "whispered poetry" in favour of literature which conveyed "truth", see ibid: 54).
148 Ibid: 54; and see Shalash, 1994: 117n33.
149 Quṭb, 1946b, 231.

150 Ibid: 230.
151 Ibid: 233.
152 Ibid: 234.
153 Ibid.
154 Nissim Rejwan, 2008. *Arabs in the Mirror: Images and Self-Images from Pre-Islamic to Modern Times*. University of Texas Press, 124.
155 Ibid: 125.
156 Musallam, 2005: 88.
157 Ibid: 228n77.
158 Ibid: 88.
159 Yūnus, 1995: 30.
160 Ibid: 45.
161 Shalash, 1994: 118.
162 Quṭb, 1962c: 15.
163 Quṭb, 2003 [1947b]: 64-5.
164 Quṭb, 1962c: 190.
165 Ibid: 193-6 (al-Aqqād's work *Allah* is quoted in the chapter entitled "*al-Wāqi'iyya*", ibid:190-211).
166 Ṭaha Ḥusayn, 1925. *Qādat al-Fikr* (Leaders of Thought). Cairo: al-Hilāl, 41.
167 Quṭb, 1962c: 89.
168 Erikson, 1994 [1968]: 184-5.
169 On this point, Yūnus contends that, even as early as the mid 1940s, Quṭb is said to have sought to get rid of al-Aqqād's "Mind", as he developed the idea that it stands as a stumbling block to the poetry of "emotive spontaneity" which allows for a strict response of intuition to the world, see Yūnus, 1995: 44.
170 'Abbās M. al-'Aqqād, 1947b. *Al-Falsafa al-Qur'āniyya: Kitāb 'an Mabaḥith al-Falsafa al-Rawḥiyya wa al-Ijtima'iyya alatī Waradat Mawḍū'atiha fī Ayyat al-Kitāb al-Karīm*. Cairo: Lajnat al-Bayān al-'Arabī:175 (by that time, Quṭb has written *Mashahid al-Qiyama fī al-Qur'ān* in which he offered a sensory perception of the afterlife).
171 Quṭb, 2003 [1947b]: 45 (In 1947, Quṭb seemed to place himself in the same league as Hardy, al-Khayām, and Tagore, who were seen by him to fill the category of "grand litterateur" (*al-adīb al-kabīr*), and whom he describes as gifted with a "grade of prophethood" (*qabs min al-nubuwwa*), see Quṭb, 1947b: 29.).
172 In his criticism of the historical method in literary criticism in the revised edition of *al-Naqd al-Adabī*, Quṭb makes the claim that "genius" is not just down to the environment, but it is rather "a matter which escapes the ordinary" (*falta*), explaining further that "genius" is a matter which could be likened to the eruption of a volcano, in so far as it is latent in humanity (for the opportune moment to erupt), see Quṭb, 2003 [1947b]: 169-170.
173 In one biography of Al-Aqqād, he is described as a "human encyclopaedia of modern Arab culture", see http://www.encyclopedia.com/doc/1G2-3435000023.html (accessed December 26/2012).
174 'Abbās al-'Aqqād, 1946b."Mawlid al-Falsafa al-Islāmiyya" in al-Ḥasanī Ḥasan 'Abdullah (ed.) *al-Islām wa al-Ḥaḍāra al-Insāniyya wa Maqalat Ukhra*. Beirut: Manshūrāt al-Maktaba al-'Aṣriyya, 7.
175 Shepard, 1996: xvn8.
176 al-Badawi, 2002: 168.
177 Ḥilmī al-Namnam, 2010: 146 (Namnam provides a list of 15 articles which were published in various publications- including *al-Akhbār*, *Rose al-Yusuf*, and *al-Risāla* – in support of Naguib between August 8 and October 20, 1952, see ibid: 215; the first such article "Istijwāb ila al-Baṭal Muḥammad Najīb" was published in *al-Akhbār* daily on August 8th (see select bibliography for a full listing of these articles; Mitchell finds that "an agreement of sorts" was reached between the military revolutionaries and some members of the Brotherhood which did not involve the latter's head at the time, Ḥasan al-Huḍaybī, concerning the part that the Muslim Brothers would play on the day of the revolution in case of the coup's failure, see Mitchell, 1993 [1969]: 103).

178 See Quṭb's article "Adab al-Inḥilāl" published in *al-Risāla* on 25 Aug. 1952, quoted in al-Namnam, 2010: 129-130.

179 Ibid: 144 (this criticism was levelled by the historian/novelist Muḥammad Farīd Abu Ḥadīd in the literary magazine *al-Thaqāfa*).

180 Quoted in al-Namnam, 2010: 146.

181 These works are included in Quṭb's bibliography but *not* referenced in the work.

182 http://www.poemhunter.com/lascelles-abercrombie/biography/ (accessed Dec. 5, 2014) *Principles of Literary Criticism* translated as *Qawā'id al-Naqd al-Adabī* by 'Awaḍ Muḥammad.

183 *The Art of Literary Study* (1924) translated by Zakī Naguib Maḥmūd as *Funūn al-Adab*.

184 *Méthode de Criticisme Littéraire* translated by Dr. Muḥammad Mandūr as *Manhaj al-Baḥth fī al-Adab*; note that Ḥusayn attended classes taught by Emile Durkheim and Gustave Lanson in the Sorbonne, see Toth, 2013: 265.

185 Quṭb, 1988 [1947c]: 33.

186 al-Namnam, 2010: 146-7.

187 As discussed in chapter 2 above, Quṭb joined a number of other intellectuals who saw a need to base social justice on Islamic foundations when they set up the journal *al-Fikr al-Jadid* in 1947, without, however, wholeheartedly committing to it himself.

188 Quṭb describes "*shi'r al-fikra*" as one which is "devoid of imagery and shadings" (*mujarad min al-ṣuwwar wa al-ẓilāl*), noting that although the poetry of both al-Mutanabbī and al-Ma'arrī fall into this category, their poems rather fall into the category of prose. See Quṭb, 2003 [1947b], 76. In contrast, Quṭb praises al-Khayām's poetry as "splendid" (*badī'*), for giving free expression to his heart rather than to his intellect (*al-dhihn*), see ibid: 78.

189 Quṭb explains that the excess of the "intellect-bent orientation" of the "Rationalist School" (of al-'Aqqād) is understandable as it unfolded in reaction to the orientation to mere craftsmanship, as in the works of al-Manfaluṭī in prose, and Shawqī in poetry, see ibid: 50.

190 In my analysis of the 2nd chapter of the 2nd edition of the work entitled "The Nature of Social Justice in Islam", I found no reference to "*taṣawwur*", whereas I counted thirteen instances when Islam is referred to as an "idea", five instances of reference to it as a "philosophy", and three instances when it is referred to as a "theory" (*naẓariyya*), see Quṭb, 1950 [1949]: 21-32; in the same chapter of the last edition of the work (1964), reference to Islam as a philosophy is omitted altogether, whereas the word "*taṣawwur*" is used fourteen times mostly in lieu of the use of the word "*fikra*", which is only used once, as is reference to "*naẓariyya*". See Quṭb, 1993 [1964a]: 20-30.

191 This point is inferred from the argument which is made by Quṭb stipulating that "humanity remained in search, over long stretches of time, of a comprehensive idea on the Creator, creation, the universe, life and humans, as it was not ready, in terms of awareness, [to attain] such an overall and comprehensive idea, until the advent of Islam". See Quṭb, 1950 [1949]: 22; this quote remains unchanged in all first five editions of the work, see Shepard, 1996: 26n20.

192 Quṭb, 1950 [1949]: 237 & Shepard, 1996: 291 (note that reference to the Roman component of European civilisation is a novelty introduced in Quṭb's Islamist discourse. As discussed above, it is clear that Quṭb assumed only the Greek component in his rebuttal of Ḥusayn's *Mustaqbal al-Thaqāfa fī Miṣr*).

193 Quṭb, 1950 [1949]: 238.

194 In all editions of *al-'Adāla*, Asad's long quote refers to the Roman "cultural legacy" of the (unchristian) Western modern civilisation, and to its "irreligious" foundations and essence, and paints a rather derogatory view of the modern Western civilisation of "matter", as both irreligious and unchristian, see ibid: 238-240.

195 Smith, 1946 [1943]. *Modern Islam in India: a Social Analysis*. London: Victor Gollancz, 148.

196 Smith, 1981 [1958]. "The Historical Development in Islam of the Concept of Islam as an Historical Development" in *On Understanding Islam*. The Hague: Mouton Publishers, 71-76 (I note here that Smith's list includes two works by al-Qaṣimī – *Shuyūkh al-Azhar wa al-Ziyāda fi al-Islām* (1932) and *al-Ṣira' Bayna al-Islām wa al-Wathaniyyīn* (1937) – as well as a 1935 translation by

al-ʻAqqād of Adams' study *Islam and Modernism in Egypt: a Study of the Modern Reform Movement Inaugurated by Muḥammad ʻAbduh* (1933); these titles must have been read by Qutb).

197 W. C. Smith, 1964: 108.

198 Quṭb is said to have completed the work, and entrusted its final draft to his younger brother, Muḥammad, following the closure of the weekly *al-Fikr al-Jadīd*, of which he was an editor, in May 1948, and right before he departed to the United States in November 1948, see Musallam, 2005: 96-7.

199 As discussed above, the dominant trend amongst the older generation of literati was toward rationalism with Ḥusayn, for instance, advocating the view in the mid 1920s that the leadership of thought passed in modern times from the hands of the poets to the hands of the philosophers, theorising further that "man requires centuries to raise himself from the superstitious perplexities of an unreasoning existence to the wisdom of an intellectual conquest". See Ṭaha Ḥusayn, 1932 [1925]: 12-3.

200 Quṭb, 1950 [1949]: 241.

201 Ibid: 242.

202 Hamilton A. R. Gibb, 1975 [1947]. *Modern Trends in Islam*. New York: Octagon Books, 46.

203 William E. Shepard, 1997."The Myth of Progress in the Writings of Sayyid Quṭb" in *Religion*, 27:3, 255.

204 Ibid: 259.

205 Wilfred C. Smith, 1946 [1943]: 73.

206 Ibid: 140.

207 Peter Coates, 2011 [2002]. *Ibn ʻArabī and Modern Thought: The History of Taking Metaphysics Seriously*. Oxford: Anqa Publishing, 179.

208 Quṭb, 1993 [1964a]: 49; translated by Shepard, see Shepard, 1996: 64.

209 Ibid.

210 Ibid: 50.

211 Barlas argues that by the 8th century, male ʻulama had managed to "dilute the egalitarian impulse in various parts of [Islamic] tradition", see Asma Barlas, 2011 [2006]. "Women's Readings of the Qur'an" in Jane D. McAuliffe (ed.) *The Cambridge Companion to the Qur'ān*. Cambridge University Press, 256.

212 Quṭb, 1950a: 16.

213 Ibid; see also Shepard, 1996: 13n59.

214 According to Roded, it was ʻAbduh who first called for the liberation of women in the Arabic-speaking world, see Roded, 2001-2006: 536; as early as 1899, Qāsim Amīn argued for the importance of educating women, arguing that "the work of women in society is to form the morals of the nation". Reflecting clear Darwinist influences, he went to describe "the decay of Islam", and attributed such a decay to the "disappearance of social virtues" which are conducive to "moral strength", see Hourani, 1983 [1962]: 164.

215 Quṭb, 1950a: 16.

216 Ibid (reference is made here to one of a number of Traditions attributed to the Prophet on learning which were quoted by the Indian thinker Amir Ali in his work *Spirit of Islam* (1891) which, according to Smith, found many sympathetic readers in the West as well as in Egypt in the 1940s, see Smith, 1946 [1943]: 55 & 317, 26; Smith remarks that Ali's glorification of the Islamic past, is to stress "the contrast between it and contemporary Europe", and the civilising power of Islam which influenced the modern civilisation of Europe, see ibid: 61-62; the ḥadīth quoted by Quṭb above reads: "Seek knowledge, even though it be in China", see ibid: 64).

217 Quṭb, 1950a: 16 (As far as I can tell this section as well as reference to the duty of Muslim women to seek knowledge were removed in the 5th and last editions of the work, see Quṭb, 1958: 15 & 1993 [1964a]:15); Shepard notes that the Ḥadīth "seek knowledge, even in China" was quoted in editions 1 & 2 only (1949-1950), see Shepard 1996, 1996: 13n59.

218 Ḥasan al-Banna, 1966a [no date]. *Mudhakkirāt al-Da'wah wa al-Dā'iya*. (2nd edition). Cairo: no publisher, 52.

219 Ibid: 27.
220 Ibid: 52.
221 Quṭb, 1950 [1949]: 245 (Shepard argues that this statement, which was made in the first five editions of *al-'Adāla,* appears to be in response to some unnamed sceptics who questioned Quṭb's call to adopt the "pure sciences" of the West, and its applications in material life, without accepting the ideological underpinnings of Western thought, see Shepard, 1996: 330).
222 'Abbās al-'Aqqād, no date [ca. 1950s?]. *Al-Tafkīr Farīḍa Islāmiyya*, 8.
223 al-'Aqqād, 1947b: 15-16.
224 Calvert, 2010: 39.
225 Kreutz, 2012: 138.
226 Quṭb, 1950 [1949]: 22; Shepard, 1996: 25n9.
227 Shepard does not indicate when the addition of al-Fārābī was made. I have seen reference to al-Fārābī in the fifth edition of the work, see Quṭb, 1958 [1949]: 21.
228 al-'Aqqād, no date [ca. 1950s?]: 73.
229 Ibid: 34-5, (the word "rhetoric" appears in English and in inverted commas in the text).
230 Quṭb, 1950 [1949]: 246.
231 Ibid: 247n1.
232 Ibid: 246.
233 Ibid: 233 (Quṭb added American colonialism in the 6th edition of the work (1964), see Shepard, 1996: 286n20).
234 Quṭb, 1950 [1949]: 233.
235 Ibid, (this section was removed from the 6th edition of the work, see Shepard, 1996: 332).
236 Quoted in Calvert, 2010: 152.
237 Quṭb, 1951b, III: 118 (It is to be noted that Quṭb did not name Huet, he, however, gave the name of the painting in Arabic).
238 Quṭb, 1950 [1949]: 237; see also Shepard, 1996:291.
239 Ibid: 236.
240 Quṭb, 1993 [1964a]: 192.
241 The quote is attributed to National Public Radio journalist Robert Siegel from an article entitled "Sayyid Quṭb's America" published in 2003, see Musallam, 2005: 118.
242 Calvert gives an account of an incident when Quṭb and another Egyptian student were denied admission into one of Greeley's cinemas on account of their dark complexions. Quṭb is said to have been left angry and indignant by the incident, see Calvert, 2010: 148.
243 Quṭb recounts that during his stay in the United States he has seen the White Americans treating people of colour in "mean arrogance" (*'ajrafa mardhūla*), and "hideous ferocity" (*waḥshiyya bashi'a*), finding that the racist "swaggering" (*ṣalaf*) of the Americans in treating people of colour is fiercer and crueller than that which was exercised by Nazis against the Jews, see *Ẓilāl*, II: 1091.
244 Calvert, 2010: 149.
245 Upon his return to Egypt, Quṭb targets the "White Man", criticising the English, the French and the Americans, along with the (westernised) Egyptians, whom he refers to as the "Brown English", linking them all to a "spiritual and intellectual colonialism of Egypt's Ministry of Education, see Quṭb, 1952a [1951]. *Ma'rakat al-Islām wa al-Ra'simāliyya*. Cairo: Dār al-Kitāb al-'Arabī, 127.
246 Quṭb, 1951a. "Aduwina al-Awal al-Rajul al-Abyaḍ" in Ṣalaḥ A. al-Khaldī, 1987, 41-2.
247 Calvert is satisfied that Quṭb made a "breakthrough" in his knowledge of English, following an eight-week course in elementary English composition in Greeley in 1949 in spite of the fact that he withdrew from all of his courses right before the final examinations, Calvert, 2010: 147.
248 The quotes are attributed to Jonathan Raban, a newspaper reporter in the Guardian, cited in Musallam, 2005: 121.
249 Ibid: 120.
250 Quṭb, 1951b: 98.

251 Quṭb, 1949a. "Ḥamā'im fī New York" in Ṣalaḥ A. al-Khaldī (1987), 141.
252 Ibid: 142-3.
253 Quṭb, 1992 [1964b]: 175.
254 Quṭb, 2005 [1962a]: 87-9 (the inverted commas are placed by Quṭb).
255 Calvert, 2010: 146.
256 Quoted in al-Khaldī, 1987: 22.
257 Musallam, 2005: 118.
258 Calvert, 2010: 141 (this is based on Quṭb's own reflections on the voyage which were made in his commentary on Q2:164 in *Ẓilāl*); I agree with Calvert that one should dismiss Quṭb's assertion that he allegedly was propositioned by a "beautiful, tall, semi-naked woman [who] was an American agent sent to engineer his moral collapse", ibid: 142.
259 As discussed above, Quṭb quotes Asad's work on the irreligious nature of the Westerner; I have also identified a passage in which Asad refers to the lack of ethical considerations in the West which is especially relevant to Quṭb's view of American pragmatism and materialism, see Asad, 2007 [1934]. *Islam at the Crossroads*. New Delhi: Kitab Bhavan, 60.
260 Asad, 2007 [1934]: 56-7 & see Quṭb, 1950 [1949]: 238-240.
261 Quoted in al-Khaldī, 1987: 105.
262 Ibid: 107.
263 Ibid: 107-8.
264 Calvert6, 2010: 153.
265 Quṭb, 1951b: 102.
266 Ibid: 99-100.
267 Ibid: 101.
268 Judy spotted a reference to Smith in the 2nd edition of Quṭb's anthology *America from Within* (1986), but this reference was removed from the 1987 edition that I analysed. See Ronald A. T. Judy, 2004. "Sayyid Quṭb's Fiqh al-Waqi'i, or New Realist Science", *Boundary 2*, 31:2, 134n10.
269 Quṭb, 1951c: 104.
270 Quṭb, 1949b: 153-4.
271 Musallam, 2005: 98.
272 http://www.acls.org/about/history/ (accessed September 2, 2012).
273 Calvert, 2010: 145.
274 Erikson, 1995 [1951]: 223.
275 Racism admittedly existed in the United States especially at the time of Quṭb's visit. However, for all of Quṭb's praise of the Islamic "humane" view which, according to him, was totally free of any tribal, religious and racist partisanship, Quṭb himself held extremely derogatory views of both the "White" Americans and the "negroes" remarking in an article on "artistic primitiveness" in America in 1951, for instance, that both "negroes" and White Americans share an inclination to primitiveness together with an animal disposition. 'The Americans are primitive in their artistic taste which favours jazz music which was created by the "negroes" to satisfy their "primitive" inclinations, "their desire for noise and to excite their animal dispositions", see Quṭb, 1951bb: 115.
276 Calvert comments on Quṭb's "obsessive concern" with moral issues, especially on matters of sexuality, as he drew a "disapproving picture" of the American woman's seductive appearance depicting her "thirsty lips", her "bulging breasts" and her "smooth legs", see Calvert, 2010: 151 & 320n35. Some of Quṭb's crude remarks certainly convey the feeling that Quṭb was not, himself, immune to the charms of the American women writing in one article, for instance, that the American girls are fully aware of their physical charms...in her "full-bosomed breasts" and her "full buttocks", and her "rounded thighs", and her "smooth legs", quoted in s al-Khaldī, 1987: 112.
277 Ibid.
278 The discussion of American pragmatism is removed from the last edition of *al-'Adāla*.
279 Quṭb, 1950 [1949]: 246 & see Shepard, 1996: 331.

280 Suraksha Bandal, V. K. Maheshwari, and Saroj Agarwal . "Pragmatism and Education" in http://www.scribd.com/doc/30853941/Pragmatism-and-Education (accessed December 17th , 2012), 5.
281 Ibid: 1.
282 Goodman, 2003: 101.
283 Wilfred C. Smith, 1959: 146.
284 Ibid.
285 Birgit Schäbler, 2012. "Humanism, Orientalism, Modernity: a Critique" in in Reichmuth, Rüsen, Sarhan (eds.) *Humanism and Muslim Culture: Historical Heritage and Contemporary Challenges.* National Taiwan University Press, 152 (Al-Aqqād offered a lengthy bibliography of Goethe which was not referenced in any of Quṭb's works).

Chapter 4

1 Quṭb, 2004 [1946]: 61.
2 Ibid: 60-1 (*awliya'*, pl. of *walī*; in popular Islam, the expression "*awliya'* Allah" (friends of God are regarded as persons of exceptional spiritual merit who are able to perform *karāmāt*, or miracles, see Calvert and Shepard: 2004 [1946]: 150).
3 Ibid: 62.
4 Gudrun Krämer, 2010: 10.
5 Calvert, 2010: 74.
6 A literal interpretation of the word *al-majdhūb* is "to be drawn"; in the above context, the word *al-majdhūb* came to be used in folk populist beliefs in reference to those who are drawn to the divine and the world beyond.
7 Quṭb, no date [1946a]: 9.
8 Ibid (translation provided by Shepard and Calvert, see Quṭb, 2004 [1946]: 1).
9 Quṭb, no date [1946a]: 9 (Quṭb describes *al-sharba* as a "bitter" and "repulsive" liquid which he was made to swallow when he once came down with a fever).
10 Ibid: 10 (Quṭb explains that "*sharbat al-wilāya*" is one which was believed to be given to some "elect servants of God" following choosing them at random in the course of a yearly meeting of the great pious *awliya* on Mount Qāf with Quṭb al-Ghawth presiding over them., ibid; In traditional Middle Eastern Muslim cosmology, Mount Qāf is "the cosmic mountain that encircles the world"; Quṭb al-Ghawth "is one name for the *wālī* who stands at the top of the invisible cosmic spiritual hierarchy that Sufis believe in", see Calvert and Shepard, 2004 [1946]: 140n3).
11 Ibid: 9 (translation provided by Shepard and Calvert with some minor alterations, see Quṭb, 2004 [1946]: 1).
12 Hoffman, 1995: 212.
13 T. C. Rastogi, 1990. *Sufism: A Dictionary with Profiles of Saint-Poets.* New Delhi: Sterling Publishers Ltd, 60; see glossary under "*sharaab*".
14 Hoffman, 1995: 208.
15 Ibid: 112.
16 "*Maqamāt*(s)" (stations or stages) provide the foundations of the Sufi path. For almost all Sufis, the first stage on the Sufi journey is repentance, and the later stages mark a Sufi's experience of "peaceful surrender and ultimately, for the blessed few, the witness of divine glory", see ibid: 156-7 (the expression "*maqamāt*(s)" is not used by Quṭb in any of his writings).
17 Febe Armanios, 2011. *Coptic Christianity in Ottoman Egypt.* Oxford University Press, 7; the *Mūlid* celebrations, in the form of popular festivals, probably date from the 13th century; they began with a celebration of *Mūlid* of the Prophet, as a response to the celebration of Christmas, see Hoffman, 1995: 355; many Muslim Sufis attend Coptic *mūlid* celebrations, and in at least one

case there is a merging of Mārī Girgis, the popular St. George and dragon-slayer and martyr, and the figure known as Khiḍr in the Qur'an (18:65-82), see ibid: 333).

18 Ibid: 6.

19 Hoffman, 1995: 328.

20 Calvert and Shepard, 2004 [1946]: XXV.

21 Baer, 1969: 218-9.

22 Armanios, 2011: 6 (the Coptic Church shares a distinctive brand of Christianity with the Armenian, Syrian and Ethiopian Churches which dissented from Rome and Constantinople at the Council of Chalcedon (451) in a dispute over the nature of Christ. The Copts and other opponents of the council favoured defining the person of Jesus as of two natures. In time, the Copts separated from Byzantine domination, and after the Islamic conquest of Egypt in 641, they became "doubly-marginalised", and "estranged as a subordinate religious community" (in their own homeland), see ibid).

23 Naguib Mahfouz is particularly critical of Quṭb, remarking that the latter refused to give a positive appraisal of the works of a Coptic writer, in spite of accepting the last's merit, fearing that in the future the unnamed Coptic writer "will slander Islamic heritage in every twisted way", see Naguib Maḥfouz, 1972 [1999]: 120 (this account is given in Mahfouz's novel *Mirrors* where Quṭb features as the fictitious fanatic 'Abd al-Wahhāb Isma'īl who accepts that, though he was a member of the Wafd party once, he does not trust people of "other" religions, see ibid); it is particularly interesting that Quṭb showed much appreciation of Sa'd Zaghlūl while ignoring one of the "brightest and most respected" leaders of the Wafd party, the Coptic Makram 'Ubayd, who acted as the Secretary-general of the party in the 1940s until his resignation in protest to the party having taken power "behind British tanks", see Goldschmidt Jr., 2004. *Modern Egypt: the Formation of a Nation-state*. Oxford: Westview, 89).

24 Quṭb, 1946b: 213; (Quṭb made these remarks in a review of Mikhā'īl Nu'ayma's work *al-Bayādir* (1945) in a chapter dedicated to a discussion of matters of the "soul" and the world under the title "Fi al-Nafs wa al-'Alam" in his work, see Quṭb, 1946b: 212-260. (I could not provide a translation for the word *Bayādir* (البيادر), it seems to be used here as a plural of *baydar* (بيدر) for threshing floors in fields used to separate grains from corn or other crops.); Nu'ayma is one of a number of "mahjari' poets who emigrated to America, and are identified by Badawī for their "idealisation of their homeland", and for setting up an opposition between the "spirituality of the East" and "the materialism of the West" which is an idea repeated "*ad nauseam*" in their works, see M.M. Badawi, 1985. *Modern Arabic Literature and the West*. London: Ithaca, 116-7; it is worthy of note that Quṭb commended Nu'ayma's work for looking at the universe and everyday problems with "the Eye of the East", see ibid: 212-3.

25 For maps of monasteries in Coptic Egypt, showing the Holy Family's path during their sojourn in Egypt, see Christian Cannuyer, 2009 [2001]. *Coptic Egypt: the Christians of the Nile*. Thames and Hudson, 135.

26 For a picture of a pilgrimage to Deir Dronka, near Asyut, see Ibid: 106.

27 I am making reference here to the claim made in 1942 by the editor of the *Yearbook of Egyptian Jewry*, Maurice Fargeon, that some Jews did not leave Egypt at the time of Moses. According to Fargeon, some Jews remained and moved to Asyut, where they formed a tribe of warriors. They were later joined by refugees, including the prophet Jeremiah and his secretary Baruch, fleeing the Babylonian conquest of Judea, see http://web.stanford.edu/group/SHR/5-1/text/beinin.html (accessed July 18, 2014); however, there appears to have been no significant Jewish population outside of Giza in upper Egypt, see Gudrun Krämer, 1989. *The Jews in Modern Egypt, 1914-1952*. London: University of Washington Press.108; It seems to be the case that Fargeon's assertions were drawn from Renan's *The History of the People of Israel*, a popular text among rationalist francophone Jews, see http://web.stanford.edu/group/SHR/5-1/text/beinin.html (accessed July 18, 2014).

28 See ibid; in 1925, a Société D'Etudes Historiques Juives presided over by Aslan Cattaoui and Chief Rabi Hayyim Nahum was established in Egypt, which, among other things, took an active

interest in the Geniza materials, see Gudrun Krämer, 1989: 100; In July 1935, a number of leading personalities of the Jewish community in Egypt, including Joseph Aslan Cattaoui and Chief Rabi Hayyim Nahum founded a youth club in the Cairo Jewish *ḥāra* called Association de la Jeunesse Juive Egyptienne (*jam'iyat al-Shubbān al-Yahūd al-Miṣriyīn*). Their slogan was "Fatherland, Faith and Culture". The group included as well Dr Hillel Farhi (see n31, chapter 2) and Dr. Israel Wolfensohn (d. 1980), a professor of literature and former student of Ṭaha Ḥusayn, see ibid: 169-170 (as we shall see in chapter 5, Quṭb demonstrates a heightened level of anxiety in relation to Chief Rabi Hayyim Nahum).

29 Mitchell, 1993 [1969]: 2 (Hoffman notes that the Wahhābīs of Saudi Arabia opposed ceremonies of *dhikr*, see Lenn E. Goodman, 2003. *Islamic Humanism*. Oxford University Press, 66).

30 Quṭb, June 1941. "Fī al-Insāniyya Khayr ma Dam Fiha Amthāl Strauss", *RS*, 414:644-5, cited in Diyāb, 1987: 317n152.

31 Quṭb, 10 Sept., 1951. "Ila Ustadhuna al-Duktur Aḥmad Amīn", *TQ*, 663: 13, cited in Yūnus, 1995: 45n1.

32 Calvert and Shepard, 2004 [1946]: XXV; Quṭb makes reference to a Shaykh 'Alī, who belonged to an unnamed Order, who is said to have managed to stand in the face of *'afārīt* who showed "strange devilish boldness" by storming some of the local mosques, see Quṭb, no date [1946a]: 112; Quṭb describes Shaykh 'Alī as a man of *al-ṭarīq* which is a word used along with the word *ṭarīqa* (plural *ṭuruq*) to designate a shaykh of a Sufi order, or Brotherhood, literally meaning path or way, see Hoffman, 1995: 123.

33 Quṭb, no date [1946a]: 104.

34 As mentioned before, Quṭb dedicated his memoirs to Ṭaha Ḥusayn. It is to be noted that both *Ṭifl min al-Qarya* and *al-Aṭyaf al-Arba'a* were first published by the publishing house, which was affiliated with King Fu'ād's (now Cairo) university, Lajnat al-Nashr li al-Jami'īn; Calvert observes that Ḥusayn's al-Ayyām encouraged several writers, including Quṭb, to choose autobiography as "a vehicle for recounting their often similar encounters with the forces of change, see Calvert: 2010, 37.

35 Ibid: 104-5 (It is not clear which edition of the work Shepard and Calvert translated as a "Child from the village". In the same paragraph, in the edition they translated of the work, reference to "the Great Cross" is removed from the work, with the sentence above reading "the name of the Pure Virgin", and "the Great Cross", if the child was a Christian" is replaced instead by "the name of the Virgin Mary and Jesus Christ, if one was Christian", see Quṭb, 2004 [1946a]: 63).

36 Smith remarks on the striking ability of two Muslim scholars to show some "feel" for Christian positions in twentieth-century literature. The first is Itrat Husain's title *The Dogmatic and Mystical Theology of John Donne* (1938) and *The Mystical Element in the Metaphysical Poets of the Seventeenth Century* (1948). The second author is the Egyptian physician, Muḥammad Kāmil Ḥusayn, whose novel *Qarya Ẓālima* (1957, translated by Kenneth Cragg as *City of Wrong* in 1959) on the Crucifixion has attracted literary attention in Egypt and theological attention in Christendom. He adds that these two authors have succeeded brilliantly in depicting the actual faith of particular Christians – "studying it in terms of what was the Christian cumulative tradition up to the time of those particular persons, see Wilfred C. Smith, 1964: 338n6; Gardet is also highly impressed by *Qarya Ẓālima*, noting the work's value as "a philosophy of conscience", albeit he finds that the work falls short from Ibn Sīnā's and al-Ghazālī's "philosophy of the self". Still, the work is especially welcomed by Gardet in comparison to the "hard and pure Islam" (l'Islam pur et dur) of the Muslim Brothers, and the use of Islam as an "ideological revolution" by Ḥasan Ḥanafī' which renders it "a temporal tool of combat" (instrument de combat temporal) at the risk of emptying it from its profound religious values, see Louis Gardet, 1979. "Des Réformistes (*iṣlāḥiyyūn*) aux Mutations en Cours" in Alford T. Welch and Pierre Cachia (eds.) *Islam: Past Influence and Present Challenge*. Edinburgh University Press, 76-9.

37 Interestingly, al-Banna makes reference in his own commentary on *al-Fātiḥa* to an instance when 'Abduh drew comparisons between the Trinity and God's attribute of mercy "*al-Raḥman,*

al-Raḥīm" in Q1:1 (otherwise known as *al-basmala*), commenting that if such an interpretation would be acceptable to the Christians than the biggest hurdle setting Christianity and Islam apart will be removed, see "Al-Imām Ḥasan al-Banna Yaktib fī 'Ulūm al-Qur'ān" (The Imām Ḥasan al-Bannā Writes on the Sciences of the Qur'ān) in http://www.ikhwanwiki.com/index.php?title=%D8%A7%D9%84%D8%A5%D9%85%D8%A7%D9%85_%D8%AD%D8%B3%D9%86_%D8%A7%D9%84%D8%A8%D9%86%D8%A7_%D9%8A%D9%83%D8%AA%D8%A8_%D9%81%D9%8A_%D8%B9%D9%84%D9%88%D9%85_%D8%A7%D9%84%D9%82%D8%B1%D8%A2%D9%86#.D8.B9.D9.86.D8.A7.D9.8A.D8.A9_.D8.A7.D9.84.D8.B3.D9.84.D9.81_.D8.A8.D9.87 (accessed September 11, 2013); I note that Quṭb makes no mention of al-Banna's commentary on *al-Fātiḥa* in his own commentary on *Sura* one in *Ẓilāl*; al-Banna's commentary on *al-Fātiḥa* was included in an important reading-list which was distributed to teachers in the Brothers Society, see Mitchell, 1993 [1969]: 323.

38 In the context of Islamic polemical literature which presented Christians' use of the cross and icons as a form of idolatry, Hawting makes reference to Dominique Sourdel's 1966 study "Un Pamphlet Musulman Anonyme D'époque 'Abbaside Contre les Chrétiens", see Gerald R. Hawting, 2006 [1999]. *The Idea of Idolatry and the Emergence of Islam: from Polemic to History*. New York: Cambridge University Press, 83n53. Hawting credits Franz Cumont's 1911 study "L'Origine de la Formule Grecque d'Abjuration Imposée aux Musulmans" for the latter's findings which suggest that Christians developed an awareness of the accusation of *shirk* made against them well before the *De Haeresibus* which is attributed to John of Damascus (d. 754), see ibid: 83-84 & 84n55.

39 Hawting finds that al-Ṭabarī gives an account of a letter in which there seems to be a denouncement of Christian Arabs, who supported a rising of the tribe of Nājiya against 'Ali, as "*mushrikūn*". See ibid: 83.

40 Hugh Goddard, 1996. *Muslim Perceptions of Christianity*. London: Grey Seal Books: 31.

41 Goddard gives the example of the title *Muḥāḍārat fī al-Nuṣrāniyya* (*Lectures on Christianity*, 1942) by al- Azhar *Shari'a* teacher, Muḥammad Abu Zahra, as an example of contemporary anti-Christian polemical literature. The work's main thesis is "the break between Jesus and the council of Nicaea", see ibid: 60 (Quṭb comes to reference the aforementioned work in *Ẓilāl* as he quotes the Gospel of Barnabas, see *Ẓilāl*, II: 802n1).

42 According to Krämer, the scope of missionary activities in al-Maḥmūdiyya was such that it warranted a counter activity by the *Ḥaṣāfiyya* Benevolent Society of which al-Banna was a member. Krämer quotes al-Banna as recounting that the aforementioned Society was to become the forerunner of the Brotherhood society, see Gudrun Krämer, 2010: 15-16.

43 Ibid: 94.

44 Reference to apocalyptic Ḥadīth here relates to some strife-related prophetic traditions in relation to the Jews, which are known as "*āḥādīth al-fitan wa āshrāṭ al-sā'a*" (the traditions of strife and the conditions of the coming of doomsday), see Ḥasan al-Banna, 1980 [1930s-early 1940s?]. *Naẓarāt fi Iṣlāḥ al-Nafs wa al-Mujtama'* (Views on Reforming the Self and Society). Cairo: Dār al-I'tiṣām, 52.

45 At times, we see al-Banna rejecting any notion of friendliness, or cooperation, with Christians and Jews as per the explicit ruling of Q5:54, albeit animosity to the Christians is linked here to missionary activities, see Ḥasan al-Banna, 1999 [ca. 1930s]: 166; almost invariably the "enmity" of the "Jew" is contrasted to the "friendliness" of the Christians as per Q5:85 in his discourse, see ibid: 134.

46 Quṭb, no date [1946a]: 123.

47 Mention of O'Leary is made by Amīn in a chapter entitled "Ṭabī'at al-'Aqliyya al-'Arabiyya" (The Nature of the Arab Mind) in which Amīn also addresses Ibn Khaldūn's criticism of the Bedouin Arab as a destroyer of civilisation, see Amīn, 2005 [1929]: 46.

48 This study by Amīn offers itself as a study of the life of the "Arab Mind" since the early days of Islam down to the end of the Umayyad state (750 A.D.), as is indicated by the long title

of the work *Fajr al-Islām Yabḥath ʿan al-Ḥayā al-Aqliyya fi Ṣadr al-Islām ila Akhir al-Dawla al-Amawiyya*.

49 Amīn, 2005 [1929]: 53.
50 Quṭb, 1947b: 189.
51 Cachia, 1990: 88.
52 Malcolm Bradbury, 1988. *The Modern World: Ten Great Writers*. New York: Viking, 3.
53 http://www.sis.gov.eg/En/Templates/Articles/tmpArticles.aspx?ArtID=1346 (accessed November 18, 2010).
54 http://csmt.uchicago.edu/glossary2004/collectiveconsciousness.htm (accessed December 17, 2013).
55 Nadav Safran, 1961: 161 (paraphrased, for original quote see chapter 1).
56 See note 87 in chapter 3.
57 Smith, 1966 [1957]: 65-6.
58 William C. Chittick, 2004. *The Sufi Doctrine of Rūmī*. World Wisdom: 1.
59 Reichmuth observes that the trend of humanism in Sufi poetry in general tends to transcend "exterior norms of Islamic behaviour in the name of universal divine love, as in the poems of Ibn al-ʿArabī, al-Rūmī and Ḥāfiẓ", see Stefan Reichmuth, 2012. "Humanism in Islam between Mysticism and Literature" in *Humanism and Muslim Culture*, 116-126; Quṭb quotes al-ʿAqqād's harsh criticism of al-Rūmī from the anthology that his mentor collected and published under the title *Ibn al-Rūmī: Ḥayātuhu min Shiʿrihu*, see Quṭb, 1947b: 232-4.
60 Wilfred C. Smith, 1981 [1963a]: "The Crystallisation of Religious Communities in Mughul India" in *On Understanding Islam*. The Hague: Mouton Publishers, 184-5.
61 I am making reference here to Quṭb's expressed view which confused Einstein's theory of relativity with Sufi "theories".
62 The Theosophical Society was co-founded in 1875 by the Russian-born Helena Blavatsky (d. 1891) who was chosen, and trained, by the Tibet-based masters of Theosophy to preserve and extend ancient wisdom. Following a two-year training in the Tibet (1868-1870), she dedicated her life to spreading the theosophical message around the world. The Theosophical Society derives its name from the term "Theosophia" used by the Neo-Platonists in reference to "knowledge of the divine", see http://www.blavatsky.net/ (accessed May 19, 2014).
63 Charles D. Smith, 1983: 220n65; al-Banna is said to have been disconcerted by the prevalence of Theosophy in Egypt's elite circles, see Calvert, 2010: 82; among the prominent Egyptians who frequented the Theosophical Society in Cairo were the politicians ʿAbd al-Khāliq Tharwat Pasha and Luṭfī al-Sayyid Bey, see ibid: 309n100.
64 http://www.ts-adyar.org/content/early-history (accessed May 19, 2014).
65 Smith, 1983: 100 (Haykal made reference to Tagore's influence on his thought in an article entitled "Al-ʿUẓamāʾ wa-l-Fikr al-Insānī" which was published in 1929, see ibid: 213n35; it is noteworthy that Shaykh Muṣṭafa al-Marāghī (d. 1945), who was the rector of al-Azhar between 1935 and 1945, wrote a laudatory introduction to Haykal's work, *Ḥayāt Muḥammad* (1935), in which he makes reference to the theosophical movement, see Charles D. Smith, 1983: 118; Shaykh al-Marāghī, who was considered by some to be ʿAbduh's "most brilliant disciple", has called for the abolition of Dār al-ʿUlūm in the 1930s, see ibid: 110; it is to be noted that Quṭb takes no notice in all of his writings of all of the devotional material contributed by the Rectors of al-Azhar which, W. C. Smith observes, aims at arousing "the love of God in men's hearts". He adds that a good example of such material is to be found in the addresses of Shaykh al-Marāghī, which he describes as "brilliant" in language, "deep" in spirit, and reflecting a "limpid and sincere" feeling, see Smith: 1966 [1957]: 131.
66 Alastair Bonnett, 2004. *The Idea of the West: Culture, Politics and History*. New York: Palgrave Macmillan: 79; According to Bonnett, this position ultimately culminated in laying the foundations for a line of dehumanising Occidentalism which was upheld by radical Islamists, and led to the creation of a "dystopian model" of Western civilisation, such as the one which was created in both Pakistan and Iran in the 1960s, see Ibid: 143 (Bonnett makes specific reference

here to the 1960s titles of [the Jewish convert to Islam] Pakistan's Maryam Jameelah *Western Civilisation Condemned by Itself*, and the Iranian Jalal Al-e Ahmad's *Plagued by the West*).

67 David Kopf, 1992. *The Brahmo Samaj and the Shaping of the Modern Indian Mind.* Princeton University Press: 287 (the *Brahmo Samāj* is a theistic movement within the fold of the Hindu tradition which was founded in Calcuta in 1828 by Rammoham Ray. The movement does not accept the authority of the Vedas, has no faith in avatars (incarnations). It discards Hindu rituals and adopts some Christian practices in its worship. Influenced by Christianity and Islam, it denounces polytheism, idol worship and the caste system, source: *The Wordsworth Encyclopedia of World Religions* (1999), 184).

68 Ibid: 291.

69 Ibid: 290.

70 Quoted in Varisco, 2007: 371n330.

71 Rabindranath Tagore, 2010 [1917]. *Nationalism.* London: Penguin Books, 43 (by "the Mohammedans of the West and those of central Asia", Tagore means "the hordes of Mughul and Pathans who invaded India" who, he accepts, India has known as human races, but not as a "nation", see ibid: 38).

72 Varisco, 2007: 391n626.

73 Tagore, 2010 [1917]: 44 (Even so, Tagore was particularly critical of England, claiming that, compared to Germany and France, England produced the smallest number of scholarly works which were dedicated to studies of Indian literature and philosophy "with any amount of sympathetic insight or thoroughness", see ibid: 73; In 1921, he founded the Institute for Asian Culture in Santinketan, see Varisco, 2007: 391n626).

74 Quṭb, 1946b: 18.

75 Rabindranath Tagore, 2013 [1915].*Selected Poems.* London: Collins Classics, 90.

76 Quṭb is said to have told al-Nadwi in 1951 that he did not find in al-'Aqqād's school of thought what satisfies the soul which prompted him to turn to studying eastern poetry, such as that of Tagore, until he found "the Book of God". Quoted in Shalash 1994: 14; Yūnus relays that following Quṭb's loss of his "god", al-'Aqqād, he is said to have explained that turning to Islam was driven by a need for a god that will protect him against worshiping other humans [most probably meaning Tagore]. Yūnus, 1995: 45.

77 Kopf, 1992: 287.

78 Quṭb was to recognise in the translated poems of Tagore "the deep, transparent and fluttering love" (*al-ḥubb al-'amīq, al-shafīf, al-rifāf*) expressed by a "human" depicting a paradise-like world, as he puts it, in the two editions of his work *al-Naqd al-Adabī* (1947), see Quṭb, 1947b: 18 & Quṭb, 2003 [1947b]: 20 (the inverted commas are placed by Quṭb).

79 Gavin Flood, 2006 [1996]. *An Introduction to Hinduism.* Cambridge University Press, 251.

80 Ibid.

81 Quṭb, 1946b: 236-44.

82 Ibid: 337 (these comments occur in Quṭb's review of Shafīq Ghurbāl's work *Muḥammad 'Alī al-Kabīr* which, Smith observes, marks a turning point in Egyptian historiography works at the time which considered the period in Egyptian history from 1517 as part of the history of Egypt, not of Islam. See Wilfred C. Smith, 1966 [1957]: 95n3).

83 Hartung, 2013: 278n35.

84 Quṭb, 1946b: 239-40 (Note that, although Quṭb uses the words "*al-būdhiyya*" and "*hindūsiyya*", which I rendered as two mere objectified/reified isms, i.e. Buddhism and Hinduism respectively, he is hardly considering these traditions as mere objects here).

85 Ibid: 238 (the inverted quotation marks are placed by Quṭb to highlight "faith in all that is Western").

86 Ibid: 240.

87 Ibid: 242.

88 Tagore reflected in *Sādhanā*, for instance, on the harmony between man and nature, see Arup Jyoti Sarma, 2012. "Humanistic Philosophy of Tagore". *Kritike*, 6:1, 53 & ibid: n11.

89 Marie Josephine Aruna. "Tagore's Philosophy of Life- a Study of Sādhanā" in http://rupkatha.com/V2/n4/11Tagorephilosohy.pdf (accessed May 19, 2014); Quṭb seems to have been particularly attracted to Tagore's idea of achieving "union with the Brahman" which he reproduced in *Khaṣṣā'iṣ* (1962) even as he adopts the doctrine of *jāhiliyya*, see Quṭb, 1962c: 216; It is noteworthy that, in discussing the Hindu and Buddhist traditions in the revised edition of *Mashāhid* (1947), Quṭb quotes from a twenty-seven page section dedicated to a discussion of Indian ancient literature in the first of a three-volume work which was co-authored by Aḥmad Amīn and Zakī Najīb Mah mūd (d. 1993), *Qissat al-Adab fī al-'Alam* (The Story of World Literature, 1943). From the aforementioned work, Quṭb quotes the Vedanta, noting that it is the "most modern" and explains that it places an emphasis on the idea that "God and the human soul form one thing; if it appears to a human that they are two different things, this is only due to the limitation of his awareness of their unity," see Quṭb, 1988 [1947c]: 28-9.

90 Quṭb, 1946b: 242.

91 Ibid: 242-3 (Several articles were published in Egypt in the early 1930s on Tagore, his concept of the New Man, and Vedantic texts, noting the esoteric-exoteric dichotomy; some of these articles were written by Fatḥī Raḍwān, see Charles D. Smith,1983: 220n64).

92 Ibid: 242.

93 This portrait is found in the Buddhist site Polonnaruwa in North East Sri Lanka (which was part of Fawzī's tour), see http://www.buddhanet.net/e-learning/history/sites.htm (accessed January 30, 2013).

94 See http://www.britannica.com/EBchecked/topic/442755/Parakramabahu-I (accessed January 30, 2013).

95 Quṭb, 1946b: 242.

96 George Gispert-Sauch, 1997. "Asian Theology" in David F. Ford (ed.) *The Modern Theologians*. Oxford: Blackwell Publishers, 462.

97 See Gavin Flood, 1996: 304-5.

98 Quṭb, 1946b: 241.

99 Karen Armstrong, 2006. *The Great Transformation: the World in the Time of Buddha, Socrates, Confucius and Jeremiah*. London: Atlantic Books, 188 (Orpheus was "a man of peace"; his poetry is said to have "tamed wild beasts, calmed the waves, and made men forget their quarrels", see ibid).

100 Quoted in Quṭb, 1946b: 241.

101 The Dravidian languages group includes the languages of Tamil, Kannada, Telegu, and Malayalam, as well as Brahui, the language of a hill people in Pakistan; the Indo-Iranian languages include Avestan which is the sacred language of the Zoroastrians, see ibid; the earliest Tamil writing is attested in inscriptions and potsherds from the 5th century BCE, see http://www.britannica.com/EBchecked/topic/581953/Tamil-language (accessed June 2, 2014); It is noteworthy that Quṭb continues to express open admiration for Tagore in *al-Naqd al-Adabī* (1947), as a grand litterateur, for having established permanent open channels with the "Great Mother" (*al-um al-Kabīra*), see Quṭb, 1947b: 29; He is probably making reference to the notion of the "Mother Goddess" of the ancient Indus Valley civilisation which is believed to owe its origin to the god Shiva of classical Hindu [ism tradition], see Armstrong, 2006, 14.

102 Flood, 1996: 27.

103 A. R. Venkatachalapathy, 2013. "'Madras Manade' – How Chennai remained with Tamil Nadu" in http://missiontelangana.com/madras-manade-how-chennai-remained-with-tamil-nadu/ (accessed June 2, 2014).

104 http://www.bharatonline.com/tamilnadu/pilgrimage.html (accessed June 2, 2014).

105 Syncretic Muslim practices included, for instance, *Dargah* worship (the adulation of saints and their tombs), see A. R. Venkatachalapathy. "The Changing Face of Tamil Nadu's Muslim Politics" in http://www.thehindu.com/opinion/interview/the-changing-face-of-tamil-nadus-muslim-politics/article4989008.ece (accessed June 2, 2014).

106 Flood, 1996: 269.

107 See http://plato.stanford.edu/entries/transcendentalism/ (accessed May 30, 2014).
108 Quṭb, 1946b:213.
109 Wilfred C. Smith, 2001 [1981b]."The History of Religion in the Singular" in Kenneth Cracknell (ed.) *Wilfred Cantwell Smith: a Reader*. Oxford: Oneworld, 86.
110 Ibid: 87.
111 Ibid: 88.
112 Charles C. Adams, 1933. *Islam and Modernism in Egypt: a Study of the Modern Reform Movement Inaugurated by Muḥammad 'Abduh*. London: Oxford University Press, 95.
113 Hourani, 1983 [1962]:143.
114 Quṭb's review of Fawzī's work was published in the newspaper *al-Thaqāfa*, see Diyāb, 1987: 319n175-6.
115 Calvert, 2010: 105.
116 Shalash remarks that Quṭb started to show an interest in the "artistic imagery" of the Qur'anic+ text in 1939, possibly after seeing the huge interest which was generated by Haykal's and Ḥusayn's writings on Islam-related topoi, see Shalash, 1994: 76.
117 As early as 1934, Quṭb took the position that, as a literary critic, he was undertaking "the difficult and sacred mission" to replace the older generation of literary critics in lieu of "ignorant journalists" who were competing with him, see Yūnus, 1995: 28; in 1944, Quṭb criticised Mandūr specifically in an article published in *al-Risāla* as someone who lacks, as a literary critic, in the ability to differentiate between "authenticity" (*al-aṣāla*) and "fallacy" (*al-zayf*), quoted in ibid.
118 Boullata, 2000: 358.
119 See n87 in chapter 1.
120 Quṭb, 1959 [1945b]: 32-3.
121 William A. Graham & Navid Kermani, 2011 [2006]. "Recitation and Aesthetic Reception" in Jane D. McAuliffe (ed.) *The Cambridge Companion to the Qur'ān*. Cambridge University Press, 130.
122 Adams, 1933, 85 (these works are *Asrār al-Balāgha* and *Dalā'il al-I'jāz*, see ibid: n6).
123 Gibb, 1963 [1926]: 88-9.
124 As discussed in chapter 2 earlier, Quṭb mentions in his memoirs that attending lessons on al-Zamakhsharī's exegesis by al-Azhar *'ulama* in the village was meant to make him feel "like a man", see Sayyid Quṭb, no date [1946a]: 52.
125 Gibb, 1963 [1926]: 122-3 (Al-Zamakhsharī's chief works included, as well, his linguistic commentary on the Qur'an, *al-Kashshāf 'an Ḥaqā'iq al-Tanzīl* (The Discoverer of Revealed Truth), and his other grammatical work, *Al-Mufaṣṣal fī 'Ilm al-Arabiyya* (Detailed Treatise on Arabic Linguistics, 1119–21) which was also known as *Kitāb al Mufaṣṣal fī al-Naḥw* (Detailed Treatise on Grammar), and is celebrated for its concise, yet exhaustive exposition, see Abu al-Qāsim Maḥmūd Ibn 'Umar al-Zamakhsharī, *Encyclopaedia Britannica*, http://www.britannica.com/EBchecked/topic/655524/Abu-al-Qasim-Mahmud-ibn-Umar-al-Zamakhshari (accessed January 23, 2013).
126 Quṭb, 1959 [1945b]: 26.
127 Ibid.
128 Ibid: 29.
129 Ibid (the inverted comas in the quote are placed by Quṭb to accentuate the word "*al-kalām*").
130 Ibid: 32 (as discussed in chapter 3 above, Quṭb makes the opposite argument in the first five editions of *al-'Adāla*, by making the argument that Islam, (as an objectified idea), came at a time of full awareness of humanity at large [to attain] such an overall and comprehensive idea).
131 By and large, Quṭb's literary writings, over the period of some two decades, failed to secure a favourable reception within the literary milieu to which he belonged. Shalash observes that it is likely that Quṭb experienced a degree of despair following the publication of *al-Taṣwīr al-Fannī* in 1945 (which was criticised in academic circles), and the failure of the work to attract the attention of leading figures in Egypt's literary circles such as al-'Aqqād, Ṭaha Ḥusayn and Aḥmad Amīn, see Shalash, 1994: 92; In an appraisal of Quṭb's literary writings, over the period of some

two decades, Calvert writes that these were "erratic and uncertain", especially compared to the works of the literary luminaries of the day, see Calvert, 2010: 11.

132 This information is according to a book which was released in Cairo in 1969, and included in Stanford University Library's book collection, *Dalā'il al-I'jāz* was included in the commentaries on the Qur'an by Abduh, Riḍā, al-Shanqitī, and al-Marāghī. See http://searchworks.stanford.edu/view/6762995 (accessed January 23, 2013).

133 Al-Jurjānī's *Kitāb al-Ta'rīfāt* provided a short dictionary of technical terms from theology, philosophy, and philology and was first edited by the German lexicographer G. Flügel in 1845, see http://www.britannica.com/EBchecked/topic/308602/al-Jurjani (accessed January 23, 2013).

134 In analysing the chapter entitled "How was the Qur'an Understood" (*Kayfa Fuhima al-Qur'ān*) in *al-Taṣwīr al-Fannī fi al-Qur'ān,* I identified one instance when Quṭb makes reference to al-Zamakhsharī's commentary on the divine attributes in *Sura* I (*al-Fātiḥa*), see Quṭb, 1959 [1945b]: 27.

135 *Ẓilāl*, VI:3990-3.

136 McAuliffe points out that much of this sort of literature, which is credited to the Prophet and his Companions, is associated with Q109. Among the most common statements about Q109 is the declaration that "the recitation of this *Sura* is equivalent to the recitation of a quarter of the Qur'an". Al-Tha'labī cites this statement on the authority of Mālik Ibn Anas (d. 769) while al-Zamakhsharī quotes the Prophet, see Jane D. McAuliffe, 2011 [2006]. "The Tasks and Traditions of Interpretation" in McAuliffe (ed.) *The Cambridge Companion to the Qur'ān*. New York: Cambridge University Press: 188.

137 Ibid: 201.

138 *Ẓilāl*, VI: 3991.

139 Ibid: 3992.

140 Gibb, 1963 [1926]: 54.

141 Ibid: 52-3.

142 Ibid: 65.

143 Goodman, 2003: 180.

144 Gibb, 1963 [1926]: 88.

145 Quṭb, 1947b: 129 (it is noteworthy that al-Manār quotes Maḥmūd Sālim, the president of the Society (Jamā'at al-Da 'wa wa al-Irshād, as expressing the opinion that "the ancients applied the ideas of Aristotle, Plato, Pythagoras, and Galen to Qur'anic exegesis, we must now do the same with G.W. von Leibniz, Auguste Comte, and Herbert Spencer, see Goldziher, 2006 [1920]. *Schools of Koranic Commentators* with an introduction on Goldziher and Ḥadīth from *Geschichte des Arabischen Schrifttums* by Fuat Sezgin edited and translated by Wolfgang H. Behn. Wiesbaden: Harrassowitz Verlag: 219).

146 Quṭb, 1959 [1945b]: 120.

147 Ibid: 122 & ibid: n1.

148 Ibid: 127.

149 This information is derived from the back cover of *Kutub wa Shakhṣiyyāt*; the third work that he intended to write is a comparative study on story-telling in the Torah and the Qur'an.

150 Smith, 1981 [1974]. "Muslim-Christian Interrelations Historically: An Interpretation" in *On Understanding Islam*. The Hague: Mouton Publishers, 249.

151 Quṭb, 2004 [1947c]: 41.

152 Unless there is a variation between the two editions of the work that I analysed, I will reference only the last revised edition of the work (1988).

153 Fazlur Rahman deems Q2:62 to be one of the Qur'anic verses, along with Q2:134 & 141, which convey "a strong rejection of exclusivism and election" in matters of faith and stress the recognition of the existence of good people in other communities such as that of Jews, Christians, and Sabians, see Fazlur Rahman, 1990. "The People of the Book and the Diversity of Religions" in Paul J. Griffiths (ed.) *Christianity through Non-Christian Eyes*. New York: Orbis Books, 254n4

(In Quṭb's commentary on Q2:62 in *Ẓilāl*, he goes against the inclusive message of the verse by implying that it was temporal. Quṭb seems to expect then that all humans should adopt Islam, as objectified and interpreted by him, as he puts forward the argument that "the Muḥammadan mission" brought a "final form of belief", see *Ẓilāl*, I:75-6).

154 In a discussion of the historical context of the Qur'an, Saeed notes that, unlike the Byzantine Empire which was on the whole Christian, the Sassanid empire was predominantly Zoroastrian, but included a number of other traditions such as the Buddhist, the Jewish, and the Christian, see 'Abdullah Saeed, 2009. "Contextualising" in Andrew Rippin (ed.) *The Blackwell Companion to the Qur'ān*. Wiley-Blackwell, 37.

155 Quṭb, 2004 [1947c]: 28 (for Quṭb's reference to "*Hindūkiyya*", as an equivalent to English Hinduism in the singular in *al-'Adāla*, see Quṭb, 1950 [1949]: 26).

156 Haykal invokes the idea of "Nirvana" in discussing the Theosophical movement in the mid-1930s, see Haykal, 1976 [1935]: 597n21.

157 Cited in Ahmad M. al-Badawī, 2002: 11 (The word "*shuhūd*" in Islamic Sufi terminology refers to a vision of God obtained by the illuminated heart of the seeker of truth. Through *mushāhada*, the Sufi acquires *yaqīn* (real certainty), which cannot be achieved by the intellect or transmitted to those who do not travel the Sufi path by going through various ritual stages (*maqām*), see http://global.britannica.com/EBchecked/topic/398862/mushahadah (accessed May 23rd, 2014); Ibn 'Arabī explains that he has not seen any of "God's friends" reaching the station of "*shuhūd*" which is only "tasted" (*dhawq*) by prophets and messengers of God, see Chittick, 1989: 44).

158 Quṭb, 2004 [1947c]: 29-30.

159 http://www.buddhanet.net/e-learning/buddhism/disciples09.htm (accessed May 23rd, 2014).

160 W. C. Smith, 1964: 240n20.

161 Quṭb notes in *Kutub wa Shakhṣiyyāt* that Amīn contributed only some scattered articles to modern literary criticism, see Quṭb, 1946b: 4.

162 It is probably the case that Amīn ceased to pose a threat to Quṭb following the former's retirement in 1946 after a twenty-year teaching career at Cairo University where he established regular contacts with European-educated Egyptians as well as European professors, see Shepard, 1982. *The Faith of a Modern Muslim Intellectual: The Religious Aspects and Implications of the Writings of Aḥmad Amīn*. New Delhi: Vikas House, 20.

163 Aḥmad Amīn and Zakī Najīb Mahmūd, 1943. *Qiṣṣat al-Adab fī al-'Alām* (The Story of World Literature). Cairo: Maṭba'it Lajnat al-Tā'līf wa al-Tarjama wa al-Nashr, I: 39-65.

164 Shepard identifies this work as one of three popular works which were co-authored by Amīn and Mahmūd to introduce Egyptians to Western heritage; the other two works are *Qiṣṣat al-Falsafa al-Yunāniyya* (The Story of Greek Philosophy, 1936), and *Qiṣṣat al-Falsafa al-Ḥadītha* (The Story of Modern Philosophy, 1936). According to Shepard, all three titles may have been inspired by Will Durant's *Story of Philosophy*, upon which the two authors rely "quite heavily" in *Qiṣṣat al-Falsafa al-Ḥadītha*, see Shepard, 1982: 23 (In the preface of *Qiṣṣat al-Adab fī al-'Ālam*, Amīn indicates that the aim of the work is to avoid committing in the modern *nahḍa* the mistake which was committed during the Abbasid *nahḍa* which neglected the translation of works of literature, see Amīn and Maḥmūd, 1943, I: II).

165 Amīn and Maḥmūd, 1943, I: 59.

166 Shepard, 1982: 84.

167 Quoted in Quṭb, 2004 [1947c]: 28 (for my interpretation of Brāhmānā as the Brahma-Mimamsa, see http://global.britannica.com/EBchecked/topic/624431/Vedanta (accessed May 30th, 2014).

168 See http://www.thebrahmosamaj.net/history/chronolgy.html (accessed May 30th, 2014); It is to be noted that the appeal of the Vedanta in the modern West, where it was interpreted under the Ramakrishna order leadership in 1930 in the direction of affirming "the oneness of existence, and the divinity of the soul", was such that a Vedanta Society was founded in the same year in Southern California; the Society expanded later by establishing other branches in other parts of the United States, see http://vedanta.org/ (accessed May 30th, 2014).

169 According to one study, some similarities have been drawn between the Vedanta philosophy, which inspired Tagore, as being pantheistic in its outlook for allowing one to become Brahma and strands of Sufism which developed into "idealistic pantheism". The argument is made that there are pantheistic elements in the belief which developed in Sufi Islam that God is imminent and that man will ultimately be absorbed unto God (*fanā' fī Allah*), as in Ibn 'Arabī's idea of "*wiḥdat al-wujūd*" and of al-Ḥallāj that he has become God, see Kavi Ghulam Mustafa. "The Idea of God and Universe in Tagore and Iqbal", in http://www.allamaiqbal.com/publications/journals/review/oct60/4.htm (accessed May 25th, 2014).

170 Carré finds that in *Ẓilāl* "Quṭb speaks more than once about the quest for contact with God, but without going into the varied Sufi techniques...", see Carré, 2003: 96; In the preface of *Muqawwimāt al-Taṣawwur al-Islāmī*, Quṭb's younger brother, Muḥammad, alludes to some comments made by some of his older brother's detractors who pointed out some ambiguity surrounding some expressions used by Quṭb in his commentary on the Qur'anic *Suras al-Ḥadīd* (Q57) and *al-Ikhlāṣ* (Q112) in *Ẓilāl* which might impress on some readers that his older brother was making reference to the doctrine of "*wiḥdat al-wujūd*", see Quṭb, 1997 [1969]: 9; indeed, Quṭb makes an explicit reference to "*aḥadiyyat al-Wujūd*" in his commentary on Q112, see *Ẓilāl*, VI: 4002; he also indicates in his commentary on Q57 that nothing else exists in reality but God, see ibid: 3479.

171 al-'Aqqād, 1947b: 165.

172 All five books are identified by Amīn and Maḥmūd as constituting the body of the Torah in the section they dedicate to discussing Hebrew literature, see Amīn and Maḥmūd, 1943: 80.

173 The omission of any mention of the story of Joseph in Genesis is particularly important since Quṭb was certainly made aware of the importance of that sacred text to his favourite, Tolstoy, who, according to Amīn and Maḥmūd, described the story of Joseph in Genesis as reaching the pinnacle of artistic perfection, see ibid: 83.

174 'Abbās M. Al-'Aqqād, 1964 [1947c]. *Allah: Kitāb fī Nashā't al-'Aqīda al-Ilahiyya* (Allah: a Study on the Genesis of the Belief in the Divine).Cairo: Dār al-Ma'ārif, 23.

175 Ibid: 118; Varisco notes that it was the publication of Müller's *Sacred Books of the East* series in 1875 which helped illuminate the previously "hidden wisdom of the East" in Sanskrit studies, see Varisco, 2007: 87; interestingly, Quṭb illuminates the myth of the flood in *Sura* LXXI, Nūḥ (Noah), in *Ẓilāl* by openly borrowing from Genesis (without referencing it) the idea that Noah lived to the age of 950 years, see *Ẓilāl*, VI, 3706; on the myth of Noah in Genesis, see Bowker, 1998: 32-3.

176 There is one instance when Quṭb is said to have been favourably impressed by a 1946 play, *The New Shylock*, by 'Ali Aḥmad Ba-Kathir, an Egyptian-based writer of Yemeni-Indonesian background, which invokes Shakespeare's problematic portrayal of the Jewish character in *The Merchant of Venice*. In a newspaper article which was published in *al-Risāla* under the title "Shylūk al-Jadīd, wa Qaḍiyyat Filisṭīn", Quṭb expresses an appreciation of the play's call for a boycott of the Zionists, quoted in Calvert, 2010: 122 & ibid: 316n78.

177 Quṭb, 1946b: 42.

178 Al-'Aqqād explains that Laurence Hope (1865-1904) is a pen-name of an English contemporary poetess who was influenced by Indian doctrines and wrote on eastern issues, including "il-Gharām al-Hindī" (The Book of Indian Love, 1905), see 'Abbās M. al-'Aqqād, 1970 [ca. early 1940s]. "Arā'is wa Shayāṭīn" (Muses and Demons) in *Majmū'at A'lām al-Shi'r*. Beirut: Dār al-Kitāb al-'Arabī, 644n1.

179 For al-'Aqqād's translation, see ibid: 644-5, for the English text see http://www.gutenberg.org/cache/epub/5125/pg5125.html (May 30th, 2014).

180 Hardy is introduced by al-'Aqqād in his anthology "*Arā'is wa Shayāṭīn*" as being perhaps the greatest early 20th-century European poet. He notes, however, that Hardy is rather inclined to sarcasm, and pessimism, see al-'Aqqād, no date [ca. early 1940s]: 649n1.

181 Professor Landow argues that, like so many Victorian authors – such as Thomas Carlyle, Gerard Manley Hopkins, John Henry Newman and John Ruskin – Hardy had little sympathy with

Evangelical Christianity. In fact, Hardy is believed to have ended up abandoning it for a belief in some "Unconscious Will", see George P. Landow "Thomas Hardy's Religious Beliefs" in http://www.victorianweb.org/authors/hardy/religion1.html (accessed June 10, 2014); An argument is also made that Hardy's "moments of vision" are comparable to what Wordsworth calls "spots of time" which, like Emily Dickinson's poetry, relate to attempting to unravel "secrets" which are concealed from us, see Andrew Bennett and Nicholas Royle, 2004 [1995]. *Introduction to Literature, Criticism and Theory*. Dorchester: Dorset Press: 244.

182 The exotic settings and passionate intensity of Hope's first volume of poetry, "The Garden of Kama" and other Love Lyrics from India, which were published in 1901, were seen as "oriental" and hardly acceptable in Victorian and Edwardian England. See http://maddy06.blogspot.co.uk/2014/03/adela-violet-florence-nicolson-laurence.html (accessed June 10, 2014).

183 John Donne is known to have been a main influence on the 1948 Nobel prize laureate, Thomas S. Eliot (b. 1888), see http://www.poets.org/poetsorg/poet/t-s-eliot (May 30th, 2014); see also Helen Gardner, 1985 [1957]. *The Metaphysical Poets*. London: Penguin Books, 309.

184 Ibid: 317-8.

185 John Donne's poem "Elegy: his Picture" is translated by al-'Aqqād, see al-'Aqqād, no date [ca. early 1940s]: 624-5 & ibid: 625n1; John Milton is mentioned by Aḥmad Amīn and Zakī Najīb Maḥmūd in the course of discussing Hebrew literature, see Amīn and Maḥmūd, 1943: 84.

186 I am drawing an analogy here from the argument made by Smith that the Qur'an should be studied mainly as "a timeless book...a living, life-giving source of the religious life of the continuing community", See Wilfred C. Smith, 1981 [1963]. "Is the Qur'ān the Word of God?" in *On Understanding Islam*. The Hague: Mouton Publishers, 295.

187 Starting the mid-1920s, Protestant fundamentalists in the United states launched a counteroffensive against modernity, and concentrated, like Haredi Jews, on creating their own defensive counterculture. By 1930, there were at least fifty fundamentalist Bible colleges in the United states. Another twenty-six were founded during the Depression years. In the counterculture that Protestant fundamentalists were creating, their colleges were considered safe, scared enclaves amid the surrounding profaneness, see Armstrong, 2001a: 214-5; after the second world war, new *yeshivot* were built in both Israel and the United States. In both countries, Torah education was generously funded and flourished as never before, see ibid: 212.

188 Quṭb, 2004 [1947c]: 32.

189 Ibid: 33 (unbeknown to Quṭb, an English edition of the Book of Job, which contained eighteen illustrations by William Blake, was published in 1825. Blake's drawings, in turn, provided the inspiration for "Job: a Masque for Dancing" by the great English composer Ralph Vaughan William (1872-1958), see Peter Calvocoressi, 1987. *Who's Who in the Bible*. Penguin Dictionaries, 114; a translation of Blake's poem "The Poison Tree" is provided by al-'Aqqād in his anthology "'Arā'is wa Shayāṭīn", see al-'Aqqād, no date [ca. early 1940s]: 733-4).

190 Quṭb, 2004 [1947c]: 33-34.

191 'Ali Adham, 1978 [1945]. *Naẓārat fi al-Ḥayāt wa al-Mujtama'*. Cairo: Dār al-Ma'ārif, 81-91.

192 The Arabic text is from a 1897 translation of the Bible by the Beirut-based Yasū'iyyīn Publishing House which is used by Adham, see Adham, 1978 [1945]: 87n1.

193 Armstrong, 2006: 171.

194 Adham, 1978 [1945]: 81 (this part is included in the two paragraphs quoted by Quṭb).

195 Ibid: 86.

196 Calvert argues that it was only after World War II, when the conflict in Palestine came to a head, that Quṭb gave the issue his full attention, see Calvert, 2010: 120.

197 Marion Woolfson, 1980. *Prophets in Babylon*. London: Faber and Faber, 12.

198 This quote is extracted by Calvert from the article "al-Ḍamīr al-Amrikanī wa Qaḍiyyat Filisṭīn," which was published in *al-Risāla* in 1946, see Calvert, 2010: 120 & ibid: 316n74.

199 There is no recognition in *Mashāhid* of any of the Old Testament three major prophets (Isaiah, Jeremiah, Ezekiel), or any of the twelve minor prophets, including Zechariah, and Jonah, and of

Old Testament prophets who are not mentioned in the Qur'an: Hosea, Nahum, Joel, Habakkuk, Amos, Zephaniah, Obadiah, Haggai, Micah, and Malachi, see Ronald D. Witherup, 1989. *The Bible Companion: a Handbook for Beginners*. New York: the Crossroad Publishing Company, 99.

200 Gershoni and Jankowski exclude Quṭb from the "supra-Egyptian nationalist ideology" which placed an emphasis on Arab nationalism in the 1930s and 1940s, see the chapter entitled "Egyptian Arab nationalism" in Israel Gershoni and James Jankowski, 1995. *Redefining the Egyptian Nation*, 1930-1945. Cambridge University Press, 117-142; Based on an analysis of Quṭb's discourse in *al-Rad 'ala Mustaqbal al-Thaqāfa fī Misr* (1939), Gershoni and Jankowski place Quṭb in the 1930s "Egyptian Easternism" movement, see ibid: 43 & 228n44; Calvert remarks that Quṭb derided the British and Americans for their complicity in the Zionist project, and was particularly critical of the 1946 report which was issued by the Anglo-American Committee of Inquiry, which recommended, at US President Truman's insistence, the immediate entry into Palestine of 100, 000 Jewish refugees from Europe and the creation of a unitary Palestinian state into which Jews would continue to be welcome to the detriment of the right of Arab primacy in Palestine and the right of Arab people to be in control of their own territory, see Calvert, 2010: 121.

201 Al-'Aqqād, 1964 [1947c]: 114.

202 Quṭb, 2004 [1947c]: 34-5 (the quote from Matthew is an insertion by Quṭb which is not included in the quote he seems to have extracted from al-'Aqqād's work).

203 Quṭb is writing against the backdrop of increasing scholarly interest in Egypt in the early 1940s in Hebrew literature and history which made a wealth of information available to Quṭb through the works of scholars, such as Muḥammad 'Aṭiya al-Ibrāshī and Fu'ād Ḥasanayn, who were recognised within Egypt's academia circles as being the authority on Hebrew literature, see Aḥmad Amīn and Zakī Najīb Maḥmūd, 1943, iii; one of the studies, which was certainly available to Quṭb in the mid-1940s, is the one which was undertaken by al-Ibrāshī, a graduate of the University of London, who taught at Dār al-'Ulūm and Cairo University upon his return to Egypt in 1930, which was published in 1946 under the title *al-Adāb al-Sāmiyya* (Semitic Literature). Al-Ibrāshī relays in the preface of the work that the study of Hebrew literature is undertaken with the view of affirming himself as an "Eastern Arab", see Muḥammad 'Aṭiya al-Ibrāshī, 1946. *al-Adāb al-Sāmiyya*. Syria: Dār Iḥyā' al-Kutub al-'Arabiyya, 3-4; al-Ibrāshī gives in the work a detailed exposé of the Old Testament books, and points out the importance of the Book of Isaiah in illuminating modern-day studies of Hebrew dialect in the South, whereas the Book of Joshua represents the dialect of the north, see ibid: 22-25. Al- Ibrāshī relies primarily on Nöldeke in his study and some other forty Orientalists.

204 Al-'Aqqād quotes Isaiah 24:21-23; 25:6; and 27:1.

205 The first part of the Book of Isaiah (chs. 1-39) ,which deals thematically with "prophecies calling for fidelity", is believed to have originated from the 8th century "Isaiah of Jerusalem"; the second part of the Book (chs. 40:1-55:13) is believed to have preserved the words of "the Second Isaiah" (ca. 540 BCE) who was a prophet of the exile in Babylon; the last part of the Book (chs. 56:1-66-24) was written when the restoration of Jerusalem was underway, see Ronald D. Witherup, 1989: 104-105, (al-'Aqqād, however, makes reference to "the Second Isaiah", noting that the Israelites came to understand the idea of "the unity of God" (*al-wiḥdāniyya*), see al-'Aqqād, 1960 [1947c]: 115.

206 Quṭb, 2004 [1947c]: 35.

207 Ibid: 37 (The same argument is made by al-'Aqqād who, however, accepts Daniel as a "prophet" and quotes Daniel 12:2, see Al-'Aqqād, 1964 [1947c]: 114).

208 Smith, 1964: 242n25.

209 al-'Aqqād, 1960 [1947c]: 172, (al-'Aqqād's remarks occur in a section of his work *Allah* which he dedicates to a discussion of "Religions after Philosophy" in which he tackles, Judaism (164-171), Christianity (172-177), and Islam (178-187), as well as the impact of "book-religions" *(al-adyān al-kitābiyya)* on philosophy (188-203) and a discussion of Sufism (204-210) in which he accepts that Buddhism is a "conquest" (in the spiritual realm), see ibid).

210 Quṭb, 1988 [1947c]: 35; It is worthy of note that Quṭb would eventually come to deprecate St. Paul in the revised edition of *al-Mustaqbal li-hadhā al-Dīn*, quoting from al-'Aqqād's section on "Christianity after philosophy" in his work *Allah* that Paul's epistles brought into Christianity the philosophy of "*ḥilūl*", and that he called himself "*rasūl Yasū' al-Masīḥ*" (the messenger of Jesus Christ), see Quṭb, 2005 [ca. 1962d]: 28.

211 Quṭb, 2004 [1947c]: 35 (neither the Sadducees, nor the Pharisees, are mentioned in the Qur'an).

212 Ibid.

213 Chadwick, 1990: 23.

214 John Bowker, 1998. *The Complete Bible Handbook*. London: Dorling Kindersley, 400 (I paraphrased Bowker and added insertions from Acts 21:28 here).

215 Smith, 1964: 243n29.

216 Ibid: 57-8.

217 Quṭb, 1950 [1949]: 9; this quote is only found in edition 1 & 2 of *al-'Adāla*, see Shepard, 1996: 3n7.

218 Bowker, 1998: 403.

219 *Ẓilāl*, V: 2961.

220 William M. Watt, 1991. *Muslim-Christian Encounters: Perceptions and Misperceptions*. London: Routledge, 47.

221 Bowker, 1998: 433.

222 Ibid: 411.

223 Quṭb, 1950 [1949]: 9 (only in the last edition of *al-'Adāla*, as Quṭb begins to objectify Islam as a system in the 1960s, he criticises Christianity for not taking the form of a system which prevails over all of life, see Quṭb, 1993 [1964a]: 8-9. In broad terms, I agree with Shepard's argument that there is a "subtle change" in Quṭb's view of Christianity which sees him depicting it in the earlier editions of *al-'Adāla* as "a religion, which by its very nature and original historical circumstances, was limited to inward spiritual and moral training and made no effort to order society", see Shepard, 1996: Iiii. As we shall see in chapter 5, Quṭb's polemics against Christianity in *Khaṣṣā'iṣ* are not targeting Paul, and rather presuppose the Christian communities which were encountered by Muḥammad, see Watt, 1991: 1).

224 Bowker, 1998: 403.

225 Goddard, 1996: 19.

226 Yūnus relays that it was probably following al-'Aqqād's refusal to write an introduction to *Mashāhid* that Quṭb severed all contact with his mentor, see Yūnus, 1995: 45n2.

227 Translation provided by Shepard with the exception that I added "empty in appearances" at the end of the sentence, see Shepard, 1996:2; see Quṭb, 1950 [1949]:6 and Quṭb, 1993 [1964a]:8.

228 Haddad notes that 'Abduh attempted to modernize Islam by disregarding "accumulated traditions" that he felt were irrelevant in the twentieth century, aiming to meet the challenge posed by Protestant Christianity and the colonial powers which judged the prevalent Islamic institutions at the time as "ossified", and essentially "irrelevant". See Yvonne Y. Haddad, 1983b: 15-16; according to Goldziher, al-Manār party was in agreement with al-Ghazālī who, eight centuries earlier, noted that the prevalent decadence of the Muslim world in "the fossilation" of the four Orthodox fiqh rites, see Goldziher, 2006 [1920]: 206; in the same vein, Ṭaha Ḥusayn writes in 1924 of a priest's activity in organizing a charitable event in France, and invites Azharite scholars to follow the example of European priests, or be "atrophied", see Rasheed el-Enany, 2006. *Arab Representations of the Occident: East-West Encounters in Arabic Fiction*. Oxon: Routledge, 58.

229 Nettler, 1987: 11.

230 Quṭb, 1969 [1939]: 21-23.

231 Quṭb, 1950 [1949]: 7-8; see also Shepard, 1996: 19-20 & 19n 89-90, 20n92.

232 Ibid: 7.

233 Ibid (I consulted Shepard's translation at times here with verses from Matthew being all translated by Shepard, see Shepard, 1996: 19).

234 al-'Aqqād, no date [ca. late 1940sa] *Falāsifat al-Ḥukm fī al-'Aṣr al-Ḥadīth* (The Philosophers on Government Theories in the Modern Age) in *al-Majmū'a al-Kāmila li Mu'alafāt al-Ustādh 'Abbās al-'Aqqād*, Vol. 14. Beirut. Dār al-Kitāb al-Libnānī, 457.

235 Ibid: 465.

236 Ibid: 467.

237 Ibid: 466.

238 Alistair Hamilton, 2007 [1996]. "Humanists and the Bible" in Jill Kraye (ed.) *Renaissance Humanism*. Cambridge University Press, 101.

239 Quṭb insists on the penalty of stoning as a means of purification in all editions of *al-'Adāla*, see Quṭb, 1993 [1964a]: 130; Shepard, 1996: xxviii (Clearly, Quṭb ignores the part in Jesus' Sermon in which he blesses those who are "pure in heart" (Matthew 5:8).

240 Shepard, 1996: xxviii.

241 Quṭb is quoted as noting in an article entitled "Hadhā al-Majalla" published on January 1, 1948 in *al-Fikr al-Jadīd* that the European Section of the Egyptian Broadcasting Company employs "a Jew who routinely sketches the Star of David alongside his signature", see Calvert, 2010: 125, and ibid: 316n89.

242 Ibid: 122.

243 Ibid (these remarks are made in an article published on 20 May 1946 in *al-Risāla* "al-Kalimat al-Yawm li al-'Arab Famadhā Hum Ṣāni'ūn", cited in ibid: 316n76).

244 J. Calvert, L. J. Greenspoon, B. F. Le Beau, Sep, 1996. "Radical Islamism and the Jews: the View of Sayyid Quṭb" **in** *Studies in Jewish civilization*, 220; the struggle for Palestine is depicted by Quṭb in a 1946 newspaper article in *al-Risāla* as being one of "a resurgent East against a Barbaric West", quoted in ibid: 220.

245 Quṭb was, however, dismayed by "the US commitment to Zionism", since he shared with other Arabs the belief that the US was committed to justice, and criticised President Truman in 1946 for pleading the entry into Palestine of 100, 000 European Jews, see ibid.

246 Quṭb's commentary on this *sura*, in terms of otherness, reveals that it was written after writing the fifth edition of *al-'Adāla* (1958) and before writing *Khaṣṣā'iṣ* (1962).

247 Erikson, 1994 [1968]: 299.

248 The detail that Lot was Abraham's nephew is an addition by Quṭb which is not mentioned in Q21:71.

249 *Ẓilāl*, 4: 2388. (Quṭb reveals here that he had gained some knowledge of biblical historiography which accepts Abraham as the first patriarch, which contradicts the Qur'anic depiction of Abraham as a "*ḥanīf*" (Q3:67) who was neither Jew nor Christian (2:140) following the rejection of Muḥammad's prophethood by Jews and Christians, see Watt, 1991: 16, and ibid: 153n8; it is noteworthy that, even as Quṭb refers to "*millet* Ibrāhim" as the "*ḥanifiyya al-Ula*" (first monotheism) in his commentary on Q2:62, he still accepts the Jews, the Christians, and the community referred to as "*al-Ṣābi'ūn*" as adhering to *tawḥīd*, see *Ẓilāl*, 1:75; elsewhere, in his commentary on Q21:52-4, Quṭb accepts, as well, Abraham, not as a "*ḥanīf*", but as "the great forefather" of the Arabs who built the holy shrine, *al-ka'ba*, and destroyed statues of false deities in Mecca, see *Ẓilāl*, 4: 2384; here, he is being more in tune with qur'anic argumentation which refers to Abraham as one who criticises the "malignity of rival deities" to God (Q26:77), see Kate Zebiri, 2009. "Argumentation" in Andrew Rippin (ed.) *The Blackwell Companion to the Qur'ān*. Wiley-Blackwell, 270-271.

250 Quṭb, 1950 [1949]: 168.

251 Quṭb, 1993 [1964a]: 146 (this argument is made in all editions of *al-'Adāla*).

252 Ed.1, ed.2 reads "i*dh'ān*" and in the 6th ed. "*taslīm*", see Shepard, 1996: 214n96; all three words clearly suggest that the non-Muslin "other" should acquiesce, or submit, to the Muslim and maintain a position of lowliness in a Muslim society; on the oppressive *dhimma* system see Bat Ye'or, 1980. *Le Dhimmī: Profil de L'opprimé en Orient et en Afrique du Nord depuis la Conquête Arabe*. Paris : Editions Anthropos.

253 http://www.bbc.co.uk/history/ww2peopleswar/timeline/factfiles/nonflash/a1143578.shtml (accessed November 2, 2014): Quṭb wrote of the Beveridge Report in 1943, see Sayyid Quṭb, May 1943. "Mashrū' Beveridge," (*MSI*), 5:21-9, cited in Muḥammad Ḥāfiẓ Diyāb, 1987: 317, n152.

254 Quṭb, 1950 [1949]: 218 (in the last edition of *al-'Adāla*, Quṭb makes the argument that 'Umar introduced the idea of "social solidarity" (*al-taḍāmun al-ijtimā'ī*) as a "right" on a "purely humane basis, see Quṭb, 1993 [1964a]: 153; clearly borrowing from Durkheim's romantic ideas on community and solidarity, see Inger Furseth and Pal Repstad, 2006. *An Introduction to the Sociology of Religion*. Hants: Ashgate, 77; as discussed in chapter 2, Durkheim is identified as one of "the three Jews" by Muḥammad Quṭb).

255 Ibid: 176; all eds. see Shepard, 1996: 220-21.

256 Bernard Lewis questions the authenticity of the "Pact of 'Umar" on the grounds that some of the measures regulating the relationship between Muslims and *dhimmīs* in this decree were really introduced by the Umayyad Caliph 'Umar II (717-720), see Lewis, 1984a: 25.

257 Ibid: 171 (Quṭb is said to have been particularly critical of the educational policies of Dunlop which provided the basis for education policies in Egypt in the early part of the 20th century, see 'Abbās Khiḍr, 1983: 58).

258 Ibid: 172 (translated by Shepard, see Shepard, 1996: 216).

259 Ibid.

260 Shepard, 1996: 216n104.

261 Quṭb, 1993 [1964a]: 149-150 (Quṭb draws a comparison here to the detriment of a coercive European civilisation, and its colonialist activities, on the one hand, and Islamic conquests, which were free of any form of "coercion", on the other; Watt notes that such an argument was put in circulation towards the 1940s by Muslim apologists, who were particularly critical of the hostility of European colonialism to Islam, while justifying "Islamic colonialism" which, he considers to have been motivated by the booty, see Watt, 1991: 59-60).

262 Norman A. Stillman, 1991. *The Jews of Arab Lands in Modern Times*. New York: The Jewish Publication Society, 17.

263 Ibid: 22.

264 Quṭb, 1988 [1947c]: 38.

265 Goddard, 1996: 105.

266 Smith, 1964: 120.

267 See Henri de Lubac's study *The Drama of Atheist Humanism* (1944).

Chapter 5

1 Emmanuel Sivan, 1990. *Radical Islam: Medieval Theology and Modern Politics*. Yale University Press, 22 (In Shi'ite Iran, Sayyid M. Taleqani (d. 1979) promoted the idea of a war against "*the new jāhiliyya*", see Buruma & Margalit, 2004: 115).

2 Shepard, 2003. "Sayyid Quṭb's Doctrine of *Jāhiliyya*". *IJMES*, 35:4, 524.

3 Karen Armstrong, 2005. *A Short History of Myth*. Edinburgh: Canongate, 142.

4 On the comparison between Quṭb's Islamism, Marxism, and Hitler's National Socialism, see Hendrik Hansen and Peter Kainz, 2007. "Radical Islamism and Totalitarian Ideology: a Comparison of Sayyid Quṭb's Islamism with Marxism and National Socialism" in *TMPR*, 8:1, 55-76. (This article relies on a diversity of primary sources including *Ma'ālim*, *Hadha al-Dīn*, *al-Mustaqbal li-Hadha al-Dīn* and *Ẓilāl* unlike another study which relies solely on the article "Ma'rakatunā Ma'a al-Yahūd" in analysing Quṭb's anti-Semitism, see Perry and Schweitzer, 2008. "Our Struggle with the Jews...the Jews...the Jews!! 1950s" in *Anti-Semitic Myths: a Historical and Contemporary Anthology*. Indiana University Press, 309-16).

5 Buruma & Margalit, 2004: 119.

6 Erikson, 1994 [1968]: 298.
7 Ibid: 298-9.
8 Ibid.
9 The eclipse of the Islamic humanist traditions in the modern age is made only too apparent when compared to the strides made in that area not only in the West, secular or otherwise, but also in comparison to the humanist impulse in the Jewish tradition, which is rooted in classical rabbinic sources, in both the Talmud and Midrash, and which placed an emphasis on a concern for man and the human condition, see Lachs, 1993: 13.
10 Reichmuth, 2012: 117 (Reichmuth is making reference here to works which were undertaken on this topic after World War II by Sir Hamilton Gibb, Jacob Landau, Louis Gardet, Joel Krämer, and more recently Lenn Goodman, see ibid: n5; it is noteworthy that the Buyid Age which is at the centre of Krämer's study *Humanism in the Renaissance of Islam* (1986), is not invoked by Quṭb in any of his writings; Krämer observes that the translators, scribes and commentators of the Buyid Age tried "to recover" the meaning of Greek thought which entailed "a hermeneutical effort of dramatic proportions, and the success was astounding", see Joel Krämer, 1992 [1986]: xv).
11 Ibid: 118 (the consensus precludes Orientalists, such as Jörg Krämer, Hellmut Ritter and Gustav von Grunebaum who expressed reservation about the very existence of a concept of Islamic humanism based on the conviction that the prevailing doctrine of "God's unique and overwhelming power" leaves minimal space for human agency, see ibid).
12 The word *jahiliyya* is not included in the glossary of Miskawayh's *Tahdhīb al-Akhlāq* which is provided by the translator of the work into English, Constantine k. Zurayk. Instead, the words "*jahl*", for "ignorance", and "*jāhil*" for "ignorant or ill-bred" are included, see Miskawayh, Aḥmad ibn-Muḥammad, 1968 [932/320H]. *The Refinement of Character* (*Tahdhīb al-Akhlāq*) translated by Constantine k. Zurayk. American university of Beirut, 212 (Arkoun points out that Aristotle's *The Nicomachean Ethics* provides the basis for Miskawayh's work, see Mohammed Arkoun, 2012: 71; he notes further that 'Abduh's reformist works bear no traces of any explicit influence by Miskawayh's *Treatise*, see ibid: 64; it is to be noted that Aḥmad Luṭfi al-Sayyid translated into Arabic all of Aristotle's works including *The Nicomachean Ethics*, see Muḥammad M. M. al-Jamāl, 2004. *Aḥmad Luṭfī al-Sayyid: Dirāsa fī al-Khāriṭa al-Ma'rifiya*. Cairo: Dār al-Amīn, 23; Quṭb does not refer to any of al-Sayyid's translation efforts although, evidently, he was rattled by the Aristotelian world-view, nor does he make any mention of Miskawayh's *Treatise* in any of his works; I note that there is some evidence that Miskawayh's *Treatise* continued to be published in Egypt in the early part of the Twentieth century albeit as an appendix in al-Ṭabarsī's *Makārim al-Akhlāq* which was published by al-Maṭba'a al-Khayriyya in Cairo in 1303H).
13 Abu Zayd argues that the whole concept of *jāhiliyya* is unknown to Ibn 'Arabī, see Nasr Ḥ. Abu Zayd, 2002. *Hakadhā Takalam Ibn 'Arabī*. Cairo: al-Hay'a al-'Āma li al-Kitāb, 35.
14 Reichmuth, 2012: 118.
15 B. Lewis, Ch. Pellat & Joseph Schacht (eds.), 1965. "Djāhiliyya", *EOI*, 383 (In Arabic literature, the word *jāhiliyya* was put in use in reference to a "time of ignorance" in the pre-Islamic period; Bauer argues that, as a term relating to literary history, Ibn Sallām al-Jumaḥī classified poets by referring to them as '*Jahilī*' and '*Islāmī*', adding that the word '*mukhaḍram*' was coined to refer to "poets whose lives extended over both periods", see Thomas Bauer, 1998. "Jāhiliyya" in Meisami, Julie Scott & Paul Starkey (eds.), *EAL*. London: Routledge, 406).
16 Muḥammad 'Abduh, 1319/1901. *Tafsīr al-Fātiḥa*. Cairo: Maṭba'it al-Mawsū'āt, 5.
17 Ibid: 18.
18 The expression "big-bang outlook" is coined by Wilfred C. Smith in his critique of the sort of distortive historiography which considers that religious traditions are initiated by their respective founders, while neglecting their historical roles in the religious life of their communities, and the "transcendent truth" (God) beyond history, see Smith, 2001 [no date]. "Sikhism's Relationship to the Guru Nanak" (excerpt from *Towards a World Theology*", 52.
19 Joel Krämer, 1992 [1986]: xviii.

20 Ibid: xix-xx.
21 Goldziher argues that Muḥammad's prophecy did away with all the "barbarous abominations" in the cult and society of the pagan Arabs as the Qur'anic message conveys an opposition between pagan and Islamic ways. He adds that both Judaism and Christianity contributed in equal measure in the Prophet's doctrines and institutions, see Ignaz Goldziher, 1981 [1910]. *Introduction to Islamic Theology and Law.* New Jersey: Princeton University Press, 13.
22 In agreement with Goldziher's findings, Izutsu argues that the word *jāhiliyya* was used in Arabic poetry in opposition to *ḥilm* to denote "the moral forbearance of the civilised man", adding that his own semantic analysis of the term reveals that its primary function was to refer to "the implacable and reckless temper of the pagan Arabs", see Toshihiko Izutsu, 2002. *Ethico-religious Concepts in the Qur'ān.* New York: Ithaca, 28.
23 Smith, 1981 [1974b]. "Faith in the Qur'ān, and its Relation to Belief" in *On Understanding Islam.* The Hague: Mouton Publishers, 121.
24 Ibid: 130.
25 'Abduh, 1972-3 [ca. 1898-1905a], 5:120.
26 Franz Rosenthal, 1970. *Knowledge Triumphant: the Concept of Knowledge in Medieval Islam.* Leiden: Brill, 32.
27 Shepard, 2003: 522.
28 Edward William Lane, 1863, 2: 477.
29 al-Khaldī, 1987: 38.
30 Specific accusations were made and questions were raised by Dr. al-Ṭāhir Makkī, a professor of Andalusian literature at Dār al-'Ulūm, who put in question the fact that, aged forty-two in 1948, Quṭb hardly qualified for a bursary which was normally awarded to younger new graduate students, and that, furthermore, no announcement of the bursary was publicised in the papers at the time, see al-Namnam, 2010: 74 (both al- Qabbānī and Ghurbāl received higher education in Britain, ibid: 75; Ghurbāl responded that both, himself and al-Qabbānī, hoped that a visit to the United States will acquaint him with Western civilisation, and "add depth to his thought, while broadening his world-view", quoted in ibid).
31 http://www.kaftoun.com/commons/documents/Point_Four_Bates.htm (accessed November 27, 2014); Truman's "Point Four Program" was criticised by Quṭb in *Ma'rakat al-Islām wa al-Ra'simaliyya* (1951) as part of the capitalist camp missionary ploy to impress "the deprived masses" in the Islamic world, see Quṭb, 1952 [1951]: 155 Musallam's analysis of a 1967 edition of *Islam and Universal Peace* (1951) reveals that Quṭb maintained the view that Truman's "Point Four Program" was part of American economic inducements to arrest the expansion of communism in the Arab world, see Musallam, 2005: 128).
32 al-Khaldī, 1987: 40.
33 'Abbās Khiḍr, 1983. *Ha'ulā' "Araftuhum.* Cairo: Dār al-Ma'ārif: 28.
34 Ibid: 58.
35 Ḥusayn A. Amīn, 2007. *Shakhṣiyyāt 'Araftuha* (Personalities I encountered). Cairo: al-'Ayn co, 36.
36 Mitchell, 1993 [1969]: 109.
37 Musallam, 2005: 142.
38 Calvert, 2010: 186.
39 Erikson, 1994 [1968]: 185.
40 Toth, 2013: 69.
41 Quṭb received a warm reception by the younger members of the Muslim Brothers upon his return to Egypt in August 1950, see Musallam, 2005: 122.
42 Murawiec finds that, at the time, the Saudi monarch King 'Abdul 'Aziz Ibn Saud have "used and abused" the central position the Saudis occupy in controlling Mecca and Medina in "an effort to seize Islam", see Laurent Murawiec, 2005 [2003] *Princes of Darkness: the Saudi Assault on the West.* Maryland: Rowman & Littlefield, 30; Murawiec notes further that "under the aegis of oil wealth, there was a gradual coming together – a federation rather than a merger – among several

Islamist movements... [which all] openly displayed hatred of the West and westernization; and an aggressive missionary program." No less than a "convergence" ensued between Wahhābism and the Deobandi and Tablighi movements* of the Indian subcontinent, on the one hand, and the salafis and the movements attached to the Muslim Brotherhood in Egypt, on the other, see ibid:36; Olivier Roy adds further that in the 20th century Wahhābism, Tablighism, and Salafism all set themselves "the same goal: to standardise the practice of Sunni Islam around an orthodoxy that is completely divorced from local cultures", see Olivier Roy, 2010. *Holy Ignorance: When Religion and Culture Part Ways*. London: Hurst & Company, 208; It is noteworthy that Nadwi is said to have presented the traditional thought of the Tabligh movement, see M. Nafeel M. Zawahir, 2008. *Comparative Study on Abul Hasan Alī Nadwī's Political Thought with Particular Reference to His Contemporaries Abul Ala Mawdūdī and Sayyid Quṭb*. Lampeter: University of Wales, ii.

43 Calvert, 2010: 157 (at a later stage, al-Nadwi is said to have strongly criticised Quṭb's and Mawdūdī's political interpretations of Islam, see Zawahir, 2008: 1; to this end, al-Nadwi dedicated in 1979 his work al-*Tafsīr al-Siyasī li al-Islām, fī Kitabat al-Ustādh Abu al-A'la al-Mawdūdī wa al-Shahīd Sayyid Quṭb*, in which he criticised Mawdūdī's so-called "four concepts of the Qur'an", "*ilah*, *rabb*, *'ibāda* and *dīn*", on the grounds that these concepts contradict the spirit of the Qur'an and Islam, and are secondary manifestations of *jāhiliyya*; the primary one being *shirk* (polytheism), see ibid: 81 & 189n159; Quṭb makes reference to this particular work by Mawdūdī as he stresses the idea of "*ḥakimiyya*" (sovereignty), and equates between "*dīn*" and "*manhaj*" in *Muqawwimat al-Taṣawwur al-Islāmī*, see Quṭb, 1997 [1969]: 33-34; al-Nadwi accused both Quṭb and Mawdūdī of "narrow thinking" and of calling on readers to worship them, instead of God, by using the concept of God's sovereignty, see Zawahir, 2008: 49).

44 There are several editions of this work including a tenth edition which was published in Cairo in 1977 by Dār al-Qalam.

45 Choueiri, 2010 [1997]: 121.

46 Ibid: 121-2.

47 Gershoni and Jankowski detect a strand of Easternism in Amīn's discourse beginning in 1933, see Gershoni and Jankowski, 1995: 39 (articles by Amīn in the Easternism vein include "Nahḍatunā al-Fikriyya," *HI*, April 1937, see ibid: 228n34 & "Bayna al-Gharb wa al-Sharq aw al-Madiyya wa al-Ruḥaniyya," *TQ*, 10 Jan. 1939, ibid: 230n113).

48 Aḥmad Amīn, 1950. "Introduction" in Abu al-Ḥasan al-Nadwī, 1950. *Madha Khasira al-'Alam bi Inḥiṭāṭ al-Muslimīn*. Cairo: Lajnat al-Ta'līf wa al-Nashr: i.

49 These articles were later published in book form as *Li-Madha Ta'akhkhar al-Muslimūn wa Li-Madha Taqaddam Ghayruhum*?(*Why have the Muslims become Backward while others Progressed*?, see Smith, 1966 [1957]:54 (the English version published in India (1944), and reprinted in Pakistan in 1952, was translated from the Malayalam, see ibid: n25).

50 Aḥmad Amīn, 1950: 17.

51 Quṭb makes no mention in any of his Islamist works of Nadwat al-'Ulamā's new educational system which aimed to amalgamate the "old" and the "modern" curricula when it was first established in north India in 1310/1892. In 1898, the society established its own educational institution, Dār al-'Ulūm, which became, in practice, yet another *madrasa* which positively discourages modern education, see Ẓafarul-Islām Khān, 1991. "Nadwat al-'Ulamā", *EOI*. Leiden: Brill, 7:874-5; I tend to disagree with Faḍl Allah's argument that the development of the doctrine of *jāhiliyya* in Quṭb's 1960s writings, such as *Mushkilat al-Ḥaḍāra*, *Ma'alim*, and *Ẓilāl*, owes its origin in al-Nadwi's thought, see Mahdī Faḍl-Allah, 1979 [1978]: 129).

52 *Ẓilāl*, VI: 3947-3953.

53 Ibid: 3948-9 (it is to be noted that Quṭb applies intra-qur'anic techniques in his commentary on this *sura* by quoting, along with 2: 113 and 5:64, 72-3, and perhaps for the first time in his writings, the key qur'anic verse 9: 30, which accuses the Jews of deifying Ezra and the Christians, likewise, of deifying Jesus; it is not, however, till Quṭb wrote *Khaṣṣā'iṣ* in 1962 that he used verse

9:30 to accuse the Christians and the Jews who encountered Muḥammad of *shirk* (polytheism) and *kufr* (unbelief), as we shall see in section two below).

54 Quṭb, 1950: 17.

55 Quṭb quotes here, as he does in all editions of *al-'Adāla* (Quṭb, 1993 [1964a]: 19) Q3:110, which confirms Muslims as God's "best *umma,*" and 2: 143, which refers to Muslims as an "*umma* of witnesses unto all people", (well before becoming acquainted with Mawdūdī's work *Witnesses unto Mankind*). The first instance I have seen Quṭb making reference to the aforementioned work which was translated into Arabic as *Shihādat al-Ḥaqq*, without, however, quoting it, occurs in the section he dedicates to a discussion of the characteristic of *al-Ijabiyya* (to be active in the world) in *Khaṣṣā'iṣ*, see Quṭb, 1962c: 184n1.

56 Quṭb, 1962c: 184 (at a later stage in the course of his Islamist career, Quṭb confirmed to his friend, 'Abbās Khiḍr, that "religion was necessary to guide the human flocks which only submit to religion", see Khiḍr, 1983: 59).

57 Norman A. Stillman, 1991. *The Jews of Arab Lands in Modern Times*. New York: The Jewish Publication Society of America, 9 (the ban imposed on the use of the derogatory term "*al-ra'āya*" was part of a number of reforms which were introduced by the "*Khaṭṭ-i Humayun*" decree (1856) which had been worked out by the ambassadors of England, France, and Austria, as the Ottoman empire's "entrance ticket to the European Concert of Powers", see ibid: 8-9).

58 Quṭb, 1950: 18.

59 The adverse content about Paul is in chapter 1 of al-Nadwi's work, see Abu al-Ḥasan al-Nadwī, 1950: 2 (See on this point Quṭb's commentary on *al-Bayina* in *Ẓilāl* discussed above, and his criticism of Paul in the last edition of *al-'Adāla, see* Quṭb, 1993 [1964a]: 8.

60 Ibid.

61 McAuliffe observes that when Quṭb discusses "the new *jāhiliyya*" (as in ignorance), he rather draws a line, not between Muslims and non-Muslims, but between "those who can justifiably call themselves Muslims and those who have surrendered any right to this identification", see McAuliffe, 2011 [2006b]: 200.

62 Quṭb, 1950: 17 (it is to be noted that Quṭb is not the first to make reference to nominal Muslims as having fallen in a *jāhiliyya*. Shepard points out that some comparisons came to be drawn in *al-Manār* between aspects of pre-Islamic *jāhiliyya* conditions and "the conservatism, injustice, superstition and secular tendencies" in Islamic society, and that references were made in this respect to "some geographical Muslims" of the age as being "more corrupt in their religion and morals" than those concerning whom Q5:50 & 5:53 were revealed, see Shepard, 2001: 39; although Riḍā fails to identify who these "geographical Muslims" are, Adams finds that by the early 1930s Ṭaha Ḥusayn's thought especially was totally at variance with that of *al-Manār*'s group. To Riḍā, Ḥusayn and like-minded members of the literati, came to represent "an aggressive atheism that is usurping the institutions of the country and the very profession of teaching, in order to poison the minds of the young men of the country with their unbelief", see Adams, 1933: 259; Additionally, Riḍā seemed to have developed a conviction that Ḥusayn's books defame the scholars of Islam, like al-Ghazālī and Ibn Khaldūn who, he notes, are "highly-valued by European scholars" while bringing forward characters, like al-Ma'arrī, who he accused of "atheism", and Abu Nuwās who he also considered to be "notorious for immorality and debauchery", see ibid; I note here that while Quṭb accepted al-Ma'arrī's poems well into the mid-1940s as one of very few "unexpected occurrences" (*falatat*) in "millions of Arab poems' verses" which were composed across the ages (Quṭb, 1946b: 35), he failed nonetheless to appreciate the humanist dimension in that Arab poet's thought. As discussed by Gibb, al-Ma'arrī stands out as "a great humanist and an incisive, though pessimistic, thinker", see Gibb, 1963 [1926], 92; Goldziher identifies in al-Ma'arrī's asceticism "principles of personal conduct and a philosophy which owe their origin in India"; he credits Alfred v. Kremer's work *Über die Philosophischen Gedichte des Abū-l-'Alā al-Ma'arrī* (1888) for identifying Indian elements in al-Ma'arrī's poems, see Goldziher, 1981 [1910]. *Introduction to Islamic Theology and Law* 141-2 & 142n81).

63 Quṭb, 1950: 20.
64 Quṭb, 5 Nov. 1951b: 97-102.
65 Quṭb, 1952 [1951]: 122.
66 The verbs "*irtaqa*" and "*taraqa*", for instance, are used in relation to a process of ascension, or in reference to acquiring a degree in knowledge or science; one may also use the verb "*taraqa*", derived from "*ruqiy*" to mean "a person exalted himself", signifying also reaching "a place of ascent", see Lane, 1863, iii: 1140.
67 Shepard, 1997: 264n10 (I note here that Quṭb's position in relation to the idea of progressive "*irtiqa*" is contrary to that of Mawdūdī; Hartung observes that, under Darwinist influences, Mawdūdī depicted the Muslim *umma* as "a community in nearly constant decline", and called for a radical reversion to its original religious constitution as the only possible cure", see Hartung, 2013: 73).
68 Quṭb's recognition of a progressive movement towards refinement in the Christian West does not translate, however, in any of his writings, to an acceptance, as early Muslims did, of its "rationalist-idealist-humanist" Greco-Roman tradition within the context of "other religious traditions of humankind"; on this particular point, Wilfred C. Smith notes in the chapter "*Philosophia* as One of the Religious Traditions of Humankind" that the rationalist-idealist-humanist Greek tradition in the West, as mediated through Rome, or the Greco-Roman tradition, "is best understood when considered within the generic context of various –other- religious traditions of humankind", see Smith, 1997: 19-20.
69 I am making reference here to Smith's use of the concept of reification in relation to the tendency in the modern age to use terms such as "Hinduism", "Confucianism", "Buddhism" to replace the earlier "the sect of the Banians", "Chinese wisdom", "the religion of Buddha", see Smith, 1964: 71.
70 The Brothers made a distinction between "Eastern" and "Western" Christianity, and called for the protection, not only of Muslims, but of local Christians against Christian missionary activities. Towards this end, it encouraged both Christian and Muslim writers who attacked Western, especially Protestant, "subversion" of the local Orthodox and Coptic heritage, see Mitchell, 1993 [1969]: 231; I note that American Presbyterian missionaries arrived in Egypt in 1854 as part of a larger Anglo-American Protestant movement aiming for worldwide evangelization, see http://press.princeton.edu/titles/8827.html (accessed Jan. 1, 2015); It is to be noted that there is some evidence that efforts were also made by missionaries in the early part of the 20th century to convert Jewish children but these were mostly unsuccessful due primarily to the well-defined ethnic and communal nature of religious identity all over the Middle East, see Stillman, 1991: 20; there is no evidence that the Brothers took a stance against any of the efforts made by missionaries to convert Jewish Egyptian children in French schools. As noted by Beinin, both Young Egypt and the Society of Muslim Brothers were antagonistic to the Jewish presence in Egypt by the late 1930s. However, even at the risk of offending religious sentiment in Egypt, the 1945-46 edition of the *Yearbook of Egyptian Jewry* reiterated the historic link between Jews and Egypt by suggesting that the source of Jewish monotheism was the ancient Egyptian cult of Ra. The anonymous author of this article claimed that many Jewish rituals, symbols, and precepts – circumcision, the candelabrum, the altar, the design of the pillars of the Temple, even several of the Ten Commandments – derived from ancient Egypt, see Joel Beinin, 1996. "Egyptian Jewish Identities: Communitarianisms, Nationalisms, Nostalgias". *SEHR*, 5:1. *Contested Polities*. 27 February, 1996. http://web.stanford.edu/group/SHR/5-1/text/beinin.html (accessed July 18, 2014).
71 Khedive Ismā'īl (1863-1979) dreamed of modernising the social and cultural life of his people, to make Egypt "a corner of Europe". In the process of attempting to modernise Egypt, he revived some of the projects which were started by Muḥammad 'Ali and encouraged the Catholic and Protestant missions to expand their educational program, giving girls, as well as boys, a chance to become educated, see Dodge, 1961: 115.
72 According to Quṭb, there were some 4,000 well-funded Catholic Church missions which are spread as far afield as in the Congo and the Tibet in the early part of the 20th century, see Quṭb, 1952 [1951]: 123.

73 Ibid: 122-3.
74 Heather J. Sharkey, 2013. *American Evangelicals in Egypt: Missionary Encounters in an Age of Empire*. Princeton University Press, 32.
75 Quṭb, 1952 [1951]: 123 (it is to be noted that Jurjī Zidān (1861-1914) deserves a mention by Wilfred C. Smith as a Christian Arab who has taken a share in the pride of Islam's historic achievements, see Smith, 1966{1957]: 94. Zidān's *History of Islamic Civilisation* (1902-06) which was widely successful due, in great part, to its Muslim readership, is recognised by Smith as a contribution to an artistic endeavour which gave expression to the malaise which followed "the disintegration of Islam's seemingly evanescent earthly greatness" in the modern age. This particular literary movement includes a diversity of works such as the poet Hali's moving lament *Musaddas* published in Delhi in 1886, Iqbal's *Shikwah* (1912), and his *Masjid-i Qurtubah* (1935), as well as Amir 'Ali's substantial *History of the Saracens* (1899), see ibid: 53-4).
76 Although Quṭb does not recognise the Ottomans as Muslims in all editions of *al-'Adāla* (Quṭb, 1993 [1964a], 185), he quotes at some length from chapter 6 of a translation of Arnold's work which deals with the first two centuries of Turkish rule, and the toleration offered by Ottoman emperors to Christian Europeans following the conquest of Greece at the end of the 14th century, see Quṭb, 1952 [1951]: 115-6. I have identified this paragraph as corresponding to the paragraph in the original (pp133-4). (It is to be noted that Arnold's work is an early major study of the spread of the Muslim message, see Irwin 2007 [2006]: 218).
77 Quṭb quotes the same paragraph from *Whither Islam?* in *al-Salam al-'Alamī wa al Islām*, see Quṭb, 1979 [1951]: 184, and in all of the first five editions of *al-'Adāla*, see, for instance, Quṭb, 1950 [1949]: 226. The paragraph is identified by Shepard, see Shepard, 1996: 326n105. (Khiḍr observes that, contrary to Renan's deprecating views of the Semitic mind and the impact of the desert environment on it, Gibb was seen as a credible and ingenuous Orientalist who devoted his works to exploring the richness of Arabic literature and its impact on Western literature, see Khiḍr, 1968: 69).
78 Note that all of al-Azhar Shaykhs, starting in 1935, and until Quṭb's death in 1966, belonged to the Ḥanafite doctrine. Eccel notes that the position of shaykh of al-Azhar was filled by shaykhs who belonged to the Shāfi'ī madhab between 1725-1870, adding that though the government was Ḥanafī under the Ottomans and the Khedives of the Muḥammad 'Ali family, no Ḥanafī was made shaykh of al-Azhar until 1870, evidencing the degree of autonomy given to al-Azhar at this time, see A. Chris Eccel, 1984: 133.
79 Quṭb cites 'Abd al-Ḥalīm al-Guindī's work *Abu Ḥanīfa: the Paragon of Freedom and Tolerance in Islam*, and 'Abd al-Ḥalīm Gouda al-Saḥār's work *The Ascetic Socialist, Abu Dhirr al-Ghafārī* in his bibliography of the 2nd edition of *al-'Adāla*,(no bibliography is supplied in the 1964 edition of the work); Ayubi notes that Abu Dhirr al-Ghafārī was invoked by militant Muslims who are particularly concerned with the cause of equality, see Ayubi, 1991: 63; on the dismissal of the four Sunni schools of *Fiqh*, and Quṭb's claim that there was no Islamic society in existence, see Quṭb, 2005 [1962a]: 196; this turn of event is significant considering the humanistic impulse which was attached to scholasticism in Islamic early history, on this topic see George Makdisi's study *The Rise of Humanism in Classical Islam and the Christian West: with Special Reference to Scholasticism* (1990).
80 Quṭb, 1950: 21.
81 Quṭb, 1952 [1951]: 126.
82 Quṭb, 1979 [1951]: 184-5 (Compare Quṭb's positive position in relation to Christian Europe to his younger brother's work *Shubuhat Ḥawl al-Islām* (1954) which was reviewed by Wilfred C. Smith as an example of literature which reflects the "vehemence", "deep" and "fierce" hatred of the West in so far as it is "bitter, blind, and furious", see Smith, 1966 [1957]: 159n203; note that this work was published firstly by Dār Wahba and consequently by Dār al-Shurūq in Cairo which is the publisher of *Ẓilāl*).
83 Diyāb, 1987: 98 & Ibid: 225n127.

84 Quṭb, 1951f. "Li al-Azhar Risāla, wa-Lakinnahū la Yu'addiha", *RS*, 937: 685-86; quoted in Musallam, 2005: 129 & ibid: 223n62.
85 See chapter 3.
86 Quṭb, 1952 [1951]: 79.
87 This statement continues to cause much dismay in some circles, see http://www.themadkhalis.com/md/articles/jevki-shaykh-hammad-al-ansari-on-the-saying-of-sayyid-qutb-that-islami-is-a-mixture-of-communism-and-christianity.cfm (accessed Dec. 17, 2014).
88 See chapter 3.
89 http://www.britannica.com/EBchecked/topic/77198/Brahmo-Samaj (accessed Dec. 17, 2014).
90 Kris Manjapra, 2010. *M.N. Roy: Marxism and Colonial Cosmopolitanism*. London: Routledge, 10.
91 Ibid: xiii. (Roy's 1920 "Supplementary Theses on the Colonial Question" are included in official communist publications as an addendum to Lenin's own official writings on the subject, and the theses stimulated African, American, Indonesian and Egyptian rejoinders, see ibid).
92 Ibid: xv.
93 Both England and France began an era of colonisation and 'improvement' with evangelical zeal at the end of the eighteenth century, see ibid.
94 Such is the interpretation given by Ibn al-'Arabī in his discussion of a *ḥadīth* about "*shafa'a*" which, he explains, refers to the deliverance of those who had knowledge of *tawḥīd*, but not faith in it, see Chittick, 1989. *Ibn al-'Arabī's Metaphysics of Imagination: the Sufi Path of Knowledge*. State University of New York: 197 (Watt argues that the intercession of Muḥammad became an "article of belief" in Sunni Islam based on early traditions, see Watt, 2009 [1998]: 138).
95 Quṭb, 1952 [1951]: 45 (As we shall see in the next section, Quṭb continues to claim the redemptive qualities of Islam even as he abandons the idea of communism being a component of Islam, and comes to recognise the French-American Catholic Christian eugenicist, Alexis Carrel, as a man of true faith while challenging Mawdūdī's deprecating views of Christianity).
96 Shepard, 2003: 523.
97 Note that Quṭb finds in *Khaṣṣā'iṣ* (1962) that both Marx's and Engels' concepts on human life to be equally "repulsive" without, however , identifying Marx as "one of the three Jews", see Quṭb, 1962c: 82; no mention is made by Quṭb of Marx, as one of "the three Jews" in his later work *Muqawwimat* even as there is an insertion of a reference to his younger brother's chapter "The Three Jews" in the work, see Quṭb, 1997 [1969]: 298.
98 *Ẓilāl*, II:1121, (on peaceful co-existence, see http://www.johndclare.net/cold_war12.htm (accessed January 27, 2014); Quṭb was particularly drawn in the early 1950s to Lenin. He makes specific reference to the latter's work *Imperialism: the Highest Stage of Capitalism* (1916) in one of his early 1950s articles "Mujtama"Alamī" published posthumously in *Naḥw Mujtama' Islāmī*, see Quṭb, 1969 [ca. early 1950sa], 94n1).
99 Stillman, 1991: 156-161; on the meaning of *Aliyah*, see https://www.google.co.uk/search?site=&source=hp&q=meaning+of+aliyah&oq=meaning+of+Aliyah&gs_l=hp.1.0.0l5j0i10j0i22i30l3j0i22i10i30.4328.16244.0.27200.35.22.6.5.6.0.512.4830.0j5j10j2j1j1.19.0.msedr...0...1c.1.62.hp..5.30.6298.MAEXHbuf9rE (March 21, 2015).
100 Quṭb, 1962c: 212-5.
101 Ibid: 217.
102 Quṭb is going further here in his criticism of the Jews for deifying Ezra than in his commentary on the Meccan *Sura* 19, Maryam (Mary), where he accuses only *some* Meccan Jews and Christians of being polytheists for deifying, respectively, Ezra and Jesus, see *Ẓilāl*, IV: 2320.
103 Quṭb, 1962c: 230-31 (Clearly, Quṭb contradicts in that statement his earlier view in *al-Taṣwīr al-Fannī* (1945) when he argued that Muḥammad's prophethood was authenticated by "the Jewish and Christian learned men" (*aḥbār al-yahūd wa al-naṣāra*) encountered by the Prophet; I note further that Christians are accused by Quṭb in the above argument of deifying Jesus, through worship and prayers, along very similar lines to those of the *Wahhābī* doctrine of "*tawḥīd al-ulūhiyya*" which is critical of "imperfect monotheists" who recognised (through

prayers, sacrifices, vows) intermediaries between themselves and God, see Hawting, 2006 [1999]: 63).

104 Calvocoressi, 1988:72.

105 Shepard, 1997: 258.

106 See the chapter "The Views of Contemporary Philosophers on the Truth of Divinity" (Ara' al-Falasifa al-Mu'āṣirrīn fī al-Ḥaqīqa al-Ilahiyya" in al-'Aqqād's work *Allah*, 'al-'Aqqād, 1964 [1947c]: 244-279; on Benedetto Croce, see http://www.britannica.com/EBchecked/topic/143635/Benedetto-Croce (accessed 24 Feb., 2015).

107 Quṭb, 1969 [ca. late 1951]: 36.

108 http://www.churchinhistory.org/pages/booklets/women-souls-1.htm (accessed 24 Feb., 2015).

109 Quṭb, 1969 [ca. late1951]: 43-4 (Quṭb appears to have borrowed this line of argument from 'Abduh polemics who argued in the same vein that women in some non-Islamic societies were considered "as possessing no immortal soul", see Hibba Abugideiri, 2008 [2004]. "On Gender and the Family" in Suha Taji-Farouki and Basheer M. Nafi (eds.) *Islamic Thought in the Twentieth Century*. London: I. B. Tauris, 227).

110 Ibid: 17 (Russell's quote is extracted from an *al-Ahrām* article which was published on August 9th, 1951, see ibid:18n1; Interestingly enough, Quṭb maintained a particular liking for Bertrand Russell at the time of his arrest in 1965. Yūnus points out that prior to Quṭb's last arrest in 1965, his "romantic dreams of grandeur" were such that he came to see himself as having been of "a great value to humanity," writing in a letter of complaint to the Egyptian police that "Bertrand Russell did not offer to his nation, or to humanity at large, even [a fraction of] what I offered it", see Yūnus, 1995: 76n1).

111 Ibid: 18.

112 Quṭb, 1951. "Idha Ja'a Naṣr Allah wa-al-Fatḥ", *RS*, 951: 1246; quoted in Musallam, 2005: 130 & ibid: 224n63 (Quṭb is making reference here to the disputed agreement between Britain and Iran which allowed the latter only 25-30 per cent of the income generated by its oil revenues, see Roy Douglas, 1986. *World Crisis and British Decline* (1929-56). London: Macmillan, 222; Quṭb must have also been disconcerted about the agreement concluded in 1950 between the Arabian American Oil Company (ARAMCO) and Saudi Arabia, under which oil incomes were equally divided between ARAMCO and Saudi Arabia, see ibid).

113 http://www.britannica.com/EBchecked/topic/393304/Mohammad-Mosaddeq (accessed Jan. 20, 2015).

114 Wilfred C. Smith remarks that oil meant "strategic importance" for Washington, which translated into its use of the CIA to pave the way for the Shah's reign, and to overthrow Iran's less westernizing reformer Musaddiq. Washington also helped train the Shah's secret police to torture and mutilate Iranian opponents, see Smith, 1997: 90.

115 On a detailed account of the cooperation between Washington-CIA and Egypt's military regime, specifically with Nasser, see chapter 5 "The 'Nasser-Type' Leader and His 'Repressive Base'" in Miles Copeland, 1969. *The Game of Nations: the Amorality of Power Politics*. London: Weidenfeld & Nicolson, 76-91 (the American administration had no qualms to beef up Nasser's "repressive base" by supplying him in 1953 with ex-Nazi German intelligence and security personnel, see ibid: 86-7; Interestingly, Copeland reveals that the "peaceful revolution" reconnaissance project in Egypt in 1951-2, which was undertaken by the CIA agent, Kermit Roosevelt, was one of the missions which, like that of ousting Musaddiq and restoring the Shah, is said to have been carried out "in the tradition of the Upton Sinclair novels", see ibid: 51).

116 Calvert, 2010: 186 (note that, during the presidency of President Eisenhower, a covert US propaganda program headed by the CIA brought over three dozen Islamic scholars and civic leaders in 1953 for what was officially an academic conference at Princeton University to promote an anti-communist agenda in the Islamic world. One of those who were invited to the conference is the son-in-law of al-Banna, Sa'īd Ramaḍān, who acted as the group's foreign minister, although the CIA described him as "a fascist interested in the grouping of individual for power". See Ian

Johnson, 2011. *Washington's Secret History with the Muslim Brotherhood* in http://www.nybooks.com/blogs/nyrblog/2011/feb/05/washingtons-secret-history-muslim-brotherhood/ (accessed Feb. 17, 2015); for an overview and a timeline of atrocities and crimes committed by the CIA to protect American business interests, see http://www.globalresearch.ca/a-timeline-of-cia-atrocities/5348804 (accessed Feb. 17, 2015).

117 Quoted in al-Khaldī, 1987: 42-3.

118 Quṭb, 30 June 1952, *RS*, quoted in al-Khaldī, 1987: 130.

119 Quṭb, 3 Nov. 1952. "'Aduwina al-Awal al-Rajul al-Abyaḍ" (Our Prime Enemy is the White Man", *RS*, 135.

120 Douglas Little, 2003. *American Orientalism: the United States and the Middle East since 1945.* London: Tauris, 41.

121 Smith, 1966 [1957]: 72n57.

122 Mitchell, 1993 [1969]: 231.

123 Ibid (Gibb's *Modern Trends in Islam* was circulated among, and discussed with interest by English-reading and speaking members of the society. Mitchell recounts that in the course of conducting his own research, he encountered members who expressed hope that Gibb's study would not "abuse Islam", see ibid: n68).

124 Musallam, 2005: 150.

125 These are listed as *al-rabbaniyya* (divinely-ordained), *al-thabat* (fixity), *al-shumūl* (comprehensiveness), *al-tawazun* (balance), *al-Ijabiyya* (to be active in the world), *al-waqi'iyya* (realism) and *al-tawḥīd* (monism).

126 This point is made plain in the concluding chapter of *al-Islām wa Mushkilat al-Ḥaḍāra* "*Ṭarīq al-Khalāṣṣ*" (The Road to Salvation/Redemption) in which Quṭb argues that the whole of humanity has reverted to the *jāhiliyya* that Muḥammad encountered when he presented to it "the method of God" (*manhaj Allah*)and that it was now time for a new procession to lead humanity just as "the first procession" (*al-qafila al-ūla*), did; "one heart" (like that of Muḥammad's), followed by a few other forming a "corps of believers" (*al-'iṣba al-mu'mina*), has to develop an awareness of the existence of (conditions of) *jāhiliyya* and lead it to the end of the long "thorny" road like "the first procession", see Quṭb, 2005 [1962a]: 199.

127 Quṭb, 1962c: 5 (It is noteworthy that Quṭb rejects specifically all of the outcome of disputations which dealt with God's attributes and essence. The explanation that he gives reduces *Sunna* to being a mere "sect" in Islam as he argues that dialectical disputations in the early days of Islam ended up creating "a variety of sects" (*firaq mukhtalifa*) including those of the *Khawārij*, *Shi'a*, *Murji'a*; *Qadariyya* and *Jabria*; *Sunniya* and *Mu'tazila*, see ibid: 9-10).

128 See n18 above.

129 Quṭb, 1962c: 15.

130 Quṭb makes reference here to the "cunning/deceit" (*kayd*) of the Jew, Ibn Sabā', see Quṭb 1993 [1964]: 161.

131 Quṭb, 1962c: 9.

132 Ibid.

133 It is noteworthy that while Quṭb took a rather inimical stance towards the Roman Church in *Khaṣṣā'iṣ*, he still clashed with Mawdūdī as he rejected the latter's criticism of "the Christian theory on women" as a "temptress", as interpreted by Tertullian (d. 240), interjecting in a footnote in the revised edition of *al-Islām wa Mushkilat al-Ḥaḍāra* (1962) the observation that "it is more to the point to refer to 'the ecclesiastical theory' (*al-naẓariyya al-kanasiyya*) and 'the ecclesiastical concepts' (*al-taṣawwurat al-kanasiyya*) which are far removed from the 'truth' (*ḥaqqīqat*) of Christianity", see Quṭb, 2005 [1962a]: 77n1 (Quṭb's observation is made in relation to a long quote which he extracted from Mawdūdī's work *Purdah and the Status of Woman in Islam* which was translated into Arabic as *al-Ḥijāb* (literally the veil), see ibid: 76-8).

134 Browers and Kurzman observe that ,like Western observers, who saw similarities between developments in Islam and Christian history, Islamic modernists, like 'Abduh and Iqbal, saw

developments in Christian history, such as the Reformation, as mirroring similar developments in Islamic history, see Michaelle Browers and Charles Kurzman, 2004. "Introduction" in *An Islamic Reformation?* Oxford: Lexington Books, 3.

135 *Ẓilāl*, II:819 (I note here that Quṭb indicates in the revised edition of his later work *al-Mustaqbal li Hadha al-Dīn* (1963) that he came to appreciate the spiritual life of the "strong-minded, inflexible Calvinist" (Goldschmidt, 2004: 122), John Foster Dulles, who served as secretary of state for six years, starting in 1953, in the Dwight D. Eisenhower administration (1953-1961). In the aforementioned work, Quṭb quotes, at some length (27 paragraphs), from chapter 11, "Our Spiritual Need", in Dulles' work *War or Peace* (1950), see Quṭb, 2005 [ca. 1963b]: 67-73; on Dulles, see http://www.u-s-history.com/pages/h1762.html (accessed January 27, 2014); interestingly, Quṭb shows no interest in the Reformation movement in England, nor in the contribution of the Oxford scholar, William Tyndale, who took the view that English and Hebrew were much more compatible than Hebrew and Greek while translating the New Testaments into English in the early part of the 16th century, see Diarmaid MacCulloch, 2003. *Reformation: Europe's House Divided* (1490-1700). London: Penguin, 203).

136 W. C. Smith, 1964: 36 & ibid 207n77.

137 Ibid: 37.

138 Armstrong, 2007: 158-9.

139 Of particular significance is Isle Lictenstadter's comparative study *Islam and the Modern Age* which is favourably reviewed by al-'Aqqād as a work which is complimentary of 'Abduh's Hermeneutics which aimed at reconciling Revelation with the requirements of the modern age by adopting the same methods as those applied by Jewish and Christian theologians in the West, see al-'Aqqād, no date [ca. 1962b]. *Ma Yuqāl 'an al-Islām* (What They Say about Islam). Cairo: Dār al-'Urūba, 23-24; al-'Aqqād makes reference also to a study on the Islamic Near East which was commissioned by Toronto University which included a panel of eight professors including Sir Hamilton Gibb and a Professor Fayḍī(?) of the University of Kashmīr; the latter is said to have found in favour of Islamic teachings as expounded by Iqbal and Azad (b. 1888), see ibid: 70; reference is also made to Eustace Haydon's Comparative Religion work *Biography of the Gods* in which the author is said to have been particularly complimentary of 'Abduh as a "man of faith" who renewed the essentials of faith in God, see ibid 45.

140 Quṭb, 1962c: 18-19 & 19n1 (Gibb observes that some of 'Abduh's followers, led by Rashīd Riḍā, continued the process of "the rationalising dialectic of the old schoolmen", which was revived by 'Abduh - especially in *Risālat al-Tawḥīd* - to a "characteristic glide toward extremism and the rigidity of the Ḥanbalite outlook", see Gibb, 1975 [1947]: 34; Mitchell observes that 'Abduh's *Risālat al-Tawḥīd* received a place of honour among a limited number of works (by Banna and Ghazālī) in the readings under general studies of faith, see Mitchell, 1993 [1969]: 323.

141 Zebiri, 1993: 28 (the then Rector of al-Azhar, Shaykh Shaltūt, and the one before him Shaykh al-Maraghī belonged to 'Abduh's school, see ibid).

142 Choueiri, 2010 [1997]: 103.

143 Ibid: 106.

144 Al-'Aqqād, no date [ca.1962b]: 97; for original quote, see Wilfred C. Smith, 1966 [1957]: 122.

145 Quṭb, 2005 [1962a]: 55-6.

146 Quṭb, 1962c: 13 (Quṭb references here Arnold's work *The Preaching of Islam* (1913), see Ibid: 13n1 (I note here that Arnold's work is referenced in *Ẓilāl* as an example of works by Orientalists who are "at war with Islam" by "corrupting its *manhaj*" of *Jihād*, see *Ẓilāl*, 1: 294n1; Arnold's work is valued to date by the *Ikhwān* as a work of "objective" Orientalism, see http://www.ikhwanwiki.com/index.php?title=%D8%A7%D9%84%D8%A5%D8%B3%D8%AA%D8%B4%D8%B1%D8%A7%D9%82 (accessed December 13, 2013).

147 Quṭb, 1962c: 13.

148 Ibid: 10.

149 Ibid: 11-12 (Obviously, reference is made here especially to al-'Aqqād. Later in *Ẓilāl*, Quṭb reveals that his animosity to his former mentor never really subsided even some twenty odd years past the time when he claimed that he stepped out of the latter's shadow in the late 1940s. In his commentary on *Sūra* XI, (*Hūd*), which presumably followed al-'Aqqād's death in March 1964, Quṭb quotes, at length, from Al-'Aqqād's work *Allah*, which is also quoted in *Khaṣṣā'iṣ*, and accuses his former mentor of destroying "the very fundamental of the Islamic creed" (*aṣl al-i'tiqād al-Islāmī*) by following research conducted by Western comparative religion scholars (those remain unnamed, but it seems to be the case that he was making reference to Wilfred c. Smith) who, he claims, "aim to destroy the basis of celestial religions and Revelation", see *Ẓilāl*, 4:1882; I note here that Carré finds that Quṭb especially attacks al-'Aqqād in *Ẓilāl* for relying on Western sources in formulating his thought, and further targets the apologetic rationalist orientation of 'Abduh's school of thought, see Carré, 2003: 23.

150 Quṭb, 1962c: 157.

151 Ibid: 27.

152 Ibid.

153 Gibb, 1975 [1947]: 81.

154 Ibid: 80-81.

155 Quṭb, 1962c: 21 (Iqbal makes reference to Hegel's philosophy in the same chapter reviewed by Gibb "His Freedom and Immortality", see Iqbal, 2012 [no date]: 111).

156 Quṭb, 1997 [1969]: 199.

157 El-Enany detects an "enormous power" of Bergson's influence on Naguib Maḥfouz in the area of morality, see El-Enany, 1993: 15; although al-'Aqqād favours the opinion of the modern-day "imām of philologists", as he calls him, German-born Max Müller (d. 1900), for the lexicographical account he gave of the process by which religions arose, he nonetheless gives a good exposé of Bergson's philosophy in his work, *Allah*, using the French philosopher's key concept "*élan vital*" which, he explains, corresponds to *ilhām*, or *kashf* (for Sufi illumination within an Egyptian context), see al-'Aqqād, 1964 [1947c]: 22-3.

158 http://plato.stanford.edu/entries/bergson/ (accessed May 25th, 2014).

159 Quṭb, 1997 [1969]: 54n1 (on Will Durant see http://www.nytimes.com/1981/11/09/obituaries/historian-will-durant-dies-author-of-civilization-series.html (accessed May 25th, 2014); Durant's work is translated into Arabic by Dr. Aḥmad Fu'ād al-Ahwānī as *Mababij al-falsafa* as part of a project undertaken by the Franklin Foundation, see ibid: 49; the content relating to Esther is not included in *The Story of Philosophy*; it may be included in Durant's other 11-volume work *The Story of Civilisation* (1935-1975), see http://www.samizdat.com/isyn/durant.html (March 5, 2015); Quṭb makes reference to a translation by the Arab League of some volumes of this last work in the revised edition of *al-Islām wa Mushkilat al-Ḥaḍāra*, where he remarks on Durant's inimical stance against Islam in particular (probably being made aware of the chapter "The Magnitude Of Muslim Atrocities" which deals with the invasion of India by Muslim conquerors, see Quṭb, 2005 [1962a]: 137 & http://www.voiceofdharma.org/books/siii/ch6.htm (March 5, 2015)).

160 Ibid: 254.

161 Quṭb, 2005 [1962a]: 138-145.

162 Although it is claimed that it was the Indian scholar al-Nadwi who initially introduced Carrel to Muslim audiences, Reggiani finds that it was Quṭb who extracted from Carrel's views a far more radical political theory to attack Western values, see Andrés Horacio Reggiani, 2007. *God's Eugenicist: Alexis Carrel and the Socio-biology of Decline*. Oxford: Berghahn Books: 171; see also Rudolph Walther, "The Strange Teachings of Doctor Carrel: How a French Catholic Doctor became a Spiritual Forefather of the Radical Islamists" in http://www.islamagainstextremism.com/articles/vhoqj-sayyid-qutb-and-the-french-connection-the-french-catholic-social-darwinist-doctor-that-influenced-qutbs-jaahiliyyah.cfm (accessed 18 December 2011).

163 Choueiri identifies three entire pages where Quṭb offers qur'anic evidence for Carrel's views. For instance, Carrel's view that "our knowledge of ourselves is still rudimentary" is substantiated in *al-Islām wa Mushkilat al-Ḥaḍāra* by quoting Q30:6-7 "Men know an outward part of the present life", and Q17:85 "You have been given of knowledge nothing", see Choueiri, 2010: 187-188.

164 Ibid: 189.

165 Quṭb, 2005 [1962a]: 73.

166 Ibid: 66-90 (out of a total of thirteen times when Quṭb makes use of the word *jāhiliyya* and its derivatives in the work, the word occurs seven times in this section).

167 Ibid: 78-82 & 86-90 (reference is made here to Quṭb's own work *Amrika alatī Ra'ayt* which was discussed in chapter 3 above).

168 Ibid: 83-85.

169 Ibid: 85.

170 Ibid: 73-75 (*Purdah* was written in Urdu in the 1930s and was subsequently translated into Arabic and then English, see Roded, 2001-2006, 5: 537; Quṭb refers to an undated edition which was translated by Muḥammad Kāẓim al-Sabāk, see Quṭb, 2005 [1962a]: 60n2).

171 Ibid: 76-78.

172 Quṭb, no date [1964b]: 138.

173 Ibid: 139.

174 Dominic Sandbrook, March 12, 2006. "It Began with one Naked Girl". *The Guardian*. http://www.theguardian.com/politics/2006/mar/12/conservatives.past1 (accessed October 10th, 2013).

175 Quṭb, no date [1964b]: 139.

176 Binder, 1988: 188.

177 Quṭb, 2005 [1962a]: 20n1.

178 Ibid: 171-172.

179 In 1903, Carrel documented in *Le Voyage de Lourdes* a journey he took in the same year to Lourdes which is said to have confirmed him as an "unorthodox Catholic with mystic and supernatural inclinations". Carrel is said to have witnessed in Lourdes the miraculous cure of a young woman who suffered from a deadly form of tuberculosis, see Reggiani, 2007:16-17.

180 Quṭb, 1992 [1964b]: 8-9.

181 Binder, 1988: 173.

182 Hartung notes that Mawdūdī "had never explicitly denounced the widespread allegation that he wanted himself to be seen as the 'Rightly Guided' saviour", adding that the concept of the *mahdī* played an important part in his idea of history, see Hartung, 2013: 83.

183 Quṭb, 2005 [ca. 1963b]: 77-88.

184 Ibid: 86 (it appears to be the case that Quṭb was not aware that both men died before he wrote *al-Mustaqbal li-Hadha al-Dīn*).

185 Ibid: 87.

186 Ibid: 25.

187 Shepard argues that when Quṭb mentions in *Ma'ālim* that some give authority to "the people" or "the party," as he formulates his doctrine of *jāhiliyya*, he clearly has "the Egypt of Gamal Abdel-Nasser in mind, as well as other contemporary Muslim countries, see Shepard, 2003: 528; he notes further that in his late writings, Quṭb frequently makes the point that people are deified when laws are accepted from them, see Shepard, 1996: xxvii.

188 Saudi radio broadcast on a regular basis segments of *Ẓilāl*, see Calvert, 2010: 238; this was attested by Quṭb himself in *Limadha A'damūnī* where he reveals that, unbeknown to him, Saudi radio broadcast excerpts from *Ẓilāl* during the time that he spent in incarceration, see Quṭb, 1965b: 77; Quṭb mentions also in the same document that a shipment of weapons, which was meant to reach the Brothers in the brief period that he was out of prison in 1965, was supposed to have been shipped to Egypt via the Sudan was organised by an (unidentified) Arab country, see ibid, 51; Qureshi and Sells observe that "the conflictual understanding of Quṭb and Ibn Taymiyya" has been spread throughout the Islamic world by the Saudi government, and wealthy Saudi princes

& other individuals, where it is taught as "the true and authentic Islam", see Emran Qureshi and Michael A. Sells, 2003. "Introduction" in *The New Crusaders: Constructing the Muslim Enemy*. New York: Columbia University Press, 32n9.

189 On the deterioration of relations between Nasser and both conservative Arab regimes and the West see Michael Sharnoff. "Looking Back: Nasser's Inter-Arab Rivalries: 1958-1967", July 30, 2011 in http:// english.alarabiya.net/articles/2011/07/30/160027.html (accessed March 5, 2015); see also chapter 10 "Aden, Yemen and the Decline of the Anglo-Egyptian Détente, 1962-63" in Robert McNamara, 2003. *Britain, Nasser and the Balance of Power in the Middle East (1952-1967)*. London: Frank Cass, 177-190 & chapter 11 "Confrontation with Nasser, 1964" in ibid: 191-206; see also chapter 5 "Between East and West" in Peter Mansfield, 1965. *Nasser's Egypt*. Middlesex: Penguin Books, 84-97.

190 Quṭb, 1992 [1964b]: 159.

191 *Ẓilāl*, I: 28; no mention is made in Quṭb's 320-page-commentary on the *sura* of his younger Brother's chapter "the Three Jews"; in fact, Quṭb argues that Freud did not dismiss visionary dreams, see ibid: 97 (a contemporary of Quṭb, the Rector of al-Azhar, shaykh Maḥmūd Shaltūt (r. 1958-1963), places an emphasis on what he refers to as the verse of piety (*birr*), Q2:177, as being "the centre-piece of al-Baqara", see Zebiri, 1993: 154).

192 Ibid: 32 (note that, in addition to *al-Baqara*, Quṭb recognises in his commentary on Q9-29-35 an anti-Jewish theme in *sura* III, *al-'Imrān*; *sura* IV, *al-Nisā'*; *sura* V, *al-Mā'ida; sura* IX, *al-Tawba*; *sura* XXXIII, *al-Aḥzāb*; *sura* LIX, *al-Ḥashr*, see *Ẓilāl*, III: 1627).

193 Ibid.

194 Hawting, 2006 [1999]: 105 & ibid n45.

195 Although 'Abduh argues that Q2:65 was occasioned by the Jews who desecrated the Sabbath, he maintains that those particular Jews were punished in line with those "who do not adhere to the proprieties set by religion", adding that those who commit such transgressions do not attain to 'human perfection', see 'Abduh, 1972-3 [ca. 1898- 1905], IV:205; applying intra-qur'anic techniques in his commentary on the same verse, 'Abduh makes reference to Mujāhid's allegorical interpretation of Q62:5 "Those who have been charged to obey the Torah, but do not do so, are like an ass..."; 'Abduh explains that Mujāhid avoided a literal reading of Q62:5, quoting the last as stating that the verse does not refer to a physical transformation of the Jews, but of a disfigurement of their hearts, adding that (only these specific) Jews are likened to asses and apes (obviously referring to Q2:65), see ibid; On Mujāhid, otherwise known as Ibn Jabr al Makkī, and his exegesis, see Goldziher, 2006 [1920]: 70.

196 *Ẓilāl*, I: 77 (Elsewhere, in his commentary on Q8:55 in *Ẓilāl*, Quṭb mentions that the word "*dawab*" (pack animals, or stumpers) relates to all that stumps on Earth, and that this word relates to the other word "*bahima*" (brute beasts) which, he claims, relates to the three Jewish tribes banū Qurayẓa, banū Qaynuqā', and banū al-Naḍīr, see *Ẓilāl*, III: 1541; note that the idea of breaking God's "covenant" is an important component of Luther's anti-Semitic doctrine; Luther also questioned the relevance of scholastic theology and philosophy, see Perry and Schweitzer, 2008. "Luther and the Jews" in *Anti-Semitic Myths: a Historical and Contemporary Anthology*. Indiana University Press, 43-4).

197 *Ẓilāl*, I: 90.

198 Ibid: 105 (note that Quṭb accepted in *Khaṣṣā'iṣ* that Abraham passed on an "un-adulterated" (*nāṣi'a*) and "all-comprehensive" monotheistic creed to his sons, and that, in turn, Jacob passed it on to his own sons, quoting Q26:69-89 and Q2:130-133, see Quṭb, 1962c: 27; in contradiction to his earlier view, when he recognised Jewish Prophets as "al-Khāṣṣa", and disregarded Ismā'īl (Ishmael) in 1945, Quṭb makes the claim in his commentary on *al-Baqara* that the redirection of the prayer to Mecca signifies that Abraham's legacy was bequeathed to Muḥammad, and the line of Ismā'īl, after the deviation of the Jews, see *Ẓilāl*, I: 34; Generally speaking, Carré notes that in *Ẓilāl* Quṭb took the position that God's promise is given to Abraham and Ishmael, and *not* Isaac, see Carré, 2003: 120).

199 Quṭb, 1992 [1964b]: 160.

200 Ibid: 161.

201 Nettler argues that in *Ẓilāl* Quṭb seemed certain that his ideas were, in fact, the Qur'an's "true message. *Sura* by *sura*, and verse by verse, covering several thousand pages, Quṭb explicated his understanding of the Qur'an in order to build a theory of, and a practical programme, for modern Islam," see Nettler, 1994. "A Modern Islamic Confession of Faith and Conception of Religion: Sayyid Quṭb's Introduction to the Tafsīr, Fī Ẓilāl al-Qur'ān". *BJMES*, 21:1, 103-4.

202 Quṭb describes Islam mostly as a "*manhaj*" in *Ma'ālim*, being described as such one hundred and thirty eight times, while it is described in the same work as a "*taṣawwur*" eighty five times, and as a "*niẓām*" sixty-three times; Binder notes, however, that the primary point being made in *Ma'ālim* is that "Islam, and competing systems, and the world in general are all conceived of as ideas", see Binder, 1988: 189.

203 See http://oxforddictionaries.com/definition/english/minhag; see also Karen Miller Jackson. "Reshut Hakallah: the Symbolism of the Chuppah" in http://www.hebrewbooks.org/33429 (accessed March 5, 2015); Lachs notes that the liberal humanists among the rabbis tended to show much concern for the needs of the governed and the importance of local custom (*Minhag*) was such that, in interpreting the Torah, they put the Law in perspective, see Lachs, 1993: 106.

204 Neal Robinson, 2001."Sayyid Quṭb's Attitude Towards Christianity: *sura* 9.29-35 in *Fī Ẓilāl al-Qur'ān*" in Lloyd Ridgeon (ed.) *Islamic Interpretations of Christianity*. Surrey: Curzon, 174; As in *Ma'ālim*, Robinson's analysis of Quṭb's commentary on *sura* nine, *al-Tawba* (repentance), in *Ẓilāl* reveals that he used the word *Minhaj* repeatedly "in the sense of a procedure, method or programme, in contexts where he wishes to contrast God's programme with the programme of *jāhiliyya*", see ibid.

205 To put Quṭb's usage of the term *jāhiliyya* in *Ma'ālim* in perspective to that of the Qur'an, Shepard counts only four instances when the word occurs in the Qur'an (3:154; 5:53; 33:33; 48:26), see Shepard, 2001-2006. "Age of Ignorance" in *EOQ*. Leiden: Brill, I:37.

206 Hartung, 2013: 205.

207 Ibid.

208 Ayubi, 1991: 3; Mitchell observes that, in both 1948 and 1954, the government charged the Muslim Brothers with being *Khawārij*, see Mitchell, 1993 [1969]: 320n63; the Supreme Council of Islamic Affairs in Egypt reviewed *Ma'ālim* and linked the work with Kharijite ideas, see Kenney, 2006. *Muslim Rebels: Kharijites and the Politics of Extremism in Egypt*. New York: Oxford University Press, 71.

209 Calvert, 2010: 198.

210 Ibid: 201.

211 Ibid: 207 (It seems to be the case that Quṭb's fellow prisoner, Yusuf Hawwash, had a dream in which the Prophet Joseph (Yusuf) told him to tell Quṭb that the answers he seeks are to be found in *sura* XII, Yusuf . see ibid).

212 As Chief Justice, Said Ashmawī, points out Muḥammad applied the penalty of stoning firstly on two Jews in Medina, in accordance to the Torah's penal code, whereas the Qur'an prescribes flogging in the case of adultery in Q24:2, see al-'Ashmāwī, 1996. *Al-Sharī'a al-Islāmiyya wa al-Qanūn al-Masrī*. Cairo: Madbūlī, 75; although Quṭb probably knew that the penalty of stoning has its origin in the Torah, and is not prescribed in the Qur'an, Carré notes that Quṭb insists on applying the penalty of stoning which, he claims, is based on an authentic Ḥadīth, see Carré 2003, 135 (see n14 in chapter 1 on the Ḥadīth by Muslim and al-Nisā'ī to this effect); Quṭb states that the "ethics of combat", as per Islamic law, put a limit to the atrocities committed in the wars of all *jāhiliyya*(s) of old and those of modern times alike, citing a prophetic Ḥadīth whereby Muḥammad is said to have forbidden such tormenting method of slow killing by the side of a sword's blade, but allowing killing by its edge, see *Ẓilāl*, I: 188.

213 Wilfred C. Smith notes that the Wahhābīs rejected "the accommodations and cultural richness of the medieval empire"; it rejected also "the introverted warmth and other-worldly piety of the

mystic way"; it also rejected "the alien intellectualism, not only of philosophy but of theology, and insisted solely on 'the Law'", see Smith, 1966 [1957]: 42.

214 Quṭb, 1950 [1949]: 8-9.

215 Quṭb, 1993 [1964a]: 8.

216 *Ẓilāl*, IV: 1881 (The book of Ezra is discussed by the Egyptian scholar Muḥammad 'A. al-Ibrāshī in his work *al-Adāb al-Sāmiya* (1946) discussed in chapter 4; al-Ibrāshī remarks that it signalled the transition from Aramaic to Hebrew following the return of the Jews from exile in Babylon (in the late sixth century BCE) and the rebuilding of the temple; see al-Ibrāshī, 1946: 26 & 29).

217 Calvocoressi, 1987: 122.

218 *Ẓilāl*, IV: 1881.

219 Nettler, 1993: 94 (Nettler observes further that Ibn 'Arabī's' incorporation of Ezra in Sufi metaphysics built on ancient traditions which has its origins in a large body of interrelated biblical, quasi-biblical, rabbinic, various Christian and Islamic, and other Near Eastern sources, see ibid: 96n36; Goldziher's study of Schools of Qur'anic commentators reveals that the Islamic tenet of intercession (*shafa'a*) of the Prophet is derived from Jewish influence, referencing R. Basset's introduction to his edition of the Ethiopian apocalypse of Ezra (*Les Apocryphes Ethiopiens*), see Goldziher, 2006 [1920]: 109).

220 Paul Nwyia, 1970. *Exégèse Coranique et Langage Mystique*. Beirut: Dar El-Machreq, 85; Nwyia notes further that in Muqātil's exegesis on Q4:153, which refers to Jews asking Moses to see God, he quotes almost verbatim from Exodus 19, 10; 20: 1-4, 18-20 and Deuteronomy 5:25-31, see ibid: 84n1; I note here that 'Abduh criticised early exegeses for not relying on the Torah and the Bible and other books which are held as "authoritative" (*al-mu'tamada*) by *Ahl al-Kitāb* and those of other communities to illuminate the Qur'an in his expanded one-hundred and twenty-seven page commentary on *sura* one, *al-Fatiḥa*, see Muḥammad 'Abduh, 1319/1901. *Tafsīr al-Fatiḥa*. Cairo: Maṭba'it al-Mawsū'āt: 7.

221 Nettler observes that it is the Saudi editor of Quṭb's anthology, *Ma'rakatuna Ma'a al-Yahūd*, who saw it "fruitful" to integrate the *Protocols* into Quṭb's thought, noting, however, the existence of a "natural confluence" of their worldviews, see Nettler, 1987: 50; the *Protocols* have also been referenced in the thirteenth (2005) edition of *al-Islām wa Mushkilāt al-Ḥaḍāra* which I analysed; in one instance, Quṭb, (or most probably his younger Brother Muḥammad), claims that the *Protocols of Zion* state that, by pushing for women's emancipation, they will destroy all the nations of the world, see Quṭb, 2005 [1962a]: 148n1.

222 "You [Prophet] are sure to find that the most hostile to the believers are the Jews and those who associate other deities with God; you are sure to find that the closest in affection towards the believers are those who say, 'we are Christians'..."; for Quṭb's commentary on this *sura* in the article "*Ma'rakatuna Ma'a al-Yahūd*", see Quṭb, 1970 [ca. mid-1960s?]: 54-61.

223 Quṭb, 1992 [1964b]: 10.

224 Ibid: 5 (I note here that Quṭb pointed out in *al-Islām wa Mushkilat al-Ḥaḍāra* that Will Durant's interpretation of history, in terms of economics, reflects an inclination to Marxism, see Quṭb, 2005 [1962a]: 139n1).

225 As discussed in chapter 2 and 4 above.

226 *Ẓilāl*, II: 961.

227 Quṭb, 1993 [1964a]: 11n1.

228 Quṭb argues in all editions of *al-'Adāla* that there is a 'truth' in the claim made by Communism that economic pressures on the individual makes him give up the justice and equality which are guaranteed to him sometimes by law on a theoretical level. He, however, argues that this is not the whole truth, see Quṭb, 1993 [1964a]: 33.

229 'Scientific socialism' is described in Nasser's National charter (1962) as "the suitable style for finding the right method leading to progress", see Choueiri, 2010 [1997]: 104.

230 Quṭb, 1992 [1964b]; 116.

231 *Ẓilāl*, IV: 1959 (as noted above, I suspect that the insertion of the Protocols are made by Quṭb's younger brother Muḥamad).

232 Goldziher remarks that the exegesis of 'Abduh and his school reads into the Qur'an modern ideas, particularly those of Charles Darwin, see Goldziher, 2006 [1920]: 223.

233 Quṭb, 1992 [1964b]: 58 (Quṭb takes a critical stance towards Darwin, Freud and Marx for degrading humans in their respective works in his other earlier revised work of the period *al-Islām wa Mushkilāt al-Ḥaḍara*, see Quṭb, 2005 [1962a]:78; Conversely, Carré observes that Quṭb is "pleased" to cite in *Ẓilāl* several Western scientists who have come to the conclusion that science and revelation are of a different order including Huxley, as well as Carrel, Frank Allen and J.B. Seathes, see Carré, 2003: 45.

234 Quṭb, 1993 [1964a]: 201-2.

235 Quṭb, 1992 [1964b]: 141.

236 Ibid.

237 Quṭb, 1993 [1964a]: 203.

238 Quṭb, 1992 [1964b]: 144.

239 Zebiri, 2001. "Muslim Perceptions of Christianity and the West" in Lloyd Ridgeon (ed.) *Islamic Interpretations of Christianity*. Surrey: Curzon, 184 (the quote is extracted from a work which was co-authored by Farrūkh and Muṣṭafa Khālidī, entitled *al-Tabshīr wa al-Isti'mār fī al-Bilād al-'Arabiyya* which was first published in 1953); Smith remarks that the aforementioned work is one example among many of "what was perhaps the essential shock of the whole Palestinian affair: the terrible discovery that the Arabs were not accepted by the West, were not regarded as members of the civilised community, see Wilfred C. Smith 1966 [1957], 100 (Quṭb references *al-Tabshīr wa al-Isti'mār fī al-Bilād al-'Arabiyya* in his commentary on *sura* IX, *al-Tawba* (Repentance), in *Ẓilāl* as he becomes aware of the danger posed by the 'Crusaderist' Wilfred C. Smith's scholarship, as we shall see below, see *Ẓilāl*, III: 1630n1&2).

240 'Ali 'Ashmāwī, no date: 85-86; Carré's analysis of *Ẓilāl* reveals that Quṭb opposes the Orientalists in general, and then the commentaries of 'Abduh and 'Abduh's "School", which he considers to be aligned with Orientalism which is presented as a European intellectual enterprise, first Jewish, then Christian, see Carré, 2003: 21).

241 Quṭb was released out of prison in May 1964, see Musallam, 2005: 165.

242 Calvert, 2010: 249.

243 It is noteworthy that Muḥammad Quṭb's book *al-Mustashriqūn wa al-Islām* (1999) is particularly critical of Gibb's school of Orientalism and his work *Modern Trends in Islam*, and of his "disciple" Wilfred C. Smith's *Islam in Modern History* (1957); like his other work, *Shubuhāt Ḥawl al-Islām*, which is identified by Smith as an example of hatred literature targeting the West, it is published by Dār Wahba in Cairo which is owned by a Saudi publishing house, aL-Mu'asasa al-Su 'ūdiyya; Gibb, as well as Smith, are listed as "fanatic" Orientalists on an Egyptian *Ikhwān* site, see http://www.ikhwanwiki.com/index.php?title=%D8%A7%D9%84%D8%A5%D8%B3%D8%AA%D8%B4%D8%B1%D8%A7%D9%82 (accessed December 13, 2013); In his commentary on Q9:36-37 in *Ẓilāl*, Quṭb describes the Canadian scholar as "an extremely cunning and profoundly evil Crusaderist [*sic.*] writer"; he also associates between "modern *jāhiliyya*" and efforts by Jews and Christians to arrest Islamic revival, see Carré, 2003: 309).

244 I find it particularly interesting that Quṭb makes no use of the term *jāhiliyya* in the section he dedicates to deprecating French women in all editions of *al-'Adāla* which suggests that, having encountered the American as a neo-colonialist brutish power, he was evidently no longer threatened by the egalitarian norms of the French Revolution as he was in the early Islamist stage of his life.

245 The head of the Iraqi military regime in the 1960s, 'Abdul Salām 'Ārif, is said to have found solace in reading *Ẓilāl* in the period that he spent under house arrest by his co-conspirator, Abd al-Karīm Qāsim, beginning in 1958 following the toppling of the Hashemite monarchy, see Calvert, 2010: 236; Islamists in Syria, Iraq, Algeria, India and Pakistan were reading Quṭb's works, see ibid: 238.

246 Smith, 1966 [1957]: 90.
247 ibid: 157 and ibid n198.
248 Smith makes reference to his review of Quṭb's work in the same footnote above in *Islam in Modern History*. See Smith, 1954. "Book Review: Sayed Kotb, Social Justice in Islam", *MEA*, 5:392-94.
249 Smith, 1954: 393.
250 Quṭb, no date [1964b], 80 (Note that Arnold's work *The Preaching of Islam* (1913) is referenced in *Ẓilāl* as an example of works by Orientalists who are "at war with Islam" by "corrupting its *manhaj*" of *Jihād*, see, l: 294n1).
251 Shepard finds that 32 out of a total of 41 paragraphs (paragraphs 140-180), which were added to the 8th chapter in the last edition of *al-'Adāla* correspond, with some slight variation in wording, to some paragraphs which constitute almost all of the chapter entitled "Al-Taṣawwur al-Islāmī wa al-Thaqāfa" (The Islamic Concept and Culture) in *Ma'ālim*, noting further that all of these paragraphs are drawn from sections in *Ẓilāl*, on which *Ma'ālim* is based, see Shepard, 1996: 300.
252 Quṭb, 1993 [1964a]: 201.
253 Ibid.
254 Ibid: 208.
255 Ibid: 212 (Shepard identifies this paragraph as one of 24 paragraphs which are extracted from Quṭb's early 1950s anthology *fi al-Tarīkh fikra wa Minhaj* and quoted in the 5th and last editions of *al-'Adāla*, see Shepard, 1996: 313).
256 Ibid: 183-184 (translated by Shepard, see Shepard, 1996: 279-280).
257 Carré, 2003: 309.
258 *Ẓilāl*, III: 1620.
259 Ibid: 1648.
260 Ibid.
261 Ayubi, 1991: 17; see also al-Rasheed, Kersten and Shterin, 2013. "Introduction" in *Demystifying the Caliphate*. London: Hurst, 1-30.
262 *Ẓilāl*, III: 1648.
263 Ibid: 1620.
264 Quṭb, 1992 [1964b], 99.
265 Smith, 1966 [1957]: 80-81n68. (Smith observes that sociology of religion and general sociology attest the tendency towards "a closed society, and that towards a religious society, referencing Emil Durkheim's *Les Formes Élémentaires de la Vie Religieuse* (1912) and Henri Bergson's *Les Deux Sources de la Morale et de la Religion* (1932), see ibid; it is arguably the case that, at this point, Quṭb became aware of Durkheim's ideas, leaving it to his younger brother Muḥammad, however, to refute the French scholar).
266 *Ẓilāl*, III: 1637 (Quṭb's argument is based on Rashid Riḍā's commentary in *al-Manār* where he makes the claim that the Jews' worship of Ezra may be close to the philosophy of the Jewish philosopher, Philo, which, in turn, is close to the philosophy of the pagans in India which provides "the source of the creed of the Christians").
267 Ibid.
268 Goldziher does not index these verses in *Schools of Koranic Commentators* (1920).
269 McAuliffe, 2011 [2006]: 200.
270 Chittick, 1989: 349.
271 Ibid: 350.
272 'Ashmāwī, no date: 90-92.
273 Stillman, 1991: 143 & see http://web.stanford.edu/group/SHR/5-1/text/beinin.html (accessed July 18, 2014).
274 'Ashmāwī, no date: 88-9 (in fact, In 1907 Rabbi Nahum was elevated to the post of Chief Rabbi for the Ottoman Empire and retained the position until 1920. It was only following the reorganization of Cairo's Jewish community that Rabbi Nahum was invited to serve as Chief

Rabbi of Egypt starting in 1924 when he arrived in Egypt, see http://web.stanford.edu/group/SHR/5-1/text/beinin.html (accessed July 18, 2014).

275 'Ashmāwī, no date: 89.

276 Ibid: 92.

277 See "Luther and the Jews" in Perry, 2008: 45-6.

278 See "The Jew and Modern Capitalism, 1911" by Werner Sombart in ibid: 83; Choueiri finds that Quṭb's commentary on the Qur'an reflects a clear imprint of ideas expounded by Sombart in *Die Juden und das Wirtschaftsleben* (1911) which was ultimately to culminate in "Hitler's diagnosis of Judaism as the originator of both capitalism and Marxism", see Choueiri, 2010 [1997]: 155.

279 'Ashmāwī, no date: 92.

280 *Ẓilāl,* VI: 3564; for Old Testament references to the word 'goyim', see http://brigperegrine.tripod.com/igedm.html (accessed March 5, 2015).

281 See n192 above.

282 Shepard, 2003: 531.

283 Nettler, 1987: 11.

284 See n 199 in chapter 4.

285 Haddad, 1983b: 25.

286 Ibid (see *Ẓilāl,* I: 136).

287 Calvert, 2010: 295n17.

288 Ibid: 276.

289 Smith, 1964: 55.

290 Diana Steigerwald, 2009 "Ismā'īlī Tā'wīl" in Andrew Rippin (ed.) *The Blackwell Companion to the Qur'ān.* Wiley-Blackwell, 397.

Conclusion

1 Smith, 1966 [1957]: 298.

2 Ayubi, 1991: 58.

3 Dodge, 1961: 113-4.

4 Ibid: 113.

5 Ibid: 115.

6 Calvert, 2010: 58.

7 Quoted in Krämer, 2010: 18.

8 Dodge, 1961: 121.

9 Goldschmidt, 2004: 42.

10 Ibid: 48.

11 Quṭb, no date [ca.1946a]: 21.

12 Dodge, 1961: 1.

13 *Ẓilāl,* III, 1637: n1.

14 Quṭb, 1969 [ca. late 1951]: 43-4.

15 Kreutz observes that Ṭaha Ḥusayn pointed out that Aristotle has obtained a great deal of reception during the Abbasid era and that his works had a considerable impact on Muslim philosophers including al-Farābī, Ibn Sinā, and Ibn Rushd to the effect that Aristotle was recognised as "the first teacher" (*al-mu'allim al-awwal),* see Kreutz, 2012: 138; on the importance of Ibn Rushd in providing a synthesis of both the Aristotelian and the Islamic legacies, see Nasr Ḥāmid Abu Zayd , 2012. "Rethinking the Qur'ān: Towards a Humanistic Hermeneutics" in S. Reichmuth, J. Rüsen, A. Sarhan (eds.) *Humanism and Muslim Culture.* Taiwan: V & R Unipress, 39-60.

16 Quṭb, 1996 [1932]: 6.

17 Michael Carter, 2009. "Foreign Vocabulary" in Andrew Rippin (ed.) *The Blackwell Companion to the Qur'ān*. Wiley-Blackwell, 130.
18 Ibid: 121.
19 Quṭb, 1959 [1945b]: 32-3.
20 Wilfred C. Smith, 1959: 146.
21 Ibid.
22 Smith, 1964: 120.
23 See Henri de Lubac's study *The Drama of Atheist Humanism* (1944).
24 Nettler, 1987: 11.
25 J. Calvert, L. J. Greenspoon, B. F. Le Beau, Sep, 1996: 220.
26 Ibid.
27 Calvert, 2010: 295n17.
28 Ibid: 276.
29 Smith, 1964: 55.
30 Diana Steigerwald, 2009: 397.

Glossary

- *Aḥbār*, plural of *Ḥibr*, is rendered in Lane's Lexicon as denoting the same meaning in the dictionary as that in Hebrew and Chaldean: "a like, an equal, a fellow".[1] (Chaldea in the Oxford dictionary is described as being an ancient country in what is now southern Iraq.)

- Deobandi & Tablighi Movements see Nadwat al-'Ulamā

- Dīwān Group, the title usually given to three Egyptian poets, 'Abd al-Raḥman Shukrī, Ibrāhīm 'Abd al-Qādir al-Māzinī and 'Abbās M. al-'Aqqād, who challenged the masters of neo-classicism during the second decade of the twentieth century. The Key points in their attack were contained in the book which gave them their name as a group, *al-Diwān: Kitāb fī al-Adab wa al-Naqd* (1921). The work of the Diwān poets illustrates the extent to which English literature had become one of the major formative influences on Arab culture. Despite the fact that several plays by Shakespeare had been available in Arabic since the late nineteenth century, the principal external cultural influence on Muṭrān and his generation had been French. Shukrī, however, attended Sheffield University College from 1909 to 1912 and all three members of the Diwān Group were closely acquainted with the English lyrical poetry contained in Francis Palgrave's the Golden Treasury, which covered the period from Shakespeare to the mid-19th century. This somewhat partial view of English poetry, together with the work of a number of 'Abbasid poets, constituted the most important materials from which the Diwān Group derived both their inspiration and their principles and theories of poetry. They were anxious to distinguish themselves from the previous generation. Al-'Aqqād led the attack on Aḥmad Shawqī, the figurehead of the neo-classical movement, by reshuffling the lines of Shawqī's "Elegy on Muṣṭafa Kāmil", thus demonstrating the lack of organic unity in the piece. Of the three members of the group, Shukrī is the poet of the greatest range and interest, while al-Māzinī and al-'Aqqād are remembered mainly for achievements other than poetry. Although al-'Aqqād published eight volumes of verse throughout his long

1 Lane, 1863, *AEL*, 2: 499.

and prolific career as a writer, it is as a critic rather than a poet that he left his mark. He proclaimed Hazlitt the primary inspiration for the new literature which he sought to promote, and in his pleas for simple, everyday subjects and language to become the raw-materials of Arabic poetry, was instrumental in changing the taste and sensibility of poets who abandoned the neo-classical style in increasing numbers after WWI.[2]

- *futuwwa* **et**hics correspond to the ancient Arab ethic known as *muru'a* (translated by Hoffman as manliness but I favour magnanimity) which upheld "virtues of courage, extravagant hospitality, and indulgence toward those who are weak."[3]

- *Ḥulūl,* Lane finds that the word came to be used in philosophy to signify temporary or separable, and permanent or inseparable, indwelling or in being; and the expression, "*ḥala bihī*" or "*fīhī*", as meaning "it had, or became in the condition of having, such indwelling or being in it" ; the expression is often used in relation to joy or grief, and the like, meaning "it took up its abode in him."[4]

- Iqbal, Muhammad (1875-1938) after a classical Islamic education, Iqbal studied at Cambridge and Munich, earning a doctorate in philosophy as well as a law degree. Conversant with western philosophical Islamic education, he studied at Cambridge and Munich, earning a doctorate in philosophy as well as a law degree. Conversant with Western philosophical and scientific thought, Iqbal advocated a fundamental rethinking of Islamic thought as reflected in his *The Reconstruction of Religious Thought in Islam*.[5]

- *Ishrāq* is defined by Arkoun as the illuminative philosophy which triumphed after Avicenna (d.1037), Suhrawardī (d.1191), and Ibn 'Arabī (d. 1240).[6] Arnaldez finds that the name *Ishrāq* was given to "illuminative Wisdom" which was advocated by Shihāb al-Dīn Shuhrawardī who indicated that his ideas are derived from a "Wisdom which, in the field of mysticism, has inspired lines of initiates comparable with the initiatory *isnāds* of the Ṣūfis, though without the explicit granting of any 'delegation' by the Masters to the disciples." Western, Greek elements, as well as Eastern elements deriving from the traditions of classical

2 R. C. Ostle, 1998: 196.

3 Hoffman, 1995: 229.

4 Lane, 1863: 2: 619.

5 John J. Donohue & John L. Esposito (eds.), 1982. "Muhammad Iqbal: a Separate Muslim State in the Subcontinent" in *Islam in Transition: Muslim Perspectives*. New York: Oxford University Press, 91.

6 Mohammed Arkoun, 1994: 75.

Persia and ancient Egypt are discernible in the (concept of *Ishrāq).* Arnaldez argues that Neoplatonism was already charged with Eastern ideas, in contrast with pure rationalist Aristotelianism, adding that there is a close link between *Ishrāq* (illumination) and Eastern Wisdom (*ḥikma mashriqiyya*). It is through Plato, Arnaldez argues, that one can best approach the philosophy of illumination which is a meditation upon propositions made in the *Republic*...An exposition of the details of Wisdom (in *Ishrāq*), would be tantamount to an exposition of the details of Suhrawardī's thinking. The play of Light and shadow, the conception of *barzakh* (screen, separation, which is utter darkness), the modes of procedure, the production of the world, all these together form a whole which can be expounded, as by Suhrawardī himself, in the terminology of the Plotiniun or Avicennian philosophy of emanation. Intellects and spheres..."a higher intuitive vision [is reached] when the *'aql* is assumed by the Spirit, in which it receives the *sakīna*, 'the placing in the direct presence on the threshold of the transcendental Being".[7]

According to Karen Armstrong, it is the Iranian Suhrawardī and the Spanish born Ibn 'Arabī who "linked Islamic Falsafa indissolubly with mysticism and made the God experienced by the Sufis normative in many parts of the Islamic empire. Like al-Ḥallāj, Suhrawardī was also put to death by the 'ulama. His life's work was to link what he called "the original Oriental religion" with Islam, thus, completing the project which was proposed by ibn Sina. He claimed that "all the sages of the ancient world had preached a single doctrine". At the point of origin, this doctrine was revealed to Hermes (whom Suhrawardī identified with the Prophet identified in the Qur'an as Idris and Enoch in the Bible); Plato and Pythagoras and the Zoroastrian Magi are said to have transmitted the same doctrine. Since Aristotle, however, it had been "obscured by a more narrowly intellectual philosophy" until it had finally reached Suhrawardī via al-Bistamī and al-Ḥallāj.[8]

- *Kharijite* the Arabic word rendered as 'Khārijites' is *khawārij*, which is the plural of the participle khārij, "one going out or seceding", though a single Khārijite is a *khārijī*. The movement is held to have begun a year or two after the accession of 'Alī when a group of his supporters, allegedly disapproving of his attitude to the Arbitration, 'went out' or 'seceded' from his army. The revolts against 'Alī show that the Khārijite movement was not specifically anti-Umayyad.[9]

7 R. Arnaldez, 1978. "Ishrāq" in E. Van Donzel, B. Lewis CH. Pellat (eds.), *EOI,* IV: 119-120.

8 Armstrong, 1999: 271.

9 Watt, 1987 [1968]: 54.

- Miskawayh (d. 1030) is one of two outstanding literary figures of the Buwaihid period, the other being the essayist Abū Ḥayyān al-Tawḥīdī (d. 1023). In addition to his influential work on ethics, largely based on the synthesis of Islamic and Hellenistic thought by al-Kindī, Miskawayh produced as well the first important book of history since Ṭabarī *The Experiences of the Nations*. Its significance in Arabic literature is that Miskawayh was an official and a courtier and a serious scholar with an exacting standard of accuracy and relative independence of judgement, allowing for some natural hero-worship of his first patron, the vizier Ibn al-'Amīd.[10] (Sections of *The Experiences of the Nations* were translated by Margoliouth and included in his work *The Eclipse of the Abbasid Caliphate* (1921).[11])

- Nadwat al-'Ulamā, a Muslim educational and reform society established at Kānpūr (Cawnpore) in north India in 1310/1892. Six years later, the society moved to Lucknow with the purpose of founding a new educational system by amalgamating the "old" and the "modern" curricula, and eliminating sectarianism among Muslims. It, however, failed to impress upon other *madrasas* to adopt its suggested curricula. In 1898, it established its own educational institution, Dār al-'Ulūm, which was to become more famous than the society itself.

  During the first half of the 19th century, English language schools had cropped up all over British India but certificates of the *madrasas* teaching basically *Dars-i Niẓāmī*, the curriculum laid down by Mullā Niẓām al-Dīn (d. 1679) to produce administrators for the Mughal state, were generally recognised up to the Sepoy Mutiny of 1857-8 as sufficient qualifications to join the state machinery. After the events of 1857 and the subsequent attitudes of disfavour towards Muslims by the British, the former started to establish private *madrasas* geared only to imparting religious education. The first such *madrasa*, Kāsim al-Ulūm (later known as Dār al-'Ulūm), was established at Deoband in north India in 1865. In addition to primary and secondary education (5 years each), the Dār al-'Ulūm awards the degree of *'Ālimiyya* after a study of 4 years in its 'Arabic', i.e. Islamic, section. After a further two years' study and presentation of a small dissertation graduates are given the degree of *faḍīla*, with specialisation in either Islamic *Shari'a* or Arabic literature. In the 1970s and 1980s Dār al-'Ulūm has seen great progress in terms of buildings, but its overall impact on the intellectual life of Muslims in India remains marginal. Dār al-'Ulūm today [1991] is in practice yet another *madrasa* which positively discourages modern education.

10 Gibb, 1963 [1926]: 95.

11 Ibid: 168.

Nadwa aroused great controversy in its early years among the Muslims of India. Opponents considered it another form of the Aligarh movement of Sayyid Aḥmad Khān.[12]

- Abu al-Hasan 'Ali Nadwi was born on December 5, 1913, in Rai-Bareli, in the state of Uttar Pardesh in North India. He was born into a family with ties to the Prophet's family and which earlier in the mid-19th century had organised a religious movement based on a Wahhābī-style Islamism. His family had strong links with the Nadwat al-Ulama (scholars circle) of Lucknow, a scholastic and reformist movement that started in 1894, and with the seminary associated with the Nadwa, Dār al-'Ulūm, which was directed by Nadwi's father. Both institutions were connected to the Deoband movement that started earlier in 1866 to promote Islamic missionary work (*da'wa* or *tabligh*) and to the Khilafat movement for reinvigorating the caliphate. Al-Nadwi received a thorough education at his father's school, but one that was anchored more to the Arab world than to India.[13] In 1984, Nadwi helped establish the League of Islamic Literature, based in Riyadh, and became its first President. Nadwi was essentially an Arabophile, showing a preference to write in Arabic instead of English or Urdu. He was also an Easternist who contrasted the spiritual East and the material West and its secular decadence. He was particularly opposed to the idea of nationalism and considered it to be "a European ruse to divide the Islamic world." His anti-nationalist stance corresponded with the anti-Nasserite Islamists in Egypt. Nadwi served as the rector of the Nadwa in Lucknow. He received the King Faisal Award from Saudi Arabia and the Sultan Hasan al-Bolkhaih International Prize from Brunei and Oxford University for his publications and services on behalf of Islam.[14]

- *Rasūl* Montgomery Watt argues that the word "messenger" or "apostle" (*rasūl*) means virtually the same as "prophet" (*nabī*), namely, one who conveys to his own people a message (*risala*) from God, noting that "the commonest title for Muḥammad in Arabic is 'Messenger of God' [*rasūl Allah*]" which tends to connote a developed conception of prophethood.[15] The argument being made here is that stories of former prophets in the Qur'an, which constitute about a quarter of the text, are meant to assert that Muḥammad had a long spiritual ancestry and

12 Khān, 1991: 7: 874-5.

13 Toth, 2013: 269 (Toth bases this information on an article by Muhammad Qāsim Zaman, 1988. "Arabic, the Arab Middle East, and the Definitions of Muslim Identity in Twentieth Century India," *Journal of the Royal Asiatic Society*, 8, 1:64, see ibid: 357, n70).

14 Ibid: 270-71.

15 Watt, 1991: 11.

that previous prophets shared similar experiences as his. In Suras 7, 11, and 26 there are parallel accounts of Noah, Lot and three Arabian prophets, Hūd, Ṣāliḥ and Shu'ayb, with reference to Moses and Abraham and other prophets being sometimes made in this context as well. Mostly, the Qur'an makes reference to a prophet as one who gathered around himself a community of first-generation believers. The argument is being made here that "men such as the book-prophets of the Old Testament would be unthinkable". Apart from Jonah, none of these prophets is mentioned in the Qur'an.[16]

Uri Rubin argues in "Prophets and Prophethood" that as in the New Testament, in which apostles seem to rank higher than prophets (e.g., I Corinthians 12: 28-31; cf. Ephesians 3:5; 4:11), in the Qur'an, too, "*rasūl*" seems to be somewhat more elevated than "*nabī*".[17]

- *Ṣāghirūn,* in Lane's lexicon the word is derived from the verb *ṣaghira* signifying "small", or "little". When used in relation to a human being, it means "he was a child". The verb, and its derivatives, refers also to a person who was "content with vileness, baseness, abasement, or ignominy, tyranny or injury.[18]

- Tagore, Rabindranath (1861-1941), was the youngest son of Debendranath Tagore, a leader of the Brahmo Samaj, which was a new religious sect in nineteenth-century Bengal and which attempted a revival of the ultimate monistic basis of Hinduism as laid down in the *Upanishads*. He was educated at home; and although at seventeen he was sent to England for formal schooling, he did not finish his studies there. In his mature years, in addition to his many-sided literary activities, he managed the family estates, a project which brought him into close touch with common humanity and increased his interest in social reforms. He also started an experimental school at Shantiniketan where he tried his Upanishadic ideals of education. From time to time he participated in the Indian nationalist movement, though in his own non-sentimental and visionary way; and Gandhi, the political father of modern India, was his devoted friend. Tagore was knighted by the ruling British Government in 1915, but within a few years he resigned the honour as a protest against British policies in India.

  Tagore had early success as a writer in his native Bengal. With his translations of some of his poems he became rapidly known in the West. In fact his fame

16 Ibid: 10.

17 Uri Rubin, 2009: 240.

18 Lane, 1863: 4: 1691.

attained a luminous height, taking him across continents on lecture tours and tours of friendship. For the world he became the voice of India's spiritual heritage; and for India, especially for Bengal, he became a great living institution.

Although Tagore wrote successfully in all literary genres, he was first of all a poet. Among his fifty and odd volumes of poetry are *Manasi* (1890) [The Ideal One], *Sonar Tari* (1894) [The Golden Boat], *Gitanjali* (1910) [Song Offerings], *Gitimalya* (1914) [Wreath of Songs], and *Balaka* (1916) [The Flight of Cranes]. The English renderings of his poetry, which include *The Gardener* (1913), *Fruit-Gathering* (1916), and *The Fugitive* (1921), do not generally correspond to particular volumes in the original Bengali; and in spite of its title, *Gitanjali: Song Offerings* (1912), the most acclaimed of them, contains poems from other works besides its namesake. Tagore's major plays are *Raja* (1910) [*The King of the Dark Chamber*], *Dakghar* (1912) [*The Post Office*], *Achalayatan* (1912) [The Immovable], *Muktadhara* (1922) [The Waterfall], and *Raktakaravi* (1926) [*Red Oleanders*]. He is the author of several volumes of short stories and a number of novels, among them *Gora* (1910), *Ghare-Baire* (1916) [*The Home and the World*], and *Yogayog* (1929) [Crosscurrents]. Besides these, he wrote musical dramas, dance dramas, essays of all types, travel diaries, and two autobiographies, one in his middle years and the other shortly before his death in 1941. Tagore also left numerous drawings and paintings, and songs for which he wrote the music himself.[19]

- *Tashbīh* (anthroporphism) was refuted by the Mu'tazilites as detracting from the doctrine of "God's unity" which was at the centre of the Mu'tazilite position by the early ninth century. The chief matters which came under this principle were the denial of God's essential attributes, such as knowledge, power and speech, the denial of the eternity or un-createdness of the Qur'ān as the speech of God, and the denial of any resemblance between God and his creation (anthroporphism).[20]

- *Wiḥdat al-wujūd:* the Encyclopedia of Islam defines the technical term of classical Sufism, "*wudjūd,* as being used primarily...as a verbal noun derived from *wadjada*, 'to find' or 'to experience'. The term already occurs in several meanings in the prose writings of such prominent Baghdādī Ṣūfis as al-kharrāz (d.890-91), and al-Djunayd (d. 910-11), as well as in a well-known *qaṣīda* generally attributed to al-Ḥallāj (d. 922). Applied to the experience of the mystic, *wudjūd* is frequently juxtaposed with *shuhūd* 'witnessing' or 'presence', and/or *wadjd*, a

19 http://www.nobelprize.org/nobel_prizes/literature/laureates/1913/tagore-bio.html (accessed May 19, 2014).

20 Watt, 2009 [1998]: 242.

crucial Ṣūfī term which, though usually translated as ecstasy, is more precisely defined as a an indescribable 'encounter of the unseen with the unseen' (*muṣādafat al-ghayb bi 'l ghayb*)."

Although Ibn al-'Arabī (d.1240) became famous as the greatest spokesman for "the unity of being" (*wiḥdat al-wujūd*), Landolt finds, that the expression has not been traced to his writings. Partly based on 'Alā' al-Dawla al-Simnānī's (d. 1336) critique of Ibn al-'Arabī's doctrine of "*wiḥdat al-wujūd*," but also as a means to assert their own identity as Muslims against a certain Indo-Muslim syncretism of their own times, later Ṣūfis such as Gisūdīrāz (d. 1422) and especially Aḥmad Sirhindī (d. 1624) formulated a doctrine which is generally referred to as "*wiḥdat al-shuhūd*."[21]

Smith observes that in the course of the process of crystallisation of religious communities in Mughul India one notices the "supersession" in metaphysics of Ibn 'Arabi's doctrine of "*wiḥdat al-wujūd*" by Sirhindi's (d. 1624) doctrine of "*wiḥdat al-shuhūd*".[22] Smith remarks that "to believe in the ultimate unity of the world", (as per "*wiḥdat al-wujūd*") is also to believe in the unity of humankind".[23]

- *Sharaab,* longing that makes the seeker restless; forgetting the self altogether he may break forth into mysterious things, love for God; and esoteric knowledge.

  1. Sharab-I-Kham: lit. Wine not well fermented. In Sufi parlance, the states overtaking seeker in the beginning.

  2. Sharab-Pukhta: lit. Well-fermented wine. Sufis use the term for "intense love for God".

  3. Sharaab-I-Saaf: pure wine; the Divine benedictions reaching the seeker direct, though no other agency, such as angels, pure souls.[24]

---

21 H. Landolt, 1991. "Wudjūd" in C. E. Bosworth, E. Van Dowell, W. P. Heinrich and Ch. Pellat (eds.), *EOI.* Leiden: Brill, XI: 217-8.

22 Wilfred C. Smith 1981 [1963a]: 190.

23 Ibid.

24 Rastogi, 1990: 60-61.

Bibliography

Abbreviations for Journals, Lexicons and Encyclopaedias

AEL	Lane's *Arabic-English Lexicon*
BJMES	*British Journal of Middle Eastern Studies*
EAL	*The Routledge Encyclopedia of Arabic Literature*
EOI	*The Encyclopedia of Islam*
EOQ	*Encyclopaedia of the Qur'ān*
IJMES	*International Journal of Middle East Studies*
JPI	*Journal of Political Ideologies*
MEA	*Middle Eastern Affairs*
MEJ	*The Middle East Journal*
SMJR	*Studies in Muslim-Jewish Relations*
TMPR	*Totalitarian Movements and Political Religions*

Akh	*al-Akhbār*
DW	*al-Da'wah*
FJ	*al-Fikr al-Jadīd*
HI	*al-Hilāl*
IM	*al-Ikhwan al-Muslimūn* (first issued on 20 May, 1954)
KM	*al-Kātib al-Maṣrī*
KT	*al-Kitāb*
MJ	*al-Majalla al-Jadīda*
MSI	*Majallat al-Shu'ūn al-Ijtimā'iyya*
MQ	*al-Muqtaṭaf*
RS	*al-Risala*
RY	*Rose al-Youssef*
TQ	*al-Thaqāfa*

Primary Sources: Sayyid Quṭb's Works and Anthologies of his Articles

- 1996 [1932]: *Muhimmat al-Sha'ir fī al-Ḥayya wa Shi'r al-Jīl al-Ḥaḍir* (The Mission of the Poet in Life and the Poetry of the Present Generation). Köln: al-Kamel.
- no date [ca.1935]: *'al-Shaṭi' al-Majhūl* (The Unknown Shore), no publisher.
- no date [ca.1935a]: "Ila al-Bilad al-Shaqīqa" (To Sister Countries) in ibid.
- no date [ca.1935b]: "al-Insān al-Akhīr"(The Last Man) in ibid, 32-7.
- no date [ca.1935c]: "*al-Gharīb* (The Stranger) in ibid, 51-2.
- no date [ca.1935]: "Ila al-Shaṭi' al-Majhūl" (To the Unknown Shore) in *al-Shaṭi' al-Majhūl,* Unknown publisher, 18-20.
- 1969 [1939]: *al-Rad 'ala Mustaqbal al-Thaqāfa fī Misr*. Jeddah: al-Dār al-Sa'ūdiyya.
- June 1941: "Fī al-Insāniyya Khayr ma Dam Fiha Amthāl Strauss", *RS*, 414: 644-5.
- May 1943: "Mashrū' Beveridge," *MSI*, 5: 21-9.
- February 1944: "Sindbād 'Aṣrī wa Sindbād Qadīm li Ḥusayn Fawzī", *TQ*, 267: 21-24.
- February 1944: "Sindbād 'Aṣrī wa Sindbād Qadīm li Ḥusayn Fawzī", *TQ*, 269.
- 1945a: *al-Aṭyaf al-Arba'a* (The Four Phantoms), first published by the publishing house, which was affiliated with King Fu'ād's (now Cairo) university, Lajnat al-Nashr li al-Jami'īn.
- 1959 [1945b]: *al-Taṣwīr al-Fannī fī al-Qur'ān* (Artistic Portrayal in the Qur'an). Cairo: Dār al-Ma'ārif.
- 2004 [1946]: *A Child from the Village,* edited, translated and with an introduction by John Calvert, and William Shepard. New York: Syracuse University Press.
- 1946: *al-Ḍamīr al-Amrikanī wa Qaḍiyyat Filisṭīn* in Ṣalāḥ A. al-Khaldī (ed.) *Amrīka min al-Dakhil bi-Minẓā*r Sayyid *Quṭb*. Jeddah: Dār al-Manāra, 1987, 124-9.
- no date [1946a]: *Ṭifl min al-Qarya* (A Child from the Village). (Third edition) Beirut: no publisher (first published by the publishing house, which was affiliated with King Fu'ād's (now Cairo) University, Lajnat al-Nashr li al-Jami'īn).
- 1946b: *Kutub wa Shakhṣiyyat* (Books and Personalities). Cairo: Maṭba'it al-Risala.
- 1946c: *al-Madīna al-Masḥūra* (The Bewitched City). Cairo: Iqrā', http://www.4shared.com/get/Nh6Xq09d/___123___.html
- Jan. 1946d: "Shylock al-Jadīd, aw Qaḍiyyat Filisṭīn- Masraḥiyya li al-Ustādh Bakthīr" (The New Shylock, or the Issue of Palestine: a Theatre Play by al-Ustādh Bakthīr) *al-rRsala,* 655: 14-17.
- February 1946e: "al-Lugha al-Waḥida alatī Yafhamuhā al-Injilīz", *al-Risala,* 659: 184.
- 20 May 1946f: "al-Kalimat al-Yawm li al-'Arab Famadha Hum Ṣāni'ūn", *al-Risala,* 672: 549-55.
- 1947a: *Ashwak* (Thorns). Cairo: Dār Sa'd Miṣr, see http//www.4/shared.com/file/30277686/987d93bb/__online.html
- 1947b: *al-Naqd al-Adabī: Uṣūluhu wa Manahijahū* (Literary Criticism: its Sources and Methods). Cairo: Dār al-Fikr al-'Arabī.
- 2003 [1947b]: *al-Naqd al-Adabī: Uṣūluhu wa Manahijahū*. Cairo: Dār al-Shurūq , 8th edition.
- 1959 [1947c]: *Mashahid al-Qiyama fī al-Qur'ān* (Scenes of the Day of Resurrection in the Qur'an). Cairo: Dār al-Ma'ārif.

- 2004 [1947c]: *Mashahid al-Qiyama fī al-Qur'ān.* Cairo: Dār al-Shurūq.
- 1 Jan. 1948: "Hadha al-Majalla", *al-Fikr al-Jadīd,* 1: 3.
- Dec. 1949a: "Ḥamā'im fī New York" (Doves in New York), *KT,* 10: 666-9 in Ṣalaḥ A. al-Khaldī (1987) pp. 141-144.
- 1949b: "Ila al-Ustadh Tawfīq al-Ḥakīm" in Ṣalaḥ A. al-Khaldī (1987).
- 1950: "Introduction" in Abu al-Ḥasan al-Nadwī *Madha Khasira -al-'Alam bi Inḥiṭāt al-Muslimīn.* Cairo: Lajnat al-Ta'līf wa al-Nashr.
- 1950 [1949]: *al-'Adāla al-Ijtimā'iyya fi al-Islām* (Social Justice in Islam). Cairo: Lajnat al-Nashr li al-Jāmi'īn (2nd edition).
- Sept. 25, 1951: "Idha Ja'a Naṣr Allah wa-al-Fatḥ", *RS,* 951: 1246.
- 10 Sept., 1951: "Ila Ustadhuna al-Duktur Aḥmad Amīn", *TQ,* 663: 13.
- 19 Nov. 1951bb: "Amrīka alatī Rā'ayt fī Mizān al-Qiyam al-Insāniyya", *RS,* 959: 1301-6 in Ṣalaḥ A. al-Khaldī (1987), 113-114.
- 1951c: "al-Bida'iyya al-Faniyya" (Artistic Primitiveness in America) in Ṣalaḥ A. al-Khaldī (ed). *Amrīka min al-Dakhil bi- Minẓ*ār Sayyid Q*uṭb.* Jeddah: Dār al-Manāra, 1987: 115.
- 1951d: "Fī al-Tarīkh Fikra wa Minhaj" (In History, there is an Idea and a Method) in Sayyid Quṭb. *Fī al-Tarīkh Fikra wa Minhaj.* Cairo: Dār al-Shurūq, 2005: 37-61.
- 1951a: "'Aduwina al-Awal al-Rajul al-Abyaḍ" (Our Prime Enemy is the White Man) in al-Khaldī, 1987, pp 41-2.
- 5 Nov. 1951b: "Amrīka alatī Rā'ayt fī Mizān al-Qiyam al-Insāniyya", *RS,* 957: 1245-7 in al-Khaldī (1987), 97-102.
- Dec. 3, 1951: "Amrīka alatī Rā'ayt fī Mizān al-Qiyam al-Insāniyya" *RS,* 961: 1357-60 in al-Khaldī (1987), 115-123.
- 1951e: *al-Salam al-'Alamī wa al Islām* (*Islam and Universal Peace*). Cairo: Dār al-kitāb al- 'Arabī.
- June 18, 1951f: "Li al-Azhar Risala, wa-Lakinnahū la Yu'addiha", *RS,* 937: 685-86.
- 1979 [1951]: *al-Salam al-'Alamī wa al Islām.* Cairo: Dār al-Shurūk (8th edition).
- 1952 [1951]: *Ma'rakat al-Islām wa al-Rā'simāliyya* (The Struggle between Islam and Capitalism). Cairo: Dār al-Kitāb al-'Arabī.
- 1982 [1951]: *Ma'rakat al-Islām wa al-Rā'simāliyya* (The Battle of Islam and Capitalism). Cairo: Dār al-Shurūq.
- 30 June 1952a :"Islām Amrikanī" (American Islam), *RS,* in al-Khaldī (1987), 130-4.
- 8 Aug.1952: "Istijwab ila al-Baṭal Muḥammad Najīb", *Akh.*
- 15 Aug. 1952: "Ḥarakat la Tukhifunā", *Akh.*
- 19 Aug. 1952: "Idha Lam Takun Thawra Faḥakimū Muḥammad Najīb", *RY.*
- 25 Aug. 1952: "Adab al-Inḥilal", *RS.*
- 26 Aug. 1952: "Min Maṣlaḥat Kibar al-Mulak an Yakhḍa'ū li al-Thawra", *RY.*
- 2 Sept. 1952: "al-Thawra Tatasaka' 'ala Abwāb al-Dawawīn", *RY.*
- 8 Sept. 1952: "Ṣaḥiḥū Akadhīb al-Tarīkh", *RS.*
- 10 Sept. 1952: "Tajrīd al-Thawra min 'Anāṣir al-Quwa al-Sha'biyya", *RS.*
- 10 Sept. 1952: "al-Jamahīr laysa laha sha' min Ṣabr Ayūb", *RY.*

- 22 Sept. 1952: "Khaṭar Ijra' al-'Amaliyya bi-Silaḥ Mulawath", *RY.*
- 22 Sept. 1952: "Akhrisū hadhihi al-Aṣwat al-Danisa", *RS.*
- 29 Sept. 1952: "Hadhihī al-Aḥzab Ghayr Qabila li al-Baqa'", *RY.*
- 6 Oct. 1952: "Sha'b wa Rajul", *RY.*
- 6 Oct. 1952: "Naḥnu al-Sha'b Nurīd", *RS.*
- 20 Oct. 1952: "Lasna 'Abīdan li-Āḥad", *RY.*
- 3 Nov.1952: "'Aduwina al-Awal al-Rajul al-Abyaḍ" (Our Prime Enemy is the White Man", *RS*, in al-Khaldī (1987), pp 135-140.
- 1969 [ca.1950sa]: "Mujtama"Alamī" (an International Society) in *Naḥw Mujtama' Islāmī*. Amman: Maktabit al-Aqṣa, 92-135.
- 1969 [ca.1951]: "al-Mustaqbal li al-Islām"(The Future is for Islam), in *Naḥw Mujtama' Islāmī*. Amman: Maktabit al-Aqṣa, 17-44.
- 1969 [ca.1950sc]: "Ṭabī'at al-Mujtama' al-Islāmī" (The Nature of the Islamic Society, n. d. [ca. late 1950s c]) in Sayyid Quṭb. *Naḥw Mujtama' Islamī*. Amman: Maktabit al-Aqṣa, no date [1969], 62-91.
- 1958 [1949]: *al-'Adāla al-Ijtimā'iyya fi al-Islām*. Syria: Dār Iḥyā' al-Kutub al-'Arabiyya (5th edition).
- 2005 [1962a]: *al-Islām wa Mushkilat al-Ḥaḍāra* (Islam and the Problems of Civilization). Cairo: Dār al-Shurūq.
- 1962c: *Khaṣā'iṣ al-Taṣawwur al-Islāmī wa Muqawwimatu*: (Characteristics of the Islamic Concept and its Essentials). Syria: Dar Iḥyā' al-Kutub al-'Arabiyya.
- ca.1963a: *Hadha al-Dīn* (This Religion,), http://www.tawhed.ws/c?i=63
- 2005 [ca.1963b]: *al-Mustaqbal li Hadha al-Dīn* (The Future belongs to this Religion). Cairo: Dār al-Shurūq.
- 1992 [1964b]: *Ma'ālim fī al-Ṭarīq* (Signposts on the Road). Cairo: Dār al-Shurūq.
- no date [1964b]: *Ma'ālim fī al-Ṭarīq*. Cairo: no publisher.
- 1993 [1964a]: *al-'Adāla al-Ijtima'iyya fi al-Islām*. Cairo: Dār al-Shurūq.
- 2009 [ca.1952-1965]: *Fī Ẓilāl al-Qur'ān* (In the Shade of the Qur'an). Cairo: Dār al-Shurūq, volumes 1-6).
- 1970 [ca.1960s?]: *"Ma'rakatunā ma'a al-Yahūd" in Mā'rakatunā ma'a al-Yahūd* (Our Battle with the Jews). Jeddah: al-Dār al-Sa'ūdiyya.
- 1997 [1969]: *Muqawwimat al-Taṣawwur al-Islāmī*, (The Essential Components of the Islamic Concept). Cairo: Dār al-Shurūq.
- 1995 [no date]: "Muḥatim al-Ṭawaghīt" (Destroyer of Tyrants or Oppressors) in *Dirāsāt Islāmiyya* (Islamic Studies). Cairo: Dār al-Shurūq.
- 1995a [ca.1950s]:"Intiṣār Muḥammad Ibn 'Abdulla" (The Victory of Muḥammad Ibn 'Abdulla) in *Dirāsāt Islāmiyya* (Islamic Studies, *DI*). Cairo: Dār al-Shurūq, 1995a [ca. early 1950s].
- 1965b: *Limadha A'damūnī.* (Why Did They Execute Me?) A publication of the Saudi Company for Research and Marketing based on a statement made by Quṭb in 1965 prior to his execution in 1966 also found @ http://www.tawhed.ws/r?i=578iq2de

Anthologies of Quṭb's Articles

- 1987 [late 1940s-early 50s]: *Amrīka min al-Dakhil bi-Minẓār Sayyid Quṭb.* (America from within as seen by Sayyid Quṭb). A collection of articles and writings on America collected & edited by 'Abdul-Fatāḥ al-Khāldī. Jeddah: Dār al-Manāra.
- 1995 [ca. early 1950s]: *Dirasat Islamiyya.* Cairo: Dār al-Shurūq.
- 2005 [1967]: *Fī al-Tarīkh Fikra wa Minhaj* (In History, [there is] an Idea and a Method). Cairo: Dār al-Shurūq, & see http://www.tawhed.ws/r?i=dm6ivfov for an Internet version.
- 1969: *Naḥw Mujtama' Islamī* Amman: Maktabit al-Aqṣa (1st ed.). For an Internet copy see http://www.tawhed.ws/r?i=22070909
- 2005 [1969]: *Naḥw Mujtama' Islamī.* Cairo: Dār al-Shurūq.
- 1982 [1951]: *al-Salam al-'Alamī wa al-Islām* (World Peace and Islam). Cairo: Dār al-Shurūq.
- 1970: *Ma'rakatuna ma'a al-Yahūd* (Our Battle with the Jews). Jeddah: al-Dār al-Sa'ūdiyya.

Secondary Sources on Sayyid Quṭb's Life and Works

Abu-Rabi', Ibrahim M.

- 1996: *Intellectual Origins of Islamic Resurgence in the Modern Arab World.* New York: State University of New York Press.

Badawī, Aḥmad

- 1992: *Sayyid Quṭb.* Cairo: al-Hay'a al-Miṣriya al-'Āmma li al-Kitāb.

al-Badawī, Ahmad M.

- 2002: *Sayyid Quṭb Naqidan* (Sayyid Quṭb the Critic). Cairo: Al-Dār al-Thaqāfiyya li al-Nashr.

Binder, Leonard

- 1988: "the Religious Aesthetic of Sayyid Quṭb: a Non-Scriptural Fundamentalism" in *Islamic Liberalism: a Critique of Development Ideologies.* Chicago: The University of Chicago Press.

Boullata, Issa J.

- 2000: "Sayyid Quṭb's Literary Appreciation of the Qur'an" in Issa J. Boullata (ed.) *Literary Structures of Religious Meaning in the Qur'an.* London: Routledge.

Bouzid, Aḥmed

- 1988: *Man, Society, And Knowledge In The Islamist Discourse Of Sayyid Quṭb* (a PhD thesis presented to Virginia Polytechnic Institute and State University) in http://scholar.lib.vt.edu/theses/public/etd-3398-184043/materials/Final.pdf

Calvert, John

- 2010: *Sayyid Quṭb and the Origins of Radical Islamism.* London: Hurst and Company.

Calvert, John & William E. Shepard

- 2004 [1946]: *A Child from the Village,* edited, translated and with an introduction by John Calvert, and William Shepard (eds.). New York: Syracuse University Press.

Calvert, John, L. J. Greenspoon & B. F. Le Beau

- 1996: "Radical Islamism and the Jews: the View of Sayyid Quṭb", *Studies in Jewish Civilisation*, 8: 213-229.

Carré, Olivier

- 2003: *Mysticism and Politics: A Critical Reading of Fi Ẓilāl al-Qur'ān by Sayyid Quṭb (1906-1966).* Leiden: Brill.

Diyab, Muḥammad Ḥafiẓ

- 1987: *Sayyid Quṭb: al-Khiṭab wa al-Aydulujiyya*. Cairo: Dar al-Thaqafa al-Jadida.

Euben, Roxanne L.

- 2003: "A Counternarrative of Shared Ambivalence: Some Muslim and Western Perspectives on Science and Reason". *Common Knowledge*, 9: 1, 50-77.

Faḍl-Allah, Mahdī

- 1979 [1978]: *Ma'a Sayyid Quṭb fi Fikrihi al-Siyasi wa al-Dīnī*. (With Sayyid Quṭb in his Political and Religious Thought). Beirut: Mu'assasat al-Risala.

Gray, John

- "How Marx turned Muslim" in http://www.islamagainstextremism.com/articles/ikvkw-john-gray-how-marx-turned-muslim.cfm (accessed 2nd January 2012). Haddad, Yvonne Y.
- 1983b: "The Qur'anic Justification of an Islamic Revolution: the View of Sayyid Quṭb". *MEJ*, 37, 1: 14-29.

Hansen, Hendrik and Peter Kainz

- 2007: "Radical Islamism and Totalitarian Ideology: a Comparison of Sayyid Quṭb's Islamism with Marxism and National Socialism", *TMPR*, 8:1, 55-76.

Judy, Ronald A. T.

- 2004: "Sayyid Quṭb's Fiqh al-Waqi'i, or New Realist Science", *Boundary 2*, 31: 2, 113-148.

al-Khaldi, Ṣalāḥ A.

- 2000: *Madkhal ila Ẓilāl al-Qur'ān: Dirasa wa Taqwim* (An Introduction to Ẓilāl al-Qur'an: a Study and an Appraisal). Amman: Dār 'Amār. (an extract from al-Khaldi's PhD thesis on *Ẓilāl* found in http://www.archive.org/stream/majmouhfidilalk/mfzq3#page/n13/mode/2up
- 1994 [1989]: *Sayyid Quṭb min al-Milad ila al-Istishhad* (Sayyid Quṭb from Birth to Martyrdom. Damascus: Dār al-Qalam. (http://www.qassimy.com/vb/showthread.php?t=445732).

Khatab, Sayed

- 2006: *The Political Thought of Sayyid Quṭb: The Theory of Jahiliyya*. London: Routledge.

Moussalli, Aḥmed S.

- 1992: *Radical Islamic Fundamentalism: the Ideological and Political Discourse of Sayyid Quṭb.* Beirut: American University of Beirut.

Musallam, Adnan A.

- 2005: *From Secularism to Jihad: Sayyid Quṭb and the Foundations of Radical Islamism.* London: Praeger.

Al-Namnam, Ḥilmī

- 2010: *Sayyid Quṭb wa Thawrat Yulyu* (Sayyid Quṭb and the July Revolution). Cairo: Madbūlī

Nettler, Ronald L.

- 1987: *Past Trials and Present Tribulations: A Muslim Fundamentalist's View of the Jews.* Oxford: Pergamon Press.
- 1994: "A Modern Islamic Confession of Faith and Conception of Religion: Sayyid Quṭb's Introduction to the Tafsīr, Fi Ẓilāl al-Qur'ān". *BJMES*, 21:1, pp. 102-114. (http://www.jstor.org/pss/195569).
- June 1996: "Guidelines for the Islamic Community: Sayyid Quṭb's Political Interpretation of the Qur'an". *JPI*, 1, 2: 183.

Perry, Marvin and Frederick M. Schweitzer (eds.)

- 2008: "Our Struggle with the Jews...the Jews...the Jews!! 1950s" in *Anti-Semitic Myths: a Historical and Contemporary Anthology*. Indianapolis: Indiana University Press, 2008: 307-336.

Robinson, Neal

- 2001: "Sayyid Quṭb's Attitude Towards Christianity: Sura 9.29-35 in *Fī Ẓilāl al-Qur'ān*" in Lloyd Ridgeon (ed.) *Islamic Interpretations of Christianity*. Surrey: Curzon.

Shalash, 'Ali

- 1994: *Al-Tamarrud 'ala al-Adab: Dirrasa fi Tajribat Sayyid Quṭb* (Rebellion against Literature: a Study in Sayyid Quṭb's Experience). Cairo: Dār al-Shurūq.

Shepard, William E.

- 1996: *Sayyid Quṭb and Islamic Activism: A translation and Critical Analysis of Social Justice in Islam*. Leiden: E.J. Brill.
- 1997: "The Myth of Progress in the Writings of Sayyid Quṭb" in *Religion*, 27: 3, 255-266.
- January 1989 "Islam as a 'System' in the Later Writings of Sayyid Quṭb", *IJMES*, 25:31-50.
- 2003: "Sayyid Quṭb's Doctrine of *Jahiliyya*". *IJMES*, 35: 4, 521-45.
- "Sayyid Quṭb". *Oxford Bibliographies Online*, (accessed 19 December 2011), http://oxfordbibliographiesonline.com/view/document/obo-9780195390155/obo-9780195390155-0072.xml

Toth, James

- 2013: *Sayyid Quṭb: the Life and Legacy of a Radical Islamic Intellectual.* Oxford University Press.

Tripp, Charles

- 1994: "Sayyid Quṭb: The Political Vision" in Ali Rahnema (ed.) *Pioneers of Islamic Revival.* London: Zed Books.

Walther, Rudolph

- July 31, 2007: "The Strange Teachings of Doctor Carrel: How a French Catholic Doctor became a Spiritual Forefather of the Radical Islamists", see http://www.islamagainstextremism.com/articles/vhoqj-sayyid-qutb-and-the-french-connection-the-french-catholic-social-darwinist-doctor-that-influenced-qutbs-jaahiliyyah.cfm (accessed 18 December 2011).

Yūnus, Sharīf

- 1995: *Sayyid Quṭb wa al-Uṣūliyya* ***al-Islamiyya*** (Sayyid Quṭb and Islamic Fundamentalism). Cairo: Dār Ṭība, http://hotfile.com/dl/62368253/56c527c/sed-qtb-w-alaswleh-alaslameh-ewn-ar_ptiff.pdf.html

General Books and Articles

'Abbās, Ṭahir

- 2007: *Islamic Political Radicalism: a European Perspective* in T. 'Abbās (ed.), Edinburgh: Edinburgh University Press.

'Abduh, Muḥammad

- 2004 [1897]: *Risalat al-Tawḥīd*, translated into English by Isḥāq Musa'ad and Kenneth Cragg. Kuala Lampur: Islamic Book Trust.
- 1972-3 [ca. 1898-1905]: *al-A'mal al-Kamila li al-Imām Muḥammad 'Abduh* (The Complete Works of the Imām Muḥammad 'Abduh), Muḥammad 'Imāra (ed.). Beirut: al-Mu'assasa al-'Arabiyya li al-Dirāsāt wa al-Nashr, vols 4&5.
- 1319/1901: *Tafsīr al-Fātiḥa* (A Commentary on the First *Sūra* of the Qur'ān). Abridged from the lectures of 'Abduh by Rashīd Riḍā. Followed by three expository articles by 'Abduh. Cairo: Maṭba'it al-Mawsū'āt.
- no date [1993]: *al-Islām bayna al-'Ilm wa-l-Madaniyya*. Cairo: al-Hay'a al-Maṣriyya al-'Ama li-l-Kitab.

Abercrombie, Lascelles

- no date: *Principles of Literary Criticism* translated as *Qawā'id al-Naqd al-Adabī* by 'Awaḍ Muḥammad.

Abu El-Faḍl, Khaled

- 2007: *The Great Theft: Wrestling Islam from the Extremists*. New York: Harper San Francisco.

Abugideiri, Hibba

- 2004: "On Gender and the Family" in Suha Taji-Farouki and Basheer M. Nafi (eds.) *Islamic Thought in the Twentieth Century*. London: I. B. Tauris, 223-59.

Abu Zayd, Nasr Ḥ.

- 2002: *Hakadha Takalam Ibn 'Arabī* (Thus, Spoke Ibn 'Arabī). Cairo: al-Hay'a al-'Āma li al-Kitab.
- 2012: "Rethinking the Qur'ān: Towards a Humanistic Hermeneutics" in S. Reichmuth, J. Rüsen, A. Sarhan (eds.) *Humanism and Muslim Culture*. Taiwan: V & R Unipress, 39-60.

Adams, Charles C.

- 1933: *Islam and Modernism in Egypt: a Study of the Modern Reform Movement Inaugurated by Muḥammad 'Abduh*. London: Oxford University Press.

Adham, 'Ali

- 1978 [1945]: *Naẓarat fi al-Ḥayat wa al-Mujtama'*. Cairo: Dār al-Ma'ārif.

Allen, Roger

- 1999: "Introduction" in Naguib Maḥfouz. *Mirrors* translated by Roger Allen. The American University in Cairo Press.

Amīn, Aḥmad

- 2005 [1929]: *Fajr al-Islām* (The Dawn of Islam). Tunis: Dār al-Ma'ārif.
- April 1937: "Nahḍatuna al-Fikriyya," *HI*, 653-6.
- 10 Jan. 1939: "Bayna al-Gharb wa al-Sharq aw al-Madiyya wa al-Ruḥaniyya," *TQ*, 2-5.

- 1950: "Introduction" in Abu al-Ḥasan al-Nadwī, 1950. *Madha Khasira al-'Alam bi Inḥiṭāṭ al-Muslimīn*. Cairo: Lajnat al-Ta'līf wa al-Nashr.

Amīn, Aḥmad and Zakī Najīb Maḥmūd

- 1943: *Qiṣṣat al-Adab fī al-'Alam* (The Story of World Literature), vol. I. Cairo: Maṭba'it Lajnat al-Ta'līf wa al-Tarjama wa al-Nashr.

Amīn, Ḥusayn A.

- 2007: *Shakhṣiyyat 'Araftuha* (Characters I have Encountered). Cairo: Dār al- 'Ayn.

al-Aqqād, 'Abbās M.

- 1924a: "Falsafit al-Mutanabbī wa Falsafit Nitsha" in *Muṭala'at fī al-Kutub wa al-Ḥayya*. Cairo: al-Maṭba'a al-Tujāriyya al-Kubra.
- 1924d: "Falsafit al-Mutanabbī, bayna Nitsha wa Darwin" in ibid, 165-6.
- 1970 [ca. early 1940s]: "Arā'is wa Shayāṭīn" (Muses and Demons) in *Majmū'at A'lām al-Shi'r*. Beirut: Dār al-Kitāb al-'Arabī.
- (1946a): "Hadhihī Hiya al-Aghlal" (These are the Shackles) in al-Ḥasanī Ḥasan 'Abdullah (ed.) *al-Islām wa al-Ḥaḍāra al-Insāniyya wa Maqalat Ukhra*. Beirut: Manshūrāt al-Maktaba al-'Aṣriyya, n. d. (originally published in *al-rRsala*, October 28, 1946).
- 1946b: "Mawlid al-Falsafa al-Islamiyya" (The Birth of Islamic Philosophy) in al-Ḥasanī Ḥasan 'Abdullah (ed.) *al-Islām wa al-Ḥaḍāra al-Insāniyya wa Maqalat Ukhra*. Beirut: Manshūrāt al-Maktaba al-'Aṣriyya, no date.
- 1947b: *Al-Falsafa al-Qur'āniyya: Kitab 'an Mabaḥith al-Falsafa al-Rawḥiyya wa al-Ijtima'iyya alatī Waradat Mawḍū'atiha fī Ayyat al-Kitab al-Karīm*. Cairo: Lajnat al-Bayan al-'Arabī.
- 1964 [1947c]. *Allah: Kitab fī Nasaā't al-'Aqīda al-Ilahiyya* (Allah: a Study on the Genesis of the Belief in the Divine).Cairo: Dār al-Ma'ārif.
- 1958°: *Bayna al-'Ilm wa al-Falsafa wa al-Fann* in *Dīn wa Fann wa Falsafa*. Cairo: al-Hay'a al-'Ama li al-Kitab, no date.
- no date [ca. 1960s]: *al-Mar'a fi al-Islām* (Women in Islam). Cairo: Dār al-Hilal.
- no date [ca. 1950s?]: *Al-Tafkīr Farīḍa Islāmiyya*. Cairo: no publisher.

Armanios, Febe

- 2011: *Coptic Christianity in Ottoman Egypt*. Oxford University Press.

Aroian, Lois A.

- 1983: *The Nationalisation of Arabic and Islamic Education in Egypt*. The American University in Cairo.

Aruna. Marie Josephine

- "Tagore's Philosophy of Life – a Study of Sadhana" in http://rupkatha.com/V2/n4/11Tagorephilosohy.pdf (accessed May 19, 2014).

Arkoun, Mohammed

- 1994: *Rethinking Islam: Common Questions Uncommon Answers*, translated and edited by Robert D. Lee. Brooklyn: Westview Press.
- 2005: *Humanisme et Islam: Combats et Propositions*. Paris : Librairie Philosophique. 2012 "The Vicissitudes of Ethics in Islamic Thought" in Stephan Reichmuth, Jörn Rüsen, Aladdin Sarhan

(eds.) *Humanism and Muslim Culture: Historical Heritage and Contemporary Challenges.* National Taiwan University Press, 61-86.

Armstrong, Karen

- 1999: *A History of God.* London: Vintage Books.
- 2001a: *The Battle for God: Fundamentalism in Judaism, Christianity and Islam.* London: Harper Collins.
- 2005: *A Short History of Myth.* Edinburgh: Canongate.
- 2006: *The Great Transformation: the World in the Time of Buddha, Socrates, Confucios and Jeremiah.* London: Atlantic Books.
- 2007: *The Bible: the Biography.* London: Atlantic Books.

Arnaldez, R.

- 1978: "Ishrāq" in E. Van Donzel, B. Lewis CH. Pellat (eds.), *EOI,* IV:119-120.

Arnold, Sir T.W.

- 1896: *The Preaching of Islam* (translated by Ḥasan I. Ḥasan, Abd-al-Majid 'Abdīn, and Ismā'īl al-Naḥrāwī as *al-Da'wa ila al-Islām*) Westminster: Archibald Constable.

Asad, Muḥammad

- 2007 [1934]: *Islam at the Crossroads.* New Delhi: Kitab Bhavan, translated as *al-Islām 'ala Muftaraq al-Ṭuruq* by 'Umar Farrūkh.

'Ashmawī, 'Ali

- no date: *Al-Tarīkh al-Sirrī li-Jama'at al-Ikhwan al-Muslimīn.*Cairo: Dār al-Hilal.

al-'Ashmawī, Muḥammad S.

- 1996 *Al-Sharī'a al-Islamiyya wa al-Qanūn al-Masrī.* Cairo: Madbūlī.

Ayubi, Nazih

- 1991: *Political Islam: Religion and Politics in the Arab World.* London: Routledge.

Al-Azm, Sadiq J.

- 2000: "Orientalism and Orientalism in Reverse" in A. L. Macfie (ed.) *Orientalism: a Reader.* Edinburgh University Press, 217-238.
- 2010: Orientalism and Fundamentalism in Islamic and Judaic Critique: a Conference Honouring Sadiq al-Azm" in *Comparative Studies of South Asia, Africa and the Middle East,* vol. 30, 1:6-13.

Badawi, M.M.

- 1985: *Modern Arabic Literature and the West.* London: Ithaca.

Baer, Gabriel

- 1969: *Studies in the Social History of Modern Egypt.* The University of Chicago Press.

Baker, Peter

- 2010: "Obama's War Over Terror". *The New York Times Magazine,* January 4, 2010, see http://www.nytimes.com/2010/01/17/magazine/17Terror-t.html?pagewanted=all&_r=0 (accessed 30 August, 2013).

Bandal, Suraksha, V. K. Maheshwari, and Saroj Agarwal

- "Pragmatism and Education" in http://www.scribd.com/doc/30853941/Pragmatism-and-Education (accessed December 17th, 2012).

al-Banna, Ḥasan

- 1999 [ca. 1930s]: *Fiqh al-Waqi'* (A Jurisprudence of Realism) Cairo: Dār al-kalima.
- 1966a [no date]: *Mudhakkirat al-Da'wah wa al-Da'iya.* (2nd edition). Cairo: no publisher.
- 1980 [1930s-early 1940s?]: *Naẓarat fi Iṣlāḥ al-Nafs wa al-Mujtama'* (Views on Reforming the Self and Society). Cairo: Dār al-I'tiṣām.

Bauer, Thomas

- 1998: "Jahiliyya" in Meisami, Julie Scott & Paul Starkey (eds.), *EAL*. London: Routledge, 406-7.

Barlas, Asma

- 2011 [2006]: "Women's Readings of the Qur'an" in Jane D. McAuliffe (ed.) *The Cambridge Companion to the Qur'ān*. Cambridge: Cambridge University Press.

Beinin, Joel

- 1996: "Egyptian Jewish Identities: Communitarianisms, Nationalisms, Nostalgias". *SEHR*, 5:1. *Contested Polities*. 27 February, 1996. http://web.stanford.edu/group/SHR/5-1/text/beinin.html (accessed July 18, 2014).

Bennett, Andrew and Nicholas Royle

- 2004 [1995]: *Introduction to Literature, Criticism and Theory*. Dorchester: Dorset Press.

Bergesen, Albert J.

- 2008: *The Sayyid Quṭb Reader: Selected Writings on Politics, Religion and Society*. New York: Routledge.

Biesterfeldt, Hinrich

- 2012: "The Perfect Man – a Humanist?" in Reichmuth, Rüsen, Sarhan (eds.) *Humanism and Muslim Culture: Historical Heritage and Contemporary Challenges*. National Taiwan University Press, 101-113).

al-Bishri, Ṭāriq

- 1996: al- Waḍ' *al-Qānūnī al-Mu'āṣir bayna al-Shari'a al-Islamiyya wa al-Qānūn al- Waḍ'ī*. Cairo: Dār al-Shurūk.

Bonnett, Alastair

- 2004: *The Idea of the West: Culture, Politics and History*. New York: Palgrave Macmillan.

Bowker, John

- 1998: *The Complete Bible Handbook*. London: Dorling Kindersley.

Burke, Jason

- 2004: *Al-Qaeda*. London: Penguin Books.

Buruma, Ian & Avishai Margalit

- 2004: *Occidentalism: The West in the Eyes of its Enemies*. New York: The Penguin Press.

Browers, Michaelle and Charles Kurzman (eds.)

- 2004: "Introduction" in *An Islamic Reformation?* Oxford: Lexington Books.

Cachia, Pierre

- 1956: *Ṭaha Ḥusayn : His Place in the Egyptian Literary Renaissance*. London : Luzac & Company Ltd.
- 1990: *An Overview of Modern Arabic Literature*. Edinburgh University Press.
- 1998: "Ḥusayn, Ṭaha (1889-1973)" in Meisami, Julie Scott & Paul Starkey (eds.), *EAL*. London: Routledge, 296-7

Calvocoressi, Peter

- 1988: *Who's Who in the Bible*. Penguin Dictionaries.

Cannuyer, Christian

- 2009 [2001]: *Coptic Egypt: the Christians of the Nile*. Thames and Hudson.

Carrel, Alexis

- 1935: *L'homme Cet Inconnu*. Translated by Shafīq A. Farīd. as *al-Insān dhalik al-Majhūl*. Paris: Librairie Plon.

Carter, Michael

- 2009: "Foreign Vocabulary" in Andrew Rippin (ed.) *The Blackwell Companion to the Qur'ān*. Wiley-Blackwell, 120-139.

Charlton, H. B.

- 1924: *The Art of Literary Study* translated by Zakī Naguib Maḥmūd as *Funūn al-Adab*.

Cherry, Kendra

- "Erik Erikson Biography (1902-1994)" in http://psychology.about.com/od/profilesofmajorthinkers/p/bio_erikson.htm (accessed September 6, 2013).

Chittick, William C.

- 1989: *Ibn al-'Arabī's Metaphysics of Imagination: the Sufi Path of Knowledge*. State University of New York.
- 2004: *The Sufi Doctrine of Rūmī*. World Wisdom

Choueiri, Youssef M.

- 2010 [1997]: *Islamic Fundamentalism: the Story of Islamist Movements*. London: The Tower Building.

Coates, Peter

- 2011 [2002]: *Ibn 'Arabī and Modern Thought: The History of Taking Metaphysics Seriously*. Oxford: Anqa Publishing.

Copeland, Miles

- 1969: *The Game of Nations: the Amorality of Power Politics*. London: Weidenfeld & Nicolson.

Coulson, Noel J.

- 1964: *A History of Islamic Law*. Edinburgh University Press.

Cracknell, Kenneth

- 2001: "Introductory Essay" in Kenneth Cracknell (ed.) *Wilfred Cantwell Smith: a Reader*. Oxford: Oneworld Publications.

The Earl of Cromer

- 1908: *Modern Egypt*. New York: the Macmillan Company.

Dajani, Zahia R.

- 1990: *Egypt and the Crisis of Islam*. New York: Peter Lang.

Dodge, Bayard

- 1961: *Al-Azhar: a Millennium of Muslim Learning*. Washington: The Middle East Institute.

Donohue, John J. & John L. Esposito (eds.)

- 1982: "Muhammad Iqbal: a Separate Muslim State in the Subcontinent" in *Islam in Transition: Muslim Perspectives*. New York: Oxford University Press, 91-3.

Douglas, Roy

- 1986: *World Crisis and British Decline* (1929-56). London: Macmillan.

Dozy, Reinhart

- 1845: *Dictionnaire Détaillé des Noms des Vêtements Chez les Arabes.*

Dulles, John Foster

- 1950: *War or Peace.* New York: the Macmillan Company.

Durant, Will

- 2006 [1926]: *The Story of Philosophy* (*t*ranslated into Arabic by Dr. Aḥmad Fu'ād al-Ahwānī as *Mabāhij al-falsafa*). New York: Simon & Schuster.
- 1935-1975: *The Story of Civilisation* (11-volumes).

Durkheim, Emile

- 1895: *Les Règles de la Méthode Sociologique* (translated as *Rules for the Sociological Method).*

Eccel, A. Chris

- 1984: *Egypt, Islam and Social Change: al-Azhar in Conflict and Accommodation.* Berlin: Klaus Schwarz Verlag.

El-Enany, Rasheed

- 1993: *Naguib Maḥfouz: the Pursuit of Meaning.* London: Routledge.
- 2006: *Arab Representations of the Occident: East-West Encounters in Arabic Fiction.* Oxon: Routledge.

Erikson, Erik H.

- 1995 [1951]: *Childhood and Society.* London: Vintage.
- 1994 [1968]: *Identity,* ***Youth*** *and Crisis.* New York: Norton & Company.

Erikson, Erik H. & Joan M. Erikson

- 1998: *The Life Cycle Completed.* London: W.W. Norton & Company.

Farhi, Hillelv

- 2003 [1914]: *Siddur Farhi*: *Daily Prayers.* New Jersey: The Farhi Foundation.

Farrūkh, 'Umar and Muṣṭafa Khālidī

- 1953: *al-Tabshīr wa al-Isti'mār fī al-Bilad al-'Arabiyya* (*Missions and Imperialism in Arab Lands*).

Flood, Gavin

- 2006 [1996]: *An Introduction to Hinduism.* Cambridge University Press.

Ford, Peter

- 27 September 2001: "Why Do They Hate Us?" *The Christian Science Monitor*, (accessed 17 December 2011), http://www.csmonitor.com/2001/0927/p1s1-wogi.html

Furseth, Inger and Pal Repstad

- 2006: *An Introduction to the Sociology of Religion.* Hants: Ashgate.

Gaultier-Kurhan, Caroline

- 2005: *Mehemet Ali et la France : 1805-1849. Histoire Singulière du Napoléon de l'Orient.* Paris: Maisonneuve & Larose.

Gardet, Louis

- 1951: *La Pensée Religieuse d'Avicenne.* Paris: Vrin.

- 1952: *La Conaissance Mystique Chez Ibn Sinā et ses Présupposés Philosophiques.* Le Caire: Institut Français d'Archéologie Orientale.
- 1953: *Expériences Mystiques en Terres non-Chrétienne.* Paris: Alsatia
- 1977: *Les Hommes de L'Islam, Approches des Mentalités.* Paris: Hachette.
- 1979: "Des Réformistes (*iṣlāḥiyyūn*) aux Mutations en Cours" in Alford T. Welch and Pierre Cachia (eds.) *Islam: Past Influence and Present Challenge.* Edinburgh: Edinburgh University Press.

Gardner, Helen

- 1985 [1957]: *The Metaphysical Poets.* London: Penguin Books.

Gershoni, Israel and James Jankowski

- 1995: *Redefining the Egyptian Nation*, 1930-1945. Cambridge University Press.

Gibb, Sir Hamilton A.R.

- 1926: *Arabic Literature: an Introduction.* London: Oxford University Press.
- 1932: *Whither Islam: A Survey of Modern Movements in the Muslim World* . edited by H.A.R Gibb (translated as *Ila Ayn Yatajih al-Islām*). London: Victor Gollancz.
- 1963 [1926]: *Arabic Literature: an Introduction.* Oxford University Press.
- 1975 [1947]: *Modern Trends in Islam.* New York: Octagon Books.
- 1970 [1949]: *Moḥammedanism.* London: Oxford University Press.

Gibb, H.A.R. & Harold Bowen

- *Islamic Society and the West: a Study of the Impact of Western Civilisation on Moslem Culture in the Near East.* London: Oxford University Press, V. II, 1957.

Goddard, Hugh

- 1996: *Muslim Perceptions of Christianity.* London: Grey Seal Books.

Goldschmidt Jr., Arthur

- 2004: *Modern Egypt: the Formation of a Nation-state.* Oxford: Westview.

Goldziher, Ignaz

- 1981 [1910]: *Introduction to Islamic Theology and Law*, translated by Andras and Ruth Hamori with an introduction and additional notes by Bernard Lewis. New Jersey: Princeton University Press.
- 2006 [1920]: *Schools of Koranic Commentators* with an introduction on Goldziher and Ḥadīth from *Geschichte des Arabischen Schrifttums* by Fuat Sezgin edited and translated by Wolfgang H. Behn. Wiesbaden: Harrassowitz Verlag.

Goodman, Lenn E.

- 2003: *Islamic Humanism.* Oxford University Press.

Gouilly, Alphonse

- 1945: *L'Islam devant le Monde Moderne* (translated as *al-Islām Ḥiyāl al-Duwal al-Kubra.* Paris: La Nouvelle Edition.

al-Guindī, 'Abd al-Ḥalīm

- no date: *Abu Ḥanīfa: the Paragon of Freedom and Tolerance in Islam.* Cairo: no publisher.

Graham, William A. & Navid Kermani

- 2011 [2006]: "Recitation and Aesthetic Reception" in Jane D. McAuliffe (ed.) *The Cambridge Companion to the Qur'ān.* Cambridge University Press.

Haddad, Yvonne Y.

- 1994: *Muḥammad 'Abduh: Pioneer of Islamic Reform* in Rahnema Ali (ed.) *Pioneers of Islamic Revival*, London: Zed Books.

Hall, Calvin S.

- 1954: *A Primer of Freudian Psychology*. New York: Mentor Book.

Ḥamdūn, Muḥammad A.

- 1976: *Islamic Identity & the West in Contemporary Arabic Literature*. Michigan: The Temple University.

Hamid, Mohsin

- 22 July 2007: "Why Do They Hate Us?" *The Washington Post*, (accessed 17 December 2011), http://www.washingtonpost.com/wp-dyn/content/article/2007/07/20/AR2007072001806.html?nav=rss_opinions/outlook?nav=slate

Hartung, Jan-Peter

- 2013: *A System of Life: Mawdūdī and the Ideologisation of Islam*. London: Hurst & Co.

Hawting, Gerald R.

- 2006 [1999]: *The Idea of Idolatry and the Emergence of Islam: from Polemic to History*. New York: Cambridge University Press.

Heyworth-Dunn, J.

- 1950: *Religious and Political Trends in Modern Egypt*. Washington: McGregor & Werner.

Hitti, Philip. K.

- 1970 [1937]: *History of the Arabs*. London: Macmillan Press.

Hodgson, Marshall G.S.

- 1974 [1961]: *The Venture of Islam: Conscience and History in a World Civilisation: the Gunpowder Empires and Modern Times*. The University of Chicago Press, III.
- 1999 (ca.1961): "Cultural Patterning in Islamdom and the Occident" in E. Burke (ed.) *Rethinking World History: Essays on Europe, Islam and World History*. Cambridge: Cambridge University Press.

Hoffman, Valerie J.

- 1995: *Sufism, Mystics, and Saints in Modern Egypt*. South Carolina: University of South Carolina Press.

Hornberger, Jacob G.

- 9 August 2006: "Why do They Hate Us?" *Freedom Daily*, (accessed 17 December 2011), http://www.fff.org/comment/com0608c.asp

Hourani, Albert

- 1983 [1962]: *Arabic Thought in the Liberal Age 1798-1939*. Cambridge University Press.
- 1991: *A History of the Arab Peoples*. London: Faber & Faber.

Hornberger, Jacob G.

- 2006: "Why do They Hate Us?" *Freedom Daily*, 9 August 2006, http://www.fff.org/comment/com0608c.asp (accessed 17 December 2011).

Hughes, Edward J.

- 1986: *Wilfred Cantwell Smith: A Theology for the World*. London: SCM Press.

Hurvitz, Nimrod

- 2002: *The Formation of Ḥanbalism: Piety into Power*. Oxon: Routledge.

Ḥusayn, Ṭaha

- 1917: *Étude Analytique et Critique de la Philosophie Sociale d'Ibn Khaldūn*. Paris.
- 1925: *Qadat al-Fikr* (Leaders of Thought). Cairo: al-Hilāl.
- 1928: "*De L'emploi dans le Coran du Prénom Personnel de la Troisième comme Démonstratif*".
- 1929: *Al-Ayyam*. Cairo: Dār al-Ma'ārif, vol. I.
- 1932 [1925]: *Leaders of Thought* (a translation of *Qadat al-Fikr* (1925) by Ḥasan A. Luṭfi). Beirut, no publisher.
- no date [ca. 1934]: *Ala Hamish al-Sīra*.
- 1933-1951: *Ala Hamish al-Sīra*. Cairo: Dār al-Ma'ārif.
- 1937: *Ḥadīth al-Arbi'a'* (the Wednesday Talk).
- 1993 [1938]: *Mustaqbal al-Thaqāfa fī Miṣr* ((The Future of Culture in Egypt) Cairo: al-Hay'a al-Maṣriyya al-'Ama li-l-Kitāb.
- 1944: *Shajarat al Bu's* (The Tree of Misery). Cairo: Dār al-Ma'ārif.
- 1947: "Tendances Religieuses de la Littérature Egyptienne" in Cahiers du Sud : L'Islam et l'Occident, 239-41.
- 2006 [1947-1956]: *al-Fitna al-Kubra* (The Great Strife), 2 volumes. Cairo: Dār al-Ma'ārif.

al-Ibrāshī, Muḥammad 'Aṭiya

- 1946: *al-Adāb al-Samiyya*. Syria: Dār Iḥyā' al-Kutub al-'Arabiyya.

Iqbal, Muhammad

- 2012 [no date]: *The Reconstruction of Religious Thought in Islam (*translated as *Tajdīd al-Fikr al-Dīnī fī al-Islām*). New Delhi, Kitab Bhavan. (chapter 6 in English p 73-74 hadha al-Din)

Irwin, Robert

- Nov 1, 2001: "Is this the Man who Inspired Bin Laden?" *The Guardian,* in http://www.guardian.co.uk/world/2001/nov/01/afghanistan.terrorism3 (accessed 17 December 2011).
- 2007 [2006]: *For Lust of Knowing; the Orientalists and their Enemies*. London: Penguin Books.

Izutsu, Toshihiko

- 2002: *Ethico-religious Concepts in the Qur'ān*. New York: Ithaca.

Jackson, Karen Miller

- "Reshut Hakallah: the Symbolism of the Chuppah" in http://www.hebrewbooks.org/33429 (accessed March 5, 2015).

al-Jamāl, Muḥammad M. M.

- 2004: *Aḥmad Luṭfī al-Sayyid: Diaāsa fī al-Khariṭa al-Ma'rifiya*. Cairo: Dār al-Amīn.

Johnson, Ian

- 2011: *Washington's Secret History with the Muslim Brotherhood* in http://www.nybooks.com/blogs/nyrblog/2011/feb/05/washingtons-secret-history-muslim-brotherhood/ (accessed Feb. 17, 2015).

Jomier, Jacques

- 1954: *Le Commentaire Coranique du Manār: Tendances Modernes de L'exégèse Coranique en Egypte*. Paris: Editions G. P. Maisonneuve.

- 1996: *Dieu et l'Homme dans le Coran*. Paris: Cerf.

Kenney, Jeffrey T.

- 2006: *Muslim Rebels: Kharijites and the Politics of Extremism in Egypt*. New York: Oxford University Press.

Kersten, Carool

- 2011: *Cosmopolitans and Heretics: New Muslin Intellectuals and the Study of Islam*. London: Hurst & Co.

Khān, Ẓafarul-Islām

- 1991: "Nadwat al-'Ulamā" in C. E. Bosworth, E. Van Dowell, W. P. Heinrich and Ch. Pellat (eds.), *EOI*. Leiden: Brill, 7: 874-5.

Khiḍr, 'Abbās

- 1983: *Ha'ula' ''Araftuhum*. Cairo: Dār al-Ma'ārif.

Knysh, Alexander D.

- 2001-2006: "Sūfism and the Qur'ān" in *EOQ*, J. D. McAuliffe (ed.), Leiden: E. J. Brill, 5: 137-159.

Kopf, David

- 1992: *The Brahmo Samaj and the Shaping of the Modern Indian Mind*. Princeton University Press.

Krämer, Gudrun

- 1989: *The Jews in Modern Egypt, 1914-1952*. London: University of Washington Press.
- 2010: *Hassan al-Banna: Makers of the Muslim World*. Oxford: One World.

Krämer, Joel

- 1992 [1986]: *Humanism in the Renaissance of Islam: the Cultural Revival during the Buyid Age*. Leiden: Brill.

Kreutz, Michael

- 2012: "Understanding the Other: Ṭaha Ḥusayn on Reason and Individualism" in S. Reichmuth, J. Rüsen, A. Sarhan (eds.) *Humanism and Muslim Culture*. Taiwan: V & R Unipress.

Lachs, Samuel T.

- 1993: *Humanism in Talmud and Midrash*. Ontario: Associated University Press.

Landolt H.

- 1991: "Wudjūd" in C. E. Bosworth, E. Van Dowell, W. P. Heinrich and Ch. Pellat (eds.), *EOI*. Leiden: Brill, XI: 216-8.

Landow, George P.

- "Thomas Hardy's Religious Beliefs" in http://www.victorianweb.org/authors/hardy/religion1.htm (accessed June 10, 2014)

Lane, Edward William

- 1863: *An Arabic-English Lexicon*. London: Norgate.

Lanson, Gustave

- no date [1920s?]: *Méthode de Criticisme Littéraire* translated by Dr. Muḥammad Mandur as *Manhaj al-Baḥth fī al-Adab*.

Lenin, V. I.

- 2010 [1916]: *Imperialism: the Highest Stage of Capitalism. London:* Penguin Books.

Lewis, Bernard

- 2000 [1982]: *The Muslim Discovery of Europe*. London: Phoenix Press.
- 1984a: *The Jews of Islam*. New Jersey: Princeton University Press.
- 1995b: *The Middle East: 2000 Years of History from the Rise of Christianity to the Present Day*. London: Orion Books.
- 2003a: *The Crisis of Islam: Holy War and Unholy Terror*. London: Weidenfeld & Nicholson.

Lewis, B., CH. Pellat & Joseph Schacht (eds.)

- 1965: "DJahiliyya", *EOI*, 383-4.

Lifton, Edward J.

- 2007: "A Clinical Psychology Perspective on Radical Islamic Youth" in T. Abbās (ed.) *Islamic Political Radicalism: a European Perspective*. Edinburgh: Edinburgh University Press.

Little, Douglas

- 2003: *American Orientalism: the United States and the Middle East since 1945*. London: Tauris.

MacCulloch, Diarmaid

- 2003: *Reformation: Europe's House Divided* (1490-1700). London: Penguin.

Maḥfouz, Naguib

- 1945: *Khan al-Khalilī*. Cairo: unknown publisher.
- 1972 [1999]: *Mirrors* (*al-Maraya* translated by Roger Allen. The American University in Cairo Press.

Makdisi, George

- 1990: *The Rise of Humanism in Classical Islam and the Christian West: with Special Reference to Scholasticism*. Edinburgh University Press.

Makkia, Kan'an & Ḥasan Munaymina

- January 4, 2002: 'Ghazuwwat al- Ḥadī 'Ashr min Aylūl fi Qira'a li Wathīqa Tu'ahil Qurā'uha al-Khaṭiffīn li al-Mawt' (The September 11 Raid: a Reading of a Document Preparing its Readers, the Hijackers, for Death). *Al-Ḥayat*.

Manjapra, Kris

- 2010: *M.N. Roy: Marxism and Colonial Cosmopolitanism*. London: Routledge.

Mansfield, Peter

- 1965: *Nasser's Egypt*. Middlesex: Penguin Books.

Marsot, Afaf L. al-Sayyid

- 2007 [1984]: *A History of Egypt: from the Arab Conquest to the Present*. Cambridge University Press.

McAuliffe, Jane D.

- 1991: *Qur'anic Christians: An Analysis of Classical and Modern Exegesis*. Cambridge: Cambridge University Press.
- 2011 [2006]: "Introduction" in Jane D. McAuliffe (ed.). *The Cambridge Companion to the Qur'ān*. New York: Cambridge University Press, 1-20.
- 2011 [2006b]: "The Tasks and Traditions of Interpretation" in Jane D. McAuliffe (ed.) *The Cambridge Companion to the Qur'ān*. New York: Cambridge University Press: 181-209.

McNamara, Robert

- 2003: *Britain, Nasser and the Balance of Power in the Middle East (1952-1967)*. London: Frank Cass.

Miskawayh, Aḥmad ibn-Muḥammad

- 1968 [932/320H]: *The Refinement of Character* (*Tahdhīb al-Akhlāq*) translated by Constantine k. Zurayk. American university of Beirut.

Mitchell, Richard P.

- 1993 [1969]: *The Society of the Muslim Brothers.* New York: Oxford University Press.

Moosa, Ebrahim

- 2000: "Introduction" in Fazlur Raḥman, 2000. *Revival and Reform in Islam: a Study of Islamic Fundamentalism* edited & with an introduction by Ebrahim Moosa. Oxford: One World.

Murawiec, Laurent

- 2005 [2003]: *Princes of Darkness: the Saudi Assault on the West* a translation of *La Guerre D'après* by George Holoch. Maryland: Rowman & Littlefield.

Mustafa, Kavi Ghulam

- "The Idea of God and Universe in Tagore and Iqbal" http://www.allamaiqbal.com/publications/journals/review/oct60/4.htm (accessed May 25th, 2014).

Nadwi, abu al-Ḥasan 'Ali

- 1950: *Madha Khasira al-'Alam bi Inḥiṭāṭ al-Muslimīn.* Cairo: Lajnat al-Ta'līf wa al-Nashr.
- 1977: *Madha Khasira al-'Alam bi Inḥiṭāṭ al-Muslimīn.* Cairo: Dār al-Qalam, (10th edition).
- 1979: al-*Tafsīr al-Siyasī li al-Islām, fī Kitabat al-Ustadh Abu al-A'la al- Mawdūdī wa al-Shahīd Sayyid Quṭb.*
- 1400/1980: *al-Tafsīr al-Siyāsī li'l Islām fi Mir'āt Kitabat al-Ustadh Abī 'l-Al'ā Mawdūdī wa'l-Shahīd Sayyid Quṭb.* Cairo: Dār Affāq al-Ghadd.

Nettler, Ronald L.

- 1993: "Prophecy, Qur'an and Metaphysics" *in Ibn 'Arabī's Discussion of 'Uzayr (Ezra)* in Ronald L. Nettler (ed.) *Studies in Muslim-Jewish Relations.* Switzerland: Harwood Academic Publishers.

Nwyia, Paul

- 1970: *Exégèse Coranique et Langage Mystique.* Beirut: Dar El-Machreq.

O'Connor, Cathleen Malone

- 2001-2006: "Amulets" in Jane D. McAuliffe (ed.), *EOQ*, Leiden: E. J. Brill, 1: 77-8.

Ostle, R. C.

- 1998: "Diwān Group" in Meisami, Julie Scott & Paul Starkey (eds.), *EAL.* London: Routledge.

Oswalt, Angela

- "Erik Erikson and Self-Identity" in http://www.sevencounties.org/poc/view_doc.php?type=doc&id=41163&cn=1310 (accessed September 6, 2013).

Perry, Marvin and Frederick M. Schweitzer (eds.)

- 2008: "Arab Theologians on Jews and Israel" in *Anti-Semitic Myths: a Historical and Contemporary Anthology.* Indiana University Press, 316-321.
- 2008: "The Jew and Modern Capitalism, 1911" in ibid, 82-9.
- 2008: "Luther and the Jews" in ibid, 43-49.

Qureshi, Emran and Michael A. Sells

- 2003: "Introduction" in *The New Crusaders: Constructing the Muslim Enemy*. New York: Columbia University Press.

al-Qāṣimī, 'Abdullah

- 2000 [1946]: *Hadhihī Hiya al-Aghlal* (These are the Shackles). Köln: al-Kamal.

Quṭb, Muḥammad

- no date [1954]: *Shubuhat Ḥawl al-Islām*.(ed. 4) Cairo: Maktabit Wahba.
- 1992 [1954]: *Shubuhat Ḥawl al-Islām*.(ed. 21) Cairo: Dār al-Shurūq.
- no date [ca.1965-6?]: "al-Yahūd al-Thalatha: Marx, Freud, and Durkheim" in *al-Taṭawwur wa al-Thabat* (Progress and Fixity). Cairo: Maktabit Wahba.
- no date [ca.1966?]: *Al-Taṭawwur wa al-Thabat*. Cairo: Maktabit Wahba.
- 1999: *al-Mustashriqūn wa al-Islām*. Cairo: Maktabit Wahba.

Rahimieh, Nasrin

- 1990: *Oriental Responses to the West: Comparative Essays in Select Writers from the Muslim World*. Leiden: Brill.

Rahman, Fazlur

- 1990: "The People of the Book and the Diversity of Religions" in Paul J. Griffiths (ed.) *Christianity through Non-Christian Eyes*. New York: Orbis Books.

al-Rasheed, Madawi, Carool Kersten and Marat Shterin

- 2013: "Introduction" in *Demystifying the Caliphate*. London: Hurst, 1-30.

Rastogi, T. C.

- 1990: *Sufism: A Dictionary with Profiles of Saint-Poets*. New Delhi: Sterling Publishers Ltd.

al-Raystūni, M. al-Muntaṣir

- 1987: *Sayyid Quṭb wa Manhajuhu fi al-Tafsir* (Sayyid Quṭb and his Methodology in [Qur'anic] Exegesis). Tiṭwān: Maṭba'at al-Nūr.

Reggiani, Andrés Horacio

- 2007: *God's Eugenicist: Alexis Carrel and the Socio-biology of Decline*. Oxford: Berghahn Books.

Rejwan, Nissim

- 2008: *Arabs in the Mirror: Images and Self-Images from Pre-Islamic to Modern Times*. University of Texas Press.

Rifaat, Muḥammad

- 1964: *The Awakening of Modern Egypt*. Lahore: Premier Book House.

Rosenthal, Franz

- 1970: *Knowledge Triumphant: the Concept of Knowledge in Medieval Islam*. Leiden: Brill.

Reichmuth, Stefan

- 2012: "Humanism in Islam between Mysticism and Literature" in S. Reichmuth, J. Rüsen, A. Sarhan (eds.), *Humanism and Muslim Culture*. Taiwan: V & R Unipress.

Reichmuth, Stefan, Jörn Rüsen, and Aladdin Sarhan

- 2012: "Humanism and Muslim Culture: Historical Heritage and Contemporary Challenges" in S. Reichmuth, J. Rüsen, A. Sarhan (eds.), *Humanism and Muslim Culture*. Taiwan: V & R Unipress, 11-24.

Robinson, F. C. R.

- 1991: "Mawdūdī" in C. E. Bosworth, E. Van Dowell, W. P. Heinrich and Ch. Pellat (eds.), *The Encyclopedia of Islam*. Leiden: Brill, 6: 872.

Roded, Ruth

- 2001-2006: "Women and the Qur'an" in *EOQ*, J. D. McAuliffe (ed.), Leiden: E. J. Brill, 5: 523-541.

Roy, Olivier

- 2010: *Holy Ignorance: When Religion and Culture Part Ways*. London: Hurst & Company.

Rubin, Uri

- 2009: "Prophets and Prophethood" in Andrew Rippin (ed.) *The Blackwell Companion to the Qur'ān*. Wiley-Blackwell, 234-247.

Safran, Nadav

- 1961: *Egypt in Search of Political Community: an Analysis of the Intellectual and Political Evolution of Egypt, 1804-1952*. Cambridge, Massachusetts: Harvard University Press.

Sandbrook, Dominic

- March 12, 2006: "It Began with one Naked Girl". *The Guardian*. http://www.theguardian.com/politics/2006/mar/12/conservatives.past1 (accessed October 10th, 2013).

Sardar, Ziauddin

- 4 October, 2004: "Why do They Hate Us?" *New Statesman*, http://www.newstatesman.com/200410040042 (accessed 17 December 2011).

Sarma, Arup Jyoti

- 2012: "Humanistic Philosophy of Tagore". *Kritike*, 6: 1.

Schäbler, Birgit

- 2012: "Humanism, Orientalism, Modernity: A Critique" in S. Reichmuth, J. Rüsen, A. Sarhan (eds.) *Humanism and Muslim Culture*. Taiwan: V & R Unipress.

Schacht, Joseph

- 1979 [1950]: *The Origins of Muḥammadan Jurisprudence*. Oxford: Clarendon Press.

Schimmel, Annemarie

- 1995: "Jesus and Mary as Poetical Images in Rūmī's Verse" in Yvonne Y. Haddad and Wadi Z. Haddad (eds.) *Christian-Muslim Encounters*. University Press of Florida.

Sharabi, Hishām

- 1970: *Arab Intellectuals and the West: the Formative Years, 1875-1914*. London: The Johns Hopkins Press.

Sharkey, Heather J.

- 2013: *American Evangelicals in Egypt: Missionary Encounters in an Age of Empire*. Princeton University Press.

Sharnoff, Michael

- July 30, 2011: "Looking Back: Nasser's Inter-Arab Rivalries: 1958-1967" in http://english.alarabiya.net/articles/2011/07/30/160027.html (accessed March 5, 2015).

Shepard, William E.

- 1982: *The Faith of a Modern Muslim Intellectual: The Religious Aspects and Implications of the Writings of Aḥmad Amīn*. New Delhi: Vikas House.
- 2001-2006: "Age of Ignorance" in Jane D. McAuliffe (ed.) *EOQ*. Leiden: E. J. Brill, 1:37-40.
- 2004: "The Diversity of Islamic Thought: Towards a Typology" in Suha Taji-Farouki and Basheer M. Nafi (eds.), *Islamic Thought in the Twentieth Century*. London: I. B. Tauris, 61-103.

Shwadran, Benjamin

- 1954: "The Anglo-Iranian Oil Dispute 1948-1953", *MEA*, 5: 193-231.

Sivan, Emmanuel

- 1990: *Radical Islam: Medieval Theology and Modern Politics*. Yale University Press.

Smith, Charles D.

- 1983: *Islam and the Search for Social Order in Modern Egypt*. Albany: State University of New York Press.

Smith, Wilfred C.

- 1946 [1943]: *Modern Islam in India: a Social Analysis*. London: Victor Gollancz.
- 1954: "Book Review: Sayed Kotb. *Social Justice in Islam*", *MEA*, 5:392-94.
- 1957: *Islam in Modern History*. New York: Mentor Books.
- 1966 [1957]: *Islam in Modern History*. New Jersey: Princeton University Press.
- 1981 [1958]: "The Historical Development in Islam of the Concept of Islam as an Historical Development" in *On Understanding Islam*. The Hague: Mouton Publishers, 41-77.
- 2001 [1959b]: "Some Similarities and Some Differences between Christianity and Islam" in Kenneth Cracknell (ed.) *Wilfred Cantwell Smith: a Reader*. Oxford: Oneworld Publications.
- 1981 [1974]: "Muslim-Christian Interrelations Historically: An Interpretation" in *On Understanding Islam*. The Hague: Mouton Publishers, 247-264.
- 1998 [1962]: *Patterns of Faith Around the World*. Oxford: Oneworld Publications.
- 1981 [1963]: "Is the Qur'ān the Word of God?" in *On Understanding Islam*. The Hague: Mouton Publishers, 282- 300.
- 1981 [1963a]: "The Crystallisation of Religious Communities in Mughul India" in *On Understanding Islam*. The Hague: Mouton Publishers, 177-96
- 1964: *The Meaning and End of Religion*. New York: Mentor Books.
- 1981 [1974b]: "Faith in the Qur'ān, and its Relation to Belief" in *On Understanding Islam*. The Hague: Mouton Publishers, 110-134.
- 2001 [1981b]: "The History of Religion in the Singular" in Kenneth Cracknell (ed.) *Wilfred Cantwell Smith: a Reader*. Oxford: Oneworld.
- 2001 [1993]: "Scriptures are not Texts" (excerpt from *What is Scripture?*) in Kenneth Cracknell (ed.) *Wilfred Cantwell Smith: a Reader*. Oxford: Oneworld Publications.
- 1997: *Modern Culture from a Comparative Perspective*. State University of New York Press.
- 2001 [no date]: "Sikhism's Relationship to the Guru Nanak" (excerpt from *Towards a World Theology*") in Kenneth Cracknell (ed.) *Wilfred Cantwell Smith: a Reader*. Oxford: Oneworld Publications.

Spencer, Jonathan

- 1995: "Occidentalism in the East: The Uses of the West in the Politics and Anthropology of South Asia" in James G. Carrier (ed.) *Occidentalism: Images of the West*. Oxford: Clarendon Press.

Steigerwald, Diana

- 2009: "Ismāʻīlī Ta'wīl " in Andrew Rippin (ed.) *The Blackwell Companion to the Qur'ān*. Wiley-Blackwell, 386-400.

Stillman, Norman A.

- 1979: *The Jews of Arab Lands: A History and Source Book*. Philadelphia: The Jewish Publication Society of America.
- 1991: *The Jews of Arab Lands in Modern Times*. New York: The Jewish Publication Society of America.

Suwif, Muṣṭafa Ismāʻīl

- no date: "Al-Taḥlīl al-Nafsī wa al-Fanān" (Psychoanalysis and the Artist). Cairo: Majallat ʻIlm al-Nafs.

Swearer, Donald K.

- 2011: "The Moral Imagination of Wilfred Cantwell Smith". *Harvard Divinity Bulletin*. Winter/spring, 39: 1&2 in http://www.hds.harvard.edu/news-events/harvard-divinity-bulletin/articles/the-moral-imagination-of-wilfred-cantwell-smith (accessed August 13th, 2012).

al-Ṭabarsī, Raḍi al-Dīn Abi Naṣr A. A.F.

- 1303H: *Makarim al-Akhlāq* Cairo: al-Maṭbaʻa al-Khayriyya.

Tagore, Rabindranath

- 2013 [1915]: *Selected Poems*. London: Collins Classics.
- 2010 [1917]: *Nationalism*. London: Penguin Books.

Tibi, Bassam

- 1991: *Islam and the Cultural Accommodation of Social Change*. Oxford: Westview Press

Varisco, Daniel M.

- 2007: *Reading Orientalism: Said and the Unsaid*. Seattle: University of Washington Press.

Venkatachalapathy, A. R.

- 2013: "'Madras Manade'– How Chennai remained with Tamil Nadu" in http://missiontelangana.com/madras-manade-how-chennai-remained-with-tamil-nadu/ (accessed June 2, 2014).
- "The Changing Face of Tamil Nadu's Muslim Politics" in http://www.thehindu.com/opinion/interview/the-changing-face-of-tamil-nadus-muslim-politics/article4989008.ece (accessed June 2, 2014).

Venn, Couze

- 2000: *Occidentalism: Modernity and Subjectivity*. London: Sage Publications.

Walther, Rudolph

- "The Strange Teachings of Doctor Carrel: How a French Catholic Doctor became a Spiritual Forefather of the Radical Islamists" in http://www.islamagainstextremism.com/articles/vhoqj-sayyid-qutb-and-the-french-connection-the-french-catholic-social-darwinist-doctor-that-influenced-qutbs-jaahiliyyah.cfm (accessed 18 December 2011).

Watt, William Montgomery

- 1987 [1968]: *Islamic Political Thought*. Edinburgh University Press.

- 1991: *Muslim-Christian Encounters: Perceptions and Misperceptions*. London: Routledge.
- 2009 [1998]: *The Formative Period of Islamic Thought*. Oxford: One World.

Wild, Stefan

- 2011b [2006]: "Political Interpretation of the Qur'an" in Jane D. McAuliffe (ed.) *The Cambridge Companion to the Qur'ān*. New York: Cambridge University Press.

Witherup, Ronald D.

- 1989: *The Bible Companion: a Handbook for Beginners*. New York: the Crossroad Publishing Company.

Woolfson, Marion

- 1980: *Prophets in Babylon*. London: Faber and Faber.

Würsch, Renate

- 2012: "Humanism and Mysticism –Inspiration from Islam" in Stefan Reichmuth, Jörn Rüsen, and Aladdin Sarhan (eds.) *Humanism and Muslim Culture: Historical Heritage and Contemporary Challenges*. Taiwan: National Taiwan University Press.

Wright, Lawrence

- 2006: *The Looming Tower: Al-Qaeda and the Road to 9/11*. New York: Vintage Books.

Zakaria, Fareed

- 22 August 2007: The Politics of Rage: Why Do They Hate Us?" *Newsweek*, (accessed 17 December 2011), http://www.fareedzakaria.com/ARTICLES/newsweek/101501_why.html

Zawahir, M. Nafeel M.

- 2008: *Comparative Study on Abul Hasan Alī Nadwī's Political Thought with Particular Reference to His Contemporaries Abul Ala Mawdūdī and Sayyid Quṭb*. Lampeter: University of Wales.

al-Ẓawahiri, Ayman

- December 4, 2001: "Fursān taḥt Rayit al-Nabbī" (Knights Under the Prophet's Banner), *Asharq al-Awsat*, (8407).

Zebiri, Kate

- 1993: *Maḥmūd Shaltūt and Islamic Modernism*. Oxford: Clarendon Press.
- 2001: "Muslim Perceptions of Christianity and the West" in Lloyd Ridgeon (ed.) *Islamic Interpretations of Christianity*. Surrey: Curzon.
- 2009: "Argumentation" in Andrew Rippin (ed.) *The Blackwell Companion to the Qur'ān*. Wiley-Blackwell, 266-281.

Zollner, Barbara

- 2007: "Prison Talk: the Muslim Brotherhood's Internal Struggle during Gamal Abdel Nasser's Persecution, 1954 to 1971" in *IJMES*, 39:411-433.

Internet Sites

General

On Al-'Aqqād, see http://www.britannica.com/EBchecked/topic/30991/Abbas-Mahmud-al-Aqqad;& http://www.sis.gov.eg/En/Templates/Articles/tmpArticles.aspx?ArtID=1346 (accessed November 18, 2010).

Introduction

http://news.bbc.co.uk/1/hi/world/americas/1567815.stm (accessed 17 December 2011).

http://www.military-quotes.com/george-bush.htm (accessed 17 December 2011).

http://www.quotationspage.com/quotes/George_W._Bush/ (accessed 17 December 2011).

For the four page document found on the September 11 attacks ringleader Muḥammad 'Aṭṭā see http://www.guardian.co.uk/world/2001/sep/30/terrorism.september113 (accessed 17 December 2011).

http://www.youtube.com/watch?v=1mXnbgsg9DM (accessed April 8th, 2013).

http://www.youtube.com/watch?v=KFyNPOstbhU (accessed 3 April, 2013).

al-Manār, 2nd ed. (1947) in http://www.waqfeya.com/book.php?bid=786 (accessed September 11, 2013).

http://www.carnegiecouncil.org/resources/transcripts/4465.html (accessed May 22, 2012).

Chapter 1

http://plato.stanford.edu/entries/lucretius/ (accessed 10 July 2012).

Chapter 3

http://objectiveart01.tripod.com/john_the_baptist.htm (accessed March 28, 2013).

http://www.egs.edu/library/sigmund-freud/articles/leonardo-da-vinci-a-psychosexual-study-of-an-infantile-reminiscence/iii/ (accessed March 28, 2013).

http://www.encyclopedia.com/doc/1G2-3435000023.html (accessed December 26/2012).

http://www.acls.org/about/history/ (accessed September 2, 2012).

http://www.encyclopedia.com/doc/1G2-3435000023.html (accessed December 26/2012).

Chapter 4

http://searchworks.stanford.edu/view/6762995 (accessed January 23, 2013).

http://www.britannica.com/EBchecked/topic/308602/al-Jurjani (accessed January 23, 2013).

http://www.bbc.co.uk/history/ww2peopleswar/timeline/factfiles/nonflash/a1143578.shtml (accessed November 2, 2014).

http://web.stanford.edu/group/SHR/5-1/text/beinin.html (accessed July 18, 2014).

"Al-Imām Ḥasan al-Banna Yaktib fī 'Ulūm al-Qur'ān" (The Imām Ḥasan al-Bannā Writes on the Sciences of the Qur'ān) in http://www.ikhwanwiki.com/index.php?title=%D8%A7%D9%84%D8%A5%D9%85%D8%A7%D9%85_%D8%AD%D8%B3%D9%86_%D8%A7%D9%84%D8%A8%D9%86%D8%A7_%D9%8A%D9%83%D8%AA%D8%A8_%D9%81%D9%8A_%D8%B9%D9%84%D9%88%D9%85_%D8%A7%D9%84%D9%82%D8%B1%D8%A2%D9%86#.D8.B9.D9.86.D8.A7.D9.8A.D8.A9_.D8.A7.D9.84.D8.B3.D9.84.D9.81_.D8.A8.D9.87 (accessed September 11, 2013).

http://csmt.uchicago.edu/glossary2004/collectiveconsciousness.htm (accessed December 17, 2013).

http://www.britannica.com/EBchecked/topic/655524/Abu-al-Qasim-Mahmud-ibn-Umar-al-Zamakhshari (accessed January 23, 2013).

http://www.blavatsky.net/ (accessed May 19, 2014).

http://www.ts-adyar.org/content/early-history (accessed May 19, 2014).

http://www.nobelprize.org/nobel_prizes/literature/laureates/1913/tagore-bio.html (accessed May 19, 2014).

http://www.buddhanet.net/e-learning/history/sites.htm (accessed January 30, 2013).

http://www.britannica.com/EBchecked/topic/442755/Parakramabahu-I (accessed January 30, 2013).

http://www.britannica.com/EBchecked/topic/581953/Tamil-language (accessed June 2, 2014).

http://www.bharatonline.com/tamilnadu/pilgrimage.html (accessed June 2, 2014).

http://plato.stanford.edu/entries/transcendentalism/ (accessed May 30, 2014).

http://global.britannica.com/EBchecked/topic/624431/Vedanta (accessed May 30, 2014).

http://www.thebrahmosamaj.net/history/chronolgy.html (accessed May 30, 2014).

http://vedanta.org/ (accessed May 30, 2014).

http://global.britannica.com/EBchecked/topic/398862/mushahadah (accessed May 23, 2014).

http://www.buddhanet.net/e-learning/buddhism/disciples09.htm (accessed May 23, 2014).

http://www.gutenberg.org/cache/epub/5125/pg5125.html (May 30, 2014).

http://maddy06.blogspot.co.uk/2014/03/adela-violet-florence-nicolson-laurence.html (accessed June 10, 2014).

http://www.poets.org/poetsorg/poet/t-s-eliot (May 30, 2014)

Chapter 5

http://www.kaftoun.com/commons/documents/Point_Four_Bates.htm (accessed November 27, 2014).

http://www.altafsir.com/Tafasir.asp?tMadhNo=3&tTafsirNo=33&tSoraNo=48&tAyahNo=26&tDisplay=yes&UserProfile=0&LanguageId=1 (accessed September 29, 2013).

http://www.studyquran.org/LaneLexicon/volume2/00000113.pdf (accessed August 10, 2012).

http://www.themadkhalis.com/md/articles/jevki-shaykh-hammad-al-ansari-on-the-saying-of-sayyid-qutb-that-islami-is-a-mixture-of-communism-and-christianity.cfm (accessed Dec. 17, 2014).

http://press.princeton.edu/titles/8827.html (accessed Jan. 1, 2015).

http://www.shapell.org/manuscript.aspx?emile-zola-dreyfus-affair (accessed Dec. 1, 2014).

http://www.britannica.com/EBchecked/topic/77198/Brahmo-Samaj (accessed Dec. 17, 2014).

http://www.pewforum.org/2009/01/15/the-religious-affiliations-of-us-presidents/ (accessed Jan. 11, 2014).
http://www.britannica.com/EBchecked/topic/393304/Mohammad-Mosaddeq (accessed Jan. 20, 2015).
http://www.poemhunter.com/lascelles-abercrombie/biography/ (accessed Dec. 5 , 2014).
http://www.u-s-history.com/pages/h1762.html (accessed January 27, 2014).
https://www.marxists.org/archive/mattick-paul/1936/inevitability.htm (accessed February 10, 2015).
http://mises.org/library/marx-and-inevitability (accessed February 10, 2015).
http://www.johndclare.net/cold_war12.htm (accessed January 27, 2014).
http://www.britannica.com/EBchecked/topic/143635/Benedetto-Croce (accessed 24 Feb., 2015).
http://www.churchinhistory.org/pages/booklets/women-souls-1.htm (accessed 24 Feb., 2015).
http://www.globalresearch.ca/a-timeline-of-cia-atrocities/5348804 (accessed Feb. 17, 2015).
http://www.u-s-history.com/pages/h1762.html (accessed January 27, 2014).
http://www.ikhwanwiki.com/index.php?title=%D8%A7%D9%84%D8%A5%D8%B3%D8%AA%D8%B4%D8%B1%D8%A7%D9%82 (accessed December 13, 2013).
http://plato.stanford.edu/entries/bergson/ (accessed May 25, 2014).
http://www.nytimes.com/1981/11/09/obituaries/historian-will-durant-dies-author-of-civilization-series.html (accessed May 25, 2014).
http://www.voiceofdharma.org/books/siii/ch6.htm (March 5, 2015).
http://www.samizdat.com/isyn/durant.html (March 5, 2015).
http://oxforddictionaries.com/definition/english/minhag (accessed March 5, 2015).
https://www.google.co.uk/search?site=&source=hp&q=meaning+of+aliyah&oq=meaning+of+Aliyah&gs_l=hp.1.0.0l5j0i10j0i22i30l3j0i22i10i30.4328.16244.0.27200.35.22.6.5.6.0.512.4830.0j5j10j2j1j1.19.0.msedr...0...1c.1.62.hp..5.30.6298.MAEXHbuf9rE (March 21, 2015).
http://brigperegrine.tripod.com/igedm.html (accessed March 5, 2015).
http://www.ipsnews.net/2014/04/erasure-exodus-forgotten-history-jews-egypt/ (March 5, 2014).

Glossary

https://archive.org/details/Tafsir_Abu_Suoud & http://shamela.ws/index.php/book/1429(accessed (accessed November 8, 2014).
http://www.nobelprize.org/nobel_prizes/literature/laureates/1913/tagore-bio.html (accessed May 19, 2014).

Other Sources

The Wordsworth Encyclopedia of World Religions (1999).